Withdrawn from University of Oregon Library

Adaptive User Interfaces

Principles and Practice

HUMAN FACTORS IN INFORMATION TECHNOLOGY *10*

Series Editors:

Hans-Jörg Bullinger

FhG-IAO
Stuttgart
Germany

Peter G. Polson

Institute of Cognitive Science
University of Colorado
Boulder, Colorado, USA

Assistant Series Editors:
Klaus-Peter Fähnrich
Jürgen Ziegler

FhG-IAO, Stuttgart, Germany

NORTH-HOLLAND
AMSTERDAM · LONDON · NEW YORK · TOKYO

Adaptive User Interfaces

Principles and Practice

Edited by

MATTHIAS SCHNEIDER-HUFSCHMIDT
THOMAS KÜHME
UWE MALINOWSKI

*Siemens Corporate Research and Development
München, Germany*

1993

NORTH-HOLLAND
AMSTERDAM · LONDON · NEW YORK · TOKYO

NORTH-HOLLAND
ELSEVIER SCIENCE PUBLISHERS B.V.
Sara Burgerhartstraat 25
P.O. Box 211
1000 AE Amsterdam
The Netherlands

Library of Congress Cataloging-in-Publication Data

```
Adaptive user interfaces : principles and practice / edited by
  Matthias Schneider-Hufschmidt, Thomas Kühme, Uwe Malinowski.
       p.   cm. -- (Human factors in information technology ; 10)
  Includes bibliographical references and index.
  ISBN 0-444-81545-7
  1. User interfaces (Computer systems)  2. Human-computer
interaction.   I. Schneider-Hufschmidt, Matthias, 1957-  II. Kühme,
Thomas, 1957-    . III. Malinowski, Uwe, 1961-   . IV. Series.
  Qa76.9.U83A33  1993
  005.1'2'019--dc20                                            93-8442
                                                                  CIP
```

ISBN: 0 444 81545 7

© 1993 ELSEVIER SCIENCE PUBLISHERS B.V., ALL RIGHTS RESERVED.

No part of this publication may be reproduced, stored in a retrieval system or transmitted in any form or by any means, electronic, mechanical, photocopying, recording or otherwise, without the prior written permission of the publisher, Elsevier Science Publishers B.V., Copyright & Permissions Department, P.O. Box 521, 1000 AM Amsterdam, The Netherlands.

Special regulations for the readers in the U.S.A. - This publication has been registered with the Copyright Clearance Center Inc. (CCC), Salem, Massachusetts. Information can be obtained from the CCC about conditions under which photocopies of parts of this publication may be made in the U.S.A. All other copyright questions, including photocopying outside of the U.S.A., should be referred to the publisher, Elsevier Science Publishers B.V., unless otherwise specified.

No responsibility is assumed by the publisher for any injury and/or damage to persons or property as a matter of products liability, negligence or otherwise, or from any use or operation of any methods, products, instructions or ideas contained in the material herein.

pp. 269-284: Copyright not transferred

This book is printed on acid-free paper.

PRINTED IN THE NETHERLANDS

Preface

The area of intelligent and adaptive user interfaces has been of interest to the research community for a long time. Much effort has been spent in trying to find a stable theoretical base for adaptivity in human-computer interaction and to build prototypical systems showing features of adaptivity in "real-life" interfaces.

In 1991 we initiated a research project on adaptive user interfaces within the system ergonomics department of Siemens Corporate Research and Development. Our aim was to explore the potential of adaptive user interfaces for industrial applications.

When starting to develop an extended state-of-the-art survey of adaptive user interfaces, we soon realized that research in this field had so far not led to a coherent view of problems, let alone solutions. After examining published results of other research projects we felt that, although each project had its own merits in the performance of research on individual problems, no common understanding or vocabulary for the description of theory and practice in the field had as yet materialized.

We subsequently organized a workshop which brought together a number of well-known researchers in the area of adaptive user interfaces. This workshop was intended to serve several purposes:

(1) to develop a coherent view of the results accomplished in the field,

(2) to organize basic ideas which might lead to a more general methodology for adaptivity in order to overcome the problem of specialized, non-generalizable solutions, and

(3) to discuss possible areas for future research in the field and to define criteria for the selection of the most promising directions of such research.

The results of the workshop are presented in this volume. We have collected papers from the participants which describe both their research and their opinion on the questions with which we have tried to deal during the workshop. Also included is a state-of-the-art report and taxonomy for the field of adaptive interfaces and a discussion summary.

This book presents a coherent and comprehensive overview of the research area of adaptive user interfaces. After some discussion we have given it the title "Adaptive User Interfaces: Principles and Practice," and we have done our best to strike the appropriate balance between theoretically oriented papers and experience reports from projects that have dealt with fundamental questions of adaptive user interfaces, in order to fulfill the promise given in this title.

Acknowledgements

Many people have supported us and helped to put together and finish this book. First of all, we would like to thank the authors of the individual papers in this book. Without their participation at the workshop and their willingness to write a book section and review the papers of their co-authors, we could not even have started the editing process.

Judy Kay, D. Peter Sanderson, Edward H. Shortliffe, and Werner van Treeck deserve to be mentioned explicitly. They contributed to this book although we could not invite them to participate at the workshop.

Siemens Corporate Research and Development supported us generously during the entire project, first by giving us the possibility to organize the workshop, and second, by creating a working environment that allowed us to work on this book for an extended period of time. In this regard our sincere thanks go to Heinz Schwärtzel, Peter Müller-Stoy, and Peter Kleinschmidt.

Hartmut Raffler helped us to define and start our research project, and especially during the start-up phase, his encouragement and support were invaluable.

Kees Michielsen from Elsevier deserves credit for the encouragement he gave us whenever we got tired of the editing and writing process.

Darin Krasle and Harmut Dieterich have helped us proofread the entire book and turn it into a homogenous entity. Darin managed to improve the readability of some of the articles without interfering with the individual style of authors, while Hartmut finalized the lay-out of the book.

There remains one important group that deserves to be mentioned: the members of our families who had to cope with the fact that we spent so many hours with our computers instead of with them: Andrea, Lea, and Max Hufschmidt, Schura Al-Asadi-Kühme, and Angelika Malinowski. Thank you all.

Matthias Schneider-Hufschmidt   *Thomas Kühme*   *Uwe Malinowski*

Many of the designations used by manufacturers and sellers to distinguish their products are claimed as trademarks. Where those designations appear in this book, and we were aware of a trademark claim, they have been marked explicitly.

Apple Macintosh™ is a trademark of Apple Computer, Inc.
Excel™ is a trademark of Microsoft Corporation
HyperCard™ is a trademark of Apple Computer, Inc.
MediaTracks™ is a trademark of Farallon Computing, Inc.
NeXT™ is a trademark of NeXt Inc.
Timbuktu™ is a trademark of Farallon Computing, Inc.
UNIX™ is a trademark of AT&T.

Contents

Introduction	1
Thomas Kühme and Matthias Schneider-Hufschmidt	
Part I: Setting the Stage	11
State of the Art in Adaptive User Interfaces	13
Hartmut Dieterich, Uwe Malinowski, Thomas Kühme, Matthias Schneider-Hufschmidt	
Shared Knowledge in Cooperative Problem-Solving Systems – Integrating Adaptive and Adaptable Components	49
Gerhard Fischer	
Experiences from the AID Project	69
Dermot P. Browne	
Spaces and Distances: Software Architecture and Abstraction and their Relation to Adaptation	79
Gilbert Cockton	
Part II: Modelling Users, Tasks, and Dialogs	109
User Modeling: Recent Work, Prospects and Hazards	111
Alfred Kobsa	
Pragmatic User Modelling for Adaptive Interfaces	129
Judy Kay	
Accommodating Individual Differences through an Adaptive User Interface	149
David Benyon	
Intelligent User Support Based on Task Models	167
H. Ulrich Hoppe	
A Demonstrator Based Investigation of Adaptability	183
Franz Koller	

A Built-in Provision for Collecting Individual Task Usage Information in UIDE: the User Interface Design Environment *Piyawadee "Noi" Sukaviriya and James D. Foley*	197

Part III: Prototypes and Systems 223

AIDA – An Adaptive System for Interactive Drafting and CAD Applications *Jairo A. Cote-Muñoz*	225
Adaptive User Interface Design and Its Dependence on Structure *D. Peter Sanderson and Siegfried Treu*	241
Adaptive Hypermedia for Support Systems *Gernoth Grunst*	269
A User-Adaptable Interface to Predict Users' Needs *Eric H. Sherman and Edward H. Shortliffe*	285

Part IV: Evaluation 317

Contributions of a Social Science Based Evaluation for Adaptive Design Projects *Christoph Grüninger and Werner van Treeck*	319

Discussion Results 331
Uwe Malinowski and Matthias Schneider-Hufschmidt

About the Authors	337
Subject Index	345

Introduction

Thomas Kühme and Matthias Schneider-Hufschmidt

Siemens Corporate Research and Development
München, Germany

Adaptive User Interfaces have been a focus of Human-Computer Interaction Research for a long time. Only in rare cases, however, the results were convincing. Despite these discouraging experiences of the past research on adaptive user interfaces may prove fruitful for the design of usable systems. The reason for the apparent failure of adaptive user interfaces can certainly not be found in a lack of technological progress. Only the concentration on usability problems that can be overcome by making interfaces adaptive will ensure the success of this research field.

In this chapter, we point to a methodological shortcoming of past research in the field and provide a framework for a rationale for building adaptive user interfaces which leads to worthwhile gains through the provision of this technology. The structure of this book and the contents of its chapters are subsequently outlined.

TECHNOLOGY-DRIVEN RESEARCH — A DANGEROUS APPROACH

As a consequence of the penetration of our daily life and work by information technology, more and more people have to use computer systems with ever increasing complexity. System designers have to cope with the fact that these users exhibit a wide range of prerequisite knowledge and individual preferences. The envisioned idea of an adaptive user interface which automatically handles all these differences in an appropriate manner has attracted many researchers. The broader approach of an intelligent user interface includes adaptive characteristics as a (if not the) major source of its intelligent behavior.

The decade of the 1980s saw a rapidly growing number of research activities in the area of adaptive and intelligent user interfaces. The publication rate of related papers in international journals, conference proceedings, and books at the end of the decade was about 20-25 times as high as ten years before. This trend continues into the 1990s. International workshops on Intelligent User Interfaces took place in 1983, 1988 [Sullivan & Tyler 91], and 1993 [Gray et al. 93], each time attracting more attention of research and industry. A book entitled Intelligent Interfaces was published in 1989 [Hancock & Chignell 89], and another one on Adaptive User Interfaces in 1990 [Browne et al. 90]. International workshops on Adaptive User Interfaces include this book's workshop in 1992 and a workshop at the InterCHI '93 conference, entitled Computer-Aided Adaptation.

Despite the long-standing efforts, adaptive user interfaces have not gone beyond the stage of prototype implementations and, consequently, have not yet found their way into practice. Looking at quite a number of outstanding research results, one might argue that this is only because of deficiencies in technology which simply do not allow for a generalization of results and their application to real world problem domains. This view would suggest that adaptive user interfaces could be led to success by strengthening research on the technological basis which, as a matter of fact, has been the major objective for many years.

However, another perspective, as supported by this book, proposes that past research was far too technology-oriented and forgot about the usability problems it was originally intended to deal with. This becomes particularly obvious with over-ambitious research goals, such as trying to build a system that provides intelligent assistance of a kind which could not even be expected from a well-trained human assistant. The main orientation of research in this line is characterized by the following description which refers to AI techniques as the technological basis: *"Intelligent interface research starts with this technological basis, and looks toward the question of how interfaces can be improved, for both users and developers, by the use of these techniques"* [Miller et al. 91].

In contrast, this book suggests putting more emphasis on the reverse approach which can be characterized correspondingly: Intelligent/adaptive interface research starts with the question of how an improved interface would behave, i.e., how it would deal with predetermined usability problems, and looks toward existing and emerging technologies that can serve as a basis for the desired improvements. A more active involvement of researchers from disciplines other than computer science and artificial intelligence, such as cognitive science, social science, psychology, or pedagogics, could greatly contribute to this approach.

A RATIONALE FOR THE DESIGN OF ADAPTIVE USER INTERFACES

Before trying to develop methods for adaptivity or implement adaptive user interfaces, one should try to answer a number of questions dealing with the rationale for an adaptive interface behavior. About what might the interface need to be adaptive? What are the usability problems which ought to be addressed by building adaptive interfaces? The latter question acknowledges that – even if there is something the interface could be adaptive about – there may be other, more sensible ways to deal with the involved problems than making the interface adaptive. In the following, we elaborate on both questions in order to provide a framework for a rationale for adaptive interfaces.

Most commonly, adaptive interfaces are meant to be adaptive to differences or changes that exist or take place within the user population of a computerized system ([Browne 93], in this book). This is the perspective of a system that has to support different and changing human users and their real world tasks. The users from their perspective, however, might want the interface to also adaptively reflect differences and changes within the system environment they are working in. We can identify four different reasons for adaptive behavior, and the examples given subsequently illustrate the various concerns.

- A system is used by users with different requirements.

  This is the most prominent reason for adaptive interfaces. Individual differences in the users' cognitive abilities and personality traits impose different requirements on the interaction and can cause usability problems if the interface does not meet these requirements ([Benyon 93], in this book). Other user characteristics relevant for interaction include any preferences and desires, as well as the users' knowledge and interest. Additionally, different users introduce different tasks and different ways of performing a particular task, in particular in the case of multi-purpose systems, e.g. in office automation. Task-oriented support addresses these differences ([Hoppe 93], in this book).

- A system is used by a user with changing requirements.

  Users are not only different, but the requirements of each particular user also change over time. Along with the usage of a system, the user's knowledge and experience evolves with respect to both the interaction with the system and the system's application domain. Most often this is regarded as a user's development from novice to expert, but also users who have been well-trained before actually using a system undergo changes in perception, understanding, and use of the system. While, in the long term, users form individual habits and preferences, they might also switch between work-related functions and respective tasks in the short term. The provision of macros for frequently used interaction sequences is an example of an interface which adapts to the long-term changes ([Cote 93], in this book).

- A user works in a changing system environment.

  Changes in a system environment are routinely caused by almost every interaction with the system. In process control applications, for instance, changes occur even without any interaction. A changing system environment can cause usability problems if the system, i.e. the user interface, fails to reflect these changes adequately. While the provision of comprehensive feedback on the application's current state is one of the major characteristics of today's direct manipulation user interfaces, all the context changes could also be used as a source for making the interface more suitable in a particular situation. For instance, context-sensitive help might give explanations individually adapted to the current context of the interaction and application ([Sukaviriya & Foley 93], in this book).

- A user works in different system environments.

    Working with different applications or with one application in different environments causes many problems. Besides rather technical problems, such as providing the same interface functionality across different environments, the question of interface consistency across different applications or environments comes up. How can we deal with inconsistencies of interfaces for a pilot who operates different airplanes? How can an interface to a new application be accommodated to a user who has been using other applications for some time?

When trying to provide solutions to any of the above described problems, one must ask if an adaptive interface can provide the most effective solution or if there are alternative approaches to be considered. So, what are possible alternatives?

Two of the approaches may be undesirable or impossible, but should certainly be considered in the first place, even if only as a way to investigate why user interface adaptation is necessary in a particular case.

- Have users adapt!

    In conventional human-computer interaction the user is the one who has the ability to adapt to his inflexible counterpart. The result of this (enforced) adaptation is in general a lower degree of usability of systems. To overcome the resulting potential usability problems, contemporary interface design tries to build systems which meet the requirements of human users (and not force users to meet the requirements of machines). Certainly this approach is more convincing and seems to be more human-centered. The human ability and the desire to learn and adapt should, however, not be underestimated. In many cases, users do want challenging interfaces which allow explorative usage. The "perfect" adaptive user interface may not only be a dream, but also uninteresting from the users' point of view.

- Build better (non-adaptive) interfaces which fit all users and situations!

    An investigation of the consequences of this approach reveals that it will not be feasible for many application systems. To foresee all possible uses of a specific system is beyond the abilities of any system designer. Additionally, modifications of the functionality of systems generally lead to user interfaces changes as a consequence. Analysis and design methods for system development, and in particular for user interface design, are not able to cope with this kind of requirement. One never should, however, absolutely rule out the possibility that a new interaction method might turn out to be generally superior to the old, even though adaptive, method, when considering a limited domain.

In those cases where neither one of these approaches seems feasible an individualized interface can be considered. A pragmatic prerequisite for any individualization is a separable user interface [Edmonds 90]. It provides the opportunity for different interfaces to the same application and for changing or exchanging the interface independently of the application program. Similarly, an adaptable interface is a prerequisite for any adaptive behavior. In order to individualize an interface, a (self-)adaptive interface is only one of several possibilities with different degrees of adaptability or adaptivity such as:

- Design different interfaces for different users (or user groups)!
- Have users (or domain experts) adapt the interface!
- Make the interface adaptive! (Have the interface adapt itself!)

Besides these, there are many variants of adaptivity which can be characterized by, for instance, who the agent of adaptation is in which stage, when an adaptation takes place, or whether an individual user or a group of users with common requirements is targeted by the adaptation ([Dieterich et al. 93], in this book). Given a problem that evidently requires an individualization, one has to look very carefully at every possible solution and its variants in order to figure out which of them has the best ratio between effort in design and gain in usability, or even more important, if there is a payoff at all with any of them. As Benyon remarks ([Benyon 93], in this book): *"There is little to be gained if expensive adaptivity mechanisms are used to achieve a minimal improvement in usability"*.

Considering the usability gain, it must not be overlooked that an adaptation may have drawbacks as it possibly introduces new usability problems while addressing those it intends to diminish. For instance, any adaptation by definition changes the interface. If users were at least partially accustomed to the old state, it would cost them some time and effort to re-adapt after the adaptation. This causes a temporary loss in usability even though the adapted interface might be more usable in the end.

The potential benefits of adaptation are further restricted by the fact that adapting an interface requires additional effort and skills by engaging the user in a dialog which goes beyond the application domain. Self-adaptive interfaces either decrease or avoid the otherwise necessary effort but often still require the user to understand the (automatic) adaptation processes. There are cases, however, in which the user might not even be aware of an adaptation taking place (e.g. eliding details from help).

Sherman and Shortliffe ([Sherman & Shortliffe 93], in this book) address this problem by designing the adaptation as a cooperative, system-supported process involving different users and user groups. By sharing the work between all users of an application system, the adaptation effort to be spent by every single user is reduced to a tolerable amount and potentially difficult-to-understand automatic adaptations are eliminated.

Finally, if all the considerations regarding the effort/gain ratio conclude with a positive result one has still to worry about negative effects or potential risks of adaptation. Mostly these are trade-offs between individualized solutions and other concerns such as compatibility issues. Considering the compatibility between interfaces, how does an adaptation to individual users comply with the development and propagation of interface guidelines and standards? How far can adaptation go if different users work simultaneously with the same system, such as in a shared working environment (e.g. in a supervisory control center), or in the case of systems for applications that require cooperative work?

Even more pressing is the question how far adaptability should and can be restricted in order to keep the interface compatible with the purpose the system was designed for. For instance, it would not be appropriate to allow the changing of colors in a text editor interface so that the text becomes illegible or for changing the presentation of alert messages in a supervisory control system so that they lose their attention-attracting characteristics. On the other hand, restrictions built into systems cannot be a substitute for responsible users. Compare this to individualized automobiles where dark colors are tolerated even though they increase the safety risks because of the poor visibility with bad weather conditions.

WHAT CAN BE GAINED WITH ADAPTIVITY IN USER INTERFACES

After all these critical questions, one might ask if there is something that we can get from adaptive user interfaces beyond gradually improved usability and fine-tuned performance characteristics, something that makes it really worth spending the effort to get around all these problems. This is probably the main question to be asked from an industrial point of view. Although there is no general answer, there are certainly a number of issues that make an engagement in adaptive user interface research interesting enough. In the following we want to reexamine the four main reasons for adaptivity and characterize what might be gained by introducing adaptive behavior:

- A system is used by users with different requirements.

    Adaptivity in systems with different users may allow more users to access the systems' functionality. It might give those users a higher degree of satisfaction by offering them an interface to the functionality that they are able to handle without extensive learning. Off-the-shelf software components may be adapted to specific situations and tasks thereby allowing a larger audience to profit from these systems.

    Another potential field for adaptive behavior is software for cooperative system use (Computer Supported Cooperative Work). In this growing field of application systems the ability to individualize interfaces while ensuring the consistency between different user interfaces for the same system may have major influence on the success of these systems.

- A system is used by a user with changing requirements.

    Users are willing and able to learn. If we can support them in an optimal way during their learning process from novice to expert system users, we will allow them to use their computers continuously with maximal efficiency. From an economic point of view, corresponding systems offer a far better ratio between required expenditures and actual period of use.

- A user works in a changing system environment.

    The characteristics of computer systems have changed dramatically. Due to their increased lifetime and complexity these systems have become part of an infrastructure; they can no longer be developed in isolated projects and be considered fixed after the end of the development process. Rather, they undergo continuous modifications, and their user interfaces have to reflect these functional changes. Adaptivity may be one important feature which helps to maintain interface consistency across these system modifications. Also, the effort of individualizing a user interface can be saved across version changes, leading to higher efficiency of system use.

- A user works in different system environments.

    Users working in different system environments have to be enabled to individualize their user interface in a consistent way across system and application boundaries. Consequences of this consistency preserving customization can be expected in a higher efficiency of usage of diverse systems combined with a lower error rate. Sometime in the future, even the old dream might come true of interfaces that automatically adapt to a "user model" which the user carries along to different systems at work, at home, or in public places.

THE PERSPECTIVE OF THIS BOOK

This book is the outcome of a workshop held in 1992 at Siemens Corporate Research and Development in Munich. This workshop was intended to serve several purposes:

(1) to develop a coherent view of the results accomplished in the field,

(2) to get basic ideas about a more general methodology for adaptivity to overcome the problem of specialized, non-generalizable solutions,

(3) to discuss possible research areas for future research in the field and to define criteria for the selection of the most promising directions.

The first part of the book describes the context and the contents of adaptivity in user interfaces. The chapter authored by *Hartmut Dieterich, Uwe Malinowski, Thomas Kühme* and *Matthias Schneider-Hufschmidt* summarizes the findings of an extended state-of-the-art study and the subsequent development of a taxonomy of adaptive user interfaces.

Gerhard Fischer characterizes application domains and their need for adaptable and/or adaptive user interfaces. *Dermot Browne* reports the results of the Alvey "Adaptive Intelligent Dialogues" project and stresses the importance of a rationale for adaptivity as the guiding principle of any user interface project developing adaptive user interfaces. *Gilbert Cockton* assesses adaptivity from the point of view of software architecture and argues, that, with the exception of simple changes in the interface, adaptation requires extensive reprogramming of interface functionality.

Part two of this volume contains studies on components, tools, and environments for adaptive user interfaces. *Alfred Kobsa* analyzes the state of the art and the prospects of user modeling in general, while *Judy Kay* applies user modeling techniques in the specific context of adaptive behavior. *David Benyon* describes the development of an adaptive user interface based on users' experiences and knowledge. *Ulrich Hoppe* reviews different aspects of representing and using task knowledge in intelligent user interfaces. The two final chapters of this part cover the topic of user interface and dialogue representation. *Franz Koller* reports on experiences with dialog modeling techniques, while *"Noi" Sukaviriya* and *Jim Foley* describe the principles and implementation of UIDE, their user interface design environment which provides automated support for collecting task-oriented information about users.

Part three of the book is dedicated to experience reports from different adaptive user interface projects. *Jairo Cote-Muñoz* describes the development of his system AIDA which allows adaptation of a CAD system's interface to the specific knowledge of its users. Next, *Peter Sanderson* and *Siegfried Treu* analyze the results of the development of their N-CHIME system and stress the importance of methodological support for the designers of adaptive user interfaces. The topic of the chapter authored by *Gernoth Grunst* is the System HyPLAN, which is able to answer unspecific help questions using knowledge about tasks and users. The last chapter, by *Eric Sherman* and *Edward Shortliffe*, describes Podium, a system that is able to tailor a predefined user interface to different subgroups of a large user community.

The final part of the volume deals with the question of evaluating the impact of adaptive user interfaces on the work process of their users. *Christoph Grüninger* and *Werner van Treeck* argue that for the design of adaptive user interface a context-specific mixture of cognitive, psychological, social, organizational, and technical factors needs to be taken into account.

In the final chapter we summarize the results of various discussions during the workshop. The two most important results of these stimulating discussions are that

(1) research and development of prototype systems have to be driven by the needs of the users and the application, and

(2) in most cases, a combination of adaptation types is appropriate.

REFERENCES

[Benyon 93]
D. Benyon (1993). *Accommodating Individual Differences through an Adaptive User Interface*. In this volume.

[Browne 93]
D.P. Browne (1993). *Experiences from the AID Project*. In this volume.

[Browne et al. 90]
D. Browne, P. Totterdell, M. Norman (eds.) (1990). *Adaptive User Interfaces*. London: Academic Press.

[Cote 93]
J.A. Cote-Muñoz (1993). *AIDA — An Adaptive System for Interactive Drafting and CAD Applications*. In this volume.

[Dieterich et al. 93]
Dieterich, H., Malinowski, U., Kühme, T., Schneider-Hufschmidt, M. (1993). *State of the Art in Adaptive User interfaces*. In this volume

[Edmonds 90]
E. A. Edmonds (ed.) (1990). *The Separable User Interface*. London: Academic Press.

[Gray et al. 93]
W. D. Gray, W. E. Hefley, D. Murray (eds.) (1993). Proceedings of the 1993 ACM International Workshop on Intelligent User Interfaces. New York: ACM Press.

[Hancock & Chignell 89]
P. A. Hancock, M. H. Chignell (eds.) (1989). *Intelligent Interfaces – Theory, Research and Design*. Amsterdam: North-Holland.

[Hoppe 93]
H.U. Hoppe (1993). *Intelligent User Support Based on Task Models*. In this volume.

[Miller et al. 91]
J. R. Miller, J. W. Sullivan, S.W. Tyler (1991). *Introduction* of [Sullivan & Tyler 91], page 2.

[Sherman & Shortliffe 93]
E. H. Sherman, E. Shortliffe. *A User-Adaptable Interface to Predict Users' Needs*. In this volume.

[Sukaviriya & Foley 93]
P. Sukaviriya & J. Foley (1993). *A Built-in Provision for Collecting Individual Task Usage Information in UIDE: the User Interface Design Environment*. In this volume.

[Sullivan & Tyler 91]
J. W. Sullivan, S.W. Tyler (eds.) (1991). *Intelligent User Interfaces*. New York: ACM Press.

Part I

Setting the Stage

State of the Art in Adaptive User Interfaces

Hartmut Dieterich, Uwe Malinowski, Thomas Kühme, Matthias Schneider-Hufschmidt

Siemens Corporate Research and Development
München, Germany

ABSTRACT

This chapter presents a review of research on Adaptive User Interfaces. It is based on nearly 200 relevant papers and is organized as a taxonomy. Classification parameters include tasks and agents, adapted constituents, considered information, goals and strategies, models and architectures, and adaptation techniques. The taxonomy is used to classify existing systems and prototypes built and to describe the differences and relations of the following chapters.

1 INTRODUCTION

In recent years an increasing number of research activities have been performed on Adaptive User Interfaces (AUIs). Adaptive User Interfaces are a promising attempt to overcome contemporary problems due to the increasing complexity of human-computer interaction. They are designed to tailor a system's interactive behavior with consideration of both individual needs of human users and altering conditions within an application environment.

Although taxonomies of AUIs can be found in the literature (see [Edmonds 86] or [Totterdell & Rautenbach 90] as examples), it seems to be reasonable to establish another taxonomy. None of the existing schemes allow a satisfying classification of the existing approaches and prototype systems because they try to cover the variation of different classification parameters by a linear scheme. We classify the approaches and prototypes regarding each aspect on its own. This results in a multi-dimensional classification scheme with the ability to classify all existing approaches and prototype systems.

The difference between Adaptive User Interfaces and Intelligent Interfaces is not yet well defined. Therefore, first of all we explain our reading of these terms. Early user interfaces (UIs) were static. The system designer built the interface and the user had to learn how to use it. Today, a more flexible interface is the state of the art. The opportunity to accommodate the interface to their own preferences is given to the users. The flexibility is usually restricted to simple changes, for instance the change of colors, size, or positions of windows.

An Adaptive User Interface either supports users in the adaptation of the interface to their own needs and preferences or performs the adaptation automatically. The focus of adaptation extends to a broader range than in current flexible interfaces by including functionality and the demands of the application.

An Intelligent Interface is the integration of an AUI both with an Intelligent Help System (IHS), making context-sensitive and active help available [Schwab 89, Wilensky et al. 84], and with an Intelligent Tutoring System (ITS) [Sleeman & Brown 82], supporting the user in learning the use of the system (see Figure 1, an elaboration of a figure in [Elkerton & Williges 89]). Our analysis of AUIs will include existing Intelligent Interfaces since adaptivity is a main characteristic of their components (IHS and ITS).

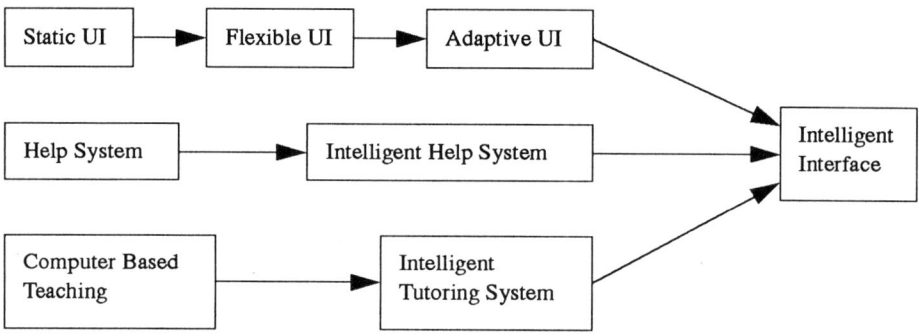

Figure 1: Terms: Adaptive User Interfaces and Intelligent Interfaces

This survey and taxonomy is influenced by the discussions of the workshop this book is based on and tries to consider the contributions of the participants that are also part of this volume. This chapter consists of three sections. While section 2 covers external aspects of adaptivity, section 3 describes the internal aspects and section 4 introduces different formalisms used in AUIs. Section 2 lists the different choices that the designer of an AUI has to make about what will change, who will perform the changes, what information has to be considered, what are the goals of an adaptation, and when will adaptation take place. Section 3 describes structural models and software structures of AUIs, which support the different types of adaptation. The range of models include task, user, dialog, and application models. A short description of architectures of existing prototypes follows. Section 4 summarizes formalisms and techniques used for the configuration of AUI components. It also contains a description of the knowledge representation techniques and the knowledge acquisition techniques used for filling and updating the models.

2 THE DESIGN SPACE FOR ADAPTIVE USER INTERFACES

The designer of an AUI has several fundamental choices to make. Firstly, who should adapt and what should their role be in the adaptation process? Secondly, what levels of the interaction should be adapted (for example presentation or functionality)? Thirdly, what information should be considered when looking for opportunities for adaptation? Fourthly, what goals should be furthered by the chosen level of adaptation when triggered by the information under consideration? Finally, when should the changes be made?

2.1 Stages and Agents in the Adaptation Process

In any adaptation process different tasks have to be performed. They can be grouped in stages that have to be considered when examining the adaptation process. While [Totterdell & Rautenbach 90] distinguish between the system-centered stages of *variation*, *selection* and *testing*, we examine stages from the user's point of view.

The first stage, called *initiative*, is the decision of one of the agents to suggest an adaptation. Subsequently, alternatives for adaptation have to be proposed (*proposal*). In the next stage one of the alternatives has to be chosen (*decision*) and finally executed (*execution*).

Possible *agents* performing or controlling these stages are the system designer, the system administrator, a local expert, the user, or the system itself. If the system designer, the system administrator, or a local expert performs the tasks of one of the stages, an adaptation can only consider the needs of user groups. Hence, the resulting interface will probably not suit the needs of an individual user. Furthermore, the user is not able to detect whether an adaptation is performed by the system, the system designer, the system administrator, or a local expert. Therefore, the most interesting agents, in the context of adaptive systems, are the *system* and the *user*.

Consequently, 16 combinations (2 agents with 4 stages) have to be considered. This can be visualized in a matrix (see Figure 2). Any combination can be illustrated by marking which agent performs which tasks.

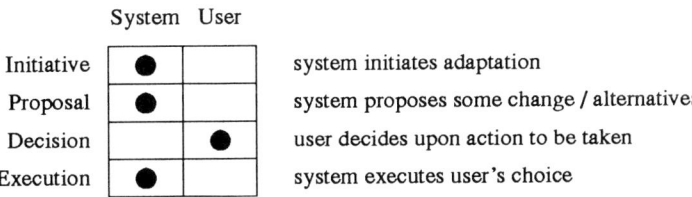

Figure 2: Tasks and Agents: Example Configuration

Among these combinations four are uninteresting: it is not reasonable to make the user execute an adaptation selected by the system, regardless of the agent performing initiative and proposal.

Asking the user to execute an adaptation proposed by the system is also a less reasonable variant. In this case, the system should be able to execute the proposed adaptation.

In the literature, no example can be found of a system which asks the user to propose alternatives and performs the other stages automatically. One can imagine a system able to evaluate proposals but unable to create them. However, it does seem more reasonable to present the evaluation of the proposals to the user and thus support his decision.

If the system performs the tasks for all stages, we call the process *Self-Adaptation*. The system observes the communication, decides whether to adapt, generates and evaluates different variants, and finally selects and executes one of them. Examples of self-adaptive systems are GUSIB (Generic User Interface Builder) [Dang 88], active context-sensitive help [Schwab 89], and error-correcting systems like FLEX [Motro 90].

Self-adaptation is particularly suitable for adapting to the requirements of the application, as in ADBS [Grimm 85]. In contrast, adaptations to the user's needs should be under user control. Such *User-Controlled Self-Adaptation* is used in POISE [Croft 84] and PODIUM [Sherman 90].

Systems using Self-Adaptation or User-Controlled Self-Adaptation should allow the user to take the initiative. Those variants are designated as *User-Initiated Self-Adaptation* and *Computer-Aided Adaptation (CAA)*, respectively. Context-sensitive help, as in UIDE [Foley et al. 91], is a kind of user-initiated self-adaptation. A system offering CAA takes on the routine tasks (Proposal and Execution) and entrusts the creative tasks (Initiative and Decision) to the user.

Lastly, all but the first stage may be left to the user. With such *System-Initiated Adaptation* the user is informed if it seems to be reasonable to tailor the system. Simple *Adaptation* gives the opportunity to the user to tailor a system to his own needs and preferences. For example, almost any window manager allows the user to change colors, sizes of windows, or the appearance of menus.

[Fischer 93] gives a comparison between adaptive and adaptable systems that is based on a different definition of terms. Speaking of adaptive systems, he means systems that would be classified as Self-Adaptive systems in this taxonomy. Systems identified as using Computer-Aided Adaptation, User-Controlled Self-Adaptation, or Adaptation, are summarized as adaptable systems by [Fischer 93].

The control of each stage by the system requires two classes of knowledge which result in a two-dimensional classification scheme. We call the dimensions *System Intelligence for Context Analysis and Plan Recognition* and *System Intelligence for Proposal Creation and*

Evaluation (Figure 3). The most interesting combinations of agents and tasks, according to the above analysis, are placed in this scheme.

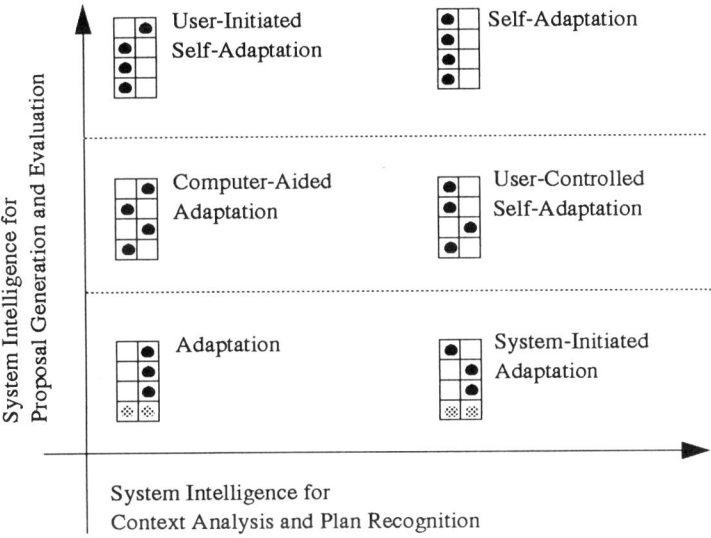

Figure 3: Classification Scheme: Tasks and Agents

This classification scheme serves to classify systems and approaches with regard to stages and agents from the user's point of view (Figure 4). For each of the systems the marked area shows the provided types of adaptation. For instance, ADBS performs Self-Adaption to the requirements of the application and gives the users the opportunity to adapt the interface to their preferences. [Fischer 93] stresses that it is not sufficient to restrict a system to one type of adaptation. Systems have to provide an integration of Self-Adaptation and Adaptability, speaking in his terms mentioned before, in order to use each of them in the appropriate situation. Figure 5 shows the subtree of the classification scheme representing the tasks and agents aspects.

2.2 Adapted Constituents

[Browne et al. 90a] state that there are no principal restrictions in the possible dimensions of adaptation. From a global point of view, two groups of adaptations can be distinguished. In a system using *adaptation of the communication*, the user has to perform the same tasks whether adaptation takes place or not. *Adaptation of functionality* gives the opportunity to the user to apply new or more complex functions.

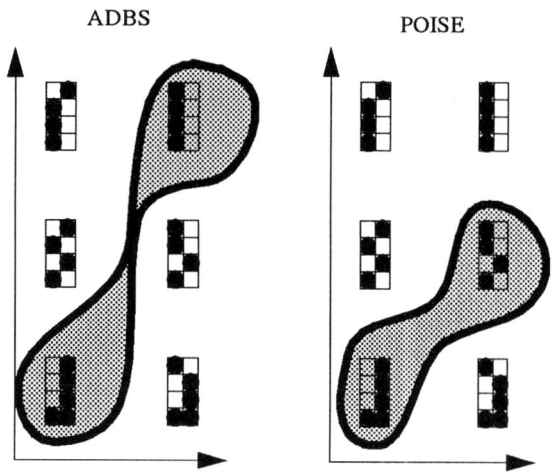
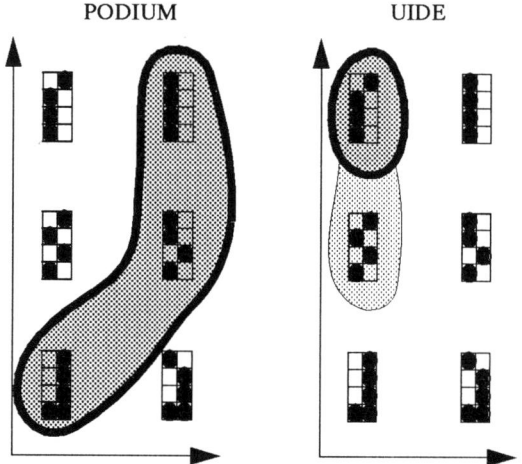

Figure 4: Examples of Classified Systems

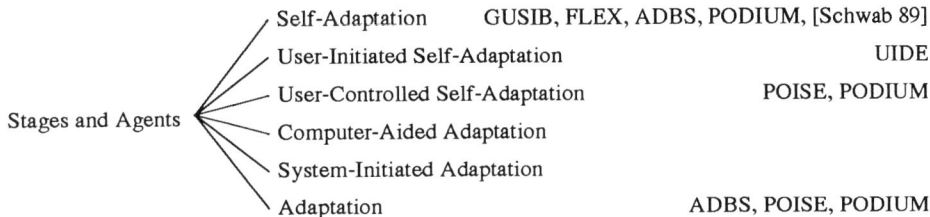

Figure 5: Stages and Agents

[Croft 84] and [Motro 90] present systems with the ability to *correct errors and inaccurate input*. [Croft 84, Dang 88, Schwab 89] and other authors describe *active help systems*. These systems try to detect errors and non-optimal plans of the user during interaction with the user. On that basis they present the most appropriate information attempting to enable the user to overcome these shortcomings on his own.

Many variants of adaptation consider *presentation*. The user's presentation of input to the system is often changed by switching between several interaction styles. [Brooks & Thorburn 88] describe a system with different interaction styles for experts, intermediate users, and novices. Another system gives the opportunity to switch between "Query and Answer", "Menu Selection", and "Command Language" [Fowler et al. 87].

The system's presentation of information to the user can be changed by either filtering or by switching between presentation styles. A system for process control described in [Grimm 85] allows the user to select the information that has to be presented and to change the presentation style for this information. However, during critical situations in the application process the user interface can decide to present information which the user normally does not want to see.

[Tyler & Treu 89] describe a context-sensitive and adaptive user interface for UNIX™. The most interesting commands are presented to the users, and they are asked for the necessary parameters. Furthermore, plans and strategies are presented if it is appropriate for the user in the current situation.

[Mason & Thomas 84] present another user interface for UNIX™. Relevant commands and accompanying information, tailored to the experience of the actual user, are presented.

A user interface for an electronic mail system selects parameters of a selected function relevant to the user, dependent on the current situation and former actions of the user [Browne et al. 86]. [Foley et al. 91] present the user interface development system UIDE. A user interface developed using UIDE provides the user with context-sensitive help.

Adaptation of functionality is even more complicated. It seems to be reasonable to allow the user to perform the creative tasks and to allocate the execution of the routine tasks to the system. [Morris et al. 85] describe a system where tasks are dynamically allocated to either the system or the user, depending on the stress of the user. The system presented in [Rouse 88] can perform complete tasks, propose solutions, or leave the complete execution to the user.

Task simplification is proposed by [Rissland 84] for the automation of routine tasks for the individual user. This can be done by macro generation. A more elegant way is a automatic macro generation with learning by example using a generalization algorithm [Hoppe & Plötzner 91, Cote 93].

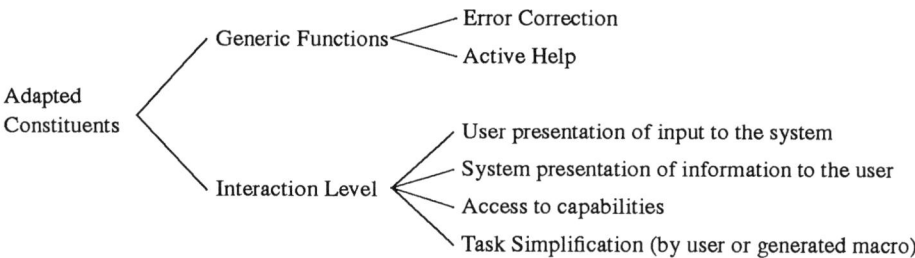

Figure 6: Adapted Constituents

Up to this point the classification aspect "adapted constituents" is inspected independently from any other aspect. Figure 7 shows the two-dimensional classification scheme with the aspects "adapted constituent" and "level of adaptation", which is described in detail in Section 3. The figure clearly shows that the aspects depend on each other.

2.3 Information Considered for Adaptation

[Benyon 93] describes a system that adapts to the differences between individual users. It tries to consider cognition and personality. The system switches the dialog style between command and menu, based on data about the spatial ability, command experience, and frequency of use.

Besides information about the user that most of the papers talk about, aspects of the application, ergonomic rules, and the user interface itself have to be considered. Although this has not been realized in prototype systems so far, it is important that all of the aspects have to be considered in each adaptation.

System designers try to consider the needs and preferences of the typical user when developing a system. Some systems allow a system administrator to customize the system to the needs and preferences of a user group.

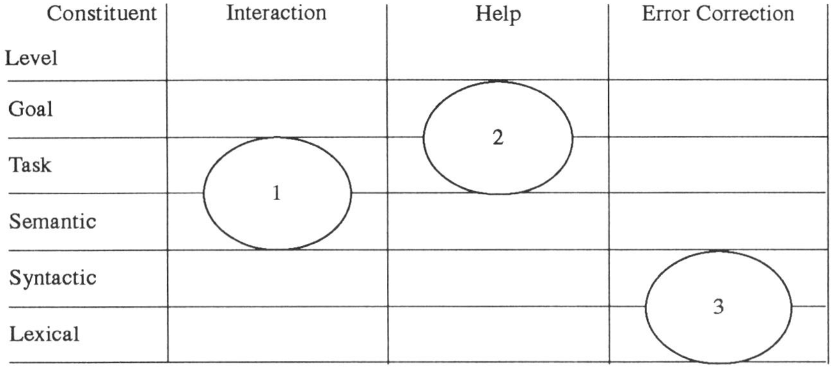

Constituent Level	Interaction	Help	Error Correction
Goal		(2)	
Task	(1)		
Semantic			
Syntactic			(3)
Lexical			

1: compare [Fowler et al. 87], [Grimm 85], [Brooks & Thorburn 88], ...

2: compare [Schwab 89], [Foley et al. 91]

3: compare [Motro 90], [Croft 84]

Figure 7: Adapted Constituents and Level of Adaptation

Information about individual users must be considered when individualizing user interfaces. The individual UI can be formed by the designer, the user, or the system itself. There is a great variety of information that has been considered in the prototypes. Frequently used terms are: needs, preferences, characteristics, abilities, interests, behavior, knowledge, experience [Brooks & Thorburn 88, Fowler et al. 87, Benyon et al. 86, van der Veer & Beishuizen 88]. The term "abilities of the user" summarizes many different aspects, from basic abilities like using the mouse, to very complex abilities like performing a specific task in the actual application context. [Fowler et al. 87] base adaptation on a choice of interaction style. The choice is made by considering the user's experience, and this also can be classified as a part of the user's domain knowledge. Furthermore, errors the individual user made while using a system have to be considered. It has to be taken into account that there are differences between individual users, and that the knowledge and preferences of the individual user change while using the system.

We have already described ADBS, a system for process control, which adapts to the individual users' typical errors. ADBS also takes into account information about the application to give the user the necessary information in critical situations. Information about the application can be related to the context of the application and to the current situation of the application.

Although not explicitly mentioned in the literature, ergonomic rules and the user interface itself have to be considered as constraints on any adaptation performed. Adaptation strat-

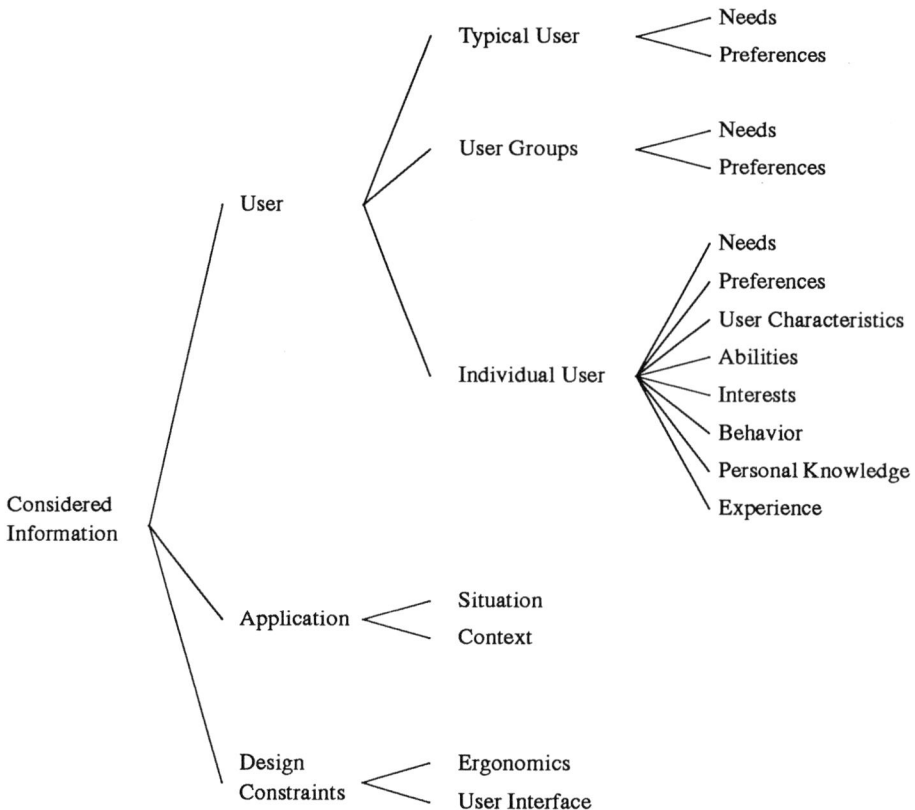

Figure 8: Considered Information

egies or rules should be consistent with ergonomic rules. The user interface as a whole has to be considered when planning any partial adaptation of the interface. In particular, the adaptation strategy has to guarantee the consistency of the user interface.

2.4 Goals of Adaptation

The main goal of adaptation is to present an interface to the user that is easy, efficient, and effective to use. A more detailed description of this main goal can be found in the literature. For instance, to give the opportunity to the user to handle complex systems, to present an interface the user wants to see, or to speed up and simplify use. To reach these goals it is necessary to have a user interface that is suitable for heterogeneous user groups and considers increasing experience of a user.

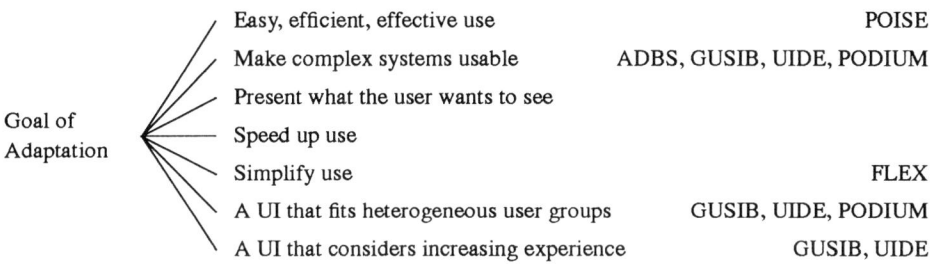

Figure 9: Goals of Adaptation

2.5 Strategies of Adaptation

There are several adaptation strategies that can be used in an AUI. They have to determine, when to interact, which information to present on the screen, and which presentation style to choose.

The strategy that is most obvious to the user is the *timing* strategy. [Rouse 88] mentions adaptation off-line prior to operation, on-line in anticipation of changing demands, and on-line in response to changes. [Cockton 87] only distinguishes within-session and between-session adaptations. The following, more detailed classification distinguishes adaptation before the first utilization of the system, during sessions, and between sessions.

Before first use of a system, several kinds of adaptation can take place. During the design of an user interface, the needs of a typical future user are to be considered. There are user interfaces that can be customized to the needs of special user groups before use. Obviously, the needs of the individual user cannot be considered in these cases. Some systems give the user the opportunity to tailor the system to personal preferences before use. This is not sufficient as that needs do appear during use. A customization with respect to the individual user happens if the user is classified on the basis of a pre-test.

Perhaps the most interesting approach is termed *adaptation during use*. The adaptation can take place continuously, on predefined junctures, after (or before) defined functions, if a special situation appears, or on user's request. Continuous adaptation can regard the current situation and the actual changes and has therefore the best chance to suit the user's needs. Furthermore, the results of the adaptation can be evaluated at once. Hence, a regressive adaptation can be obtained. The risk is a possible confusion of the user, caused by an interface changing just at the moment that the user thought to understand it. Furthermore, adaptation during use can result in a so-called *hunting* [Browne 90]: the system tries to adapt to the user, the user tries to adapt to the system; they will never reach a stable configuration.

Adaptation between two sessions allows the calculation of very complicated adaptation strategies. A major problem, however, is that the adaptation will always regard the user's needs at the end of the last session. The conflict becomes obvious, if the user has not used the system for a long time

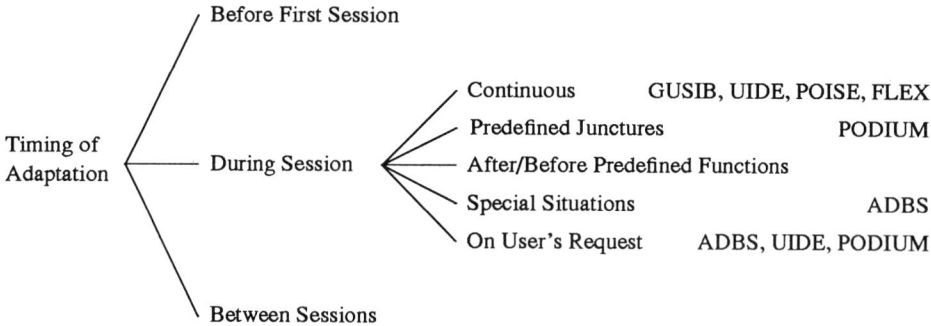

Figure 10: Timing of Adaptation

3 MODELS FOR SOFTWARE STRUCTURE

[Hartson & Hix 89] argue that "structural, descriptive models of the human-computer interface ... serve as frameworks for understanding the elements of interfaces and for guiding the dialogue developer in their construction". While [Hartson & Hix 89] focus on simple, non-adaptive dialogs, in this section structural modeling of human-computer interfaces is discussed with special consideration of adaptivity aspects in the interface. Within the model of an adaptive user interface, the pure dialog model is only one (functional) part among others. In the following we focus on a functional, user-centered approach to structuring software [Cockton 91]. Possible functions of adaptive user interfaces are summarized, and it is discussed how these functions are reflected by related software components and the overall architecture of the interface.

3.1 Functions of Adaptive User Interfaces and their Related Software Components

In order to realize adaptive, intelligent behavior, an interface has to deal with a large variety of problem domains and levels. Therefore, an adaptive interface must have access to many different knowledge sources (see [Rissland 84] for examples). Correspondingly, the structural model of the interface can be described as composed of elementary models which focus on the various functional aspects relevant to adaptive interaction (see Figure 11).

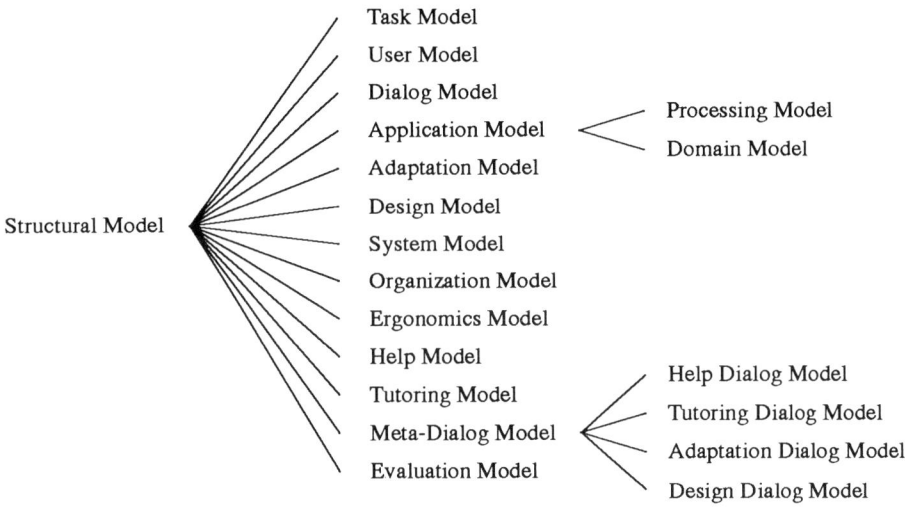

Figure 11: Elements of the Structural Model of an AUI

All these models are "embedded models" in the sense of being physically instantiated within and owned by the interface system (the notion of "embedded user models" in [Murray 87]).

The models can be implicitly contained in the interface program code or explicitly represented as a knowledge base or part of one. They can be distributed across the whole interface or centralized in separated components of the interface. In particular, the structural model can distinguish functions, i.e. elementary models which need not map directly onto distinct software components; some models might also be expressed by the overall architecture of the interface or by the functional relations between its components. Only a minority of all conceivable models (such as those listed in Figure 11) are explicitly considered in current adaptive interface prototypes. Most approaches propose at least three components dealing with a user model, a task model, and a dialog model. In addition, sometimes an application modeling component is included (see Figure 12). Elements of the adaptation model, such as levels and methods of adaptation, are often considered in connection with the dialog model. In this subsection, only these basic models and related components of AUI prototypes are briefly discussed, concentrating on their general purpose with respect to the structure of the interface as a whole. Formalisms and techniques which can configure these components are discussed in section 4.

It is widely accepted that a system which is intended to adapt to users and their tasks needs to model those aspects in some way. [Wahlster & Kobsa 89] distinguish between a user

	Task Model	User Model	Dialog Model	Application Model	
AIDA [Cote 90]	●	●	○		dialog model provided by a UIMS and a "monitor"
MONITOR [Benyon & Murray 88]	●	●	●		
PODIUM [Sherman 90]		●	●		
POISE [Croft 84]	○	○	○	○	knowledge base containing tasks, users, objects and tools
TELECOM GOLD [Totterdell et al. 90]	●	●	○	●	dialog controller
UIDE [Foley et al. 91]	○	○	○	○	interface representation with elements of task/appl. models

●   The model is explicitly implemented in the system.

○   The information that is normally represented in this model can be obtained from a knowledge source in the system.

Figure 12: Components of example prototype systems

model and a user modeling component: "A *user model* is a knowledge source ... which contains assumptions on all aspects of the user that may be relevant to the dialog behavior of the system. ... A *user modeling component* is that part of a dialog system whose function is to incrementally construct a user model; to store, update, and delete entries; to maintain the consistency of the model; and to supply other components with assumptions about the user." A similar distinction could be made for the task model. While the task model contains information about the tasks which can be performed in using the system, the task modeling component is involved in maintaining and supplying this information. However, the separation of a "passive" model and an "active" modeling component is not imperative: active, object-oriented models might be reasonable.

A dialog model describes the interactive behavior of a user interface. In the context of adaptive interfaces it is essential that the dialog model is flexible enough to permit changes of the user interface for reasons of adaptation [Browne et al. 90b]. The user interface designer must be able to specify design alternatives that can be selected at run-time by the user or through self-adaptation. Therefore, the dialog model has to provide a design space which gives the designer the opportunity to make decisions about the range, content, and control of strategies to be built into the system [Totterdell & Rautenbach 90]. In the same way [Cockton 87] points out that "flexible abstractions for executable dialogue specifications" are a "necessary condition for the success of adaptable human-computer interfaces". [Foley 91] goes in the same direction with a unified representation for user interfaces which comprises aspects of the dialog model that are particularly relevant to adaptation.

Besides being flexible, the main function of the dialog model is to form a basis for observing the dialog and collecting information about it. In particular, this information is needed to build up a user model. In the MONITOR prototype of an adaptive interface the dialog model, called an "interaction" model, includes additional information about individual sessions and a collated history of the dialog [Benyon & Murray 88]. For the same purpose, a monitoring component in conjunction with a UIMS is used in the AIDA system [Cote 90].

In the case of the dialog model, another, orthogonal dimension of software structuring can be considered: a structuring with respect to different interaction levels and the information flow between them [Cockton 91]. Several models have been proposed which divide human-computer interaction into layers [Nielsen 86]. They agree in distinguishing at least two coarse-grained layers (see Figure 13): a logical (also called invisible or symbol level) and a physical layer (also called visible or signal level). A refinement leads to a variety of different layers including, for instance, task level, semantic level, syntactic level, and lexical level.

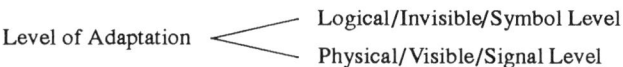

Figure 13: Levels of Adaptation

Adaptation processes can be assigned to these interaction levels. For instance, a syntactic level adaptation takes place on the basis of counting the interaction steps. A higher level adaptation on the task level intends to adapt the functionality of the system to the user's needs considering actual goals and tasks. Hence, if the interface needs to be adapted at a particular level, the corresponding level has to be modeled as a basis for this adaptation process.

Like adaptation levels, adaptation methods are an example for the adaptation model being part of or interfering with the dialog model. [Cockton 87] lists four basic methods of adaptation: *enabling*, *switching*, *reconfiguring*, and *editing* (Figure 14). Enabling is adaptation by activation or deactivation of components and features like indicators in process control systems. Switching is adaptation by selecting one of several different user interfaces, pre-configured user interface components (dialog configuration), or user interface settings (colors). Adaptation by reconfiguring is the modification of a user interface using pre-defined components. Editing is adaptation without any restrictions on the basis of the dialog model.

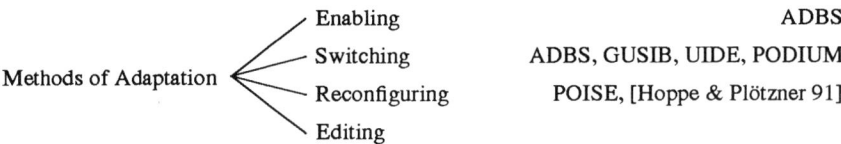

Figure 14: Methods of Adaptation

The provision of dialog independence, i.e. the separation of user interface and application program, becomes particularly important in the case of an adaptive user interface. [Browne et al. 90b] state that "adaptive user interfaces are dynamic by design and it is essential that this dynamism not be compromised by application software dependencies". They describe an example application modeling component (called *application expert*) which provides a mapping of logical user commands onto application specific functions. In the POISE prototype a sort of application model is given through a knowledge-based description of the available tool set [Croft 84].

3.2 Architectural Abstractions

While subsection 3.1 covers the components an AUI could consist of, this subsection addresses how these components could be fitted together to form the system's overall architecture. In the past, there have been several attempts to extract a reference model from concrete user interface architectures in order to understand and to classify existing architectures and to guide the construction of user interface software. The best known architectural models of user interfaces include the Seeheim model [Green 85] and the IFIP model [Dzida 87]. However, they (as others) do not consider adaptivity aspects. In the AUI literature almost no architectural abstractions can be found. Mostly, particular prototype architectures are reported instead of abstract models. Unfortunately, there is no clear pattern in them, as can be seen from Figures 15 to 17.

Figure 15 depicts the AID phase 1 architecture of an adaptive frontend to the Telecom Gold system described in [Totterdell et al. 90]. Besides containing the components mentioned

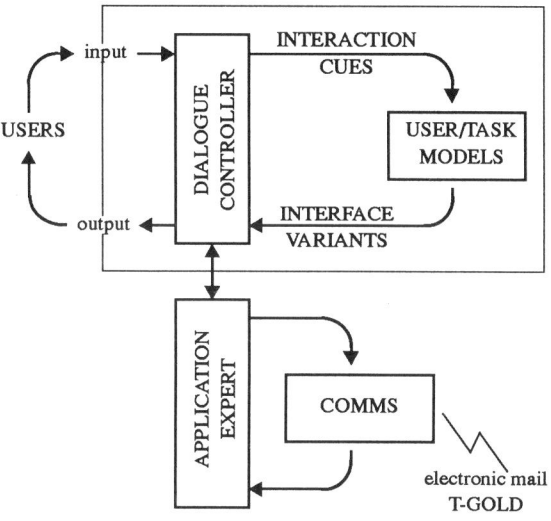

Figure 15: AID Phase 1 Architecture [Totterdell et al. 90]

above, this architecture includes an adaptation model sketched by the arrows to and from the user/task models. The AIDA architecture [Cote 90] suggests the integration of a UIMS and a knowledge base (see Figure 16). [Elkerton & Williges 89] introduce an architecture for an intelligent interface which lays stress on the provision of alternative dialogs (Figure 17).

4 REPRESENTATION AND ACQUISITION OF MODELS IN AUIS

4.1 User Modeling

One of the essential sources of information which strongly influences the process of adaptation is the user. In order to provide an individualized user interface, an adaptive system must possess knowledge about the user, i.e. relevant user characteristics.

In literature the term *"user model"* is charged with many different meanings. [Murray 87] lists some of them and in addition introduces the notion of an *"embedded user model"* which is "the System's Model ... of user characteristics for the purpose of tailoring the interaction or making the dialog between the user and system adaptive." This is the kind of model we have in mind when talking about user models. In addition, it should be mentioned that embedded user models should not be hard-wired in the program code, but represented instead as a separate piece of knowledge in order to allow dynamic updates.

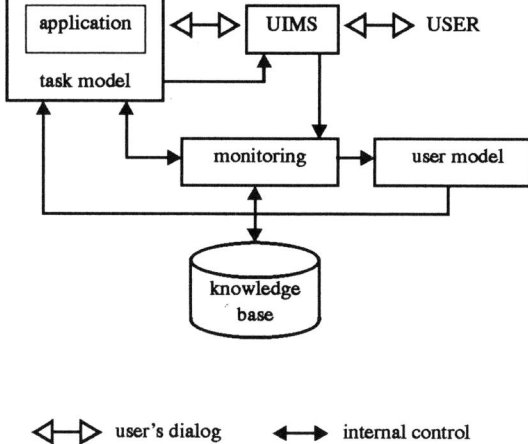

Figure 16: AIDA Architecture [Cote 90]

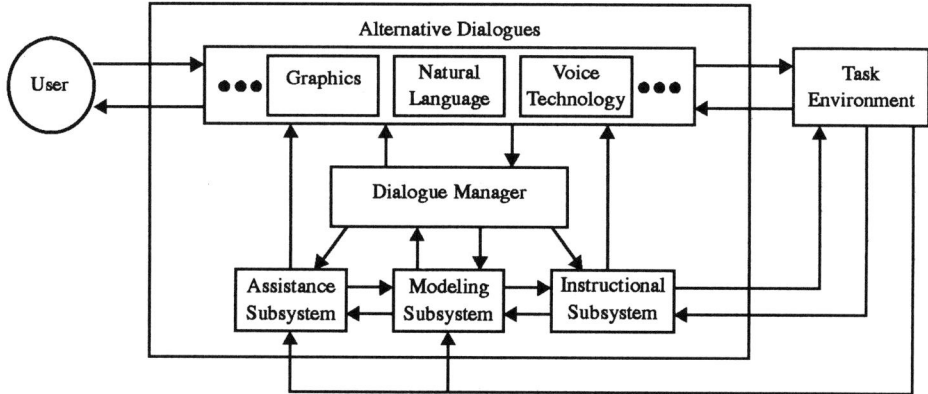

Figure 17: Architecture for an Intelligent Interface [Elkerton & Williges 89]

4.1.1 User Characteristics

The user characteristics reflected in a user model can be separated into categories. Among the application dependent characteristics are: prior experience with computers; knowledge of the present system and application; and goals, intentions, and expectations [Morris 87]. Among the application independent characteristics are preferences, psycho-motor skills, capabilities, cognitive and learning abilities, understanding, and motivation [Browne et al. 90b].

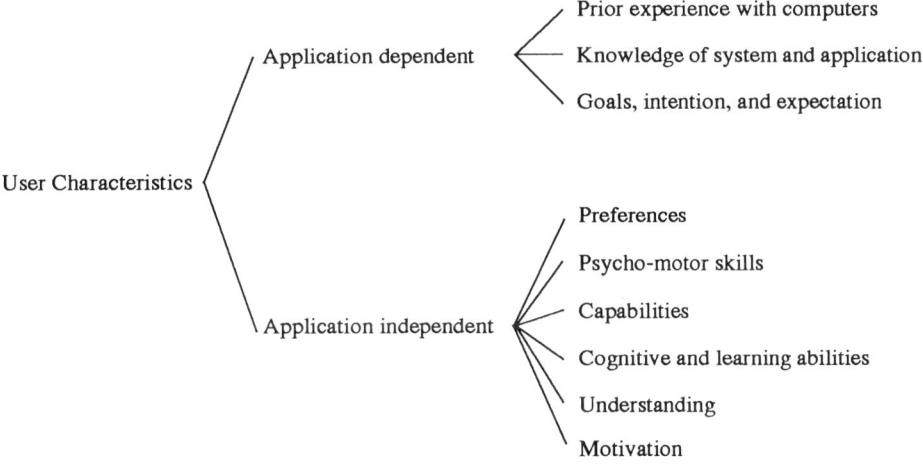

Figure 18: Contents of a User Model (User Characteristics)

4.1.2 Classification Dimensions of User Models

One of the first classification schemes of user models can be found in [Rich 79]. [Kass & Finin 88], [Schwab 89], and [Brajnik et al. 90] present refinements of this scheme. According to these, at least three dimensions can be identified.

One criterion to distinguish different user models is *granularity* [Rich 83]. The scale ranges from a single model for all users, a so-called *canonical* user model, to models for each *individual* user. In between, there are models for groups of users which have some characteristics in common. Using a canonical model is simplest because it allows the designer to complete the model during implementation. Canonical user models are of limited value in systems which are used by a heterogeneous user community. The other extreme, a model for each user, may be expensive and very difficult to achieve. For this reason often the *stereotypical* approach is chosen [Mason & Thomas 84, Bodendorf 90, Cote 90].

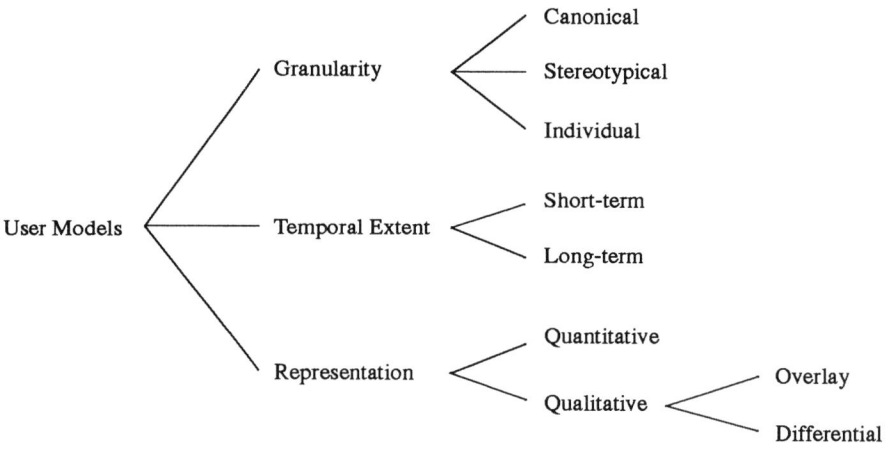

Figure 19: Dimension of User Models

Another criterion is *temporal extent* of the data acquired during a session. On the one hand, there are facts which are valid only in the current context or session (*"short-term* data"), for instance references to earlier situations in the present dialog, the last sentence typed in, or the user's topical level of attention and concentration. This aspect of a user model overlaps with what is often referred to as a "discourse model" [Rich 89], Schuster et al. 88]. On the other hand, there is information which should be kept beyond the current session (*"long-term* data") and, therefore, be saved on a permanent storage medium [Rich 83]. The latter category includes aspects like user's preferences, experience, and capabilities.

Knowledge about the user can be represented by *a quantitative* or *qualitative* model. The first type of user model contains quantitative data like the user's error rate, the number of help requests, or the amount of time which the user has spent with the system. SAUCI [Tyler 88] and GRUNDY [Rich 79] employ this kind of model. Within the qualitative category one can distinguish between *overlay models* - they encode the user's knowledge as a subset of the knowledge of an expert -, and *differential models* which contain the differences of the user's knowledge from that built into the system [Clowes et al. 85]. Systems like AIDA [Cote 90], or those described in [Mason & Thomas 84] and [Bodendorf 90], use qualitative models.

The actual model instantiation, i.e. the knowledge acquisition or "active" user modeling, can be achieved in different ways. One can start with an *empty* model; try to classify the user at the very first session into one or more *stereotypical* categories as in PODIUM [Sherman 90] or GRUNDY [Rich 79]; or build an initial *individual* model based on a preliminary question-answering session (SAUCI [Tyler 88]). During the interaction with the user these can be refined in the light of further information.

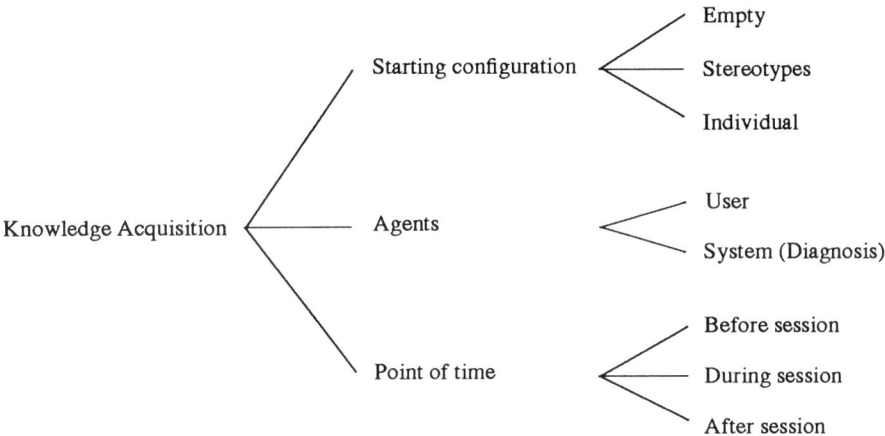

Figure 20: Knowledge Acquisition

There are two possible agents that can incrementally update the user model, either during use of the system or between sessions. One possibility is to make the *users* themselves do it, i.e. they are responsible for the explicit construction of their own "user profiles". This approach is quite simple provided the system is equipped with the necessary flexibility. This, however, puts an additional burden onto the user. In particular, novices who do not know what can be modified and how this can be achieved may be overcharged by this task. The other possibility for a user model is for the system to (incrementally) collect facts about the users. This knowledge acquisition can be achieved either directly by questioning the users at the beginning of a session or the first time they interact with a given system (cf. GRUNDY, PODIUM), or indirectly by monitoring the user interaction with the system, i.e. during the session.

The inferential approach is afflicted with uncertainty and possibly contradicting results may be derived, so one must provide a conflict resolution strategy. But also the other way, i.e. asking the user directly, does not necessarily lead to unbiased and consistent descriptions. [Rich 83] cites psychological studies which show that people are not very reliable sources of information about themselves. In both cases care must be taken that the resulting model will be consistent.

4.1.3 Representation Techniques

There are several ways to implement user models. The earlier prototypes use the traditional knowledge representation techniques of artificial intelligence like *frames* (MONITOR [Benyon 85]). With the advent of *object-oriented* software techniques, results from this field have been used to implement user models (SAUCI [Tyler 88]).

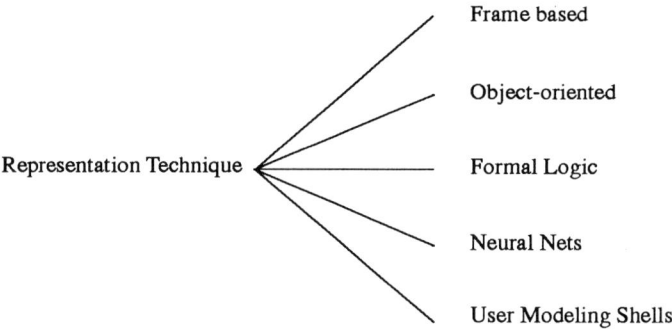

Figure 21: Representation Techniques

Due to the inherent property of formal logic to infer new facts from given ones and the simplicity of manipulating logical expression by computers there are some prototypes using this technique [Allgayer et al. 92, Kobsa 92].

Recently, new approaches like *neural nets* [Bodendorf 90] and *fuzzy logic* [Katz & Lesgold 92] have been used. These techniques allow coping with the "fuzzyness" and uncertainty of information about the user.

With the increase of systems using user models it was realized that the same steps of implementing these models from scratch were taken over and over again. To avoid this repetitive work the idea of generic shell systems was taken from the area of expert systems. Among these *user modeling shells* are: GUMS [Finin 89], MODUS [Schwab 89], BGP-MS [Kobsa 90], UM-Tool [Brajnik et al. 90, Brajnik & Tasso 92], UM [Kay 90].

4.2 Task Modeling

There is a large number of modeling techniques which emphasize different aspects of the relationship between the properties of a system and the user performance. [Wilson et al. 88] and [Green et al. 88] provide a good comparative survey of many of them. [Hoppe 93] gives a survey on representation, interpretation, and acquisition of task models. [Wilson et al. 88] differentiate them into four groups: models which analyze the knowledge content of real world tasks (e.g., TAKD [Johnson et al. 85], CLG [Moran 81]);

models to predict difficulties from interface specifications (ETIT [Moran 83], TAG [Payne 85], GOMS [Card et al. 83]); models which analyze the users' conceptual structures (Task Analysis for Information Structure Description [Wilson et al. 85], Analysis for Menu Systems [Young & Hull 83]); and models which analyze the cognitive activities (CTA [Barnard 87], Decomposition of mental activities [Norman 86]).

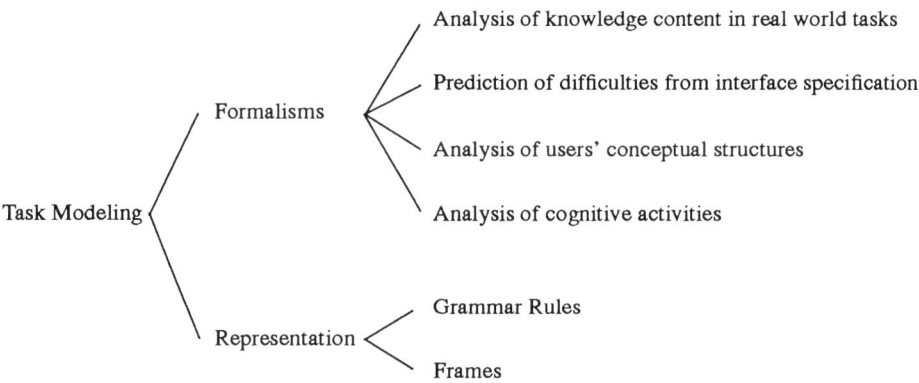

Figure 22: Task Modeling

Despite the variety of task modeling formalisms, [Benyon et al. 87] state that they have turned out to be inappropriate for practical use in adaptive user interfaces mostly because they do not provide means to handle modern interactive interfaces which are based on windows, icons, menus, and pointing devices ("WIMP-systems"). Many lack, for example, the possibility to describe parallelism and interrupts. Also, as [Cote 90] mentions, these models are static. There is evidence that the design of most prototypical adaptive systems is not explicitly based on task modeling.

In order to make these models operational on a computer, they have to be transformed into an executable form. For the representation either grammar rules (LEXITAS [Hoppe 88] which is a variant of TAG [Payne 85]), or frames (DELTA [Schwab 89]) have been used.

[Hoppe 93] describes some of the limitations and necessary extensions of task-oriented support provided by a user interface. It is argued that LEXITAS provides the means to handle the necessary extensions.

4.3 Dialog Modeling

Dialog models which are used to describe the structure of the dialog between a user and an interactive computer system can be specified in various ways. Dialog modeling is still a field of research as Cockton notes: "Intuitive approaches still dominate dialogue design"[Cockton 87]. There are several different models, but none of them have proved so far to be the best for all purposes. [Cockton 87a] lists five models adopted from formal computer science (Backus-Naur-Form (BNF), the class of transition networks, Petri Nets, production rules, and Hoare's Communicating Sequential Processes (CSP)) and discusses their strengths and weaknesses.

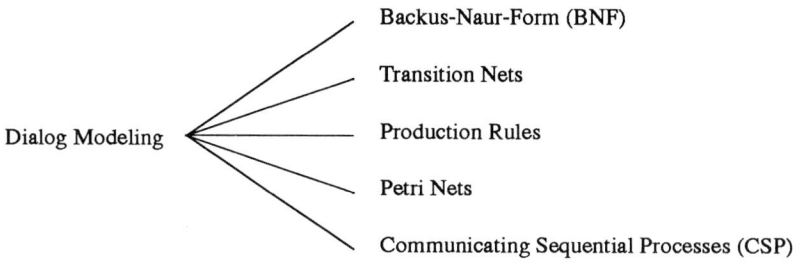

Figure 23: Dialog Modeling

Some of the criteria he uses in his comparison apply to all kinds of dialog control models; for example, *expressive power* which determines the structural complexity that can be described, or *parameterized modularization*, or *executability*. Although all UIMS require the executability of their underlying models, it is especially true for dynamically adaptable systems because in order to allow for within-session adaptation the dialog specifications must not be "configuration files for general purpose dialogue managers, or ... explicit unexecutable references for implementations ... [or] implicit and hard-wired into the code of specific dialogue managers", but must be contained in an operational form within the system [Cockton 87].

Other criteria are more important with respect to adaptivity of dialogs: *switchability*, *context sensitive branching* (which depends on user profiles and past input) as well as *explicit, labeled interaction points*. Given an executable "dialogue sequence description" one can achieve adaptation, for example, by enabling or disabling different paths through the dialog net of all possible dialogs, or by switching to "micro-dialogues" or context sensitive "meta-dialogues" [Cockton 87a]. [Alty 85] follows a similar strategy; CONNECT, the system he describes, monitors the users' interactions, and, based on production rules, opens or closes arcs in the network thereby altering its topology. *Avoidance of explicit ordering* is also an important feature of a given model because it is impossible to consider and implement all theoretically possible combinations of ordered sequences of user-actions which may occur during the interaction. Another vital property of a dialog model is its possibility to allow for the *description of parallelism*, i.e. of multi-threaded dialogs, interruption and resumption of a suspended main-dialog.

Each model has its strengths and weaknesses (also [Green 86] or [Scott & Yap 88]) and despite the fact that some of the limitations of each of the models cited above can be removed by extensions of the basic model, there is - similar to task models - no "winning" model but the designer has to decide upon the model which he considers to be most suitable in a given situation. [Browne et al. 90b], for example, mention their use of state transition networks as well as event-based models on their AID project, depending on the granularity of adaptation. This decision is not always made solely on hard facts but may also be influenced by human aspects like ease of use and understanding of a model, or by some subjective judgement based on the designer's preferences or familiarity with a specific model.

4.4 Plan Recognition

Plan recognition is closely related to both user and task aspects of adaptation. Its main goal is to recognize users' plans or parts thereof, in order to obtain further information for adaptation or to infer new tasks.

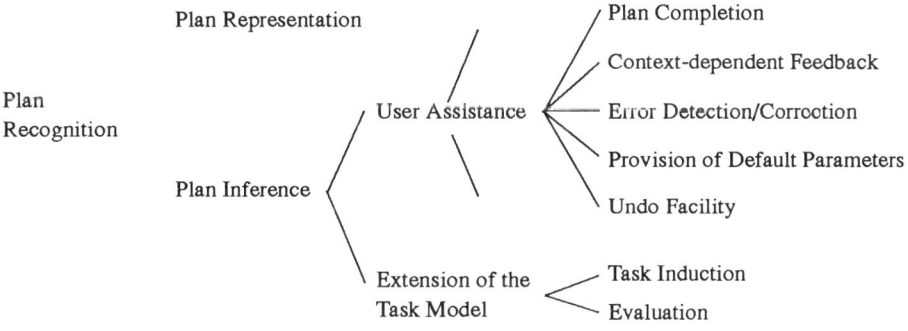

Figure 24: Plan Recognition

By monitoring the users' activities and inferring their intended plans, the system can give helpful *assistance* to the user: present possible *completions* of sub-plans; supply *default parameters*; offer *context-dependent feedback* (like appropriate error messages or help); provide a more reasonable *undo facility*; or *detect* and try to *correct global errors* (i.e., errors in user plans that otherwise would not be regarded as mistakes) [Pavlin 90, Tyler et al. 91].

[Schwab 89] describes an application-independent modeling shell called MODIA which consists of a knowledge base of all plans (formulated in the *plan representation* language DELTA), a plan recognition component, a plan completion component, and a structure containing information about the current state of the dialog. MODIA's plan recognizer is able to monitor several active plans in parallel.

In addition, [Hoppe & Plötzner 91] state that in the course of time (i.e., while working with the system), new tasks continuously come up which the designer could not anticipate. In traditional systems this will result in the need for repeated task analysis and redesign. Therefore, they propose to enable a computer system to *extend* its own *task model* automatically. This implies that the system has a component capable to infer new tasks, for example, by combining sequences of input primitives which occur frequently into new, higher-level task schemata ("*task induction*"), and possibly also a facility that *evaluates* the new tasks according to specific rules, for example, to prevent the incorporation of an apparently "new" but structurally equivalent task [Zinßmeister & Hoppe 89].

5 EXAMPLE CLASSIFICATIONS

The presented survey of projects and systems in the AUI research area is organized as a taxonomy resulting in a large classification tree. Considering each aspect on its own is important in order to investigate the immense variety of relevant issues. Since some of the aspects are orthogonal and others are not, the classification scheme is very complicated and makes it hard to obtain a general view on all the approaches. However, it is well suited to perform a comparative analysis of different approaches with respect to the diverse aspects. This is illustrated by the following example classifications of several systems.

Table 1 shows the classification of prototypes that are mentioned in papers included in this volume. Hopefully this will help the reader to get an idea of the relation between the different papers of different authors dealing with different themes. All of them have the common goal to provide means for the development of Adaptive User Interfaces. Table 2 gives the classification of systems that are mentioned in previous chapters of this paper. The examples are restricted to the aspects which can be extracted from the examined papers.

User interfaces generated with UIDE [Sukaviriya & Foley 93] provide context-sensitive help on the basis of a task and user interface description. The automatically generated help can answer the questions: Why is a command disabled? How can this command be enabled? What commands are available on an object?

A user interface designer uses PODIUM [Sherman 93] to generate a generic user interface for an application. The users can adapt the interface to their own preferences. Later on the system proposes further adaptations which have been chosen by several users of the application system. The user can accept or reject the proposed changes.

AIDA [Cote 93] provides a user interface for a CAD application that adapts to the users' skills and their methods of working. The user is provided with new functions that are constructed from the observation of the dialog with the system. If a user uses a sequence of commands several times, a new function, consisting of the sequence of commands, is automatically generated.

Aspect	UIDE	PODIUM	AIDA	Telecom Gold
Stages and Agents	User-Initiated Self-Adaptation	Self-Adaptation and User-Controlled Self-Adaptation	Adaptation and User-Controlled Self-Adaptation	Adaptation and Self-Adaptation
Adapted Constituents	system presentation of information	system presentation of information	task simplification	system presentation of information error correction
Considered Information	application context	preferences of a user group preferences of an individual user	individual user's experience, knowledge, and needs	application context individual knowledge and experience
Goal	make complex systems usable fit heterogeneous user groups consider increasing experience	make complex systems usable fit heterogeneous user groups	easy, effective, efficient use speed up use	consider increasing experience simplify use fit heterogeneous user groups
Method	switching	switching		switching
Timing	continuous on user's request	predefined junctures on user's request	on user's request special situations	continuous special situations
Models	task dialog application	user dialog	user application	user application

Table 1: Example Classification: Prototypes from this Volume

In the framework of the AID project [Browne 93] an adaptive user interface for the electronic mail system Telecom Gold was developed. It was mainly based on an application expert. The goal of the development of this system was to hide any system specifics from the user and provide a generic electronic mail interface. Furthermore, user commands were semantically analyzed to correct errors before submitting a group of commands to the application system. The whole communication with the application system is handled by the interface to hide any problems that are not task related from the user.

ADBS [Grimm 85] is a user interface for a process control application. Manner and contents of information presentation is adapted to the context and the previous dialog between user and application. The system provides adaptability without programming, adaptation by user identification, and high-level adaptation to changed tasks.

The user interface management system GUSIB [Dang 88] provides a dialog specification using the specification language DCG. The adaptation is based on users' experience with the system and their preferences. Their focus of interest considering current context is inferred from a dialog record.

Aspect	ADBS	GUSIB
Stages and Agents	Self-Adaptation and Adaptation	Self-Adaptation
Adapted Constituents	system presentation of information	system presentation of information
Considered Information	application context application situation user's needs and preferences	application context user preferences
Goal	make complex systems usable	make complex systems usable fit heterogeneous user groups consider increasing experience
Method	enabling & switching	switching
Timing	special situations on user's request	continuous
Models	user, application	dialog, user

Table 2: Example Classification: Prototypes from Literature

6 CONCLUSIONS

Looking at the classifications in Table 1 and Table 2 as examples for typical AUI research activities, two general conclusions can be drawn. Firstly, much work concentrates on self-adaptation that tries to automatically infer from dialogs all the information relevant for adaptation. Corresponding projects are quite ambitious. However, they all fail to prove that the results really match the users' needs and that these results are worth the additional, considerably large effort which has to be spent on their realization. Other approaches which give the users more control over the adaptation process and effectively support them in adapting the interface on their own seem to be more promising. In our analysis, the terms Computer-Supported Adaptation and User-Controlled/-Initiated Self-Adaptation were assigned to the related work.

Secondly, most projects concentrate on some singular aspects of adaptivity and/or on a specialized application. Results of preceding projects are exploited only to a minimal extent. Contemporary user interface technology is rarely taken into account. The time should have come now to make use of the experience previously gained by building up a framework in which a variety of aspects and applications can be considered. More effort should be spent on the integration of developed adaptivity mechanisms into common user interface design and management tools.

Thirdly, current prototypes use switching as an adaptation method and the adaptation space is therefore restricted to the dimensions predefined by the system designer.

Besides these more general issues there are still many open questions with respect to adaptation mechanisms. Several of these gaps have been identified by examining our multi-dimensional taxonomy. Examples include the questions "what kind of information has to be considered in the adaptation process" and "when should adaptation occur in order to be most successful". Another unresolved problem is the inadequacy of user models with respect to their extent and depth. The entire area of design constraints and the impact of ergonomic rules on adaptivity has not yet been dealt with. Furthermore, aspects of user acceptance and the evaluation of adaptation, which have been neglected in the past, need far more attention.

Inspecting the taxonomy we identified several aspects on which research effort should be spent. Nevertheless, it seems to be much more important to relate all the aspects mentioned in the taxonomy within a coherent development methodology for adaptive systems.

When starting to work on this taxonomy it was one of the expectations to identify promising directions for research in the AUI field. The taxonomy was built by inspecting current prototypes and the literature related to this field. The identification and characterization of different styles of adaptivity on the basis of the stages and agents distinction may help to focus our research and the work of others. On this basis we have come to the opinion that Computer-Aided Adaptation as described above is the most promising approach in order to obtain a user interface that will help the user to perform his tasks in a pleasant and effective way.

REFERENCES

[Allgayer et al. 92]
 J. Allgayer, H. J. Ohlbach, C. Reddig: *Modelling Agents with Logic*. In: [André et al. 92], pp. 22-34.

[André et al. 92]
 E. André, R. Cohen, W. Graf, R. Kass, C. Paris, W. Wahlster (Eds.): *UM 92 - Third International Workshop on User Modeling. Proceedings*, DFKI-Document D-92-17, 1992.

[Alty 85]
J. L. Alty: *Use of Path Algebras in an Interactive Adaptive Dialogue System.* In: [Shackel 85], pp.351-354.

[Barnard 87]
P. J. Barnard: *Cognitive Resources and the Learning of Human Computer Dialogues.* In: J. M. Carroll (Ed.): Interfacing Thought: Cognitive Aspects of Human-Computer Interaction. pp. 112-158, MIT Press, Cambridge, Mass., 1987.

[Benyon 85]
D. Benyon: *MONITOR: A Self-Adaptive User-Interface.* In: [Shackel 85], pp. 335-341.

[Benyon 93]
D. Benyon: *Accommodating Individual Differences through an Adaptive User Interface.* In: this book.

[Benyon & Murray 88]
D. Benyon, D. Murray: *Experience with Adaptive Interfaces.* The Computer Journal 31 (5), pp. 465-473, 1988.

[Benyon et al. 86]
D. Benyon, P. Innocent, D. Murray, J. Shergill: *Experiments in Adaptive Interfaces.* In: Proceedings IEE Colloquium on "Adaptive Man-Machine Interfaces" (Digest No 110), pp. 5/1-5/7, London, UK, 1986.

[Benyon et al. 87]
D. Benyon, P. Innocent, D. Murray: *System Adaptivity and the Modelling of Stereotypes.* In: [Bullinger & Shackel 87], pp. 245-253.

[Bodendorf 90]
F. Bodendorf: *Benutzermodellierung mit Hilfe Neuronaler Netze.* In: A. Reuter (Ed.): GI - 20. Jahrestagung II, pp. 349-358, Springer, Berlin, 1990.

[Brajnik et al. 90]
G. Brajnik, G. Guida, C. Tasso: *User modeling in Expert Man-Machine Interfaces: A Case Study in Intelligent Information Retrieval.* In: IEEE Transaction on Systems, Man, and Cybernetics, Vol. 20, No. 1, January/February 1990, pp. 166-185.

[Brajnik & Tasso 92]
Giorgio Brajnik, Carlo Tasso: *A Flexible Tool for Developing User Modeling Applications with Nonmonotonic Reasoning Capabilities.* In: [André et al. 92], pp. 42-66.

[Brooks & Thorburn 88]
A. Brooks, C. Thorburn: *User-driven Adaptive Behaviour, A Comparative Evaluation And An Inductive Analysis.* In: D. Jones, R. Winder (eds.): People and computers IV. Proceedings of the Fourth Conference of the British Computer Society (Univ. of Manchester, UK, Sept. 5-6, 1988), pp. 237-255. Cambridge University Press, New York, 1988.

[Browne et al. 86]
D. P. Browne, B. D. Sharrat, M. A. Norman: *The Formal Specification of Adaptive User Interfaces Using Command Language Grammar.* SIGCHI Bulletin 17 (4), pp. 256-260, April 1986.

[Browne 90]
D. Browne: *Conclusions.* In: [Browne et al. 90], pp. 195-212.

[Browne 93]
D. Browne: *Experiences from the AID Project*. In: this book.

[Browne et al. 90]
D. Browne, P. Totterdell, M. Norman (Eds.): *Adaptive User Interfaces*. Academic Press, London, 1990.

[Browne et al. 90a]
D. Browne, M. Norman, D. Riches: *Why Build Adaptive Systems?*. In: [Browne et al. 90], pp. 15-57.

[Browne et al. 90b]
D. Browne, M. Norman, E. Adhami: *Methods for Building Adaptive Systems*. In: [Browne et al. 90], pp. 85-130, 1990.

[Bullinger & Shackel 87]
H.-J. Bullinger, B. Shackel (Eds.): *Human-Computer Interaction - INTERACT'87*. Elsevier, Amsterdam, 1987.

[Card et al. 83]
S. K. Card, T. P. Moran, A. Newell: *The Psychology of Human-Computer Interaction*. Lawrence Erlbaum, Hillsdale, N.J., 1983.

[Clowes et al. 85]
I. Clowes, I. Cole, F. Arshad, C. Hopkins, A. Hockley: *User Modelling Techniques for Interactive Systems*. In: P. Johnson, S. Cook (Eds.): People and Computers: Designing the Interface, pp. 35-45. Proceedings of the Conference of the British Computer Society, Human Computer Interaction Specialist Group, 1985.

[Cockton 87]
G. Cockton: *Some Critical Remarks on Abstractions for Adaptable Dialogue Managers*. In: [Diaper & Winder 87], pp. 325-343.

[Cockton 87a]
G. Cockton: *Interaction Ergonomics, Control and Separation: Open Problems in User Interface Management*. Information and Software Technology 29 (4), pp. 176-191, 1987.

[Cockton 91]
G. Cockton: The Architectural Bases of Design Re-use. In: D. A. Duce, M. R. Gomes, F. R. A. Hopgood, J. R. Lee (eds.): User Interface Management and Design, Proceedings of the Workshop on User Interface Management Systems and Environments, Lisbon, Portugal, June 4-6, 1990, pp. 15-34, Springer-Verlag, Berlin, 1991.

[Cote 90]
J. A. Cote Muñoz: AIDA - *Ein an den Benutzer angepaßtes Graphisch-Interaktives System*. Doctoral Thesis (german). Darmstädter Dissertation D17, TH Darmstadt, 1990.

[Cote 93]
J. A. Cote Muñoz: *AIDA - An Adaptive System for Interactive Drafting and CAD Applications*. In: this book.

[Croft 84]
W. B. Croft: *The role of context and adaptation in user interfaces*. Int. J. Man-Machine Studies 21, pp. 283-292, 1984.

[Dang 88]
W. Dang: *Intelligence in a User Interface Management System.* ERGO-IA '88. European Colloquium - Ergonomics and Artificial Intelligence. Proceedings. CNRS, Univ. de Paris-Sud, Orsay, France, 1988.

[Diaper & Winder 87]
D. Diaper, R. Winder (Eds.): *People and Computers III.* Proceedings of the Third Conference of the British Computer Society, Human Computer Interaction Specialist Group, University of Exeter, Sept. 7-11, 1987.

[Dzida 87]
W. Dzida: *On Tools and Interfaces.* In: Psychological Issues of Human-Computer Interaction in the Work Place, M.Frese, E.Ulich, W.Dzida (eds.), North Holland, pp. 339-355, 1987.

[Edmonds 86]
E. A. Edmonds: *Towards a Taxonomy of user interface adaptation.* In: Proceedings IEE Colloquium on "Adaptive Man-Machine Interfaces" (Digest No 110), pp. 3/1-3/6. London, UK, 1986.

[Elkerton & Williges 89]
J. Elkerton, R. C. Williges: *Dialogue Design for Intelligent Interfaces.* In: [Hancock & Chignell 89], pp. 213-264.

[Finin 89]
T. W. Finin: *GUMS - A General User Modeling Shell.* In: [Kobsa & Wahlster 89].

[Fischer 93]
G. Fischer: *Shared Knowledge in Cooperative Problem-solving Systems - Integrating Adaptive and Adaptable Components.* In: this book.

[Foley 91]
J. Foley: *User Interface Software Tools.* In: J. Encarnaçao (Ed.): Telekommunikation und multimediale Anwendungen der Informatik, Proceedings GI-21.Jahrestagung, pp. 3-18. Springer, Berlin, 1991.

[Foley et al. 91]
J. Foley, Won Chul Kim, S. Kovacevic, K. Murray: *UIDE - An Intelligent User Interface Design Environment.* In: [Sullivan & Tyler 91], pp. 339-384.

[Fowler et al. 87]
C. J. H. Fowler, L. A. Macaulay, S. Siripoksup: *An Evaluation of the Effectiveness of the Adaptive Interface Module (AIM) in Matching Dialogues to Users.* In: [Diaper & Winder 87], pp. 345-359.

[Green 85]
M. Green: *Report on Dialogue Specification Tools*, In: G. E. Pfaff (Ed.): User Interface Management Systems, pp. 9-20, Springer, Berlin, 1985.

[Green 86]
M. Green: *A Survey of Three Dialogue Models.* ACM Transactions on Graphics 5 (3), pp. 244-275, 1986.

[Green et al. 88]
T. R. G. Green, F. Schiele, S. J. Payne: *Formalisable Models of User Knowledge in Human-Computer Interaction.* In: [van der Veer et al. 88], pp. 3-46.

[Grimm 85]
R. Grimm: *ADBS: A Tool for Designing and Implementing the Man-Process Interface for Different Users.* In: Analysis, Design and Evaluation of Man-Machine Systems, pp. 287-291. Proceedings of the 2nd IFAC/IFIP/IFORS/IEA Conference, Oxford, England, 1986.

[Hancock & Chignell 89]
P. A. Hancock, M. H. Chignell (Eds.): *Intelligent Interfaces: Theory, Research and Design.* North-Holland, Amsterdam, 1989.

[Hartson & Hix 89]
H. R. Hartson, D. Hix: *Human-Computer Interface Development: Concepts and Systems for Its Management.* ACM Computing Surveys 21 (1), pp. 5-92, March 1989.

[Hoppe 88]
H. U. Hoppe: *Task-Oriented Parsing - A Diagnostic Method to be used in Adaptive Systems.* In: Proceedings of CHI'88, Washington. pp. 241-247, 1988.

[Hoppe & Plötzner 91]
H. U. Hoppe, R. Plötzner: *Inductive Knowledge Acquisition for a UNIX Coach.* In: M. J. Tauber, D. Ackermann (Eds.): Mental Models and Human-Computer Interaction 2, pp. 313-335. Elsevier, Amsterdam, 1991.

[Hoppe 93]
H. U. Hoppe: *Intelligent User Support Based on Task Models.* In: this book.

[Johnson et al. 85]
P. Johnson, D. Diaper, J. B. Long: *Tasks, Skills and Knowledge: Task Analysis for Knowledge Based Descriptions.* In: [Shackel 85], pp. 499-503.

[Kass & Finin 88]
R. Kass, T. Finin: *Modeling the User in Natural Language Systems.* In: Computational Linguistics, Vol 14, No. 3, Sept. 1988, Special Issue on User Modeling.

[Katz & Lesgold 92]
S. Katz, A. Lesgold: *Approaches to Student Modeling in the Sherlock-Tutors.* In: [André et al. 92], pp. 205-230.

[Kay 90]
J. Kay (1990): *um: A Toolkit for User Modelling.* In Proc. of the Second International Workshop on User Modeling, pp. 1-11, Honolulu, HI.

[Kobsa & Wahlster 89]
A.Kobsa, W. Wahlster (Eds.): *User Models in Dialog Systems*, Springer, Berlin, 1989.

[Kobsa 90]
A. Kobsa: *Modeling the user's conceptual knowledge in BGP-MS, a user modeling shell system.* In: Computational Intelligence, Vol. 6, 1990.

[Kobsa 92]
Alfred Kobsa: *Towards Inferences in BGP-MS: Combining Modal Logic and Partition Hierarchies for User Modeling.* In: [André et al. 92], pp. 35-41.

[Mason 86]
M. V. Mason: *Adaptive command prompting in an on-line documentation system.* Int. J. Man-Machine Studies 25, pp. 33-51, 1986.

[Mason & Thomas 84]
> M. V. Thomas, R. C. Thomas: *Experimental adaptive interface*. Information Technology 3 (3), pp. 162-167, 1984.

[Moran 81]
> T. P. Moran: *The Command Language Grammar: a representation for the user interface of interactive computer systems*. Int. J. Man-Machine Studies 15, pp. 3 - 50, 1981.

[Moran 83]
> T. P. Moran: *Getting into a System: External / Internal Task Mapping Analysis*. In: CHI'83, Conference on Human Factors in Computing Systems, Boston, 1983. pp. 45-49, ACM, New York, 1983.

[Morris et al. 85]
> N. M. Morris, W. B. Rouse, S. L. Ward: *Experimental Evaluation of Adaptive Task Allocation in an Aerial Search Environment*. In: Analysis, Design and Evaluation of Man-Machine Systems, pp. 67-72. Proceedings of the 2nd IFAC/IFIP/IFORS/IEA Conference, Oxford, England, 1986.

[Morris 87]
> A. Morris: *Expert Systems - Interface Insight*. In: [Diaper & Winder 87], pp. 307-324.

[Motro 90]
> A. Motro: *Flex: A Tolerant and Cooperative User Interface to Databases*. IEEE Transactions on Knowledge and Data Engineering 2 (2), pp. 231-246, June 1990.

[Murray 87]
> D. M. Murray: *Embedded User Models*. In: [Bullinger & Shackel 87], pp. 229-235.

[Nielsen 86]
> J. Nielsen: *A virtual protocol model for computer-human interaction*. Int. J. Man-Machine Studies 24, pp. 301-312, 1986.

[Norman 86]
> D. A. Norman: *Cognitive Engineering*. In: D. A. Norman, S. W. Draper (Eds.): User Centered System Design, pp. 31-61. Lawrence Erlbaum Assoc., Hillsdale, N.J., 1986.

[Pavlin 90]
> J. Pavlin: *Task-aware user interfaces*. SIGCHI Bulletin 22 (1), pp. 55-60, July 1990.

[Payne 85]
> S. Payne: *Task-action Grammars*. In: [Shackel 85], pp. 527-532.

[Rich 79]
> E. A. Rich: *Building and exploiting user models*. PhD Thesis, Carnegie Mellon University, 1979.

[Rich 83]
> E. Rich: *Users are individuals: individualizing user models*. Int. J. Man-Machine Studies 18, pp. 199-214, 1983.

[Rich 89]
> E. Rich: *Stereotypes and User Modeling*. In: [Kobsa & Wahlster 89], pp. 35-51.

[Rissland 84]
   E. L. Rissland: *Ingredients of intelligent user interfaces*. Int. J. Man-Machine Studies 21, pp. 377-388, 1984.

[Rouse 88]
   W. B. Rouse: *Adaptive Aiding for Human/Computer Control*. Human Factors 30 (4), pp. 431-443, 1988.

[Shackel 85]
   B. Shackel (Ed.): *Human-Computer Interaction - INTERACT'84*, Elsevier, Amsterdam, 1985.

[Schuster et al. 88]
   E. Schuster, D. Chin, R. Cohen, A. Kobsa, K. Morik, K. Sparck Jones, W. Wahlster: *Discussion Section of the Relationship between User Models and Discourse Models*. In: Computational Linguistics, Vol. 14, No. 3, (Special Issue on User Modeling), pp. 79-103, 1988.

[Schwab 89]
   T. Schwab: *Methoden zur Dialog- und Benutzermodellierung in adaptiven Computersystemen*. Doctoral Thesis (german). Institut für Informatik, Universität Stuttgart, 1989.

[Scott & Yap 88]
   M. L. Scott, S. Yap: *A Grammar-Based Approach to the Automatic Generation of User Interface Dialogues*. In: CHI'88 Conference Proceedings of Human Factors in Computing Systems, pp. 73-78, 1988.

[Sherman 90]
   E. H. Sherman: *A User-Adaptable Interface to Predict Users' Needs*. Knowledge Systems Laboratory, Report KSL-90-56, Medical Computer Science, Stanford University, August 1990.

[Sherman 93]
   E. H. Sherman: *A User-Adaptable Interface to Predict Users' Needs*. In: this book.

[Sleeman & Brown 82]
   D. Sleeman, J. S. Brown: *Introduction: Intelligent tutoring systems*. In: D. Sleeman, J.S. Brown (Eds.): Intelligent Tutoring Systems. pp. 1-11, Academic Press, London, 1982.

[Sukaviriya & Foley 93]
   P. Sukaviriya, J. Foley: *A Built-in Provision for Collecting Individual Task Usage Information in UIDE: the User Interface Design Environment*. In: this book.

[Sullivan & Tyler 91]
   J. W. Sullivan, S. W. Tyler (Eds.): *Intelligent User Interfaces*. ACM Press, New York, 1991.

[Totterdell & Rautenbach 90]
   P. Totterdell, P. Rautenbach: *Adaptation as a Problem of Design*. In: [Browne et al. 90], pp. 59-84, 1990.

[Totterdell et al. 90]
   P. Totterdell, P. Rautenbach, S. O. Anderson: *Adaptive interface techniques*. In: [Browne et al. 90], pp. 131-160, 1990.

[Tyler 88]

S. W. Tyler: *SAUCI - A Knowledge-based Interface Architecture*. In: CHI'88 Conference Proceedings of Human Factors in Computing Systems, pp. 235-240, 1988.

[Tyler & Treu 89]

S. W. Tyler, S. Treu: *An interface architecture to provide adaptive task-specific context for the user*. Int. J. Man-Machine Studies 30, pp. 303-327, 1989.

[Tyler et al. 91]

S. W. Tyler, J. L. Schlossberg, R. A. Gargan, L. K. Cook, J. W. Sullivan: *An Intelligent Interface Architecture for Adaptive Interaction*. In: [Sullivan & Tyler 91], pp. 85-109.

[van der Veer & Beishuizen 88]

G. C. van der Veer, J. J. Beishuizen: *Computers and Education: Adaptation to Individual Differences*. In [van der Veer et al. 88], pp. 251-278.

[van der Veer et al. 88]

G. C. van der Veer, T. R. G. Green, J.-M. Hoc, D. M. Murray (Eds.): *Working with Computers: Theory versus Outcome*. Academic Press, London, 1988.

[Wahlster & Kobsa 89]

W. Wahlster, Alfred Kobsa: *User Models in Dialog Systems*. In: [Kobsa & Wahlster 89] pp. 4-34.

[Wilensky et al. 84]

R. Wilensky, Y. Arens, D. N. Chin: *Talking to UNIX in English: An Overview of UC*. Comm. of the ACM 27, pp. 574-593, 1984.

[Wilson et al. 85]

M.D. Wilson, P. J. Barnard, A. MacLean: *User learning of core command sequences in a menu system*. IBM Hursley Human Factors Report HF 114, IBM UK Lab. Ltd., Winchester, 1985.

[Wilson et al. 88]

M. D. Wilson, P. J. Barnard, T. R. G. Green, A. Maclean: *Knowledge-Based Task Analysis for Human-Computer Systems*. In [van der Veer et al. 88]], pp. 47-87.

[Young & Hull 83]

R. M. Young, A. Hull: *Categorisation Structures in Hierarchical Menus*. In: Proceedings of the Tenth International Symposium on Human Factors in Telecommunications, Helsinki. pp. 111-118, 1983.

[Zinßmeister & Hoppe 89]

G. Zinßmeister, H. U. Hoppe: *Acquisition of Task-Knowledge for an Adaptive User Interface*. GMD-Report, GMD-IPSI, Darmstadt, 1989.

ND

Shared Knowledge in Cooperative Problem-Solving Systems – Integrating Adaptive and Adaptable Components

Gerhard Fischer

University of Colorado at Boulder
Boulder, USA

ABSTRACT

Integrated, domain-oriented, knowledge-based design environments are examples of cooperative problem-solving systems relying on shared knowledge. Research goals pursued in the context of design environments are to support human problem-domain communication, to make information relevant to the task at hand, and to tailor information to a specific user or class of users.

The shared knowledge between a user and a system will not be static, but it will increase and change over time. There are two major ways that this can be achieved: by making systems *adaptable* (e.g., by supporting end-user modifiability), and *adaptive* (e.g., systems act differently based on a model of a specific task situation or a specific user).

We have developed prototypes of design environments that (1) demonstrate the need for shared knowledge, (2) support the incremental growth of shared knowledge, and (3) use the shared knowledge to make the interaction more user-specific and more task-oriented. Adaptable and adaptive mechanisms are used to achieve these goals.

ACKNOWLEDGMENTS

The author would like to thank the members of the Human-Computer Communication group at the University of Colorado, who contributed to the conceptual framework and the systems discussed in this paper. The research was supported in part by the National Science Foundation under grants No. IRI-9015441, MDR-9253425, and CDA-8922510, by the NYNEX Science and Technology Center, and by Software Research Associates.

1   COOPERATIVE PROBLEM-SOLVING SYSTEMS

Cooperative problem-solving systems [Stefik 86, Hill 89, Fischer 90] are knowledge-based environments supporting users in a symbiotic relationship to generate a product of their common effort. Knowledge-based systems can be designed to interact with their users in a cooperative fashion using several different interaction paradigms: doing, deciding, advising, tutoring, and critiquing. The main emphasis of our work has been to augment and empower human designers with domain-oriented design environments [Fischer 92] containing an embedded critiquing component [Fischer 91a].

Models [Norman 82] are of greater importance in cooperative problem-solving systems than in autonomous systems because the problem-solving activity and knowledge is shared by the cooperating agents. Two models are of special interest for shared knowledge systems [Fischer 91a]:

- M_1 : the users' models (the models that users have of systems and tasks), and
- M_2 : the systems' models (the models that systems have of users and tasks).

Cooperative problem-solving systems are *designed* systems. Comprehending designed systems requires an understanding of the goals, functions, and adaptive capabilities for which they can be used. The models associated with these systems are part of the design (i.e., they have to be designed too), and they can and should provide important requirements for the design.

High-Functionality Systems. Cooperative problem-solving systems require high-functionality systems for their realization, creating the following dilemma: on the one hand, these are systems where good models are most urgently needed; but on the other hand, it is unclear how these systems can be designed so users will be able to build models for them. Models for high-functionality computer systems cannot be deduced merely from experience because there are too many experiences to go through [Norman 86]. Learning complex systems is an incremental, indefinite process requiring an understanding of how users increase their knowledge and understanding of them in naturalistic settings over long periods of time.

High-functionality systems confront users with too much information. The challenge is to make the information relevant to the task at hand – i.e., delivering the right knowledge, in the context of a problem or a task, at the right moment for a human professional to consider [Fischer et al. 93]. Making information relevant to the task at hand poses many challenges for the design of interactive computer systems and it sets computer systems truly apart from other technologies (e.g., an example discussed in [Norman 93] is the printed version of the Official Airline Guide compared to (1) the electronic access to it allowing the display of results in a variety of ways, and (2) FlightFax providing schedule and fare information customized to a person's itinerary and delivering it with fax machines).

To develop better design requirements for high-functionality systems, usage patterns of them (as shown in Figure 1) provide important insights [Draper 84, Fischer 91a]. This qualitative analysis of users' knowledge about complex systems reveals two interesting findings:

Shared Knowledge in Cooperative Problem-solving Systems

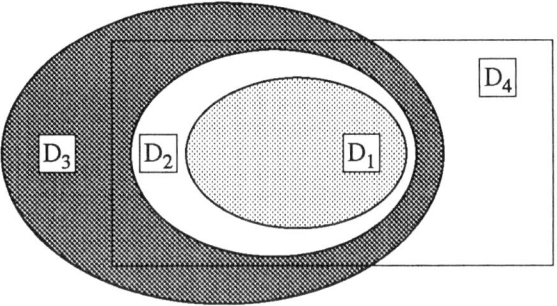

Figure 1: Levels of System Usage

In this figure the rectangle represents information embodied in a system (the system image) and ovals represent user knowledge about the system's information space.

D_1: The subset of concepts stored in the system's information repository that users know well and can use easily without the need for reference material.

D_2: The subset of concepts that users know vaguely and use occasionally. Users do not have complete understanding of the concepts, often requiring them to look the information up in manuals, etc.

D_3: The set of concepts that the user believes exist in the system. Note that some of the concepts lie outside of the actual information space.

D_4: The full set of concepts stored in the information repository of the system.

- The users' model of the system contains concepts that do not belong to the system (the part of D_3 that is not part of D_4).

- There are system parts of which users are unaware (the part of D_4 that is not part of D_3).

The former issue requires facilities assisting users in incrementally bringing their M_1-type models closer in accordance with the actual system. To address the latter issue, intelligent support systems are needed that rely on M_2-type models pointing out to users existing functionality that may be useful for their tasks.

M₁: The Users' Models of Systems. A user's model of a complex system is a cognitive construct that describes a user's understanding of a particular content domain in the world. These models are formed by experience, self-exploration, training, instruction, observation, and accidental encounters. In systems that operate at the "human-computer communication" level, the model will be centered around the properties of a computer system. An advantage of this type of model (representing a general computational environment) is that it is uniform across domains. In systems that operate at the "human problem-domain communication" level (giving users the feeling that they interact with concepts and representations drawn from the problem rather than from the computer domain [Fischer & Lemke 88]), users are able to form models using concepts much more closely related to an application domain.

M₂: The Systems' Models of Users and Tasks. There are a number of efforts to incorporate models of users into knowledge-based systems [Rich 83, Clancey 86, Kass & Finin 87, Fain-Lehman & Carbonell 89, Chin 89, Kobsa & Wahlster 89]. In our own research, we have investigated systems' models of users in connection with active help systems [Fischer et al. 85] and critics [Fischer 87, Fischer et al. 91a]. M_2-type models for critic systems pose specific demands. Unlike tutorial systems, which can track a user's expertise over a path of instruction, computer-based critics must work with users having a variety of background experiences. To operate effectively, critics should have a model of the task space in which the users operate. Having an adequate model, systems would allow for the (1) customization of explanations [Moore 89, Fischer et al. 90] so they cover exactly what users need to know; (2) provision of differential descriptions of new concepts in relationship to known concepts; (3) presentation of information through user-specific filters focusing on the parts that seem to be most relevant for a user [Fischer & Nakakoji 91]; and (4) they would keep active systems quiet most of the time [Fischer et al. 85].

Critics as Embedded System Components in Cooperative Problem-Solving Systems. Critiquing systems were first developed as stand-alone systems [Fischer 87]. Our current prototypes demonstrate that they are more powerful as embedded systems: critiquing is used as an interaction technique within integrated, domain-oriented design environments [Fischer et al. 91a, Fischer et al. 93]. The target audience for such systems is knowledge workers in application domains. Most domains have grown so complex that no single person can be considered an expert familiar with all aspects of the domain [Draper 84]. Support tools must include explanations of domain-specific knowledge and how this knowledge can assist users by critiquing their work. Experimental use of these prototypes demonstrated that in order for these systems to be truly cooperative, they must be tailored to the specific tasks and knowledge backgrounds of individual users.

As cooperative problem-solving systems move away from fine-grained analysis of simple interactions with a computer toward a focus on skilled users of high functionality systems, an essential characteristic of these systems will be their ability to adapt to their users. Systems' models of users in support of cooperative problem solving need to be dynamic, persistent, and domain-oriented. Achieving these goals requires co-adaptive systems [Mackay 92] that transcend system architectures based on a static user and static software environment.

The Desirability of Malleable Systems. Malleable systems are desirable for the following reasons: (1) to support mutual intelligibility (reciprocal recognizability of our actions, enabled by common conventions for the expression of intent, and shared knowledge about typical situations), (2) to support communicative economy (if the premises or rationale of an action can be assumed to be shared, they can be left unspoken), and (3) to achieve that tools and artifacts become ready-to-hand and invisible allowing users to communicate more directly with the task.

2 INTEGRATED, DOMAIN-ORIENTED, KNOWLEDGE-BASED DESIGN ENVIRONMENTS

Based on a number of design efforts in specific domains (e.g., kitchen design [Fischer et al. 89], user interface design [Lemke & Fischer 90], and computer network design [Fischer et al. 92]), we have developed a general architecture for integrated, domain-oriented, knowledge-based design environments (see Figure 2).

Our architecture currently consists of five components and three integrating mechanisms. The five components are:

- A *construction kit* [Fischer & Lemke 88] is the principal medium for modeling a design. It provides a palette of domain concepts and supports construction using direct manipulation and electronic forms.

- An *argumentative hypertext system* [Fischer et al. 91b] contains generic issues, answers, and arguments about the design domain. Users can annotate and add argumentation as it emerges during the design process.

- A *catalog* [Fischer et al. 92] is a collection of prestored designs illustrating the space of possible designs in the domain, and supporting reuse and case-based reasoning [Riesbeck & Schank 89]. By serving as a group memory, catalogs support long-term indirect communication among groups of designers. Group memories contain a collection of shared information repositories [Resnick 91] containing a cumulative record of rationale, solution components, information about prior projects, and other information resources for collaboration. There are two crucial issues concerning such a memory: (1) how information gets into the memory and how it accumulates, and (2) how information in the memory is made available to the individual designer.

- A *specification component* [Fischer & Nakakoji 91] allows designers to describe characteristics of the design they have in mind. The specifications are expected to be modified and augmented during the design process, rather

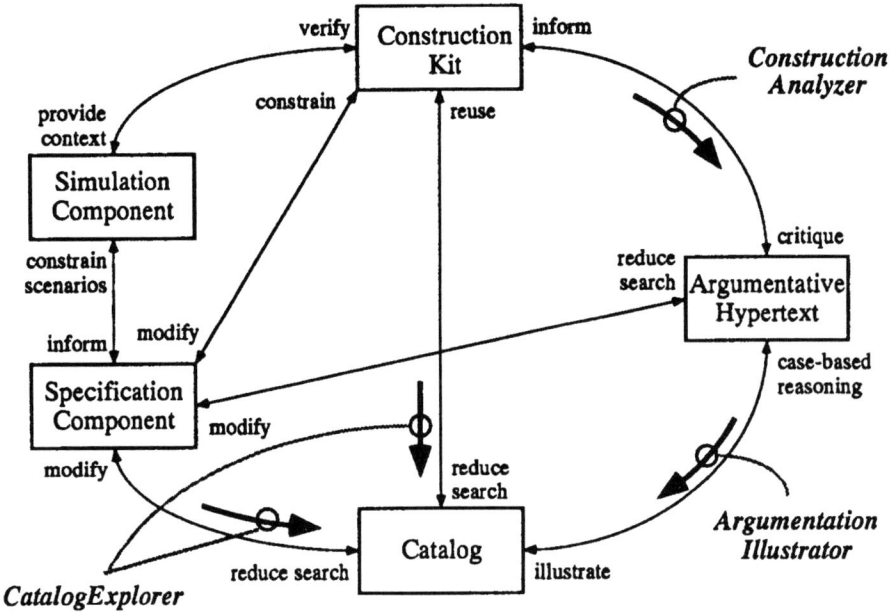

Figure 2: A Multifaceted Architecture

The components of the multifaceted architecture. The links between the components are crucial for exploiting the synergy of the integration.

than to be fully articulated at the beginning. They are used to retrieve design objects from the catalog and to filter information in the hypertext.

- A *simulation component* allows designers to carry out "what-if" games – that is, to simulate various usage scenarios involving the artifact being designed.

At each stage during the design process, the partially completed design embedded in the design environment serves as a stimulus suggesting to users what they should attend to next. To exploit the full power of the multifaceted architecture, the individual components need to be integrated. Currently the architecture supports the following linking mechanisms (see Figure 2):

- CONSTRUCTION ANALYZER. Users need support for construction, argumentation, and perception of breakdowns. Breakdowns are identified by the CONSTRUCTION ANALYZER operating as a critiquing system [Fischer et al. 91b]. The firing of a critic signals a breakdown and provides entry into the argumentative hypermedia system at which the corresponding argumentation is located. Accessing useful knowledge has as a prerequisite that the demand be noticed by the user, requiring that the situation talks back [Schoen 83]. For users who do not have extensive experience in the domain, the situation is often mute unless the environment has a component that speaks up and points out issues that the designer may otherwise not have considered. Critics can fulfill this role. Critics point out suboptimal aspects of the artifact and know the places where the corresponding issues are discussed in the argumentation component [Fischer et al. 91b].

- ARGUMENTATION ILLUSTRATOR. The explanation given in the form of argumentation is often highly abstract and conceptual. Concrete design examples matching the explanation help users to understand the concept. The ARGUMENTATION ILLUSTRATOR helps users to understand information given in the argumentative hypertext by finding a catalog example that illustrates the concept.

- CATALOGEXPLORER. CATALOGEXPLORER helps users search the catalog space according to the task at hand [Fischer & Nakakoji 91]. It retrieves design examples similar to the current construction and specification. The catalog and the CATALOGEXPLORER are used to explore the roles of examples.

3 WHY DESIGN ENVIRONMENTS NEED TO BE ADAPTIVE AND ADAPTABLE

Adaptive systems change themselves based on the user's behavior [Fischer et al. 85]. An adaptive system must contain models of the domain, of the task, and/or of the users to adapt appropriately. Adaptive systems have among their goals (1) to filter information in a user- and task-specific way (so the "knowledge in the head" of a specific user is complemented naturally by the "knowledge in the world" offered by the system [Norman 93]), and (2) to present to users information of which they are not aware of (represented by the part of D_4 that is not part of D_3 in Figure 1) thereby supporting learning on demand. Adaptable systems are systems that can be modified by users in non-obvious ways (e.g., beyond the choosing of certain parameter settings [Henderson & Kyng 91]). The goals of adaptable systems include (1) making the system fit new requirements by adding or changing knowledge structures, and (2) evolving seeds by creating functional enhancements [Fischer et al. 92].

Adaptable systems allow users to modify the systems while working with them (examples for adaptable systems are Microsoft Word, EMACS [Stallman 81], NoteCards [Trigg et al. 87], BUTTONS [MacLean et al. 90], and OBJECT-LENS [Lai & Malone 88]). Adaptable systems allow users to change the domain model (i.e., D_4 in Figure 1). A specific approach making systems adaptable is supporting end-user modifiability [Fischer & Girgensohn 90, Girgensohn 92].

A Comparison Between Adaptive and Adaptable Systems. Adaptable and adaptive systems can and should be used complementarily. Figure 3 gives a high-level comparison between adaptive and adaptable systems.

	Adaptive	Adaptable
Definition	• dynamic adaptation by the system itself to current task and current user	• user changes (with substantial system support) the functionality of the system
Knowledge	• contained in the system • projected in different ways	• knowledge is extended
Strengths	• little (or no) effort by the user • no special knowledge of the user is required	• user is in control • system knowledge will fit better • success models exist
Weaknesses	• user has difficulty developing a coherent model of the system • loss of control • few (if any) success models exist (except humans)	• systems become incompatible • user must do substantial work • complexity is increased (users need to learn and know to interact with the adaptation component)
Mechanisms Required	• models of users, tasks, and dialogs • knowledge base of goals and plans • powerful matching capabilities • incremental update of models	• layered architecture • human problem-domain communication • "back-talk" from the system • design rationale
Application Domains	• active help systems • critiquing systems • differential descriptions • user interface customization	• end-user modifiability • tailorability • information filtering • design in use

Figure 3: A Comparison Between Adaptive and Adaptable Systems

Why Design Environments Need to Be Adaptive. Design environments are high-functionality systems. The need for adaptive mechanisms is illustrated by the following example: the critiquing component of our systems encodes generic design knowledge about domains (e.g., such as "the stove should be in front of a window" or "the work-triangle should be less than 23 feet" in the kitchen design domain [Fischer et al. 89]). Without a

Shared Knowledge in Cooperative Problem-solving Systems 57

specification component, the system will be stuck with generic advice, and it will be unable to respond to user-specific situations, such as "a person in the household is only 5 feet tall" or "the family has a large number of small children"). If the system has this knowledge, critic messages and example selections can be made adaptive to the specific design situation. To support this adaptivity, we have developed a specification component [Fischer & Nakakoji 91] allowing users to describe the unique features of their design situation to the system. Specification components are explicit knowledge acquisition components in support of making systems more responsive to the task at hand (see Figure 4).

```
Specification sheet.
□Size of family?      Small  Medium  Large  Do-Not-Care
 Do both husband and wife work?        Either  Both  Do-Not-Care
 Who does the cooking?       Husband  Wife  Senior  House-Maid  Do-Not-Care
 Cook's approximate height?     -5'   5'-5'6"   5'6"-6'   6'-   Do-Not-Care
 Right Handed or left handed?      Right  Left  Do-Not-Care
 How many meals are generally prepared a day?     1  2  3  More  Do-Not-Car
 Size of meals?       Big  Medium  Small  Do-Not-Care
 Do kids help cook or bake?       Often  Sometimes  Never  Do-Not-Care
 Do you usually use a dishwasher?       Yes  No  Do-Not-Care
 Is safety important to you?      Yes  No  Do-Not-Care
□Are you interested in an efficient kitchen?       Yes  No  Do-Not-Care
  Done                              Abort
```

(a): Specification Sheet

```
Specify the factor of importance for each specified item.   Least                Most
Size of family?  Small
Do both husband and wife work?  Both
Who does the cooking?  Wife
Cook's approximate height?  5'-5'6"
Right Handed or left handed?  Left
How many meals are generally prepared a day?  2
Do you usually use a dishwasher?  No
Is safety important to you?  Yes
Are you interested in an efficient kitchen?  Yes
             Do It □                               Abort □
```

(b): Weighting Sheet for the Specification

Figure 4: Specification Component of a Design Environment for

(a): The Specify command in CATALOGEXPLORER provides a specification sheet in the form of a questionnaire.

(b): After specification, users weigh the importance of each specified item.

Why Design Environments Need to Be Adaptable. Design environments must be adaptable because (1) human knowledge is tacit [Polanyi 66] (i.e., humans know more than they can say), and (2) the domain that the environments model changes over time.

End-user modifiable systems support their users in modifying systems according to their own needs. End-user modifiability allows users to tailor a system to pursue additional tasks, to have different preferences, and to adapt the system to changing needs over time in the real world. The intended users of end-user modifiable systems are knowledgeable in the application domain but unable or unwilling to modify a system on the programming language level.

Malleable Systems: Integrating Adaptive and Adaptable Components. Our design environments integrate adaptive and adaptable components in a variety of ways. The construction situation and the specification component are sources of information for adaptive features (e.g., influencing the set of active critics, and making information in the catalog and in the argumentation component relevant to the task at hand). Figure 5 illustrates that system architectures integrating adaptive and adaptable components are based on shared decision making requiring shared knowledge.

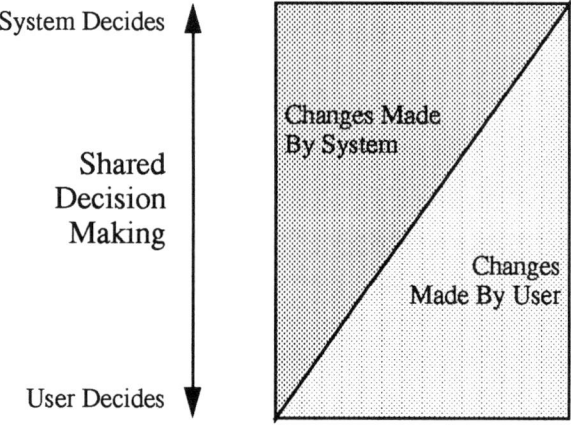

Figure 5: Integrating Adaptable and Adaptive Components

There is a broad spectrum of shared decision making between purely adaptive and purely adaptable systems in which users and system components contribute to the modification of a system.

The integration can be illustrated by showing how a standard critiquing system can be extended to a conditional one. A critiquing system that criticizes all designs based on the same standards is based on standard critics [Fischer et al. 93]. Design domains often have a basic set of rules that all artifacts in that domain should follow (e.g., in kitchen design [Fischer et al. 89] there are building codes, safety regulations, and functional principles; and in computer network design [Fischer et al. 92] there are standards established by committees). Standards that apply to all designs in a domain are important for designers to understand and follow. Novices especially need to be reminded when their design violates the design standards, but even for experts this type of support is necessary in situations where there is too much detail for one person to process.

Although standard critics are good at enforcing a set of rules that may be applied to all designs for a domain, they do not fully support design processes. Design theorists [Schoen 83, Rittel 84] tell us that each design project should be seen as unique. It is the responsibility of the designer to understand the unique characteristics of the design situation and to formulate a solution that address the unique characteristics.

Obeying general rules and design standards is necessary but not sufficient for good design. Design environments must support the designer in seeing the situation at hand as unique. Domain standards can help constrain designs, but at the same time standards alone do not determine a design solution. For interesting design domains, generic design rules play only a part in the final product of design. Conditional critics allow a design environment to evaluate design situations in accordance with partial specifications [Fischer et al. 93]. The partial specification represents a set of goals articulated by the user. Each specification item corresponds to a set of critics, which detect design situations relevant to that specification item. The set of specification items chosen by the designer determines which critics are active. Only active critics participate in the evaluation of design situations.

The partial specification is a resource for both the system and the designer (and is thereby an important part of the shared knowledge): (1) it allows the system to generate design-specific (rather than domain-specific) critiquing, and (2) it allows the designer to understand the design in terms of its unique characteristics rather than its common ones.

Conditional critics can detect design situations where one specification item conflicts with another, creating trade-off situations. To resolve a trade-off between conflicting goals, the designer must decide which goal (articulated as one specification item) is more important. To support this type of reasoning, specification items can be weighted. Being able to quickly manipulate the specification allows the designer to investigate the implications of different priority schemes. Support for understanding trade-offs is vital for complex problems where goals and priorities cannot be known a priori.

Machine learning can be seen as another approach for integrating adaptive and adaptable systems. It can be defined operationally to mean the ability to perform new tasks that could not be performed before or perform old tasks better as a result of changes produced by the learning process [Carbonell 89]. Machine learning can be integrated into end-user modifiable systems. If users want to introduce new concepts to the system, they could show the system examples and counterexamples for this concept, and the system would learn these concepts by example (see Figure 6).

Other Possibilities for Integrating Adaptable and Adaptive Systems. Modification critics [Girgensohn 92] are adaptive system components that critique the adaptations of users. Adaptive components can be used to "suggest" to users how to adapt systems [Fi-

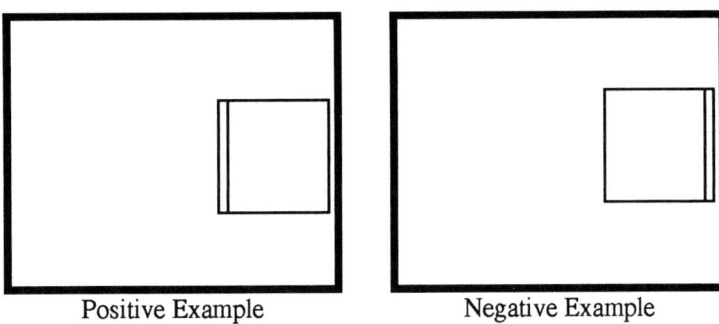

Positive Example   Negative Example

Figure 6: Learning a Rule with Examples

Our design environment for kitchen floorplans supports the creation of positive and negative examples, which can be used to integrate new knowledge into the system.

scher et al. 91a, Thomas & Krogsæter 93, Oppermann 92]. Adaptable systems could benefit from adaptive explanation components. It would also be beneficial if the interface for adaptations were adaptive to some extent so that it would be easier for users with different skills to do adaptations. In adaptive systems, it would be helpful if the users could adapt the parameters for the adaptation of the system, e.g., when to use which stereotype.

Other Efforts Integrating Adaptable and Adaptive Systems. InVision [Kass & Stadnyk 92] combines adaptable and adaptive mechanisms to address the information overload problem as it occurs in organizations (e.g., "who do I tell" and "who do I ask" type questions). InVision relies on explicitly represented models of the knowledge and information needs of members of the organization. It supports simultaneously the "computer as tool" paradigm (users explicitly build models using a specification by reformulation approach) and "computer as agent" paradigm (the system infers users' information needs based on observations of their interactions with data base systems) and it supports conflict resolution techniques for resolving contradicting information.

INFOSCOPE [Fischer & Stevens 91, Stevens 93] allows users to evolve the predefined system structure (for reading Usenet News) to suit their own semantic interpretations. Users can define virtual newsgroups. To do so, they can exploit information provided by agents who observe their behavior over periods of time and accumulate it in an M_2-type model. INFOSCOPE illustrates how adaptive components can be used to drive the adaptation of a system.

Shared Knowledge in Cooperative Problem-solving Systems 61

FLEXCEL [Thomas & Krogsæter 93] is a research effort to add flexibility to a commercially available software systems (EXCEL). An empirical investigation of FLEXCEL [Oppermann 92] has shown that adaptive and adaptable systems are not alternatives, but are most promising when both features are linked to cooperate. Adding adaptable components to EXCEL demonstrated that such components (1) do not come for free (neither for designers nor for the users), (2) require users to shift from their tasks to a meta-task, and (3) will not be successful without extensive support mechanisms. The adaptive component of FLEXCEL assists users in the adaptation process by (1) preparing them to adapt the system, (2) presenting clues when to turn from the domain task to the meta-task of adaptation, and (3) achieving a balance between massive interruption and merely mute potential.

4 SHARED KNOWLEDGE SYSTEMS

Wittgenstein: "If a lion could speak would we understand her?"

Figure 7 illustrates communication breakdowns caused by a lack of shared understanding. The visitor cannot build up a coherent model. More of the information provided should

Figure 7: Lack of Shared Understanding

Drawing by Stevenson; © 1976 The New Yorker Magazine

have been put into the world (e.g., by drawing a map, thereby grounding the mutual understanding with a shared artifact). The structural model provided by the policeman is too detailed; it may be possible to avoid this by tailoring the explanations more to the goals and objectives of the visitor. The policeman could have reduced the complexity of his description using layers of abstractions or by providing minimalist explanations [Black et al. 87, Fischer et al. 90]. The policeman (by seeing the visitor the first time) is unable to model the background knowledge of the visitor, indicating that shared understanding is not a one-shot affair but a cooperative problem-solving effort [Moore 89, Fischer 90, Fischer & Reeves 92] requiring follow-up questions and detail-on-demand.

Adaptive and adaptable systems are desirable for the following reasons: (1) to support mutual intelligibility and reciprocal recognizability of our actions, enabled by common conventions for the expression of intent, and shared knowledge about typical situations, and (2) to support communicative economy (if the premise or rationale of an action can be assumed to be shared, it can be left unspoken). Design environments can be interpreted as shared knowledge systems [Resnick 91] at several levels:

- The domain-orientation of the design environments supports human problem-domain communication [Fischer & Lemke 88] by eliminating the need for users to deal with low-level computer-specific programming concepts, thereby allowing users to communicate directly with the problem domain rather than with the computer.

- The construction and the specification component allows users to articulate their specific problem-solving situation.

- Other system components (critics, catalog, argumentation, and simulation) illustrate the system's knowledge to users in the context of their task at hand.

Adaptive and Adaptable Components in the Context of Design Environments. Opponents of adaptive components based on M_2-type models [Dumais 90, Hollan 90] have argued that there is little evidence from real systems that such models can be successfully constructed or exploited to enhance cooperative problem-solving activities. This criticism is justified by the lack of assessment studies analyzing the strength and weaknesses of systems' models of users as well as the absence of a true success story of such a system beyond research environments. These opponents are more in favor of adaptable systems and support mechanisms to enhance M_1-type models. This view is based on the belief that (1) users know more about their interests, goals, and state of knowledge than what can be communicated, defined, abstracted, and exploited by most modeling mechanisms; and (2) knowledge is tacit, requiring the back-talk of the situation to trigger additional knowledge.

Design environments provide unique opportunities to enhance and integrate adaptive and adaptable components by exploiting shared knowledge structures:

- their domain orientation [Fischer 92] establishes a restricted set of objectives and goals, which users pursue in using them,

- the systems are used repeatedly over long periods of time by domain workers (making techniques such as "Edit Wear and Read Wear" [Hill et al. 92] an important information source to drive modifications),

- the design artifact is present in the design situation [Reeves & Shipman 92] (indicating some of the goals of users), and

- the specification component allows users to articulate the specifics of a design situation [Fischer & Nakakoji 91].

The shared knowledge is used (1) to make information more relevant to the task at hand (e.g., by prioritizing information structures in the palette, catalog, and argumentation), (2) to help users to create better artifacts, and (3) to support learning on demand [Fischer 91b].

5 CONCLUSIONS

Interaction between people and computers requires essentially the same interpretive work that characterizes interaction between people, but with fundamentally different resources available to the participants [Suchman 87]. People make use of linguistic, nonverbal, and inferential resources in finding the intelligibility of actions and events, which are in most cases not available and not understandable by computers. Cooperative problem-solving systems need to take this asymmetry seriously and find alternative ways to enhance effective problem-solving activities rather than just relying on the simulation of human communication. Design environments offer interesting possibilities for integrating adaptive and adaptable components to increase the shared knowledge between users and computers.

REFERENCES

[Black et al. 87]
J.B. Black, J.M. Carroll, S.M. McGuigan, *What Kind of Minimal Instruction Manual Is The Most Effective*, Human Factors in Computing Systems and Graphics Interface, CHI+GI'87 Conference Proceedings (Toronto, Canada), ACM, New York, 1987, pp. 159-162.

[Carbonell 89]
J.G. Carbonell, *Introduction: Paradigms for Machine Learning*, Artificial Intelligence, Vol. 40, No. 1-3, 1989, pp. 1-9.

[Chin 89]
D.N. Chin, *KNOME: Modeling What the User Knows in UC*, in A. Kobsa, W. Wahlster (eds.), *User Models in Dialog Systems*, Springer-Verlag, New York, 1989, pp. 74-107.

[Clancey 86]
W.J. Clancey, *Qualitative Student Models*, Annual Review of Computing Science, Vol. 1, 1986, pp. 381-450.

[Draper 84]
S.W. Draper, *The Nature of Expertise in UNIX*, Proceedings of INTERACT'84, IFIP Conference on Human-Computer Interaction, Elsevier Science Publishers, Amsterdam, September 1984, pp. 182-186.

[Dumais 90]
S.T. Dumais, *Panel: User Modeling and User Interfaces*, Proceedings of AAAI-90, Eighth National Conference on Artificial Intelligence, AAAI Press/The MIT Press, Cambridge, MA, August 1990, pp. 1135-1136.

[Fain-Lehman & Carbonell 89]
J. Fain-Lehman, J.G. Carbonell, *Learning the User's Language: A Step Toward Automated Creation of User Models*, in A. Kobsa, W. Wahlster (eds.), *User Models in Dialog Systems*, Springer-Verlag, New York, 1989, pp. 163-194.

[Fischer 87]
G. Fischer, *A Critic for LISP*, Proceedings of the 10th International Joint Conference on Artificial Intelligence (Milan, Italy), J. McDermott (ed.), Morgan Kaufmann Publishers, Los Altos, CA, August 1987, pp. 177-184.

[Fischer 90]
G. Fischer, *Communications Requirements for Cooperative Problem Solving Systems*, The International Journal of Information Systems (Special Issue on Knowledge Engineering), Vol. 15, No. 1, 1990, pp. 21-36.

[Fischer 91a]
G. Fischer, *The Importance of Models in Making Complex Systems Comprehensible*, in D. Ackerman, M. Tauber (eds.), Mental Models and Human Computer Communication: Proceedings of the 8th Interdisciplinary Workshop on Informatics and Psychology (Schaerding, Austria), Elsevier Science, Amsterdam, 1991, pp. 3-36.

[Fischer 91b]
G. Fischer, *Supporting Learning on Demand with Design Environments*, Proceedings of the International Conference on the Learning Sciences 1991, Evanston, IL, August 1991, pp. 165-172.

[Fischer 92]
G. Fischer, *Domain-Oriented Design Environments*, Proceedings of the 7th Annual Knowledge-Based Software Engineering (KBSE-92) Conference (McLean, VA), IEEE Computer Society Press, Los Alamitos, CA, September 1992, pp. 204-213.

[Fischer et al. 85]
G. Fischer, A.C. Lemke, T. Schwab, *Knowledge-Based Help Systems, Human Factors in Computing Systems*, CHI'85 Conference Proceedings (San Francisco, CA), ACM, New York, April 1985, pp. 161-167.

[Fischer et al. 89]
G. Fischer, R. McCall, A. Morch, *JANUS: Integrating Hypertext with a Knowledge-Based Design Environment*, Proceedings of Hypertext'89 (Pittsburgh, PA), ACM, New York, November 1989, pp. 105-117.

[Fischer et al. 90]
G. Fischer, T. Mastaglio, B.N. Reeves, J. Rieman, *Minimalist Explanations in Knowledge-Based Systems*, Proceedings of the 23rd Hawaii International Conference on System Sciences, Vol III: Decision Support and Knowledge Based Systems Track, Jay F. Nunamaker, Jr (ed.), IEEE Computer Society, 1990, pp. 309-317.

[Fischer et al. 91a]
G. Fischer, A.C. Lemke, T. Mastaglio, A. Morch, *The Role of Critiquing in Cooperative Problem Solving*, ACM Transactions on Information Systems, Vol. 9, No. 2, 1991, pp. 123-151.

[Fischer et al. 91b]
G. Fischer, A.C. Lemke, R. McCall, A. Morch, *Making Argumentation Serve Design*, Human-Computer Interaction, Vol. 6, No. 3-4, 1991, pp. 393-419.

[Fischer et al. 92]
G. Fischer, J. Grudin, A.C. Lemke, R. McCall, J. Ostwald, B.N. Reeves, F. Shipman, *Supporting Indirect, Collaborative Design with Integrated Knowledge-Based Design Environments*, Human-Computer Interaction, Special Issue on Computer Supported Cooperative Work, Vol. 7, No. 3, 1992, pp. 281-314.

[Fischer et al. 93]
G. Fischer, K. Nakakoji, J. Ostwald, G. Stahl, T. Sumner, *Embedding Computer-Based Critics in the Contexts of Design*, Human Factors in Computing Systems, INTERCHI'93 Conference Proceedings, ACM, 1993, (in press).

[Fischer & Girgensohn 90]
G. Fischer, A. Girgensohn, *End-User Modifiability in Design Environments, Human Factors in Computing Systems*, CHI'90 Conference Proceedings (Seattle, WA), ACM, New York, April 1990, pp. 183-191.

[Fischer & Lemke 88]
G. Fischer, A.C. Lemke, *Construction Kits and Design Environments: Steps Toward Human Problem-Domain Communication*, Human-Computer Interaction, Vol. 3, No. 3, 1988, pp. 179-222.

[Fischer & Nakakoji 91]
G. Fischer, K. Nakakoji, *Making Design Objects Relevant to the Task at Hand*, Proceedings of AAAI-91, Ninth National Conference on Artificial Intelligence, AAAI Press/The MIT Press, Cambridge, MA, 1991, pp. 67-73.

[Fischer & Reeves 92]
G. Fischer, B.N. Reeves, *Beyond Intelligent Interfaces: Exploring, Analyzing and Creating Success Models of Cooperative Problem Solving*, Applied Intelligence, Special Issue Intelligent Interfaces, Vol. 1, 1992, pp. 311-332.

[Fischer & Stevens 91]
G. Fischer, C. Stevens, *Information Access in Complex, Poorly Structured Information Spaces*, Human Factors in Computing Systems, CHI'91 Conference Proceedings (New Orleans, LA), ACM, New York, 1991, pp. 63-70.

[Girgensohn 92]
A. Girgensohn, *End-User Modifiability in Knowledge-Based Design Environments*, Unpublished Ph.D. Dissertation, Department of Computer Science, University of Colorado, 1992, Also available as TechReport CU-CS-595-92.

[Henderson & Kyng 91]
A. Henderson, M. Kyng, *There's No Place Like Home: Continuing Design in Use*, in J. Greenbaum, M. Kyng (eds.), *Design at Work: Cooperative Design of Computer Systems*, Lawrence Erlbaum Associates, Hillsdale, NJ, 1991, ch. 11, pp. 219-240.

[Hill 89]
W.C. Hill, *The Mind at AI: Horseless Carriage to Clock*, AI Magazine, Vol. 10, No. 2, Summer 1989, pp. 29-41.

[Hill et al. 92]
W.C. Hill, J.D. Hollan, D. Wroblewski, T. McCandless, *Edit Wear and Read Wear*, Human Factors in Computing Systems, CHI'92 Conference Proceedings (Monterey, CA), ACM, May 1992, pp. 3-9.

[Hollan 90]
J.D. Hollan, *User Models and User Interfaces: A Case for Domain Models, Task Models, and Tailorability*, Proceedings of AAAI-90, Eighth National Conference on Artificial Intelligence, AAAI Press/The MIT Press, Cambridge, MA, August 1990, pp. 1137.

[Kass & Finin 87]
R. Kass, T. Finin, *Modeling the User in Natural Language Systems*, Computational Linguistics, Special Issue on User Modeling, Vol. 14, No. 3, 1987, pp. 5-22.

[Kass & Stadnyk 92]
R. Kass, I. Stadnyk, *Using User Models to Improve Organizational Communication*, Proceedings of 3rd International Workshop on User Modeling (U M'92), The German Research Center for Artificial Intelligence, Dagstuhl, Germany, August 1992, pp. 135-147.

[Kobsa & Wahlster 89]
A. Kobsa, W. Wahlster (eds.), *User Models in Dialog Systems*, Springer-Verlag, New York, 1989.

[Lai & Malone 88]
K.-Y. Lai, T.W. Malone, *Object Lens: A "Spreadsheet" for Cooperative Work*, Proceedings of the Conference on Computer-Supported Cooperative Work (CSCW'88), ACM, New York, September 1988, pp. 115-124.

[Lemke & Fischer 90]
A.C. Lemke, G. Fischer, *A Cooperative Problem Solving System for User Interface Design*, Proceedings of AAAI-90, Eighth National Conference on Artificial Intelligence, AAAI Press/The MIT Press, Cambridge, MA, August 1990, pp. 479-484.

[Mackay 92]
W.E. Mackay, *Co-adaptive Systems: Users as Innovators*, CHI'92 Basic Research Symposium, 1992.

[MacLean et al. 90]
A. MacLean, K. Carter, L. Lovstrand, T. Moran, *User-Tailorable Systems: Pressing the Issues with Buttons*, Human Factors in Computing Systems, CHI'90 Conference Proceedings (Seattle, WA), ACM, New York, April 1990, pp. 175-182.

[Moore 89]
J. Moore, *Responding to 'HUH': Answering Vaguely Articulated Follow-up Questions*, Human Factors in Computing Systems, CHI'89 Conference Proceedings (Austin, TX), ACM, New York, May 1989, pp. 91-96.

[Norman 82]
D.A. Norman, *Some Observations on Mental Models*, in D. Gentner, A.L. Stevens (eds.), *Mental Models,* Lawrence Erlbaum Associates, Hillsdale, NJ, 1982, pp. 7-14.

[Norman 86]
D.A. Norman, *Cognitive Engineering*, in D.A. Norman, S.W. Draper (eds.), *User Centered System Design, New Perspectives on Human-Computer Interaction*, Lawrence Erlbaum Associates, Hillsdale, NJ, 1986, pp. 31-62, ch. 3.

[Norman 93]
D.A. Norman, *Things That Make Us Smart*, Addison-Wesley Publishing Company, Reading, MA, 1993, Expected publication, early 1993.

[Oppermann 92]
R. Oppermann, *Adaptively Supported Adaptability*, Sixth European Conference on Cognitive Ergonomics, Human-Computer Interaction: Tasks and Organization (Balatonfuered, Hungary), September 1992, pp. 255-270.

[Polanyi 66]
M. Polanyi, *The Tacit Dimension*, Doubleday, Garden City, NY, 1966.

[Reeves & Shipman 92]
B.N. Reeves, F. Shipman, *Supporting Communication between Designers with Artifact-Centered Evolving Information Spaces*, Proceedings of the Conference on Computer-Supported Cooperative Work (CSCW'92), ACM, New York, November 1992, pp. 394-401.

[Resnick 91]
L.B. Resnick, *Shared Cognition: Thinking as Social Practice*, in L.B. Resnick, J.M. Levine, S.D. Teasley (eds.), *Perspectives on Socially Shared Cognition*, American Psychological Association, Washington, D.C., 1991, pp. 1-20, ch. 1.

[Rich 83]
E. Rich, Users are Individuals: *Individualizing User Models*, International Journal of Man-Machine Studies, Vol. 18, 1983, pp. 199-214.

[Riesbeck & Schank 89]
C. Riesbeck, R.C. Schank, *Inside Case-Based Reasoning*, Lawrence Erlbaum Associates, Hillsdale, NJ, 1989.

[Rittel 84]
H.W.J. Rittel, *Second-Generation Design Methods*, in N. Cross (ed.), *Developments in Design Methodology*, John Wiley & Sons, New York, 1984, pp. 317-327.

[Schoen 83]
D.A. Schoen, *The Reflective Practitioner: How Professionals Think in Action*, Basic Books, New York, 1983.

[Stallman 81]
R.M. Stallman, *EMACS, the Extensible, Customizable, Self-Documenting Display Editor*, ACM SIGOA Newsletter, Vol. 2, No. 1/2, 1981, pp. 147-156.

[Stefik 86]
M.J. Stefik, *The Next Knowledge Medium*, AI Magazine, Vol. 7, No. 1, Spring 1986, pp. 34-46.

[Stevens 93]
C. Stevens, *Helping Users Locate and Organize Information*, Unpublished Ph.D. Dissertation, Department of Computer Science, University of Colorado, 1993.

[Suchman 87]
L.A. Suchman, *Plans and Situated Actions*, Cambridge University Press, Cambridge, UK, 1987.

[Thomas & Krogsæter 93]
C.G. Thomas, M. Krogsæter, *An Adaptive Environment for the User Interface of Excel*, Proceedings of the 1993 International Workshop on Intelligent User Interfaces, Orlando, Fl, 1993, ACM Press.

[Trigg et al. 87]
R.H. Trigg, T.P. Moran, F.G. Halasz, *Adaptability and Tailorability in NoteCards*, Proceedings of INTERACT'87, 2nd IFIP Conference on Human-Computer Interaction (Stuttgart, FRG), H.-J. Bullinger, B. Shackel (eds.), North-Holland, Amsterdam, September 1987, pp. 723-728.

Experiences from the AID Project

Dermot P. Browne

KPMG Management Consulting
London, UK

1 INTRODUCTION

The Adaptive Intelligent Dialogues (AID) project was part of the United Kingdom's Alvey program which sponsored collaborative research between academia and industry. The project ran for four years beginning in 1984. The collaborators were STC Technology Ltd., Data logic Ltd., British Telecommunications plc, University of Hull, University of Strathclyde and University of Essex. What follows is a brief insight into some of the lessons learned during the project as seen through the eyes of one researcher.

The objectives of the project were to:

- research the principles of intelligent adaptive behaviour,
- build and evaluate exemplars demonstrating adaptive behaviours,
- produce tools to assist in the development of adaptive user interfaces.

It may seem odd but one of the most pervasive lessons learned was also a most obvious one. Do not forget why you are researching adaptive dialogues! That is, what is the objective of building adaptation into any system? While the project may have naively begun by believing that the answer to this question was independent of the system in question it soon learned that this was not the case.

> Worthwhile adaptation is system specific. It is dependent on the users of that system and requirements to be met by that system. For instance, when building system X we built in adaptive behaviours so that users could work more productively.

A second lesson learned and one that we sometimes had to re-learn was that there has to be a reason for the adaptation. This reason has to be based on discernible differences or changes that exist or take place within the user population of the system.

> There has to be something to adapt to.

This latter lesson can be made more specific as we found to our cost. It has to be possible for the adaptive system being built to identify the variance in the user population or their interactions with the system and these variances had to be reliable.

> An adaptive system must be able to identify reliable variances in its user population. For instance, users can be reliably classified as field dependent or independent.

A further lesson learned was that the user interface of the system under consideration must be able to modify itself in a directed manner. These modifications must be responsive to the user variances identified. The objective of these adaptive changes must be to improve interaction in some definable manner. Only if there is some predicted relationship between the changes and the user variances will it be possible for any observer to assess the value of the adaptations.

> There must be some definable relationship between the adaptations made by the system and the user variances. For instance, increasing the amount of Help messages given to a user decreased their error rates.

It was the experience of the AID project, or at least that of this author, that testing our work against the above statements made our research more focused and effective. As a result of learning these lessons, the hard way, the project availed itself of both a method for developing Adaptive Intelligent Dialogues (MAID) and a set of metrics for clarifying our understanding.

2 METRICS

The AID project developed a set of metrics to make explicit the categories of data that were found to be elements of an adaptive system [Browne et al. 1987]. These metrics were found useful when planning, designing, building and evaluating adaptive systems. Importantly the metrics allowed us to ask rudimentary questions about the viability of possible systems. They allowed us to be critical of designs, they focused our development work and guided our evaluations.

The six categories of metric are described below.

Objective Metric (Obj.M)

An Objective Metric provides the purpose of the adaptations. If the purpose were to increase a user's productivity with a system then Obj.M might be a time measure for the completion of some standard tasks. Clarifying the purpose of the adaptations in this way may lead a design team to specify that a time measurement facility be built into the software of the adaptive system.

Theory Assessment Metric (Tass.M)

A Theory Assessment Metric is required when the success of the system, in meeting its objective, is only indirectly related to the attribute of user interaction which the adaptations are attempting to affect. The relationship between Tass.M and Obj.M may be theoretical and untested. For instance it might be posited that user satisfaction will be more positive

Experiences from the AID Project

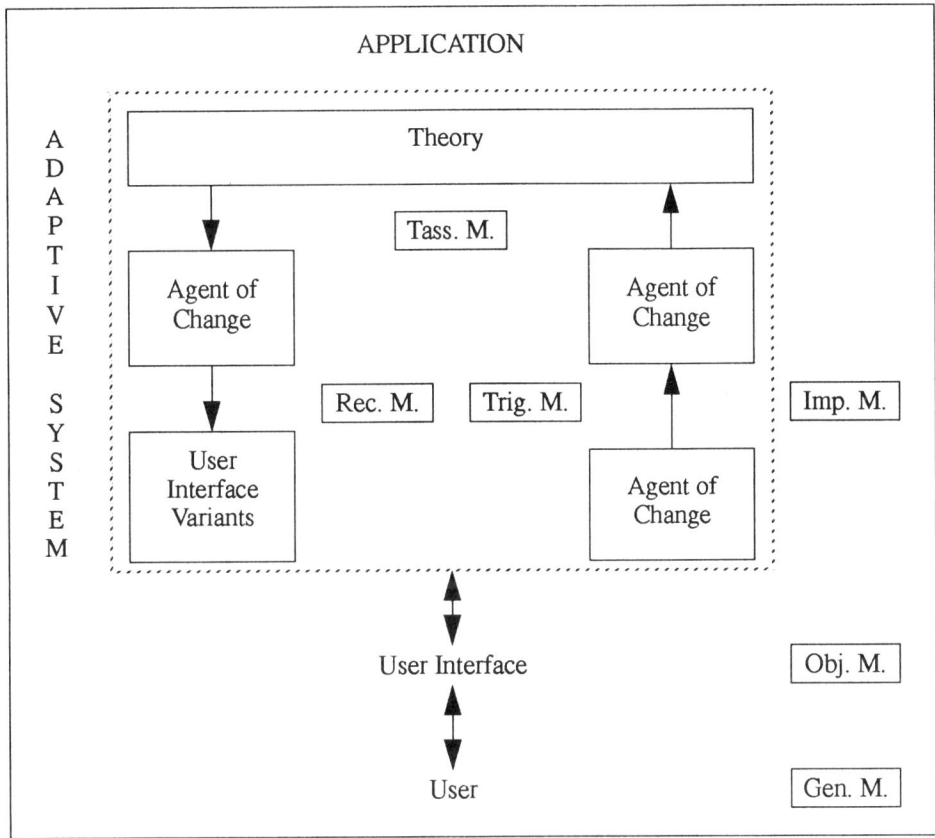

Figure 1: The Six Metrics of an Adaptive System

(Obj.M) if error rates are decreased (Tass.M). The relationship between these factors may be unknown and therefore the theory will need to be tested. The test will depend on not only collecting user satisfaction ratings but also error rate data.

Trigger Metric (Trig.M)

The Trigger Metric quantifies those aspects of user interaction that will be used as a basis for adaptations. Such triggers can be various. Error rates or even changes in error rates could provide triggers for adaptations. Other examples could include requests for help, typing rate, sequences of data retrieval and accesses to particular functions. Triggers are the sources for adaptations and so the developers must assure themselves that the chosen triggers can be captured by the system.

Recommendation Metric (Rec.M)

This metric quantifies the adaptations being made by the system. Adaptations can take many forms such as changes to screen formats, changes to the level of help provided, alterations to data structures or modifications to command sets. Whatever the change it should be quantified as far as possible. Only by so doing will it be possible for evaluators to explain the effects of the adaptations.

Generality Metric (Gen.M)

This category of metric aims to qualify the applicability of the adaptive systems. An adaptive system might be found to work for persons under twenty years of age performing tracking tasks in game like scenarios. From such findings it is not possible to make any definitive statements about other user groups or even the same user group under different environmental conditions. Thus researchers of adaptive systems wishing to understand and share their findings should qualify the generality of their work by collecting Generality Metrics.

Implementation Metric (Imp.M)

Finally, the development team should aim to estimate the impact of having embedded adaptation. Rendering a system adaptive can be expensive in terms of processing power and may cause delays in system response times. Such side effects of adaptation should be quantified. In fact if estimates can be provided in advance of development occasions may be found where a pointless development exercise can be terminated in a cost-effective manner.

Importantly, the metrics listed above can be estimated at various stages during the development of an adaptive system. The value of this is that flawed designs can be terminated early, saving valuable resources and allowing effort to be re-directed. As the following sections will show, the metrics provide a framework for justifying, designing, constructing and evaluating of adaptive systems.

Figure 1 depicts, in abstract, the relationship of the six metrics to the adaptor module of an adaptive system. The interaction between the user and the user interface provide cues for adaptations. These cues are described by Trig.M. These cues are used to populate models describing the user, their tasks or both. The actual changes that take place at the user interface are described by Rec.M. The relationship between the recommendations made by these models and the expected effects they will have on user interaction are assumptions that are described by Tass.M. Apart from the metrics describing the adaptor module of an adaptive system three metrics are used to describe the environment in which the adaptive system exists. Imp.M describes aspects of implementing the adaptations that might impact success of those adaptations. Obj.M simply describes the purpose of the adaptations; the positive impacts that it is hoped will be experienced by users. Finally Gen.M provides data that define the circumstances in terms such as user populations and types of tasks for which the adaptations have been tried.

3 METHOD FOR ADAPTIVE INTERFACE DESIGN

Having availed itself of a set of metrics to describe its work the AID project then developed a methodology that utilised these metrics and gave rigour to our work. This method (MAID) is briefly described below.

The stages of the methodology are shown in Figure 2. Each of these stages is subdivided into steps.

3.1 Requirements Analysis

The first stage is Requirements Analysis.

Firstly the developers should ascertain the *Requirement(s)* for the system in general and any adaptation in particular. For instance, the objective might be to increase productivity or extend the system's life span. The developers should also establish the generality of the required system; who is it for and under what circumstances will it be used. At this early point in a development both the objective (Obj.M) and the generality (Gen.M) of the system must be established. If the Requirements for adaptation are unclear then do not continue.

The next important question related to *Variability*. What variability exists within the user population or the tasks they are expected to perform that might usefully provide triggers (Trig.M) for adaptation? Again the reader may think these are obvious questions but it is all too easy to happily embark on a development in the mistaken belief that user differences can be reliably captured. If no bases for making adaptations can be found then do not continue.

Next a sort of cost-benefit analysis should be performed to assess the *Acceptability* of the development. This analysis should seek to quantify the costs of developing the adaptive system in terms of resources and time against the expected benefits as indicated by the objectives of having the system. If the costs of providing adaptations is too high then stop.

The final part of Requirements Analysis seeks to establish criteria, in terms of *Usability*, by which the success of the final system can be judged.

Having clarified the potential and worth of developing and adaptive system the developers should now progress to questioning the viability of such an endeavour.

3.2 Viability Analysis

This stage aims to establish the relationship between the variability in the user population identified previously with worthwhile changes at the user interface.

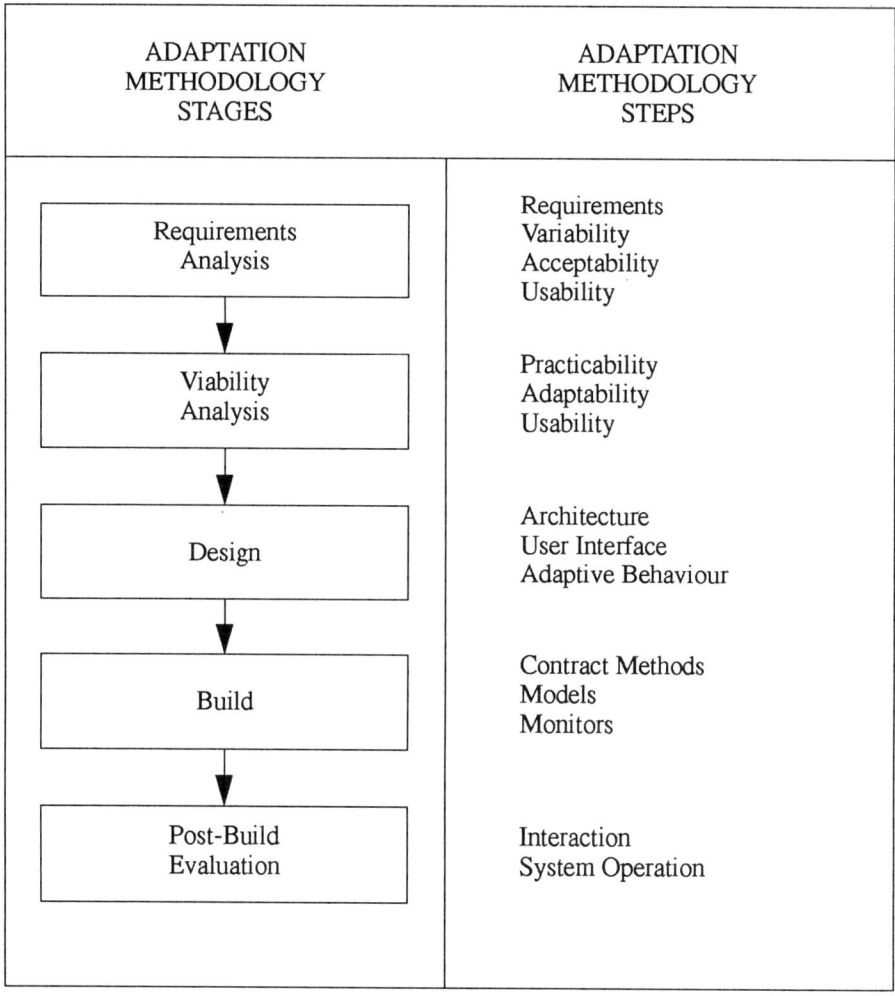

Figure 2: Method for Adaptive Interface Design

Developers must convince themselves of the *Practicability* of rendering the system adaptive. For the adaptations to be practical it must be possible to:

- capture triggers upon which adaptations can be based (Trig.M),
- determine what changes will take place at the user interface as a result of the adaptations and whether these changes can actually be supported (Rec.M),
- document any assumptions that are being made about the relationship between the triggers and the interface changes (Tass.M).

Experiences from the AID Project 75

In essence the assessment of Practicality is questioning the theory that will be embodied by the adaptive module of the system. Such theories need to have data (Trig.M) on which to operate, they must make proposals (Rec.M) and they are probably based on some assumptions (Tass.M).

The means by which the trigger data is collected largely determines the *Level of Adaptability* of the system. Triggers might be collected through negotiation with the user, by the system automatically, or by a combination of the two. Higher levels of adaptation may be achieved if the system collects data on how effective the adaptations actually are and then uses this high level information to determine subsequent adaptations. The *Usability* criteria by which the system will also be judged may also be further refined during this stage.

Taken together Requirements Analysis and Viability Analysis provide a necessary feasibility assessment before embarking on the design of an adaptive system. By so doing they enable researchers and developers to exclude pointless avenues of work and concentrate on those directions that have most potential for success. At the end of the Viability Analysis the project should have availed itself of a set of metrics by which design efforts can be guided and evaluations can be structured.

3.3 Design

Having established the practicality of and the theory to be embedded in the adaptive system, design can begin. The *Architecture* of the system can be designed in the knowledge of likely performance problems (Imp.M). Adaptive systems will typically have to:

- parse input
- identify triggers and send them to a user/task model,
- send the input to an application model, which will in turn pass input to application software,
- take data/messages from the application model which will have checked it for syntactic and semantic errors,
- pass data/messages to the dialogue controller, and
- the dialogue controller may then take recommendations from the adaptor module before updating the user interface.

Each of the above can constitute significant processes that may take time to conclude and adversely effect system response time. Basically, attention must be given to designing a viable architecture.

The design must accommodate the *User Interface Variability*. This variability must be captured in a computer executable form. For instance, if the Help to be given to users is to be adapted then will this be in terms of time of presentation, physical amount of text, information content or something else. Whatever aspect of the adaptation dimension (ie Help) is to be adaptive the potential for it must be stipulated and coded.

The design must also specify the *Adaptive Behaviour* of the system. That is the design must specify the relationship between interaction triggers (Trig.M) and user interface modifications (Rec.M). For any one adaptive system a number of adaptive behaviours might be exhibited, each of which would have to be specified. The expected relationship and any implicit assumptions (Tass.M) between the user interface modifications (Rec.M) and the objectives of the adaptations (Obj.M) should also be made explicit at this stage to permit subsequent evaluation of the theory upon which the adaptations are based.

3.4 Build

Following design attention turns to Building the system. On the basis of the Requirements Analysis and Variability Analysis the need for models will have been determined. These models may be of user behaviours, tasks and possibly applications. The data for populating these models will be the Triggers (Trig.M) as previously identified. For instance, a user model would have to maintain a description of those dimensions of user variability that have been determined as being worthy of being adapted to. A task model may be required to record those tasks which users have performed. An application model might hold historical information and state information. Historical information on the sorts of tasks that can be supported by application software and state information such as what files are presently open and to which mailboxes a user has access.

In order to provide the input for these models there may be a requirement for Monitor software. Most obviously a monitor would be required to identify the triggers in user interaction, such as the commission of errors. A monitor for a sophisticated adaptive system might also collect data on user performance for assessing whether the adaptations are being effective (Obj.M).

3.5 Evaluation

Once the system is operational it is essential to perform an evaluation to assess the suitability of the system. Suitability will be assessed in terms of the system's usability as determined by the previously stated usability criteria, the utility of the adaptations (Obj.M), and possibility the general applicability (Gen.M) of the adaptiveness. The system itself may collect some of the data for the evaluations but other data such as user satisfaction, may need to be collected off-line. It is essential that the utility of the adaptations is assessed but it also important that the generality of the adaptations is established. For instance, it might be found that the adaptations are only applicable to tasks that require a significant amount of data entry, or to users whose typing speed is over thirty words per minute.

The designers of the system will also, quite rightly, be interested in knowing whether the system has adapted as designed. This is assessed by comparing the data constituting the triggers (Trig.M) against the adaptive changes made to the user interface (Rec.M). The validity of assumptions (Tass.M) should also be assessed. For instance, if the assumption is that increasing the amount of Help (Rec.M) will decrease the number of errors (Tass.M) made then these data sets can be compared to see whether the assumption was correct.

3.6 Summary of MAID

By adopting the MAID method, the AID project eased the problems encountered when attempting to provide adaptive systems. For instance, it permitted us to curtail non-viable endeavours in a cost-effective manner, helped the project better understand the potential benefits of adaptation. In addition, the AID project gained a clearer understanding of what constitutes both adaptation and an adaptive system. The adoption of metrics also provided a valuable framework for planning developments and evaluations. The metrics were also found to be invaluable in clarifying a number of questions, including:

- How will the adaptive system behave (Trig.M + Rec.M)?
- What effect is the theory having (Tass.M + Rec.M)?
- Is the adaptive system succeeding (Obj.M)?
- What are the processing implications of providing the adaptations (Imp.M)?
- Under what circumstances are the adaptations useful (Gen.M)?

The benefits to designers of adopting MAID include:

- Highlighting areas of difficulty such as triggers that cannot be monitored.
- The identification and stating of assumptions that will need to be validated.
- Clarification of the cause and effect relationships underlying the adaptive behaviours.
- Formalisation of the way in which findings can be reported. As a consequence research findings are rendered more open to replication.

While it might be thought that good research into adaptive systems would be exemplified by providing answers to the question "Is the adaptive system succeeding?", the AID project realised that more such research begs other important questions. By providing ourselves with a method based approach to our work and identifying categories of data -metric- to be collected and analysed we found that our efforts were both more focused and rewarding.

4 CONCLUSION

This short paper, based largely on work to be found in [Browne et al. 1990], does not provide an example of a particular project on adaptive system development. This omission is forgivable because a fine example of such research which demonstrates many of the best practices identified by AID is offered in the paper by Benyon ([Benyon 93] in this volume).

For instance, Benyon's work began by identifying those characteristics of users that might be used as the basis for adaptations. Preliminary work allowed many candidate individual differences to be discounted at an early stage. A second example of good practice as found in Benyon's paper is how apparently successful adaptations are judged within the context of the overall usability and success of users with the system. Adaptation for adaptations sake is pointless it must provide some benefit over and above what could be achieved through non-adaptive means such as good user interface design.

If only two messages could be broadcast as a result of the AID project then in my judgement they should be:

- do not forget why you are providing adaptations.

- do not try to provide adaptive behaviours that analysis prior to development could have shown were impractical.

This last message reminds me of one outcome of an early piece of work on the AID project. We built an adaptive user interface to an electronic mail system. The adaptations were driven by a plan recognition model. The proposal was that if we could predict the tasks user were going to perform simply on the basis of the first few elements of the task then the user interface could be adapted in such a manner as to ease the user's completion of the task. Many persons worked simultaneously on developing this adaptive user interface. Only after the evaluation of the system, which showed that the adaptations were largely unsuccessful, did anyone ask the question of whether a human could have predicted the tasks users were going to perform if they had monitored user interaction. One of the project's members confidently replied NO and stated that this had been evident from the analyses that had been performed of user interaction with the native mail system. Why then did we attempt to build something that was so likely to fail? At that time we had little understanding of adaptation and no method to help us rationalise our work.

Hopefully the MAID method can help present and future efforts at building useful adaptive systems.

REFERENCES

[Benyon 93]
D. Benyon (1993). *Accommodating Individual Differences through an Adaptive User Interface*. In this volume.

[Browne et al. 1987]
D P Browne, R Trevellyan, P A Totterdell, M A Norman: *Metrics for the building, evaluation and comprehension of self-regulating adaptive systems*, Proceedings of INTERACT '87, Elsevier-North Holland, Amsterdam.

[Browne et al. 1990]
D P Browne, P A Totterdell, M A Norman: *Adaptive User Interfaces*, Academic Press, London.

Spaces and Distances: Software Architecture and Abstraction and their Relation to Adaptation

Gilbert Cockton

Glasgow **I**nteractive **S**ystems cen**T**re (GIST), The University
Glasgow, Scotland, UK

ABSTRACT

The software medium deserves more attention, since the practicality of much adaptation depends directly on its properties – adaptive systems are software too! This chapter builds on my earlier attempt to understand effort and wisdom in adaptation: how hard is it to make a software adaptation? what ways of doing it should be favoured or avoided? The two separate analyses in [Cockton 87a] are now fused in an outline of five dimensions of software adaptability. Before this, the potential of higher-order parameters is shown by briefly reporting potential advances in software components for *graphical input and output*. An analysis of menu configuration then shows that maximum flexibility requires *explicit dialogue configurations* which can be fully accessed by an agent of adaptation. An agent which must configure widgets via parameters cannot always be given enough flexibility. The need for configurable dialogue components points to a need for a whole spectrum of *component provision*. This is presented as a dimension of software adaptability. The companion architectural dimension of *component composition* is also outlined. These dimensions provide an analytical framework within which notions of *adaptation distance* can be explored. An analysis of simple changes in dialogue style illustrates the value of the framework. Even though the space of software configurations for interactive systems is not thoroughly mapped out, it is clear that apparently simple design intentions can result in extensive software disruption. The gulf of execution for any agent of adaptation thus cannot be predicted from the adapting intention alone.

1 INTRODUCTION: STILL TRYING TO MAP OUT SOFTWARE ADAPTATION

This chapter is a personal reworking of an old and damaged paper [Cockton 87a]. I wrote it, so I will make frequent references to it and to subsequent analyses by myself. I also feel that such a writing register is apt for a searching contribution to a workshop. Some readers may object on principle to such apparently self-centered self-citation, but I feel that this is an honest way to present this work. I hope such readers can suspend their requirements for third person objectivity, balance, and anonymity and read through to the arguments in their various stages of development.

Adaptive systems implement theories. Theories link independent variables to dependent variables, in this case, system features to user performance metrics. In the AID project [Browne et al. 90], a key concept was the monitoring of *trigger* metrics, which may be surrogates for dependent variables under (attempted) manipulation (*objective* metrics). If triggers reach a certain value, systems generate internal *recommendation* metrics. The effectiveness and applicability of theories were also measured in the AID project (*theory assessment* and *generality* metrics). The AID project thus elaborated the need for metrics for: when changes should be made; what changes should be made; what the changes are trying to change; whether they are changing them; and when such changes can be expected to have their intended effects.

The AID project represents one of the most extensive projects to date on adaptive user interfaces. It exemplifies a proper emphasis on theories and their implementation in terms of metrics and adaptable system features. The implementation of theories has received much attention, making the design and construction of user modelling and task modelling components a major topic in adaptive user interface research. In contrast, the software medium where adaptations are made has received little attention. The AID project did consider the cost of theory implementations (*implementation* metric), but even so, problems here are generally a consequence of monitoring triggers and recommending adaptations, and not of actually carrying them out. How to change things has received limited attention in the literature, although the topic of implementing, rather than recommending or selecting, changes cannot be ignored. Still, the focus of adaptive user interface research should be on theories, their validity, and their implementation. There is little value in making ineffective changes, still less, ones that degrade interaction.

I have written one of the few papers on implementing adaptations [Cockton 87a]. It was a cryptic survey, somewhat rushed and lacking in polish. Even so, few improvements on it are recorded in the survey in this volume ([Dieterich et al. 93] – which does improve on it!). This chapter is a reworking and update of my original analysis. It tries to map out a space within which software adaptations, self-adaptive or otherwise, can be made. Such a map would let us classify some adaptations as easy and others as hard in relation to the distance between a recommendation and its implementation.

The limited attention given to implementing changes may be the result of not appreciating the gulf of execution for the implementor of adaptations. This can be just as great as the gulfs of execution experienced by inexperienced end-users [Norman 86]. For some recommendations, such as changing the level of help text, there is no gulf of execution: if the help text is not generated but canned, then the recommendation is mapped into changing a scalar global variable. For other recommendations, such as adapting command syntax to accommodate user 'errors' [Senay 90], there is a considerable gulf.

One way to formalise this gulf is to think of the distance between the system's software before and after an adaptation. This distance can be expressed in terms of a space of possible software configurations. There are clear benefits in a better understanding of the software medium where adaptations are made, since this will improve our understanding of such distances. My 1987 analysis was not based on this single goal of understanding distances in software adaptation. Instead, I explored the interaction between dialogue abstractions and three dimensions of adaptation: *agents*, *mechanisms*, and *timings* of adaptation (see [Dieterich et al. 93] in this book for a refinement of within-session adaptation). An accompanying evaluation of software abstractions for graphical media drew on a hierarchy of parameter types (scalar types < structured types < higher-order types).

This chapter fuses the two separate 1987 analyses. In section 2, the limits of parameterisation are re-visited in an analysis of the configuration of menu widgets, using examples in an imperative, rather than the original functional programming style. This extended analysis considerably reduces confidence in the ability of any parameter type to maximise adaptability in interactive software. An alternative to parameterisation is required. Section 3 locates this alternative within an extended framework for the analysis of software adaptation. The framework is formed by complementing the three dimensions from 1987 with two extra dimensions: *architectural* variations of inter-component level composition, and the configurational variations due to intra-component *abstractions*. The original contrasts between different configuring abstraction *categories* become a fourth dimension which subsumes the original differences between parameterisation constructs.

The extra two dimensions form the starting point for mapping out a software space within which adaptation effort can be at least assessed, if not yet measured, in terms of some distance. The value of this approach is demonstrated in section 4. A case study indicates that adaptation distance can be much 'bigger' than expected for apparently simple design changes. The framework clearly identifies the extent of this distance for the adaptations in the case study. With the value of the initial framework established, section 5 uses the framework to order adaptations on the basis of the resulting distance between software before and after recommended changes. Section 6 concludes with positions on adaptation in general and specific hypotheses on the software engineering of self-adaptive systems.

2 THE LIMITS OF PARAMETERISATION

We can distinguish two *categories* of software abstraction. The abstractions underlying dialogue components differ from others (e.g., display and input managers). Dialogue abstractions have complex static structures, but are simple in their basic behaviour. They generate patterns of behaviour. Only one operation is generally required to achieve this (called the 'interpret' function in [Cockton 87a]). Other abstractions support many operations (e.g., setting attributes, or attaching and removing subcomponents in a display model). This distributes parameterisation of the underlying data structure(s), reducing the grain of each operation's interface. With dialogue abstractions, the configurer is, and should be, aware of their full structure, since it embodies the possibilities in an interactive dialogue. Dialogue configurations are constructed off-line as an entity, whereas other user interface components are effectively edited by run-time manipulations.

With non-dialogue software components, the configurer is generally unaware of their full structure. They are built incrementally and their full structure may be irrelevant. Such components fix the *content* of an interactive dialogue. The difference between dialogue structure and dialogue content can be clearly illustrated by contrasting the configurations of menu widgets. Before presenting this analysis however, the value of the hierarchy of parameter types in non-dialogue components can be illustrated. Some extensions to two existing abstractions for graphical media make better use of higher order parameters such as functions and predicates. These are reported first.

2.1 More adaptable abstractions for graphical media

Two common abstractions for graphical media are hierarchies for output (e.g., persistent display models such as PHIGS [Shuey et al. 86] and PRESENTER [Took 88, Took 90]), and event queues for management [Newman & Sproull 79].

In my 1987 analysis, the limitations of then current display hierarchies were noted. Potential adaptations were limited by the available set of attributes and tree manipulation operations. The IDEAL graphics language [van Wyk 82] was an interesting alternative, using constraints to describe pictures. This is one of the earliest examples of the use of higher order objects in a user interface component. Such a display language places few limits on possible display adaptations. This makes constraint-based display components more flexible than display hierarchies, which only offer a choice of scalar, set, or linear attribute values.

Display hierarchies can have functions and predicates as attribute values (and thus, via predicates, constraints). In existing hierarchical display models, such as PHIGS and PRESENTER, the synthesis operations are implicit, a situation akin to an attribute grammar [Watt 80] without rule annotations for the productions. A rare example of explicit operators is the ability to specify *rasterops* at PRESENTER nodes, which can be regarded as altering the painting operations from the default 'source only' operation (obscure existing parts of an image with a new image). Otherwise, the operations are fixed. Coordinates are always treated as offsets in the coordinate space inherited from a parent. Translations for x and y dimensions are thus added to the inherited value. The synthesis function here is $\lambda x.\lambda y.x+y$. There is no way to set absolute coordinates other than setting the root offsets to 0 and to attach the required subpicture as a child of the root.

When attributes can be operations as well as operands, then absolute coordinates can be achieved by resetting the offset combining operation to the function $\lambda x.\lambda y.y$. Similar flexibility is gained when the combining operations for other attributes can be changed. The combining operation for boolean visibility attributes is generally $\lambda x.\lambda y.y$, i.e., a lower setting to true or false always overrides a setting higher in the tree. This is a sensible default behavior, but it requires whole substructures to be traversed to make them all invisible. Traversal can be avoided by changing the combining operation to an 'enforce' function, i.e., $\lambda x.\lambda y.x$. For this to work, the current operation value must be inherited. Furthermore, the combining operation must not be reset below the enforcing node. In this example, the operation is more like a global control flag. There are clearly pitfalls associated with this increase in power, but theoretically, it points to unexplored possibilities in hierarchical display models. To summarise, the values of an attribute's final value at a leaf need not only be due to a homogeneous computation involving only one operation. Further details of an initial study are reported in [Cockton 93].

More extensive use of higher order objects (i.e., functions, predicates and procedures) can thus be made in software components for graphical display management. The same holds for graphical input components. Use of higher order objects here, such as the constraints in GRINS system [Olsen et al. 85], are rare. The logical input devices (LIDs) of graphics standards use mostly scalar parameters. They are notoriously limited and inflexible [Baecker 80]. Because Apple Macintosh™ applications are unconstrained by GKS [Enderle et al. 84] or PHIGS, objects can be picked by clicking, double-clicking, entering with the mouse down, entering regardless of the mouse state, shift-clicking, and rubber-boxing. There are many further possibilities involving further modifier keys (i.e., option, command, caps lock), time thresholds, and even cursor keys. Yet in graphics standards, all of these are a pick input. Standards implementations are unlikely to support all these variations as different logical pick devices. Yet it is also difficult to see how LID parameters such as prompt and echo styles could be used to parameterise these variations. Lastly, in GKS and PHIGS, there is no LID concept of *de-selection*, yet this is clearly critical to the smooth running of interaction in nearly every Macintosh application.

My 1987 survey overlooked the simplest input abstraction, the event queue. It appears to be a good place to start when adding more sophisticated capabilities. The first extension is the provision of some list operations, such as removal from within the queue. Such extensions cannot be achieved by a queue's standard parameters, or indeed by any parameters at all. Object-oriented programming capabilities provide one solution, but complex class hierarchies have created major learning and usage problems with programmers. Furthermore, only the most sophisticated (and highly experimental) environments allow run-time extensions of operations [Stemple et al. 92]. The advantages of object-oriented solutions are thus effectively limited to one agent of change, the computer specialist, and one time of change, between sessions. Furthermore, computer specialists who can manage the demands of complex class hierarchies appear to be a rare breed.

Input managers can thus start with an extended queue (or a restricted list) structure: extending it at run-time is generally unfeasible. Flexibility can be added by associating *rules* with each update operation. In practice, rules appear to be most useful for when events are added to the input list. These rules can rewrite a terminal subsequence of the event list under certain conditions. Side effect actions associated with these rewrites can configure immediate lexical feedback.

Event management production rules (EMPRs) have names These are used for enabling and disabling by a client object (e.g., dialogue component). This lets the grain of event synthesis be adapted during an interactive session. Events retrieved from the front of the event list can thus be anything from a raw event such as a locator displacement to a fully processed logical interaction such as a pick triggered by a 'mouse down enter'. This latter event would be synthesised by an EMPR that takes adjacent locator positions and compares their display contexts (selectable regions in a hierarchical display model). If the contexts are different and the mouse button is down, then a pair of exit and enter events is appended to the event list. The originating device is a synthetic one (e.g., MouseDownEnterPick) and the event value is the region's identifier (e.g., PHIGS path). The appropriate highlight or attention seeking animation can be specified as a rule action.

Other EMPRs can generate pick events triggered by exiting a region with the mouse button up or down, (double-)clicking on a region, or by any of the interaction techniques listed earlier. Considerable flexibility thus results from being able to associate two subsequences (one for triggering the rule, the other for specifying the rewrite), a predicate (for refining the trigger), and a procedure (for immediate lexical feedback) with update operations on event lists. The value of higher order objects is again clear. In practice, the interface between an input manager is much smaller, as rules are enabled and disabled by a name, not a tuple of subsequences, a predicate, and a procedure. Examples of rules in a frame-based syntax and an outline of the interface to rule-based event lists (RBELs) can be found in [Cockton 93].

An interactive system is composed from more than graphical media and dialogue managers. My 1987 survey briefly noted the need for one or more components that model the application's functionality and link the user interface to the implementing routines ('linkage' components, [Cockton 87b]). The survey also gathered other objects under the headings of "dialogue state structures" and "session data bases." This was subsequently refined to distinguish application-independent kernel objects for user support (e.g., help, history, undoing, programming by demonstration) from dialogue-dependent objects in the user interface (session state or 'content' objects as opposed to session/dialogue 'structure', [Cockton 91a]). This chapter does not cover state objects in the user interface or user support objects. The latter should be well covered by other contributions, since they are the major components of adaptive user interfaces.

2.2 Dialogue structure and the limits of parameterisation

This section addresses adaptation mechanisms for dialogue structures. A dialogue *structure* is a (partial) ordering of dialogue *steps*. Each dialogue step has a specific dialogue *content*. The step is best specified in terms of its *intention*, e.g., to enter the number of hard copies or to popup a menu. Dialogue content instantiates a step intention with a particular method. Dialogues can thus have identical structures in terms of step ordering and step intentions, but differ in step content.

The operational simplicity of dialogue components makes their structures unsuitable for extensive parameterisation. The structure of nearly every interactive dialogue is fixed in advance. In conventional programming language implementations, the dialogue structure is contained within the control structures of the whole program. Few programming languages let these control structures be parameterised. After all, were these parameterisable, it would be difficult to see what would be left to fix in a general procedure: everything could collapse into the apply function. The program would be wholly within its parameters, raising the question of how we should parameterise the parameters!

Dialogue structures will thus generally be preconfigured rather than adapted at run-time. The only use for parameterisation in dialogue structures is off-line generation. Interestingly, this use has not yet been reported in the mainstream UIST literature, although it could be useful in the automatic generation of user interfaces. The issue for adaptive systems becomes: how should variations be composed within preconfigured dialogue structures? Four possible mechanisms were identified in [Cockton 87a]: reconfiguring, enabling, switching, and editing. The first mechanism is better called *step* reconfiguring, since changes here may have no effect on the overall dialogue structure. Instead, the behaviour of an object in one, several, or all dialogue steps is altered. Thus it is not a mechanism for adaptation of dialogue structures, but for adapting other user interface components under the control of the dialogue manager. Parameterisation is a key technique here.

2.2.1 Exploiting parameterisation in dialogue steps

The hierarchy of parameters determines the grain of adaptation at the software implementation level. The more powerful the parameter, the greater the changes that can be effected in a change to a single dialogue step. This is not only beneficial to self-adaptive systems where it results in compact implementations of recommendations. It is also beneficial for any interactive system, since it increases the flexibility of preconfigured software components. This can be illustrated by two PASCAL headings for a menu procedure. The first heading (Figure 1), has only three parameters: an option count, an array of option strings, and an option index. The last parameter is set to the index of the selected option in the array (0 if the interaction is cancelled). With these scalar and structured parameters, the configurer can only change the content of the menu. Most of its appearance and all of its behaviour are fixed within the procedure body. Greater flexibility requires the use of functional and procedural parameters.

The second PASCAL heading (Figure 2), has eight additional parameters: three pairs of functions and procedures corresponding to conditions and actions for tentative selection, selection and quit transitions in the underlying transition network (Figure 3), plus a (possibly null) procedure for displaying the menu and a record parameter containing formatting and menu state data. By altering transition conditions and actions, the configurer can

procedure DoMenu (NumOptions : OptionIndices;
            TheOptions : OptionArrays;
        var TheSelection : OptionCounts);

Figure 1:   PASCAL heading for inflexible menu procedure

adapt the appearance and behaviour of the underlying menu. Options could be stacked, arranged in rows, or displayed in a matrix. Tentative selections could be triggered by cursor keys, keying, or dragging. Final selections could be triggered by keys (e.g., return), completion of the option selection code, or releasing a button. Quitting could be triggered by keys (e.g., escape) or dragging off and releasing a button. Recommendations for adaptation can thus be implemented by step reconfiguration of higher-order parameters. One alternative mechanism, switching between complete menu procedures, is not viable, as it could lead to an explosion of alternative menu procedures and yet still be unable to support a required recommendation that could have been supported by some combination of eight separate parameters.

procedure DoMenu (NumOptions : OptionIndices;
    TheOptions : OptionArrays;
    var TheSelection : OptionCounts;
    var m : MenuData;
    function   TentSelectDetect : boolean;
    function   SelectDetect : boolean;
    function   QuitDetect : boolean;
    procedure DoFormat (o : OptionArrays;
            var m : MenuData);
    procedure DoTentSelect (**var** m : MenuData);
    procedure DoSelect (m : MenuData);
    procedure DoQuit (m : MenuData));

Figure 2:   PASCAL heading for flexible menu procedure

At the limit of parameterisation, a procedure will contain no constant values or fixed operators. It is then a *combinator*, a function from functions to functions. For the menu example, the combinator's structure can be represented by a transition network (Figures 3 and 4). Myers has attempted to represent a generic LID or 'widget' structure in this manner

[Myers 90]. His new model for input combines the transition life cycles for several widgets into a single automaton. Condition and action slots for transitions have default values which can be overridden by setting them to function values.

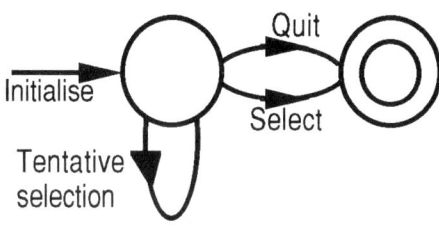

Figure 3: Underlying state machine for inflexible and flexible menu procedures

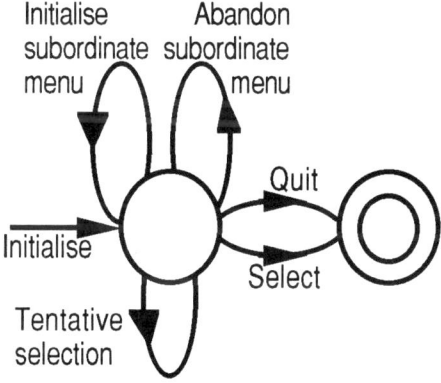

Figure 4: Underlying state machine for walking menus

Myers reported difficulties with walking menus. Functions for tentative selection were very complex. This is no surprise, as walking menus have a more complex state transition structure (Figure 4). By not adding extra transitions to the model, Myers forces initialisation and abandoning of subordinate menus into the condition and action for a single transition.

The underlying combinator structure of a software component sets the upper limit on its parameterised flexibility. There is no absolute cutoff, since the provision of higher-order parameters makes everything possible. After all, Myers model can be reduced to a single state with one looping transition and still 'work'. However, as each transition parameter is worked harder (and in the one state and transition limit, absurdly so), the complexity and risk of an adaptation increases too. So, problems begin to arise when states or transitions are missing. The limit of higher-order parameterisation is the limit of our imagination. Problems will not arise if we can anticipate the state transition life cycle of every future widget or LID. This seems unlikely.

The use of transition networks to represent the fixed structure of user interface components thus allows considerable insight into the limits of higher order parameterisation. Once the causes of configurational *viscosity* [Green 91] are understood (here, missing states and/or transitions), we can look for further ways to stretch the capabilities of the second menu procedure above (and thus also Myers' new model for input).

Examples beyond walking menus are easy to find or imagine. Tear-off menus, as in Apple's HyperCard, require a dragged state and transitions to and from it. These too will be difficult to configure in Myers' reported model and in the PASCAL menu above. We could also refine selection transitions in palette, nonwalking, and walking menus by introducing a cancel state for 'dangerous' operations. On selection, a cancel button and a simple clock icon would appear for 500ms (or whatever, it would be parameterised). The user could double click within 500ms to cancel the selection. A graphical count down on the clock icon would indicate the remaining delay. Such a refinement would seriously overload selection condition and actions in both Myers' model and the dedicated menu procedure (Figure 2). Another possible refinement would alter the initialisation transition so that it would not display the menu until the mouse stops moving. The intention here is to support expert selection. When combined with a refined selection, we could have blind menus that work better than previous attempts[1]. This requires a condition that is not supported in the Figure 2 menu. Without it, the DoFormat procedure would become very unwieldy.

What is to be done? Any attempt to encapsulate even one type of choice LID, the menu widget, is vulnerable to oversight as well as innovation (the analysis has also been repeated for panning widgets, [Cockton 93]). Any attempt to encapsulate all LIDs is doomed to failure – we can always take the underlying state machine and think of ways of requiring extra states and transitions. The examples above were not forced. They immediately sprang to mind when the principle of state transition combinator structures was understood. When transitions and/or states are missing, the affected higher order parameters will have to implement their own internal finite state machines or little event handlers. They will either simulate network behaviour or represent states using flags. If we effectively pass transition networks as parameters, we may as well make them explicit. Perhaps there was something in that Seeheim model and syntax after all!

---

[1] William Newman described an attempt in a course on user interface design [Beta Chi 87].

2.2.2 Adapting dialogue structure

The underlying transition network in any widget component, if fixed, will always be a source of inflexibility. If the transition network is a parameter, we end up with a classic Seeheim model UIMS. Despite some anti-Seeheim vogues, flexibility can be delivered by such structures which widget components cannot provide. Widgets are most flexible when they are composed from general-purpose components such as media managers, dialogue managers, and application linkage managers. Indeed, this is so for all levels of user interface management above and alongside widgets.

Since step reconfiguration of parameters cannot deliver the flexibility required by many recommendations, this leaves only three adaptation mechanisms to consider. The differences between each are due to the numbers of *implicit* and *explicit* dialogues. With *enabling* as a mechanism, several implicit dialogues are composed within a single explicit dialogue configuration. A recommendation can be specified as a change to a variable that will cause separate paths in the dialogue to be taken. With *switching* as a mechanism, separate dialogues require separate explicit configurations. A recommendation is specified as a replacement of the current dialogue configuration with another. With *editing* as a mechanism, the number of implicit dialogues in each explicit configuration can change. This may happen during an interactive session following a generated recommendation, or between sessions (human or system reconstruction). In either case, the steps in a dialogue and/or its structure are changed.

The two approaches have problems. Switching can result in repetition of subconfigurations that does not arise with enabling [Cockton 87a]. Within-session editing of dialogue structures is risky for all five key dialogue abstractions. Although one abstraction was thought safe in [Cockton 87a], production systems (or event-response systems), turn out to be equivalent to 'safe' Petri Nets (see appendix). As editing the latter is not safe, editing production rules is also risky.

Thus reconstruction (between-session editing), replacement (between- or within-session switching), and enabling (within-session extensions and restrictions) are the only safe mechanisms for any agent of adaptation.

3 TWO FURTHER DIMENSIONS OF ADAPTATION

Flexibility at all levels of user interface management is maximised when components are formed from general purpose lower level components. Adaptations can thus be implemented as changes to one or more components. Alternatively, adaptations can be implemented as changes to the way(s) in which these components are *composed*. This introduces two further dimensions of adaptation: the components that can be changed; the manner of their composition. It is these dimensions which map out the space of software adaptation. The complexity of any adaptation should be reflected in the distance that a system moves through this space following adaptation.

With the three and a half dimensions from [Cockton 87a], we now have five dimensions of adaptation. The fourth dimension was almost explicit in the 1987 contrast of two abstraction *categories* – "control sequence" and "object" classes (hence "and a half"). As well as identifying a high level partition of software components, widgets were also rejected as a serious input abstraction, since they were clearly inflexible at the time of the initial analysis. Still, it was not until later analyses of software structure that the relevance of *component provision* became apparent. A fifth dimension of adaptation was not anticipated until my analysis of software structure [Cockton 91a], where it is refined into two dimensions, *topology* and *inter-component communication*.

The space for software adaptations is defined by these fourth and fifth software structure dimensions. Holding the agent, timing, and mechanism of adaptation constant, we can look at the 'distance' between software configurations before and after adaptation. Hopefully this distance should give us some feel for the disruptiveness of an adaptation. The cost of an adaptation will be relative to a distance based on the changes to software components and on the changes to their composition. Disruptive adaptations will alter several components and inter-component links.

No adaptation mechanism identified in [Cockton 87a] is completely suitable for implementing disruptive changes. *Enabling* requires all possible links to be in place. *Editing* will generally be laborious, and without some form of change management it could be very error prone. Crude *switching* between coarse components seems to be the only viable mechanism, but this is still not ideal since it can result in much repeated code. At some levels of disruption, even within-session switching may not be feasible. Effective adaptation could be reduced to system programs that select the best version of an application for users in between interactive sessions.

Adaptation distances are thus two dimensional vectors defined by changes to software components and their links. For the simplest adaptations, no links are affected. The shortest adaptation distances can thus correspond to the hierarchy of parameter classes. As the lowest level components (leaves) of a software structure may fall within this hierarchy, these classes also subsume the editing of non parameter values. Above the lowest level of software structure, all such changes become restricted to the internals of client software components.

The simplest software adaptation will thus involve a trivial change to a *scalar* type instance. This may be a parameter or a leaf component. Moderate changes arise when *structured* or *higher-order* type instances are edited. Complete component instances which are composed around a dialogue structure can be changed by switching mechanism. This is hardly more disruptive than step configuration. However, larger changes are entailed by the need to *add* or *remove* complete component instances: the greater the number of components involved, the greater the adaptation distance. Changes become even more substantial when *new component types* (e.g., task modellers, plan recognisers, active help managers) are needed to implement an adaptation. New types could also be needed to implement the monitoring components that generate the adaptation recommendation.

Any changes to *links* result in moderate disruption or worse. The smallest possible change is the redirection of an inter-component link. Adding and removing links becomes necessary when components are added and deleted. This could become very complicated when new component types are involved. The switch to new link types will be even more disruptive, for example, from parameter or message passing to events, active values or constraints [Cockton 91a]. Yet an adaptive system would need these advanced link types, if, for example, it were to recommend any presentation that used asynchronous view updates.

Only one adaptation mechanism can handle the most disruptive changes. This mechanism was not identified in [Cockton 87a]. It follows from the two new software structure dimensions. The new mechanism is *re-composition* – the addition or removal of components or links.

One new mechanism apart, the two new dimensions do not radically alter the space of possible software adaptations. Differences in adaptation are due to the changing agent, the time of the change, what is changed (content and structure), and how it is changed. This space of possible adaptations is shrunk by interactions within dimensions. For example, provision of the user support components central to self-adaptive systems (user monitors, plan recognisers, adaptation managers) is incompatible with the simpler architectural topologies and inter-component links [Cockton 91a].

Interactions between mechanisms and components were explored in [Cockton 87a]. The determining factor here, however, is not the type of the component, nor its distribution, but the *abstraction* which is used to configure component. Analyses of interactions between five structuring abstractions for dialogue components and the agent, timing, and mechanism of adaptation formed the second part of [Cockton 87a].

Further interactions arise for the two new dimensions. Not all agents of adaptation will be equally comfortable with re-composition as an adaptation mechanism. The interactions here are between the agent of adaptation and both the component and link dimensions. For example, component abstractions may be far too technical for end-users and local experts, e.g., BNF [Olsen 84], CSP [Alexander 90], Petri Nets [Pilote 83] and event-response systems [Hill 87]. All human agents will benefit from straightforward configuration checkers, and dialogue components based on transition networks offer the most here [Feycock 77, Alty 84, Thimbleby 93]. Furthermore, creating new component types that differ radically from those within an existing architecture seems to be restricted to computer experts. End-users and local experts are unlikely to be at home with, for example, active values as an inter-component links. Lastly, the creation of new link types is as good as impossible for self-adaptive systems – the mechanisms must be implemented in advance by a computer expert.

The relationship between the 'old' and 'new' dimensions is thus generally one of restriction. For most agents of change, the full space of software adaptations is not available. Availability is also restricted for adaptation timings (e.g., the difficulties of editing dialogue structures well into an interactive session [Cockton 87a]).

Mapping out dimensions is only a preliminary to getting a grip on disruption distances for software structure and content. For some agents, certain distances appear to be insurmountable obstacles. If this is correct, then there are clearly limits to the recommendations that a self-adaptive system can put into effect. Still, the work reported here is largely at the level of insights and hypotheses. The hard work lies in firming it up. However, such work need not be attempted if the outlined framework has no identifiable predictive, explanatory, or analytical power. The next section explores the power of the framework in a small gedanken experiment (now an actual experiment) into the disruptiveness of dialogue style changes in a very simple interactive system.

4 A CASE STUDY IN DISRUPTION

Imagine a very simple statistics system for central tendency analysis. Only three functions are supported: mean, median and mode. Imagine that there are three versions of this simple system that vary only in their 'user interfaces': one has a question and answer (Q&A) interface; one has a command and response language (CRL) interface; one has a direct manipulation graphical user interface (DM GUI). The three user interfaces are illustrated in Figures 5, 6 and 7.

Figure 5:   Sample interaction with question and answer interface

Spaces and distances: software architecture and abstraction 93

The Q&A interface (Figure 5) has two prompts: one for operation names (**?**); and one for data elements (**>**). The system prompts for an operation name. On input of an acceptable name, it prompts for data elements until an empty line is input, indicating the end of the data. Only digits and the first decimal point are echoed and appended to the input data string. A wait message is displayed if at least one acceptable data element has been entered, otherwise an error message is displayed and the system returns to the operator prompt. On completion of the calculation, a carriage return moves the cursor to the next line and the result is displayed as a number (or for mode, a list of comma separated numbers) without additional explanation. All system output is emboldened.

The CRL interface (Figure 6) has only one prompt (**>**) prefixed with the current operation. A start up message draws attention to this default. Users may input a new operation name, a line of white-space separated data items, or both (name then data). Only valid data characters are echoed and appended to the input. If data has been entered on the current or a previous line, a wait message, carriage return, and result message are output as for the Q&A interface, except that the user is again reminded of the current operation by prefixing its name and = before the result. The CRL interface thus introduces the concepts of *current operation* and *current data* into the interaction.

```
Default operation is mean
mean> 5.0 10.0 15
Wait...
mean = 10.0
mean> median
Wait...
median = 10.0
median> 2 4 6
Wait...
median = 4.0
median> mode 2 4 6 2
Wait...
mode = 2.0
```

Figure 6: Sample interaction with command and response interface

The DM GUI (Figure 7) displays three operator areas above a scrolling row of data cells. Each operator area contains an icon and a result box. The mode result box has two stepping buttons for browsing multi-modal results. Operator areas are greyed out initially. They are filled in when the user selects them by pointing and clicking. If there is at least one data element, the result of applying the enabled operation to the data will be displayed above

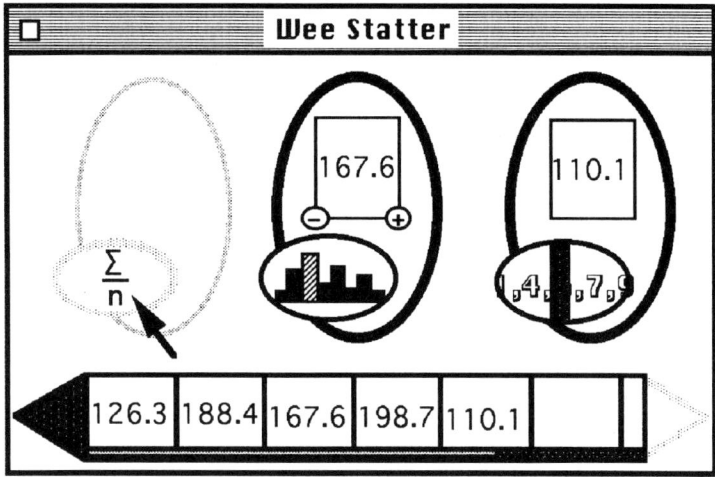

Figure 7: Sample snapshot of direct manipulation graphical interface

the icon. If there are no data items, then the operator will be disabled after the user has acknowledged a pop-up message from the system. The user can add new data elements in empty cells, change the data element in an existing cell, or delete an existing cell. This is achieved by a dialogue box which is popped up when the user points at and clicks on a cell (the delete command button is disabled for the last remaining data element). All enabled operator results are updated after any change to a data element. Users can scroll through the data elements by pressing the arrow areas to their left and right or by dragging the scroll 'elevator' below them. The width of the 'elevator' in relation to its enclosing bar is proportional to the portion of the data elements that are visible. Arrow areas are greyed out when the visible elements are a prefix or suffix of the data.

The DM GUI introduces several new functional concepts: list editing operations (add, change, delete element); list navigation operations (scrolling and stepping); and persistent operations (and toggling rather than requesting operations). It is the introduction of these extra concepts beyond mean, median, and mode that results in more software disruption than might be expected from a straightforward change in dialogue style.

A change in dialogue style must clearly affect the presentation and dialogue components in an interactive system. We should expect the operations and objects local to these components to change substantially. Indeed, we should not be surprised if whole components are completely replaced. However, we might expect higher level components to remain unchanged. This expectation can be recast in terms of the GOMS model [Card et al. 83]. In this task analysis formalism, tasks can be analysed at different grains of analysis. The grain of analysis is determined by the duration and effect of the operator. Most changes to presentation components affect operators at the finest grained *keystroke level* of interaction. Changes to the dialogue affect the *argument level*. The next coarser level defined for a GOMS analysis is the *functional level*. If dialogues style are solely concerned with representing objects and operations at the functional level (as display objects and command sequences at the argument and keystroke levels), then a change in dialogue style should have no effect on these objects and operations.

The functional level in a GOMS model is similar to the interface between the Application Interface Model and the dialogue component in the Seeheim model [Green 85]. The Application Interface Model is a software component that maps between the designer's intended conceptual model (DICM) for a system and two other system substructures: the presentation and dialogue which animates this model within the system image; and the underlying functionalities that implement the core capabilities of a system. We might expect the DICM to be unaffected by changes in dialogue style. However, this is not the case.

Figures 8, 9 and 10 show the functional level of coarse grained objects and operations for each of the three systems. The move from a Q&A interface to a CRL interface adds objects but leaves the number of operations unchanged since result computation is generalised as a result of having a current operation and data. The move from a CRL interface to a DM GUI is much more dramatic: the current data is joined by a current element; the current operation becomes three operation statuses. Three extra objects are thus added, and with them 7 completely different operations.

Why is this? My hypothesis is that dialogue styles are stereotypical collections of design preferences that go beyond the representation of objects and operations to include user support features. Each dialogue style brings with it its own set of expectations. These are social phenomena, arising from interactions between designers, users, and extant artifacts. Persistent, user-definable defaults are thus expected in command languages, but not in Q&A interfaces. Rapid, incremental operations are expected in DM GUIs, as are persistent concurrent operations and direct editing of parameters. All are possible in CRLs, but the demand for them is less strong. Similarly, cut, paste, copy, clear, and undo are essential components of any GUI, but we would not expect these operations in a text-only, CRL interface.

We can of course rise above these expectations. There are nine potential systems here (cross product of three styles and three DICMs). However, the expectations for each style would reassert themselves after each mixed marriage. A Q&A interface to the DM DICM would be cumbersome ("Edit current element, reselect current element, or edit operation statuses?"). A CRL interface might quickly fuse reselection of the current element and editing it (e.g., "add 4" replaces the current element with 4, whereas "add #3 4" would set the current element to the third item and change it to 4). A GUI to the Q&A DICM would look ridiculously primitive – a text widget plus three command buttons. A GUI to the CRL DICM would be a slight improvement – a text widget plus operation radio buttons plus an

Objects (3)

>mode, median, and mean result

Operations (3)

>compute mode, median, and mean result of a number list

Figure 8: Objects and actions for question and answer interface

Objects (5)

>current data
>current operation
>mode, median, and mean result

Operations (3)

>reset current data
>reset current operation
>compute current operation of current data

Figure 9: Objects and actions for command and response language interface

Objects (8)

>current data
>current data element
>mode, median, and mean statuses
>mode, median, and mean result

Operations (7)

>add, change, and delete current data element, recomputing enabled operations of current data
>reset current data element to new selection
>toggle mode, median, and mean statuses

Figure 10: Objects and actions for direct manipulation graphical interface

"OK" command button. But could we really leave them like that? Each style has its own pull. DM GUIs curiously may encourage more complex DICMs, although their generally superior ease of use is most noted. This is due more to finely grained operators than to any effective extension of functionality.

The value of the framework in this gedanken experiment is that it identifies the extent of disruption clearly. However, it does not predict the extent or explain it. The explanation for the functional (DICM) expectations associated with dialogue styles was a sociological one. The effect of DICM changes on overall software structure is predicted by a separate theory of user interface separability [Cockton 87b, Cockton 91a, Cockton 93].

The experiment has revealed a problem with the general application of the framework as a predictive tool for assessing the feasibility of theories of adaptation. The experiment shows that there is no automatic correlation between the simplicity of a design intention and the means of its implementation. The design changes made by human agents can become pervasive. This implication can clearly be expected to scale up from the trivial example to larger systems (unlike positive results with toy problems!)

We must thus look elsewhere for explanations and predictions. However, the taxonomic potential of the framework can be put to good use. The framework lets us try to reduce the apparent disruption in the experiment. It has been claimed that major and extensive disruption can result from adaptations to dialogue style. This disruption is due to the extent of the affected components. Changes to the DICM take changes beyond the expected ones, i.e., changes to presentation and dialogue components. The Application Interface Model also changes (to use its Seeheim name, this software component is also known as the 'linkage', 'semantic support component', 'Model' (MVC), 'top level Abstraction' (PAC), or 'semantic object' (MoDe)).

Disruptions due to changes in dialogue style seem to require nothing short of switching all three types of component (presentation, dialogue, and linkage). The value of the framework developed here is that it can guide us in the falsifying attempt to show that: fewer component types need be changed by switching; that only one needs to be changed by switching; that the changes can be effected by one or several step reconfigurations of higher-order, structured, or scalar parameters. There are clearly radical differences in dialogue structure across the three versions, so step configuration must be inadequate. Clearly, in a monolithic user interface with considerable semantic knowledge, only one component type would be changed. However, this would require editing or enabling to be used as the adaptation mechanism. Such software restructuring can thus change the logical classification of a software adaptation, but the alternative restructuring results in a worst case of the lesser adaptation. The shift is thus academic. We should only be concerned with what is possible in a well modularised interactive system. Not only are adaptive systems software, but they also, no less than any other system, need to be *good* software. Whatever we propose should be consistent with sound software engineering principles.

The value of the framework is thus that it admits critical reflection on any assessment of disruptiveness. The framework can be used to guide attempts to reduce the apparent disruption by exploring logically less disruptive positions within the space of possible software adaptations. If no convincing reassessment of disruptiveness is possible, then confidence in the initial assessment is increased.

The framework supports establishment of the minimal software disruption, consistent with sound software engineering principles, that will result from implementing recommendations for adaptations. It does not support prediction of the extent of the disruption from the underlying design intention, nor does it explain why an adaptation is disruptive as it is. The framework thus has value, but it cannot be applied until a software design is well-advanced. It is therefore best used as a heuristic tool, and thus the pay-off for extensive formalisation will be limited.

The next section therefore does not attempt to iron out every crease or patch every hole in the framework. Given the developmental leverage that it supports, this is adequate. It is also adequate as a research tool that can expose tractable parts of the space for adaptation that do not seem to have been fully explored in self-adaptive systems.

5 UNEXPLORED REGIONS OF THE SOFTWARE MEDIUM

The basic concepts for describing software media are component instances, component types (with their subdimension of flexibility), link instances, and link types. A recommendation for adaptation will have to be mapped into operations on instances and types. Instances and types can be added, changed, or deleted. For each component type, we need to consider where it lies on the hierarchy of parameterisation (scalar, structured, higher order, partially and fully parameterised combinator structures).

Any change to a user interface component via its parameters will be an example of a step reconfiguration, since such components will be composed around a dialogue structure. The effect of the parameter change will be to reconfigure the content of a dialogue step. Dialogue structures themselves are not parameterised, and thus the potential interaction supported by a component will generally not be changed by parameterisation.

The simplest adaptation in software terms is to change a scalar parameter or global object. This is probably the most used implementation mechanism for adaptations (e.g., level of help and other messages). It is well supported in all implementation environments. Step reconfigurations here may interact with the pre-configured enabling mechanisms in a dialogue structure, enabling or disabling a previously (un)available interactive potential.

The next level of software adaptation in software terms is to change a structured parameter or global component. Such components are also generally 'not so deep' leaves of a software structure. Such changes are also well used as an implementation mechanism for adaptations (e.g., adaptive menu option ordering, adaptive menu tree structures). They are well supported in most implementation environments. Changes are rarely used to enable previously unavailable interactive potential. Instead, they reformat display objects and other structured presentation objects. They could be used to adapt structures deeper in the interaction, for example default tables, or inferred command synonyms or syntax [Senay 90].

The next level of software adaptation in software terms is to change a higher order parameter, as in Myers model for input [Myers 90]. This is still an example of step reconfiguration, although the substitution of simple boolean constants for predicates can interact with the pre-configured enabling mechanisms in a dialogue structure. Both uses can be seen in the flexible menu example. A false quit predicate can restrict menu abandoning to a selection of a specific option. Changing any higher order parameter in the flexible menu only changes the condition or action for a single dialogue step. It cannot add to or diminish the pre-configured dialogue structure.

Higher order parameterisation does not seem to have been used in self-adaptive systems. The flexibility it offers in Myers model is clear, even though this flexibility is bounded. There is thus a potential here that need not be restricted to computer experts as an agent of change. Even the latter agents could make more use of this level of parameterisation, for example, by using the higher order extensions to display models and event queues outlined in section 2.1 above.

The above three adaptation distances – changes to scalar, structured and higher-order objects – are all examples of the step reconfiguration mechanism. When design changes require restructuring of the pre-configured dialogue, then mechanisms such as switching (during an interactive session) or editing (between interactive sessions) are required. There is also the unexplored option of parameterisation of components composed around a dialogue structure, but this is restricted to between session generation (interaction with timing dimension). In all cases, the links to the switched components may be unaffected.

Links will be affected when a component is added or deleted. Computer experts do this all the time during maintenance. Adding or deleting component instances will require the addition or deletion of inter-component links. Such dynamic adaptation of a system's software structure does not yet seem to have been attempted in self-adaptive systems. Since there is no clear correspondence between design or adaptive intentions and software disruption, we have no systematic way of exploring what this mechanism may be used for. Clearly, it is needed for switches of dialogue style. It could also possibly be required for major changes in presentation style. It should have the advantage of not slowing down display updates, as an intermediate layer would were it to direct system data to the currently appropriate presentation manager.

As we move into higher levels of adaptation, the uses of major disruptions and extensions to software structure become even less clear. It should be possible to create new types of components, but such a mechanism comes close to the maintenance activities of a UIMS or UIDE support team. Since so few computer experts perform such a function, it is difficult to see how a self-adaptive system could mimic this behaviour. It is not a well understood task.

Lastly, the creation of new inter-component link types seems very unlikely, since these are part of the basic software architecture of the development environment for an interactive system. There are currently only a handful of such types (subprogram call, message, broadcast event, addressed event, active value, constraint). Their proper uses and their advantages and disadvantages are still not understood, but automatic generation of such links may have a place in systems which automate the generation of visualisations. The Iconographer system [Gray et al. 90] supports editing of the data flow links between visualisation components. Techniques used here may transfer to self-adaptive systems.

The notion of adaptation distance is therefore a useful concept. Its full implications are not yet clear, but it is possible to not only to establish minimum levels of software disruption for a design intention, but also to identify unexplored mechanisms for software adaptation. Under-used mechanisms in self-adaptive (and other) interactive systems are:

- step reconfiguration of higher-order objects (also under-used by computer experts and in UIMSs, UIDEs etc.)

- parameterisation of components composed around a dialogue structure (between session generation only)

- recomposition of components composed around a dialogue structure

- addition and deletion of components composed around a dialogue structure

- redirection of inter-component links

- addition and deletion of inter-component links

The first two under-used mechanisms could be used without obvious problems in self-adaptive interactive systems. The last four mechanisms become increasingly challenging. The last three mechanisms require programming language facilities such as *reflection* [Stemple et al. 92] for within-session adaptation, so we can hardly expect them to be widely used even by computer experts, still less within self-adaptive systems. However, for between-session adaptation, adding and re-linking software components does not seem to have been attempted in self-adaptive systems.

The framework thus does expose mechanisms which are under-used by all agents of adaptation. Some are currently used by computer experts, but there are clearly opportunities here in mainstream UIST work. Anything that makes recomposition quicker and safer is going to improve software tools for iterative participative development.

6 CONCLUSIONS

This chapter has developed a framework for the analysis of adaptation in interactive systems. It supports evaluation of the current state of the art and suggests new directions for research into adaptivity in interactive systems. Its utility is not wholly negative. It does expose limits of adaptation, which must be useful – forewarned is forearmed. However, it also exposes tractable parts of the space for adaptation that do not seem to have been explored in research into self-adaptive systems.

The most flexible forms of parameterisation fix very little in a software component. Yet even the most flexible parameters can be inadequate, since what is left fixed in a highly abstract component may still be too restrictive. The *practical* value of parameterisation appears to be limited to the manipulation of very low level user interface components in dialogue 'steps'. Even so, this has not been fully exploited in self-adaptive systems.

The alternative to parameterisation, mainly for within-session adaptation of dialogue 'structure', is re-composition. The requirements for tailorability and reconfigurability in user interfaces are such that complete rebuilding of higher level components appears to be a more effective, flexible and even more efficient technique than navigating the possible changes to a rich, ever-developing and never-closing set of parameters.

The design adaptations that can be made by human agents have motivated forms of adaptation in interactive systems. However, there are neither obvious nor straightforward correspondences between these design intentions and the architectural compositions and component configurations of software structures. These poor correspondences suggest that self-adaptive systems may be unable to emulate everything that can be achieved by a human computer expert, especially when what starts out as a very simple design change can require most, if not all of the software to be rewritten. In such cases, adaptation becomes complete substitution!

The recommendations of self-adaptive systems will always be crude by comparison with the capabilities of computer experts. This is important, because a motivation for adaptive systems is the ability to respond to human variability. I doubt that any current self-adaptive system will have much of a repertoire here. That does not however invalidate them: they may be able to do little things very well and we may be glad of that.

6.1 A wider programme

Having gathered together the main conclusions for this paper, I would like to place the work reported here in its actual context. I do not work on self-adaptive systems. I was briefly involved in the AID project [Browne et al. 90], but my real interest is in software adaptation by computer experts. I feel that both mainstream UIST and self-adaptive systems work could benefit from better cross-fertilisation of ideas. What I have attempted to do above is draw out hypotheses for self-adaptive systems from work that originally focused on non-adaptive software.

A key goal in my work is trying to get the 'U' into UIST. This is not straightforward. Only a few examples of the relationship between design goals and software structure could be presented in my attempt to expose relationships between HCI design goals and implementation in interactive systems [Cockton 91b]. Like other attempts to 'apply' human factors, the process has been opportunistic and over-dependent on personal knowledge and experience [Barnard 91]. Work which has tried to ground requirements for software architectures and component abstractions in the context of design and usage of interactive systems does not overwhelm the reader with a feast of human factors insights [Cockton 93]. However, the programme is still worthwhile, whatever the variability and unpredictability of its yield.

One of the key points of this chapter is that, while adaptive systems try to make the changes that observant developers would make without them being there to observe and change, the disruption of an adaptation is unpredictable. This has two clear implications for the development of self-adaptive interactive systems. Firstly, confidence in the *feasibility* of any self-adaptive design is considerably delayed. Although theory assessment metrics can be built into self-adaptive systems, as in the AID project, this does not address the software implementation costs. These may not be known until well into the software design phase. Secondly, *change management* practices and tools are going to be severely tested. The problems which arise with radical systems maintenance will also apply to self-adaptive systems which rebuild major subcomponents. Developers of self-adaptive systems need tool support here. However, current change management tools may need to be revised and extended before they can be used to guide the development of self-adaptive systems.

Now, although it may be possible to live with both of these problems of delayed feasibility and premature change management, they are both clearly undesirable. Once again, the wider programme becomes attractive: if we can ground requirements for software architectures and component abstractions in the context of design and usage of interactive systems, then we can bring the structure of interactive software closer to the structures that arise in design, and closer to the topology of design problems that are exposed by usage. If we could create software structures isomorphic to design structures, as explored in [Cockton 91a] and [Cockton 91b], then we can take the one cast-iron approach to prediction[2]: the best way to predict the future is to invent it.

One reliable way to reduce uncertainty about the gulf between design and implementation is to bring the latter closer to the former. If this is possible, then the goal of self-adaptive systems – to make the changes that observant developers would make without them being there to observe and change – may come within the reach of other agents of change such as end-users and local experts. Attempts to make self-adaptation easier, if successful, may make it obsolescent!

---

[2] Apologies to Alan Kay for borrowing his talk title.

ACKNOWLEDGEMENTS

I would like to thank Siemens for their invitation to their workshop which was the starting point for this book. I am particularly indebted to the editors for their exceptional patience, without them this paper would not have been initiated, never mind completed. Vielen Dank! Once again, I would like to acknowledge Glasgow University's GIST group as the long suffering test ground for all my presentations. Lastly, I would like to thank Fraser Hamilton, the final year student who turned the gedanken experiment in section 4 into a real one, for several insights that have arisen from his work.

REFERENCES

[Alty 84]
    Alty, J.L., 1984, *The Application of Path Algebras to Interactive Dialogue Design*, Behaviour and Information Technology, 3(2), 119–132.

[Alexander 90]
    Alexander, H., 1990, *Structuring dialogues using CSP*, in *Formal Methods in Human-Computer Interaction*, eds. M. Harrison and H. Thimbleby, Cambridge University Press: Cambridge 272–295.

[Baecker 80]
    Baecker, R., 1980, *Towards an Effective Characterisation of Graphical Interaction*, in *Methodology of Interaction*, eds. R.A. Guedj, P.T.W. ten Hagen, F.R.A. Hopgood, H.A. Tucker and D.A. Duce, North-Holland, 127–147.

[Barnard 91]
    Barnard, P., 1991, *Bridging between Basic Theories and the Artifacts of HCI*, in *Designing Interaction, Psychology at the Human-Computer Interface*, ed. J. Carroll, Cambridge University Press, Cambridge, 103–122.

[Beta Chi 87]
    Beta Chi Design Ltd., 1987, *Course Notes on User Interface Design*.

[Browne et al. 90]
    Browne, D., M. Norman and D. Riches, 1990, *Why build adaptive systems?*, in *Adaptive User Interfaces*, Academic Press: London, 15–57.

[Card et al. 83]
    Card, S.K., T.P. Moran and A. Newell, 1983, *The Psychology of Human-Computer Interaction*, Lawrence Erlbaum.

[Cockton 87a]
    Cockton, G., 1987, *Some Critical Remarks on Abstractions for Adaptable Dialogue Managers*, in *People and Computers III*, eds. D. Diaper and R. Winder, Cambridge University Press: Cambridge, 325–344.

[Cockton 87b]
    Cockton, G., 1987, *A New Model for Separable Interactive Systems*, in *Human-Computer Interaction - INTERACT'87*, eds. H.-J. Bullinger and B. Shackel, North Holland: Amsterdam, 1033–1038.

[Cockton 91a]
Cockton, G., 1991, *The Architectural Bases of Design re-use*, in *User Interface Management and Design*, eds. D.A. Duce. M.R. Gomes, F.R.A. Hopgood and J.R. Lee, Springer Verlag: Berlin, 15–34.

[Cockton 91b]
Cockton, G., 1991, *Human Factors and Structured Software Development: the Importance of Software Structure*, in *People and Computers VI*, D.Diaper and N. Hammond, Cambridge University Press: Cambridge, 57–72.

[Cockton 93]
Cockton, G., 1993, *Architecture and Abstraction in User Interface Management*, PhD thesis, Heriot-Watt University, Edinburgh, Scotland.

[Dieterich et al. 93]
Dieterich, H., Malinowski, U., Kühme, T., Schneider-Hufschmidt, M. (1993). *State of the Art in Adaptive User Interfaces*, In: this book

[Enderle et al. 84]
Enderle, G., Kansy, K. and Pfaff, G., 1984, *Computer Graphics Programming. GKS – The Graphics Standard*, Springer Verlag: Berlin.

[Feycock 77]
Feycock, S., 1977, *Transition diagram based CAI-HELP system*, International Journal of Man Machine Studies, 9, 339–413.

[Gray et al. 90]
Gray, P.D., K.W. Waite and S.W. Draper, 1990, *Do-It-Yourself Iconic Displays*, in *Human-Computer Interaction – INTERACT'90*, eds. E D. Diaper, D. Gilmore, G. Cockton and B. Shackel, North-Holland: Amsterdam, 639–644.

[Green 85]
Green, M., 1985, *Report on Dialogue Specification Tools*, in *User Interface Management Systems*, ed. G. E. Pfaff, Springer Verlag, 9–20.

[Green 91]
Green, T.R.G., 1991, *Describing Information Artifacts with Cognitive Dimensions and Structure Maps*, in *People and Computers VI*, eds. D. Diaper and N. Hammond, Cambridge University Press: Cambridge, 297–316.

[Hill 87]
Hill, R.D., 1987, *Event-Response Systems – A Technique for Specifying Multi-Threaded Dialogues*, Human Factors and Computing Systems – CHI+GI'87, ACM, 241–248.

[Myers 90]
Myers, B.A., 1990, *A New Model for Input*, Transactions on Information Systems, 8(3), ACM, 289–320.

[Newman & Sproull 79]
Newman, W.M. and R.F. Sproull, 1979, *Principles of Interactive Computer Graphics*, 2nd. edition, McGraw Hill.

[Norman 86]
Norman, D.A., 1986, *Cognitive engineering*, in *User-Centred Systems Design*, eds D.A. Norman and S.W. Draper, Erlbaum Associates, Hillsdale, NJ, 31–61.

[Olsen 84]
  Olsen, D.R. Jr, 1984, *Pushdown Automata for User Interface Management*, Transactions on Graphics, 3(3), ACM, 177–203.

[Olsen et al. 85]
  Olsen, D.R. Jr, E.P. Dempsey and R. Rogge, 1985, *Input/Output Linkage in a User Interface Management System*, Computer Graphics, 19(3) (Proc. SIGGRAPH '85), 191–197.

[Peterson 77]
  Peterson, J.L., 1977, *Petri Nets*, Computing Surveys, 9(3), ACM, 223–252.

[Pilote 83]
  Pilote, M., 1983, *A Programming Language Framework for Designing User Interfaces*, ACM SIGPLAN Notices, 18(6), (Proc. Symp. on Programming Language Issues in Software Systems), 118–136.

[Senay 90]
  Senay, H., 1990, *Fuzzy Command Grammars for User Modelling in Intelligent Interfaces*, in *Engineering for Human-Computer Interaction*, ed. G. Cockton, North-Holland: Amsterdam, 313–327.

[Shuey et al. 86]
  Shuey, D., D. Bailey and T.P. Morrissey, 1986, *PHIGS: A Standard, Dynamic, Interactive Graphics Interface*, Computer Graphics and Applications, IEEE, 50–51.

[Stemple et al. 92]
  Stemple, D. R.B. Stanton, T. Sheard, P. Philbrow, R. Morrison, G.N.C. Kirby, L. Fergaras, R.L. Copper, R.C.H. Connor, M.P. Atkinson and S. Alagic, 1992, *Type Safe Linguistic Reflection: A Generator Technology*, Report FIDE/92/49, FIDE Report Co-ordinator, Department of Computing Science, University of Glasgow.

[Thimbleby 93]
  Thimbleby, H.T., 1993, *Literate using for finite state machines*, Department of Computer Science, University of Sterling, Scotland (submitted to HCI'93).

[Took 88]
  Took, R.K., 1988, *Presenter: Programmer/User Manual*, Department of Computer Science, University of York, Heslington, York, YO1 5DD.

[Took 90]
  Took, R.K., 1990, *Surface Interaction: Separating Direct Manipulation Interfaces from their Applications*, Ph.D. Thesis, Department of Computer Science, University of York.

[van Wyk 82]
  van Wyk, C.J., 1982, *A High-Level Language for Specifying Pictures*, Transactions on Graphics, 1(2), ACM, 163–182.

[Watt 80]
  Watt, D.A., 1980, *Rule splitting and attribute-directed parsing*, in *Semantics-Directed Compiler Generation*, ed. N.D. Jones (LNCS 94), Springer-Verlag.

APPENDIX: EQUIVALENCE OF TAGGED EVENT RESPONSE SYSTEMS AND SAFE PETRI NETS

An event-response system is a 5-tuple, $<S, P, W, w_0, w_f>$ where

S is the set of *event symbols*,

$P \varepsilon P(S) \times P(S)$ is the set of *event response rules* ($P(S)$ is the power set of S, $P(S) = \{ x \mid x \subseteq S \}$),

$W \varepsilon P(S)$ is the *working memory*,

$w_0 \varepsilon P(S)$ is the *initial configuration* of the working memory,

$w_f \varepsilon P(S)$ is the *accepting configuration* of the working memory.

Each rule in P has a set of symbols on its left and right sides (a rule is written $l_1 \ldots l_n \to r_1 \ldots r_n$, so the symbols $tl_1 \ldots l_n$ are called the *left* of the rule and the symbols $r_1 \ldots r_n$ the *right*), sometimes called the antecedent and the consequent of the rule. An event response system starts with $W = w_f$. P is then searched for rules, $L \to R$, where $L \subseteq W$. All such rules are marked. When all rules in P have been examined, all the marked rules are fired. As each rule is fired, $L \to R$, the working memory is updated to become $(W-L) \cup R$. If this new value for $W \subseteq w_f$, then the event response system has reached an accepting state. If not, then rules in P are then searched again, with the mark and fire cycle continuing until $W \subseteq w_f$.

An event response system can be used to specify the temporal behaviour of an interactive system by partitioning the set of symbols, S, into user, interaction, and system events. User and system events only appear in the left of rules. Interaction events are introduced in the right of rules and then trigger other rules by appearing on their left sides.

A safe Petri Net is a 7-tuple, $<N, T, I, O, M, \mu_0, \mu_f>$ where

N is the set of *places*,

T is the set of *transitions*,

$I \varepsilon T \to P(N)$ is the *input function* which gives the incoming places for a transition,

$O \varepsilon T \to P(N)$ is the *output function* which gives the outgoing places for a transition,

$M \varepsilon P(N)$ is the *marking* for a Petri Net,

$\mu_0 \varepsilon P(N)$ is the *initial marking*,

$\mu_f \varepsilon P(N)$ is the *accepting marking*.

Each transition in T has incoming and outgoing places which are identical in function to the left and right sides of an event-response rule. A Petri Net starts with $M = \mu_f$. T is then searched for transitions, t, where $I(t) \subseteq M$. In some interpretations, only one such transition is fired, changing the marking to $(M-I(t)) \cup O(t)$. However, all such *enabled* transitions could be fired, as in an event-response system. If the new marking $M \subseteq \mu_f$, then the Petri has reached an accepting state. If not, then transitions in t are then searched again, with the enable and fire cycle continuing until $M \subseteq \mu_f$.

A safe Petri Net is one where markings are sets and not bags. In the initial formulations of Petri Nets, markings were represented by placing *tokens* on places. A place can thus have more than one token on it, and thus continue to enable transitions even after an outgoing transition has fired. This is necessary for some modelling tasks. However, the use of sets for the domain marking in the above definition, and the corresponding use of set union in the transition function ensures that the defined Petri Nets are safe.

A Petri Net system can be used to specify the temporal behaviour of an interactive system by partitioning the set of places, P, into user, interaction and system places. User and system places only have outgoing transitions. Interaction places can have both incoming and outgoing transitions.

Safe Petri Net				Tagged ERS
Places	N	S		Symbols
Transitions	T	R		Rule names
input function → output function	$I(t) \rightarrow O(t)$	$P(r)$		Rule function
Marking	M	W		Working memory
Initial marking	μ_0	w_0		Initial configuration
Accepting marking	μ_f	w_f		Accepting configuration
Enabling predicate	$E(t) = I(t) \subseteq M$	$M(L \rightarrow R) = L \subseteq W$		Marking predicate
Firing transition	$F(t) = M \rightarrow (M-I(t)) \cup O(t)$	$F(L \rightarrow R) = W \rightarrow (W-L) \cup R$		Firing transition

Table 1: Equivalence between safe Petri Nets and tagged event-response systems

There are clear similarities between event-response systems and safe Petri Nets. These similarities can be turned into an equivalence by extending event response systems into a 6-tuple, $<S, R, P, W, w_0, w_f>$ where S, W, w_0 and w_f are as in the initial definition, and

R is the set of *rule names*,

P ε R $\rightarrow P(S) \times P(S)$ is the *rule function* which maps from rule names to productions.

Such automata will be called *tagged* event-response systems. The equivalence between safe Petri Nets and tagged event-response systems is shown in Table 1.

This equivalence provides event-response systems with their missing graphical representation (Petri Nets have always been drawn as marked graphs with two node types, places, and transitions). This has already proved useful in debugging students event-response configurations. It also provides them with the wide range of analysis techniques and complexity theory results from Petri Net research over the last 30 years. Useful constructs such as *zero transitions* [Peterson 77] are easily transferred to event-response systems. Unfortunately, it also brings with it all the known disadvantages of Petri Nets.

Part II

Modelling Users, Tasks, and Dialogs

Adaptive User Interfaces
M. Schneider-Hufschmidt, T. Kühme & U. Malinowski (Editors)
© 1993 Elsevier Science Publishers B.V. All rights reserved.

User Modeling: Recent Work, Prospects and Hazards

Alfred Kobsa

University of Konstanz
Konstanz, Germany[1]

ABSTRACT

User modeling has made considerable progress during its existence now of more than a decade. In this paper, a survey of recent developments will be presented, which concentrates on the modeling of a user's knowledge, plans, and preferences in a domain, on the exploitation of new sources of information about the user, on issues of representation, inference and revision, on user modeling shell systems and servers, and on the verification of the practical utility of user models. Research trends and research deficiencies in these areas will be outlined, and potential risks described.[2]

1 INTRODUCTION

User modeling has made considerable progress during its existence now of more than a decade. Particularly in the last few years, the need for software systems to automatically adapt to their current users has been recognized in many application areas. Consequently, research on user modeling (which originated in the field of natural-language dialog systems) has spread into many disciplines which are concerned with the development of computer systems that are to be used by heterogeneous user populations. These fields include Human-Computer Interaction, Intelligent Interfaces, Adaptive Interfaces, Cognitive Engineering, Intelligent Information Retrieval, Intelligent Tutoring, Active and Passive Help Systems, Guidance Systems, Hypertext Systems, and Expert Systems, to name just the most prominent application areas.

Several introductory surveys on user modeling have already appeared in the last few years (see, e.g., [Kass & Finin 88, Kobsa & Wahlster 88, Kobsa & Wahlster 89, Norcio & Stan-

---

[1] Alfred Kobsa is currently a visiting researcher at the Department of Computer Science, Columbia University, New York, NY 10027.
[2] The research described here has been supported by the German Science Foundation through Grant No. Ko 1044/2-4, and by the University of Konstanz through Grant No. AFF 17/92. An extended abstract of this paper appeared in the Proceedings of the Workshop on User Adapted Interaction, Bari, Italy, May 1992.

ley 89, Kok 91]). This paper therefore concentrates on more recent research trends and describes interesting developments as well as research deficiencies. Examples include the currently very popular stereotype approach, a technique that has been frequently employed for the modeling of users' domain knowledge. Another very active area at the moment is plan recognition, albeit mostly from a research perspective and not so much from an application perspective. The interest in the modeling of user preferences has also sharply risen, particularly as far as the users' information preferences are concerned. New techniques and information sources for acquiring assumptions about the user are being explored. These techniques link user modeling research more closely to modern user interfaces than did previously employed techniques that relied strongly on a (fictional) natural-language interaction. The increased demand for expressive representation systems for user models, powerful general inference mechanisms, and the need for assumption revision in user models led to a transfer of AI techniques into user modeling research. Integrated representation, reasoning, and revision tools (so-called 'user modeling shell systems') are being developed that should facilitate the deployment of user modeling components in application systems. Finally, the empirical validation of the utility of developed adaptive systems has strongly gained in importance. The first results suggest that users will indeed profit from systems that adapt to their needs.

2 USER KNOWLEDGE

The stereotype approach to user modeling (which was proposed by [Rich 79a, Rich 79b, Rich 89] and later refined, e.g., by [Chin 89]) has proven very useful for application areas in which a quick, but not necessarily completely accurate, assessment of the user's background knowledge is required. In this approach, the developer of a user modeling component in an application system has to fulfill three tasks:

- *User subgroup identification*: The user model developer must identify subgroups within the expected user population whose members are very likely to possess certain homogeneous application-relevant characteristics. The user population of a statistical database with national hospitalization data for cancer patients could, for instance, be divided into medical professionals, scientists, and statisticians, and on a more specific level, doctors, nurses, medical statisticians, actuaries, hospital managers, and policy makers.

- *Identification of key characteristics*: The user model developer should identify a small number of key characteristics which allow one to identify the members of a user subgroup (the presence or absence of these characteristics should be recognizable by a computer system). In the example of the hospitalization database, such characteristics could be the kind of questions users ask, the terminology they employ, the kind of statistical information they seek, the level of help they request, etc.

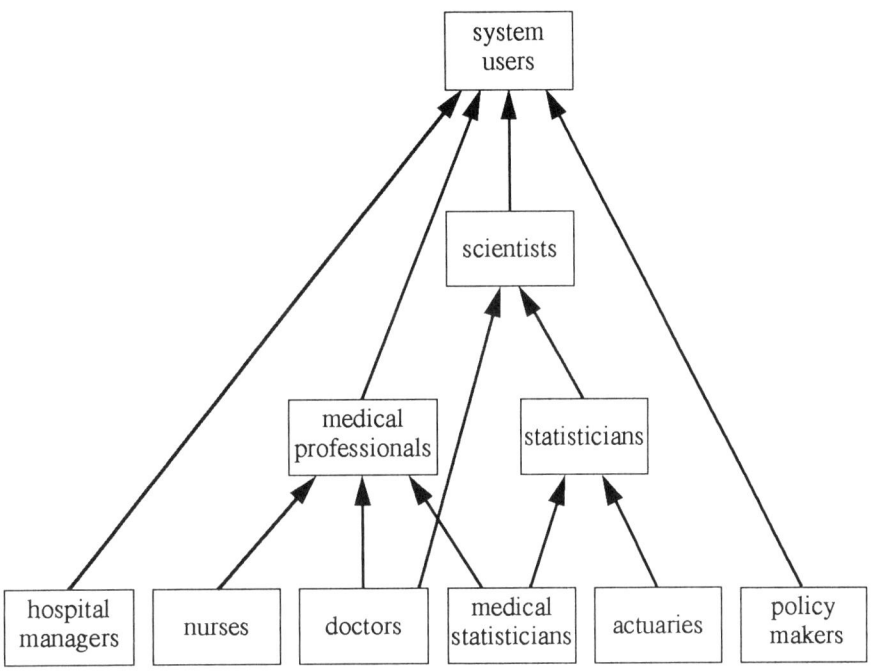

Figure 1: Example stereotype hierarchy in a medical domain

- *Representation in (hierarchically ordered) stereotypes*: The application-relevant characteristics of the identified user groups must be formalized in an appropriate representation system. The collection of all represented characteristics of a user subgroup is called a stereotype for this subgroup. If the contents of one stereotype form a subset of the contents of another stereotype, stereotype hierarchies may be constructed in which the contents of superordinate stereotypes become inherited by the subordinate stereotypes and hence need only be represented once. In Figure 1, stereotypes were developed for the user subgroups in the hospitalization domain (they contain, for instance, assumptions about the technical terms that are familiar to these subgroups). The stereotypes are ordered in a hierarchy. The universal characteristics of all system users are contained in the topmost stereotype only, and become inherited by its subordinate stereotypes. The stereotypes named 'medical professionals', 'scientists', and 'statisticians' contain a representation of the characteristics of the respective subgroups. Their contents become again inherited by their subordinate stereotypes.

Stereotypes for user groups with different background knowledge have been specifically employed for user-adapted information and advice on operating systems [Chin 89,

Nessen 89, Boyle & Encarnacion 93]. Most authors postulate a linear hierarchy of stereotypes corresponding to beginners, intermediates, and experts. However, it is doubtful whether such a simple classification of users can be empirically justified. [Sutcliffe & Old 87], for instance, found that the modeling of users' familiarity with operating system commands requires the identification of coherent knowledge clusters in the user, rather than levels of user expertise.

Since stereotypical assumptions are particularly prone to inaccuracy, considerably more attention is paid to allowing users to inspect and possibly also modify their system's model of them (see, e.g., [Kay 90, Orwant 91, Rosis et al. 92, Boyle & Encarnacion 93]). [Kobsa 90b] questions, however, whether this will also be possible for more general user models which will contain a far larger number of mostly trivial and low-level assumptions. Moreover, these assumptions are hard to translate from the formal representation language employed (e.g., modal logic) into a language that is comprehensible to the user.

3 USER PLANS

Much emphasis has been recently put on the recognition of users' plans, where a plan is a sequence of user actions that achieve a certain goal. Plan recognition systems observe the user's input actions and try to determine all possible user plans to which the observed actions can be complemented. This set of candidate plans for the unknown user plan can be further narrowed down as soon as new user actions occur.

While the basic algorithm is fairly simple and straightforward, serious combinatorial problems arise when it is practically employed, due to the following reasons:

   (a) it is often unclear when the user commences a new plan;

   (b) actions and short action sequences may often be part of more than one plan;

   (c) users may interrupt or suspend the execution of their current plans (for various reasons, such as when issuing the 'date' command or when replying to an e-mail message which they just received);

   (d) there is often more than one action sequence for achieving a (sub-)goal (i.e., there can be variations of user plans).

Two kinds of techniques are mainly employed for the recognition of users' plans:

- *Plan libraries*: In this approach, all possible user plans are already pre-stored in a so-called plan library (possibly, these plans contain open variables which have still to be instantiated). The observed user action sequence is compared with these pre-stored plans, and all plans are selected whose beginnings match the observed user input. In this approach, it is difficult to take the possibility of plan variations into account. All permissible deviations from a plan would have to be stored as separate plans.

- *Plan construction*: In this approach, the system possesses a library of all possible user actions, together with the effects and the preconditions of these actions. The observed user action sequence is completed by all possible user action sequences which fulfill the requirement that the effects of preceding actions meet the preconditions of subsequent actions.

The generality of the plan library approach is restricted by the requirement that all possible user plans must already be specified beforehand. However, this need not be a problem in small domains in which users can only pursue a limited number of goals. The plan construction approach is problematic from a complexity point of view. Often the number of possible extensions to observed user input that can be constructed from action operators is very large, particularly since the length of the user's plan is unknown. Recent work therefore investigates focusing heuristics that favor the further analysis and expansion of certain plan candidates over others, based on domain knowledge. [Appelt & Pollack 92] present a framework for choosing among competing plan ascriptions based on weighted abduction. [Raskutti & Zukerman 91] address the same problem by measuring the coherence and information content of the ascribed plan using Bayesian probability theory. [Mayfield 92] investigates when to terminate the plan-goal explanation chain based on concepts of explanation completeness and the system's expectations and curiosity.

Other authors deal with the problem that the user's actions may not necessarily be correct. One should therefore be hesitant to exclude plan candidates that do not match the user's input if the mismatch is only small. In this vein, [Eller & Carberry 92] provide a unified framework for recognizing plans from slightly ill-formed and well-formed dialogs using meta-rules to relax constraints when necessary.

4 USER PREFERENCES

Until recently, little attention has been paid to the modeling of user preferences. One of the few exceptions is the HAM-ANS system which modeled users' preferences with respect to hotel rooms they could book through the system (this work is summarized in [Morik 85]). [Morik & Rollinger 85] modeled a real estate agent that made assumptions about the preferences of clients who looked for apartments to rent.

Recently, however, considerably more work is being spent on the modeling of user preferences, particularly their information preferences. In the area of intelligent information retrieval, [Brajnik et al. 87] envisages a comprehensive natural-language access system to bibliographic databases that models the user's information needs. [Botman et al. 89] developed an access system to relational databases that draws assumptions about the user's interests based on the requested information, and volunteers additional information in which the user might be interested as well.

In the area of information filtering, [Jennings & Higuchi 93] developed a personalized electronic news server that is based on a connectionist network architecture. In the learning phase, the network is supplied with a sample of electronic news articles that the user finds interesting. Nodes and link weights adapt to the frequency of information-bearing words in these articles and the probability of their co-occurrence, respectively. After the learning phase, the network is used for determining which news articles should be presented to the user. The adapted network can be regarded as containing the user's information preferences with respect to news articles, represented by the concepts that are likely to occur in such articles. In a similar vein, [Kass & Stadnyk 92] propose to monitor users' access to technical component databases in order to determine who is interested in certain parts, and who should therefore receive company-wide distributed e-mail messages with engineering change notices.

In the area of adaptive hypertext systems, [Kaplan et al. (forthcoming)] developed the HYPERFLEX system that recommends information to users based on their specific informational needs and preferences. The system is based on associative matrices that record the hypertext frames which users with certain goals usually inspect, and bases its advice to new users on this past history.

5 USER MODEL ACQUISITION

Important changes can be observed concerning the sources of information that user modeling components exploit for drawing assumptions about the user. While early research focused strongly on natural-language input, a much wider variety of knowledge sources have been employed recently. These include, among others,

- the observation of users' direct-manipulative interaction with software systems such as
  - text editing in a WYSIWYG editor [Hirschmann 90, Krause et al. (forthcoming)],
  - navigation in a hypertext system ([Kaplan et al. (forthcoming)],
  - stretchtext activation in a hypertext system [Boyle & Encarnacion 93],
  - usage of a command-based interface [Benyon (forthcoming)],
- the analysis of the information which a user retrieves from a database [Botman et al. 89, Kass & Stadnyk 92],
- the analysis of electronic news in which the user is interested [Jennings & Higuchi 93],
- a number of other information sources, particularly UNIX™ resource files [Orwant 91].

Although natural language is seemingly a very rich information source for the acquisition of assumptions about a dialog partner (see [Kobsa 83] for many examples), this recent liberation from the burden of natural-language analysis seems very important for the practical applicability of user modeling techniques. It can be anticipated that the first commercial systems will most likely not rely on natural-language input.

Other novel research trends in the acquisition of user models can be observed on the interaction level. Acquisition so far was mostly either explicit (i.e., the system asks the user for information about him/her) or implicit (i.e., the system performs user modeling based exclusively on its normal interaction with him/her). Work by Wu [Wu 91] and Shifroni and Shanon [Shifroni & Shanon 92] is concerned with mixed-mode acquisition of assumptions about the user, and particularly with decision strategies on when the system should initiate an explicit acquisition phase.

6 REPRESENTATION, INFERENCE, AND REVISION

Issues of formal representation and reasoning did thus far not play an important role in the field of user modeling. With the exception of KL-ONE-like languages (which were used for instance by [Kobsa 85, Paris 89, Kobsa 90a, Kass 91]), formal representations have hardly been employed. This situation changed recently due to increased representational and inferential demands that are imposed on user models. Currently investigated representations include the following:

- *PROLOG* [Finin 89, Eydner & Vergara (forthcoming)], which offers a comparatively rich representation language with "built-in" backward reasoning and the possibility of a smooth migration from knowledge representation to programming;

- *Predicate logic* [Appelt & Pollack 92, Kobsa 92, Fink & Herrmann 93] which offers more expressiveness than PROLOG, as is needed in many application domains;

- *Languages with second-order predicates* [van Arragon 91] and *modal logic* [Kobsa 92], which allow one to represent assumptions about (nested) beliefs and goals of different agents in the same representation language;

- *Connectionist networks*, which have been particularly employed for classification tasks [Bodendorf et al. 90, Jennings & Higuchi 93].

Entries in user models are mainly assumptions and not confirmed facts, and possibly must later be revised when new information about the user becomes available. A problem arises if such assumptions were already used for inferring additional assumptions about the user. In this case, not only the original assumptions, but also all inferences based on them must be retracted, unless they are supported by other assumptions. Ongoing research concerns the development of reason maintenance systems [Huang et al. 91, Brajnik & Tasso 92, Eydner & Vergara (forthcoming)] that record the dependencies among assumptions. When conflicts are detected among the assumptions about the user, these systems determine which assumptions should be retracted to resolve the conflict.

7 USER MODELING SHELL SYSTEMS AND SERVERS

User modeling components in software systems are often expensive to develop. Thus far, system developers essentially have to start from scratch each time. Research on user modeling shell systems aims therefore at the development of integrated representation, reasoning, and revision tools that form an "empty" user modeling mechanism. When filled with application-dependent user modeling knowledge, these shell systems would fulfill essential functions of a user modeling component in an application system. Parallels to this line of research can be found, e.g., in the field of expert systems in which the experience gained from individual expert systems lead to the development of expert system shells. In return, the availability of these shells considerably stimulated the development of application systems.

In the next few subsections, the 4 major user modeling shell systems that have been developed to date will be surveyed. Orwant's "personalization server" will then be briefly described which is the first instance of a user model server, i.e. a user modeling system that is not part of an application system but rather an independent process that communicates with all applications that the user is interacting with, and supplies them with assumptions about the user [Orwant 91].

7.1 GUMS

The GUMS system [Finin 89], which is based on Prolog, is aimed at providing a set of services for the maintenance of assumptions about the user's beliefs. GUMS does not draw assumptions itself. Instead, it accepts and stores new facts about the user which are provided by the application system, verifies the consistency of a new fact with the currently held assumptions by trying to deduce the negated fact from the current assumptions, informs the application system about recognized inconsistencies, and answers queries of the application concerning its current assumptions about the user.

The shell system allows for the definition of a stereotype hierarchy (however, the hierarchy is constrained to a tree, and only a single stereotype may apply to the user at a time). The initial stereotype pertaining to the user must be selected either by the user model designer or the application program. Each stereotype includes a number of definite facts about the user; if one of these facts is contradicted with new information about the user, the stereotype is abandoned. It is then replaced by the most specific direct or indirect superordinate stereotype that does not contain the contradictory fact (stereotypes in parallel paths are not considered).

Two types of inference rules are supported by GUMS, namely definite rules and default rules. These are processed in a backward chaining mode when GUMS answers queries of the application system concerning the deducibility of a given fact from the current assumptions about the user, and when GUMS determines whether a new fact about the user is consistent with the current assumptions by trying to deduce the negation of this fact from its current assumptions. In both cases, negation by failure is possible if a predicate that has been asked for has been declared as closed, i.e., as defined by the current system knowledge pertaining to it. The use of default rules requires GUMS to continue to search for a goal until one is found that is not based on defaults, or until all solutions have been checked. The result of a query to the knowledge base is never recorded. Thus, no truth maintenance is needed since no assumptions exist in the knowledge base that were deduced from other assumptions.

7.2 UM

UM [Kay 90] is intended to become a toolkit for user modeling. It is still in an experimental stage at the moment and its architecture is considerably simpler than those of all other user modeling shell systems. The system offers two principal mechanisms for the development of user modeling components, namely

- *structured text files* organized in a directory hierarchy, each of which collects details of various aspects of the user's knowledge in one subdomain, and

- a *rule interpreter* which executes rule-like programs that amend the user model.

Each entry in a text file of the user model contains the following information:

- a knowledge "component" (in Kay's terms) with which the user is assumed to be familiar or not familiar,

- a list of information which supports this assumption (six different information sources with different degrees of reliability are distinguished), and

- a list of information which negates this assumption.

Individual user models that can be constructed using UM are thus thematically organized (the hierarchy reflects no inheritance relationship). There exists no representation system within the user model; instead, the interpretation of the entries is left to the programs that retrieve assumptions about the user. UM also does not contain any stereotype hierarchy, although a stereotype may be one of the above-mentioned knowledge sources which support or negate an entry in the user model. Any kind of retrieval or updating of information in the user model has to be performed by application programs that may be written in the format executable by UM's rule interpreter.

An interesting aspect of UM's user models is that these are regarded as belonging to the respective users who can access them and, if they wish, modify them. The fact that users may possibly "sabotage" their own models is tolerated. This approach has interesting consequences as to the control of users over the models of them which the system constructs (see section 9).

7.3 UMT

UMT [Brajnik & Tasso 92] allows the user model developer to define user stereotypes that contain the characteristics of user subgroups in the form of attribute-value pairs. Stereotypes can be ordered in arbitrary hierarchies, which support the inheritance of stereotype contents. Each stereotype possesses an activation condition which specifies when the stereotype can be applied to the current user. UMT also puts a rule interpreter at the disposition of the user model developer which allows for the definition of user modeling inference rules. Possible contradictions between assumed user characteristics also have to be explicitly defined using rules.

Like GUMS, UMT does not draw assumptions itself, but accepts and stores new assertions about the user which are provided by the application system (depending on the reliability of these assertions, they can be regarded as invariable *premises* or as (later still retractable) *assumptions*). Stereotypes that become activated due to the new assertions about the user add still more assumptions (namely the feature-value pairs describing the characteristic of the respective user subgroups). Some of these assumptions may possibly be contradictory. UMT then applies all inference rules (including the contradiction detection rules) to the set of premises and assumptions, and records the inferential dependencies.

A reason maintenance component in the system then determines all possible user models, which are all consistent sets of assertions containing the premises, a subset of the assumptions, and all inferences derived from these premises and assumptions. The Current User Model will be selected from the set of possible user models using preference criteria (such as assumptions which were reported to the system by the application have a higher weight than assumptions from stereotypes). If inconsistencies with new information from the application is later detected (or if the application disconfirms advice from UMT concerning the user), the assumptions on which the offending assertion was based can be easily detected (since inferential dependencies become recorded), and the set of possible user models will be revised and re-evaluated to find the new Current User Model.

7.4 BGP-MS

BGP-MS [Kobsa 90a, Kobsa 92], which is currently under development, offers a "partitioned" user model which allows for the representation of more than one type of assumption about the user, notably the user's beliefs, goals, and abilities. Assumptions about the user may include the user's presumed assumptions about other agents, e.g. the user's beliefs about the system's goals (arbitrary nesting is possible). Emphasis is being put on distinguishing whether assumptions are privately held or shared between the user and the system.

The stereotypes which BGP-MS provides can also be ordered in an arbitrary hierarchy, with inheritance, stereotype activation rules, and independent retraction rules being supported (an optional set of predefined rules is available for the definition of activation and retraction conditions). Global parameters allow the user model developer to fine-tune the operation of the stereotype mechanism, for instance, by determining its precision, its recall, and the frequency of user reclassification.

Assumptions about the user can be communicated to BGP-MS in a first-order language with modal operators (if possible, they will become translated into representationally weaker but computationally more efficient internal representations, like SB-ONE [Kobsa 91] and KN-PART [Fink & Herrmann 93]). The deduction mechanism OTTER [McCune 90] is available for drawing inferences from initial assumptions. Strong emphasis is put on assisting the user model developer in the definition of the user-modeling knowledge pertaining to the application domain. Graphics-based interfaces will be available for the definition of the stereotype hierarchies, their contents, and the activation and retraction rules.

Like all other shell systems, BGP-MS also requires that assumptions about the user must be made by the application system. In addition, though, it offers a library of domain-independent assumptions about the user that can be drawn when certain communication acts occur in the interaction between the user and the system [Kobsa 83, Kutter 93]. The application must then only notify BGP-MS about the communication act that took place, and the resulting domain-independent inferences will be made by the shell system and become entered into the user model. For instance, if the system communicates to the user that it declines his or her goal p and informs BGP-MS that this communication act took place, then BGP-MS will draw the assumption that from now on it is mutually believed that the user wants p, and that the system does not want p to be the case. These communication acts are independent of the interaction language or medium that is employed by the user and the system.

7.5 User model servers

A complementary, yet partly competing proposal to user modeling shell systems is that of user model servers. User modeling shell systems, when filled with application-dependent user modeling knowledge, become part of the application, i.e. they receive information about the user from this application only and supply only this application with assumptions about the user. In contrast, user model servers would be centralized user modeling components for more than one application (possibly for all applications with which the user interacts). It seems that the capabilities of user model servers would then be restricted to domain-independent (i.e., fairly shallow) user modeling, unless they incorporate all the domain-dependent user modeling knowledge which would be necessary if each of these applications would employ a user modeling shell system.

To date, the idea of user model servers has not been worked out very thoroughly. The only exception is [Orwant 91] who envisages a central "personalization server," which constantly gathers information about computer users from their everyday workplace activities. Independently, client systems that want to adapt to users make requests to this server for information about these users. A success or failure feedback report of the client systems is not yet foreseen, but could probably be added.

8 UTILITY OF USER MODELS

Except for Rich's empirical evaluation of her library recommendation system that bases its advice concerning books to read on a model of its current user, hardly any verification of the utility of user models was performed during the eighties [Rich 79a]. Fortunately, the concern for empirical questions has considerably increased in the last few years. Several investigations into the usefulness of user models in interactive software systems have been carried out recently, including the following:

- *Context-sensitive help in a WYSIWYG text editor* [Hirschmann 90, Krause et al. (forthcoming)]: it was shown that the adaptation of help menus in a WYSIWYG text editor to the user's current error improved significantly the task performance, and decreased the redundancy and the error rate.

- *Navigational help in a hypertext system* [Kaplan et al. (forthcoming)]: it was shown that navigational aid based on experiences with previous users and information about the current user's goal can significantly reduce the time searching for information.

- *Adaptive hypertext* [Boyle & Encarnacion 93]: it was shown that the comprehension and search speed were significantly improved in a hypertext system that adapted its text to the user's level of expertise.

- *Personal news filter* [Jennings & Higuchi 93]: it was shown that the precision and recall of an electronic news filter that was based on a connectionist user model was satisfactory for many users.

These positive results in several application areas for user modeling are contrasted by possibly negative findings in the area of preference modeling. [Allen 90], who had subjects predict other people's interests in newspaper articles, claims that the outcome of his experiments casts doubt on whether information preferences can be predicted at all by people, let alone by computer systems.

The question of whether user models and adaptive interactive computer systems offer sufficient enough advantages for their users such that the costs for their development are outweighed by their benefits can only be empirically determined. Further empirical work to this end is thus urgently needed. The first results for various types of applications were certainly promising, but at the moment one should not over-generalize them. Possibly results will be available in the future concerning the classes of applications which are amenable to user modeling, and application classes for which adaptivity is not so beneficial.

9 GUIDELINES TO PREVENT POTENTIAL ABUSES

Thus far, user modeling has been almost exclusively used for making computer systems more cooperative. Of course, user models could also support a system in pursuing non-cooperative interests. A small example is HAM-ANS [Jameson & Wahlster 82] which, in its non-cooperative mode, will deliberately misguide the user in order to "positively" influence his/her decisions concerning particular hotel rooms to book.

While user modeling is certainly an important contribution to making computers accessible to casual users (particularly to the general public), it is also subject to potential misuse like many other new technologies. Certain guidelines should therefore be observed both in research and in practical applications, in order to resist these dangers already in an early stage (see [Kobsa 90b] for a more detailed discussion):

- Users should be made aware of the fact that a computer system contains a user modeling component. In many applications, the presence of such a component may not be obvious, particularly not to casual users. The user's awareness of the user modeling abilities of a system is, however, a necessary prerequisite in order that he or she can decide whether or not to consent to being modeled by the system.

- Users should be instructed that computer systems might make errors. User modeling components draw mostly *assumptions* about the user, which may not necessarily be correct. User modeling therefore inherently involves the risk of misunderstandings (as is the case in normal communication between people). It is therefore only prudent to encourage the user to guard against possible misconceptions of the system, as he or she is used to anyway, when communicating with other people.

- Users should be instructed that a computer system might pursue non-cooperative interests. User models may not only be employed by a computer system for supporting the users' goals in a cooperative way, but also for influencing users according to other interests, e.g., of some company. If one does not regard a computer system as an objective expert, but rather as a representative of a concern, then one can rely on the strategies which one normally uses to protect oneself against the influence of other people.

- Users should have the possibility to inspect and, if necessary, also to change their user models. It can be anticipated, however, that in many applications user models will often comprise an enormous amount of fairly trivial assumptions, which are moreover difficult to translate into ordinary English. It will therefore often be difficult to render user models comprehensible to their owners.

- If technically possible, users should be able to "switch off" a user modeling component if he or she does not consent to being modeled. It is by far not clear, however, whether it is possible to separate the user modeling component from the remaining system in such a way that the user can in fact relinquish it. In many application domains, user modeling is not only a prerequisite for a system's cooperativeness, but even for its ability to conduct a coherent intelligent interaction at all.

- Long-term user characteristics should be modeled with caution since their misuse is probably more serious than the misuse of transient user characteristics. Moreover, long-term user characteristics are often regarded as more "personal" than short-term user characteristics.

- Goal and plan recognition should not be used for screening the user as to whether or not his/her goals in accessing a computer system are admissible.

- Results in user modeling research should be made accessible to the general public, which will eventually be affected by them.

REFERENCES

[Allen 90]
R. B. Allen (1990): *User Models: Theory, Method, and Practice*. International Journal of Man-Machine Studies, 32:511-543.

[Appelt & Pollack 92]
D. E. Appelt and M. E. Pollack (1992): *Weighted Abduction for Plan Ascription*. User Modeling and User-Adapted Interaction, 2:1-25.

[Benyon (forthcoming)]
D. Benyon (forthcoming): *Adaptive Systems: A Solution to Usability Problems*. To appear in User Modeling and User-Adapted Interaction.

[Bodendorf et al. 90]
F. Bodendorf, H.-G. Lindner, and H. Linß (1990): *Benutzermodellierung mit Hilfe Neuronaler Netze: Ein Prototyp fur OS/2-Nutzer*. Arbeitspapier 4/1990, Abteilung Wirtschaftsinformatik, Universität Erlangen-Nürnberg, Erlangen, Germany.

[Botman et al. 89]
A. M. Botman, A. J. Kok, and L. Siklossy (1989): *Methods for User Modelling in an Intelligent Interface for Data Retrieval*. Unpublished Manuscript, Department of Mathematics and Computer Science, Free University, Amsterdam, Netherlands.

[Boyle & Encarnacion 93]
C. D. B. Boyle and Antonio O. Encarnacion (forthcoming): *An Adaptive Hypertext Reading System*. Submitted to User Modeling and User-Adapted Interaction.

[Brajnik et al. 87]
G. Brajnik, G. Guida, and C. Tasso (1987): *User Modeling in Intelligent Information Retrieval*. Information Processing & Management, 23:305-320.

[Brajnik & Tasso 92]
G. Brajnik and C. Tasso (1992): A *Flexible Tool for Developing User Modeling Applications with Nonmonotonic Reasoning Capabilities*. Proceedings of the Third International Workshop on User Modeling, Dagstuhl, Germany, 42-63.

[Chin 89]
D. N. Chin (1989): *KNOME: Modeling what the User Knows in UC*. In A. Kobsa and W. Wahlster (eds.): *User Models in Dialog Systems*, pp. 74-107. Springer, Berlin, Heidelberg.

[De Rosis et al. 92]
F. De Rosis, S. Pizzutilo, A. Russo, D. C. Berry, and F. J. Nicolau Molina (1992): *Modeling the User Knowledge by Belief Networks*. User Modeling and User-Adapted Interaction, 2:367-388.

[Eller & Carberry 92]
R. Eller and S. Carberry (1992): A *Meta-Rule Approach to Flexible Plan Recognition in Dialogue*. User Modeling and User-Adapted Interaction, 2:7-53.

[Eydner & Vergara (forthcoming)]
G. Eydner and H. Vergara (forthcoming): *A User Modeling Truth Maintenance System Based on Prolog and KN-PART* (working title). Master thesis, Dept. of Information Science, University of Konstanz, Germany.

[Finin 89]
T. W. Finin (1989). *GUMS: A General User Modeling Shell*. In A. Kobsa and W. Wahlster (eds.): *User Models in Dialog Systems*, pp. 411-430. Springer, Berlin, Heidelberg.

[Fink & Herrmann 93]
J. Fink and M. Herrmann (1993): *KN-PART - Ein Verwaltungssystem zur Benutzermodellierung mit prädikatenlogischer Wissensrepräsentation*. WIS Memo Nr. 5, WG Knowledge-Based Information Systems, Dept. of Information Science, University of Konstanz, Germany.

[Hirschmann 90]
A. Hirschmann (1990): *Das Hilfesystem MATHILDE*. PhD Thesis, Philosophische Fakultät, Universität Regensburg, Regensburg, Germany.

[Huang et al. 91]
X. Huang, G. I. McCalla, J. E. Greer, and E. Neufeld (1991): *Revising Deductive Knowledge and Stereotypical Knowledge in a Student Model*. User Modeling and User-Adapted Interaction, 1:87-115.

[Jameson & Wahlster 82]
A. Jameson and W. Wahlster (1982): *User Modelling in Anaphora Generation: Ellipsis and Definite Description*. In Proc. of the 5th European Conference on Artificial Intelligence, pp. 222-227, Orsay, France.

[Jennings & Higuchi 93]
A. Jennings and H. Higuchi (1993). A *User Model Neural Network for a Personal News Service*. To appear in User Modeling and User-Adapted Interaction 3(1).

[Kaplan et al. (forthcoming)]
C. Kaplan, J. Fenwick and J. Chen (forthcoming): *Adaptive Hypertext Navigation Based on User Goals and Context*. Submitted to User Modeling and User-Adapted Interaction.

[Kass & Finin 88]
R. Kass and T. Finin (1988): *Modeling the User in Natural Language Systems*. Computational Linguistics 14(3):5-22.

[Kass 91]
R. Kass (1991): *Building a User Model Implicitly from a Cooperative Advisory Dialog*. User Modeling and User-Adapted Interaction, 1:203-258.

[Kass & Stadnyk 92]
R. Kass and I. Stadnyk (1992): *Using User Models to Improve Organizational Information*. In Proceedings of the 3rd International Workshop on User Modeling, Dagstuhl, Germany.

[Kay 90]
J. Kay (1990): *um: A Toolkit for User Modelling*. In Proc. of the Second International Workshop on User Modeling, pp. 1-11, Honolulu, HI.

[Kobsa 83]
A. Kobsa (1983): *Präsuppositionsanalyse zum Aufbau von Dialogpartnermodellen*. Conceptus, 17(40/41):165-179.

[Kobsa 85]
A. Kobsa (1985): *Benutzermodellierung in Dialogsystemen*. Springer, Berlin, Heidelberg.

[Kobsa 90a]
A. Kobsa (1990a): *Modeling the User's Conceptual Knowledge in BGP-MS, a User Modeling Shell System*. Computational Intelligence, 6:193-208.

[Kobsa 90b]
A. Kobsa (1990b): *User Modeling in Dialog Systems: Potentials and Hazards*. AI & Society: The Journal of Human and Machine Intelligence, 4:214-231.

[Kobsa 91]
A. Kobsa (1991): *Utilizing Knowledge: The Components of the SB-ONE Knowledge Representation Workbench*. In: J. Sowa, ed.: *Principles of Semantic Networks: Explorations in the Representation of Knowledge*. San Mateo, CA: Morgan Kaufmann.

[Kobsa 92]
A. Kobsa (1992): *Towards Inferences in BGP-MS: Combining Modal Logic and Partition Hierarchies for User Modeling* (Preliminary report). In Proceedings of the 3rd International Workshop on User Modeling, Dagstuhl, Germany, pp. 35-41.

[Kobsa & Wahlster 88]
A. Kobsa and W. Wahlster, eds. (1988): *Computational Linguistics 14(3): Special Issue on User Modeling*. MIT Press, Cambridge, MA.

[Kobsa & Wahlster 89]
A. Kobsa and W. Wahlster (1989): *User Models in Dialog Systems*. Springer, Berlin, Heidelberg.

[Kok 91]
A. Kok (1991): A *Review and Synthesis of User Modeling in Intelligent Systems*. The Knowledge Engineering Review, 6:21-47.

[Krause et al. (forthcoming)]
J. Krause, A. Hirschmann and E. Mittermaier (forthcoming): *The Intelligent Help System COMFOHELP: Towards a Solution of the Practicability Problem for User Modeling and Adaptive Systems*. Submitted to User Modeling and User-Adapted Interaction.

[Kutter 93]
O. Kutter (1993): *Aufbau eines Benutzermodells durch Analyse von Kommunikationsakten.* Projektarbeitsbericht, AG Wissensbasierte Informationssysteme, Informationswissenschaft, Universität Konstanz.

[Mayfield 92]
J. Mayfield (1992): *Controlling Inference in Plan Recognition.* User Modeling and User-Adapted Interaction, 2:83-115.

[McCune 90]
W. W. McCune (1990): *OTTER 2.0 Users Guide.* Technical Report ANL-90/9, Argonne National Laboratory, Mathematics and Computer Science Division, Argonne, IL.

[Morik 85]
K. Morik (1985): *User Modelling, Dialog Structures, and Dialog Strategy in HAM-ANS.* In Proc. of the 2nd EACL, pp. 268-273, Geneva, Switzerland.

[Morik & Rollinger 85]
K. Morik & C.-R. Rollinger (1985): *The Real Estate Agent: Modeling Users by Uncertain Reasoning.* AI Magazine 6, 44-52.

[Nessen 89]
E. Nessen (1989): *SC-UM: User Modeling in the Sinix Consultant.* Applied Artificial Intelligence, 3:33-44.

[Norcio & Stanley 89]
A. F. Norcio and J. Stanley (1989): *Adaptive Human-Computer Interfaces: A Literature Survey and Perspective.* IEEE Transactions on Systems, Man, and Cybernetics, 19: 399-408.

[Orwant 91]
J. L. Orwant (1991): *The Doppelganger User Modelling System.* In Proc. of the IJCAI Workshop W4: Agent Modelling for Intelligent Interaction, pp. 164-168, Sydney, Australia.

[Paris 89]
C. L. Paris (1989): *The Use of Explicit User Models in a Generation System for Tailoring Answers to the User's Level of Expertise.* In A. Kobsa and W. Wahlster (eds.): *User Models in Dialog Systems,* pp. 200-232. Springer, Berlin, Heidelberg.

[Raskutti & Zukerman 91]
B. Raskutti and I. Zukerman (1991): *Generation and Selection of Likely Interpretations During Plan Recognition in Task-Oriented Consultation Systems.* User Modeling and User-Adapted Interaction, 1:323-353.

[Rich 79a]
E. Rich (1979a): *Building and Exploiting User Model.* PhD thesis, Department of Computer Science, Carnegie-Mellon University, Pittsburgh, PA.

[Rich 79b]
E. Rich (1979b): *User Modeling via Stereotypes.* Cognitive Science, 3:329-354.

[Rich 89]
E. Rich (1989): *Stereotypes and User Modeling.* In A. Kobsa and W. Wahlster (eds.): *User Models in Dialog Systems,* pp. 35-51. Springer, Berlin, Heidelberg.

[Shifroni & Shanon 92]
    E. Shifroni and B. Shanon (1992): *Interactive User Modeling: An Integrative Explicit-Implicit Approach*. User Modeling and User-Adapted Interaction 2:287-330.

[Sutcliffe & Old 87]
    G. Sutcliffe and A. C. Old (1987): *Do Users Know They Have User Models? Some Experiences in the Practice of User Modelling*. In H.-J. Bullinger and B. Shakel (eds.): Human-Computer Interaction: INTERACT'87, pp. 35-41. North-Holland, Amsterdam.

[van Arragon 91]
    P. van Arragon (1991): *Modeling Default Reasoning Using Defaults*. User Modeling and User-Adapted Interaction, 1:259-288.

[Wu 91]
    D. Wu (1991): *Active Acquisition of User Models: Implications for Decision-Theoretic Dialog Planning and Plan Recognition*. User Modeling and User-Adapted Interaction, 1:149-172.

Pragmatic User Modelling for Adaptive Interfaces

Judy Kay

University of Sydney
Sidney, Australia

ABSTRACT

This paper describes the way that user models can support adaptivity of several classes of interfaces. To highlight the similarities and differences between the different classes, the same user model is used to illustrate each. The classes of systems have been defined so that they cover much of the current work in systems whose adaptivity is driven by a user model. These are: advisors, consultants, and help systems; systems that use filtering to help the users find what they need and want; systems that tailor the output they produce to the particular needs of the individual; systems that tailor the interaction and modality so that it better matches the user's preferences, goals, task, needs, and knowledge; and finally, the intelligent teaching systems that aim to teach, as any good teacher does, matching the teaching content, style, and method to the domain and the individual student.

Viewing these classes of systems as defining the types of high level goals of adaptive systems, the paper describes the more primitive functional roles a user model can play in an adaptive system and the degree of importance each role has in the various classes of adaptive systems. Next, we examine the tasks involved in the user modelling process itself. And finally, we discuss a range of issues that will become of increasing importance as user-model driven adaptation moves from the research laboratories into practical use.

1   INTRODUCTION

The principal motivation for adaptive interfaces is that users differ. This applies to the individual across a range of different tasks, as his goals, needs, and knowledge change. It also applies to a whole community of users as they may differ along these same dimensions. This paper is concerned with interfaces where different users may be treated differently and the same user may be treated differently in different contexts and at different times.

The goals of adaptivity are to improve the efficiency and effectiveness of the interaction. As has been observed elsewhere [Malinowski et al. 92], this means that adaptive systems aim to make complex systems more usable, present the user with what he wants to see, as well as speed up and simplify interactions. This paper focuses on the way that a user model can support such adaptivity.

The paper is structured in terms of three layers we can identify in building such systems. Figure 1 shows the relation of these to the user model itself. The lowest layer consists of the tasks needed to construct and maintain a user model. The upper levels all rely on the user model. The common roles for the user model define the elementary sets of functions that are combined in creating adaptive systems. The paper starts at the top layer since this provides motivation for the whole process.

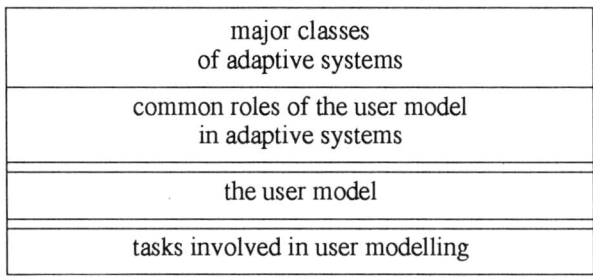

Figure 1: Levels of tasks for adaptivity based on user models

2 GOALS OF MAJOR CLASSES OF ADAPTIVE SYSTEMS

Every program embodies some model of the likely user population and the programmer makes many design decisions based on this. However, such a model is rarely specified and it is not kept as a distinct entity within the system.

In this paper, the term 'user model' means a collection of information that constitutes a model of the user. This information is explicit and it is a separate entity (rather than interspersed throughout the whole system). This follows the definitions of [Norman 83] and [Wahlster & Kobsa 86]. It is emphasized that this model, like all models, attempts to represent only some aspects of the user, namely those that are relevant to the domain at hand. A 'consumer' of the user model is a program that adapts its interaction.

To make the discussion concrete, this section introduces an example. This is based on current work in which several systems are being developed around models for over a thousand users over a three-year period [Thomas et al. 91]. The domain is a powerful mouse and window based text editor, **sam** [Pike 87]. The user models are maintained using the **um** toolkit [Kay 90, Kay (forthcoming)]. Figure 2 shows an hypothetical user's model derived from those actually constructed in these research projects.[1]

For the present, we will ignore the actual representation used for this information and the basis for drawing the conclusions shown for the particular user. Instead, we will discuss the information kept in the parts of the user model shown in Figure 2. Then we will introduce the uses that can be made of such modelling information by consumers created by various research communities concerned with adaptive interfaces.

Detailed knowledge of various aspects of the editor
1.1 believes that killing the window is a good way to quit
1.2 knows how to quit safely and sometimes does
1.3 has been told twice about the benefits of the safe quit method
1.4 probably does not know how to make multiple windows on a file
1.5 has been told once how to make multiple windows on a file

Some general attributes of the user
2.1 writes C programs
2.2 dislikes using a mouse
2.3 seems to only want to know the minimum about **sam**
2.4 claims to be a sophisticated user of the text editor **vi**
2.5 fast typist
2.6 prefers terse explanations and descriptions

User's current goal
3.1 currently typing a set of additions to a large program
3.2 currently adding code to a function (exprn) in the file parse.c

---

Figure 2: Example of parts of a user model

The first block of statements is taken from some of the 'components' that represent the user's detailed knowledge of the editor. So, for example, the statement 1.1 represents an incorrect belief that the user appears to have. (It is incorrect because the proper method of quitting is safer than the method she believes to be appropriate.) Statements 1.2 and 1.3 also relate to the user's knowledge about quitting. A quite different aspect of the user's knowledge is represented in the fourth and fifth statements.

The second block of statements about the user reflects her attributes and preferences. These can be quite specific to **sam** (like 2.3) or more general (2.5, 2.6).

Finally, statement 3.1 represents the user's current short term goal in this session. Statement 3.2 is an even shorter term goal within this context.

---

[1] In fact, the current model represents all the forms of conclusion shown except 2.2, 3.1, and 3.2. The former happens not to have been needed in the applications to date. Hence it has not been determined. The latter are short term goals and the current **um** structure is not used for these. Instead, they are normally handled by the particular consumer.

In the actual models we build, there can be many components organized into several 'partial models', each of these having collections of closely related components. The parts shown in Figure 2 are drawn from several of the partial models for this user so that the discussion can focus on the small parts of the model that are useful for illustrating the classes of systems described in the remainder of this section.

Each of the following subsections has a similar format. It starts with a characterization of the class and the role a user model can play in terms of the example in Figure 2. Then there is a general discussion of the broader range of systems in that class, including examples of systems that have user models to support that class of system.

Advisory, Consultant, and Help Systems

To see the way that an advisory system might use the information in Figure 2, consider the following situation. The user had invoked the editor twice on the same file so that she could see the global declarations in the file while she edited the relevant function. (She did not realize she could have created a second window on the same file from one invocation - this is consistent with 1.4 in the model for the user.) She makes the intended changes then confuses the two editor windows and kills the one from which the changes were made without first writing out that file. Then she realizes her error.

If there were an advisory program she could invoke at this point, it could use the data in Figure 2 in several ways. Firstly, it would be helpful for interpreting the user's query. Then it could help the user retrieve the lost file (because the editor saves such files in a standard place). Then it could advise the user about avoiding this problem in future. This involves using the safe quit command because it would have reported unwritten file buffers. The advisor could also explain the benefits of having two windows on the one file (because it would avoid the problem). All the knowledge in the first part of the model would be helpful in interpreting the problem and the query as well as generating the advice.

The advisor could use 2.1 to make the advice more relevant, by casting it in terms relevant to a C programmer. (In fact, one of the most convenient uses for multiple windows is just that of seeing both global declarations and code further down the file.) The information in 2.3 and 2.4 enables the advisor to explain aspects of **sam** in terms of both similarities to and differences from **vi** and 2.3 suggests that the system may need to motivate the user to see the merits of learning new aspects of **sam**. In addition, 2.6 indicates that the text presented to the user should match her preference for terse prose.

The user's short terms goals (3.1, 3.2) could help the advisor identify the problem. They also make it possible to cast the advice in terms of the user's current task.

This example describes a very sophisticated advisor. There are many possible levels of *advisory, consultative,* and *help systems* which can usefully provide various parts of this. However, the example was constructed to illustrate the various roles the user model can play for such systems. To really help a user, a system can benefit from knowledge about:

- what the user knows,
- what task she intended to do,
- what goals she intended this task to serve,
- how that relates to the best way for this user to achieve those goals, and
- how to communicate information to the user, taking account of such aspects as the user's motivations and goals, the gap between what she knows and would benefit from knowing, and the appropriate trade-off in complexity against conciseness.

There are many systems that have tackled the challenging, but potentially rewarding goal of creating helpful advisory systems. Of those that have employed user models, an exemplar is the Unix Consultant [Wilensky et al. 88, Chin 89, Quilici 89]. This gives users advice about the UNIX™ operating system. It supports short term modelling of the user's current goals as well as longer term aspects like her detailed knowledge and level of expertise. It accepts English requests, determines what the user really wants to know, and gives advice in a form that is appropriate to that user's knowledge and level of expertise. A similar set of goals were behind EUROHELP [Breuker 90] which represents an ambitious series of projects providing help for users aided by a user model. This research project developed help for a UNIX™ operating system and tools like the mail system.

Although there has been much research into advisors for computer systems, many other classes of advisors have been studied, especially in the creation of natural language based systems which model user's goals. For example, Carberry's system advises students about course enrolments, modelling their overall plans and intent to give advice that serves these in addition to the direct English requests made by the user [Carberry et al. 92].

Filtering Systems

Using the model of Figure 2 to characterize the way that a filtering system might exploit a user model, suppose we had a large on-line manual with information on all the facilities of **sam**. The user who is modelled in Figure 2 would, most likely, find this daunting to read and would have trouble finding parts that were relevant. Moreover, (noting that they are not committed to learning more than necessary about **sam**) they would not be keen to browse opportunistically.

So, a quite simple filtering system could accept requests for information about parts of **sam**. Suppose that the user simply issued a request for "something useful to know about **sam**." The filter system would then have the task of taking each aspect in its database of information about **sam** and assessing its utility to this user. Much of the information in the second part of the user model (2.1-4) would aid the system in this. In addition, information of the character of that shown in the first part of Figure 2 would help the system assess which aspects the user appeared to know about and which not. Finally, the user's goals (3.1 and 3.2) could serve to select aspects that are of value to the user right now.

In general, the role of a filter is take large amounts of information and help the user find relevant parts. Filtering is an important concern in intelligent information retrieval and database search systems, as well as filtering of on-line mail, news, and other network services. The essential elements are that:

- there is a large static database of information,
- only small parts are of interest to each user, and
- the user's preferences, interests, and knowledge (and, to a lesser degree, her current goals) define the parts of the database that should be allowed through the filter.

Filtering is an extremely promising area for development of pragmatic systems that can adapt to the individual user's needs and preferences. Some of the earliest research applying user models was Rich's GRUNDY [Rich 83]. This developed a user model to recommend books that the user would likely enjoy. As such, it acted as a filter on the full set of books. There has been a wide variety of other work including, for example, the filtering of on-line news [Bender et al. 91, Jennings et al. 91]. Also, there has been considerable activity in filtering in association with hypertext systems, as an example, the work of [Boy 91] which helps users retrieve documents relevant to them from a very large set of documentation. In the area of user modelling to aid in using a database is work like [Brajnik et al. 90a].

Tailoring Output

To illustrate the way a tailoring system can take advantage of information from Figure 2, suppose that user has specified that she wants to know about quitting the text editor. A tailoring system will aim to present the information in a form suited to the user's level of knowledge and her interests and goals. The user model indicates that this user is not motivated to learn more than necessary (2.3), she knows how to quit safely (1.2) and has been told about the benefits of this method (1.3) and yet holds a misconception about it (1.1). The tailor may need to help the user appreciate the misconception as such.

Tailored examples in terms of the current task (3.1, 3.2), the user's normal activity (2.1), and related knowledge (1.2 and 2.4) may enable her to learn where a standard form of documentation may not help.

Tailoring systems tackle the problem of production of information. So, for example, the text presented can include definitions of terms the user does not know, presented at a level suited to her understanding. It can order and organize the presentation to match the user's knowledge and needs. For example, a sophisticated user of **sam** can be presented with a terse, dense, and abstract presentation of the details she is likely to forget and needs to look up. By contrast, a novice making the same inquiry can be given a simple presentation of introductory concepts with examples rather than abstract descriptions.

A tailoring system may be viewed as a very specialized form of filtering system. Whereas the filter selects parts of a larger body of information, a tailor will be choosing between alternatives, all serving the same purpose but with each suiting only some of the users.

There is a wide range of tailoring systems supported by user modelling. For example, there is an active research area in the generation of natural language that is tailored to the individual. This includes such work as TAILOR [Paris 88, Paris 89] which can describe complex devices at a level appropriate to the user's level of expertise and the SERUM [Haimowitz 90] system which generates empathetic dialogue in a medical context. In tailored hypertext systems is the work of Encarnacion and Boyle which provides a pragmatic system for UNIX™ documentation individualized to the user's level of expertise [Encarnacion & Boyle 90].

Tailoring Interaction and Modality

Let us see how this might operate for the user of Figure 2 in the context of various ways to move around in a text. The **sam** editor is fairly modeless and was designed to make heavy use of the mouse: small movements in the text are effected by moving the cursor with the mouse; and clicking on the scroll bars achieves large movements in the text. Now, the user of Figure 2 dislikes using a mouse (2.2) and can type quickly (2.5). She also claims to use **vi** (2.4) which is highly moded. The user is likely to prefer a moded system or special keys to move around the file.

So, we might add such facilities for this user. Note, however, that we would retain the current, more intuitive interface for novices who might be confused if they were to accidentally change modes.

Systems that tailor the interaction and modality can alter the way that the user is required to interact with a program. This might permit interaction including such varied possibilities as natural language text or speech, various menus, special keys, and the use of eye-movement. One such application is the work of [Benyon 93].

A sophisticated system that tailors interaction is CHECS, a **C**hemical **E**ngineering **C**AD **S**ystem [Goodman & Litman 92], which supports a helpful interface in several ways. It can identify which actions within the interface are legal. It then ensures that only these actions are available and it alters the menus so that inappropriate actions are made dim. This is similar to the way menus operate on systems like the Apple Macintosh. The difference is that CHECS does not hard code this into the system; rather, it calculates the appropriate menus at runtime in terms of the user's current goal. CHECS also aids in task completion based on recognizing a user's goals. It supports users in doing designs and as a user creates his partial design, it can show the user designs in the system's library that have matching underlying plans. CHECS' model of the user's plan also supports its error handling.

Intelligent Teaching System - ITS

To see how the user model of Figure 2 could be used in an ITS, consider a system that aims to teach the user about several aspects of **sam**, including the use of multiple windows and to quit safely, both areas where this user has problems. First, the ITS needs to select which aspect to teach first, taking into account that the user has already been told about both (1.3 and 1.5). Since the user is unwilling to learn about **sam** (2.3) and she knows **vi** (2.4), the ITS might decide to teach the multiple windows concept first because this is a considerable strength of **sam**, compared to **vi** (for C programmers - 2.1). In addition, the user's current goals (3.1 and 3.2) make multiple windows likely to be useful now.

Having selected a teaching goal, the ITS may formulate its presentation of information to the user. As in the case of the advisor, there are issues of motivation and the user's level of knowledge which can support this stage.

The user model in an ITS is generally called a *student* or *learner* model. It can help define the intended learning goals and sequence. It can also tailor its presentation of information. The critical distinction between this system and the advisor is that the ITS sets the agenda and selects the teaching goals. From that point on, there is strong similarity with the advisor.

The ITS *actively* supports users in learning. (Clearly, an advisory system can also support learning, but it does so at the behest of the user.) Such systems might operate by selecting a series of goals for the user (student) to learn. Alternately, they might offer the user the option of selecting the aspects he would like to learn about. They may even provide a game that takes the user through a sequence of entertaining activities that require him to learn about **sam**. As in the example above, it could watch his use of **sam** and, like a sports coach, offer advice and direction on how to improve **sam** skills.

Much of the work in ITS relies on a user model of some sort. So, for example, a survey book like Wenger describes many ways that a user model supports the actions of an ITS [Wenger 87]. For most of these systems, the user model is *not* the focus of the research. By contrast, some recent systems have concentrated on developing the role of the user model. For example, Huang, McCalla, Greer, and Neufeld developed a sophisticated user model to support a programming tutor [Huang et al. 91], Nwana's system for teaching fractions [Nwana 91] developed an elegant approach for representing what the user knows and decides what to teach, while London's IMAGE system [London 92] can employ various teaching methods based on the user model.

3   COMMON ROLES OF THE USER MODEL IN ADAPTIVE SYSTEMS

This section identifies four functions that a user model is required to serve. They are in two pairs. The first is supporting the interpretation of user input. The second is the symmetric role of driving the adaptivity of the system's own actions.

The other two functions also form a symmetric pair. The first is the task of enabling the system to operate as a cooperative agent. The other concerns the system's goal of altering the user being modelled.

Whereas Section 2 described the high order goals of the system, this section describes the tasks that systems need to do to achieve them. Much current research work is at the stage of building prototypes to support research into these tasks that support the high order goals. Accordingly, the tasks in this section are often the focus level of research projects and their reports in the literature.

Interpret User Actions during Interactions

There are two levels of user actions that may be subject to analysis supported by the user model. First, there are the direct user inputs to the consumer system as, for example, when the user makes a request of a **sam** advisor. The primary benefit of a user model in this case is in helping the advisor make sense of the user's actual query. In addition, it helps the system give genuinely helpful responses because it can go beyond a direct answer to the specific question asked and provide information that the user really needs or wants.

The second level of user actions is the *dialogue history* in using **sam** itself. The user model can help the system interpret this and determine what the user is actually trying to do at various times.

The importance of interpreting user actions varies across the classes of systems described in the last section. For example, in advisory, consultant, and help systems like the Unix Consultant [Wilensky et al. 88] and EUROHELP [Breuker 90] this is a critical aspect.

By contrast, there is a far smaller role in filtering systems such as those mentioned in Section 2. Similarly, research in systems that tailor output focus on that part of the problem and have little need to interpret the user's actions.

As we saw in the description of CHECS [Goodman & Litman 92], interpretation of the user's actions can play an important role in systems aiming to tailor interaction and modality.

The importance of this aspect for Intelligent Teaching System ranges considerably. It can be central as, for example, in the systems of [Huang et al. 91], [Nwana 91], and [London 92] of Section 2. This is not the case in other systems where the ITS sets the context with a series of tasks and the user needs only to make one of a limited set of responses.

Generate System Actions

This aspect is common to all the classes of systems. In a simple form, most software provides adaptivity at this level and in systems where there is a user model to support the adaptation, this appears to be a common function.

[Malinowski et al. 92] distinguish between the deeper *logical* level that defines *what* the system will present to the user and the surface, *physical* level which defines *how* the system will present it. Most of the systems described in Section 2 represent a research emphasis on the logical level. This reflects the utility of the user model, particularly for logical level adaptation of the system's actions.

Attempt to Cooperate with the User

This aspect is common to all the systems but the emphasis varies across the classes of systems. In general, an important role for the user model is to enable the system to operate more cooperatively because it is better able to determine how to do this.

In the advisory systems, cooperativeness is an essential element. This places quite substantial demands on the user model which must have sophistication in the representation of the user's current goals as well as longer term attributes and knowledge. Systems that tailor the interaction also have a primary goal of cooperativeness.

By contrast, in many ITSs this is not important. In these, there is a tendency for the system to assume that the user will cooperate with the system's goals and directions.

The other classes lie somewhere inbetween. In systems that filter output, cooperation plays a role in formulating the goals of the tailoring and filtering. This is an important part of systems like those of [Bender et al. 91] and [Jennings et al. 91] from Section 2. Similarly, the output-tailors aim to be cooperative.

Attempt to Alter the User

This aspect represents the opposite intent from cooperation. A highly cooperative system alters itself to meet the user's needs and preferences. By contrast, a system that attempts to alter the user will adapt, but only in order to achieve its larger goal of altering the user.

In this aspect, we see a continuum across the classes of systems of Section 2. At one extreme is the ITS. The driving force behind most ITSs is a set of internal goals that the user is supposed to achieve. Since the user model represents the current state of the user, it plays a critical role in the system's definition of how to help the user learn more and in monitoring this.

To a lesser degree, any system that aims to help the user learn must formulate internal goals intended to achieve this. As we saw in Section 2, the advisory systems may need to alter the users' goals and develop their knowledge and understanding. To a lesser degree, this also applies to the output tailoring and filtering systems.

At the other extreme, the systems that tailor their interaction or modality are driven primarily by the users' goals and aim to match their preferences.

4 TASKS INVOLVED IN USER MODELLING

This section moves from the goals and functions of adaptive systems to the methods underlying the user modelling. Since this is closer to the detailed techniques, it describes another dimension along which one finds research about user model based adaptation.

Acquisition of the User Model

This can be viewed as a specialized problem in knowledge acquisition for knowledge based systems. In teaching systems, the task of constructing a model of a learner's knowledge is frequently described as *diagnosis*. In general, the acquisition of modelling information is a difficult and important task.

Depending upon the particular application, tools for acquiring the model may be extremely important or not. For example, in a natural language system, the dialog itself is the logical source of modelling information. On the other hand, an ITS will typically benefit from powerful diagnosis tools that help construct the user model.

Information about the user is available from many sources. The external sources used to create the model of Figure 2 include:

- information *given*, be it by the user, some other person, or some records (for example, 2.4 was given by the user);

- *observations* which include the dialogue history and monitoring the user's actions on the system (1.2, 1.4, and 2.5 were derived this way);

- *told-about*, which describes information that has been communicated to the user and which they therefore may know about (1.3, 1.5);

In addition, the model can be constructed on the basis of *inferences* as discussed in the next sections.

Representation of the User Model

Many user models are simple collections of unstructured scalars (also called a *scalar* or *parametric*). This may simply be a collection of flags. Each flag indicates whether the user should be treated as though they have the attribute represented by the flag. Where there is a weight on the flag, it indicates the degree to which the flag applies to the user. For example, we could view 2.2 in Figure 2 as a flag representing the user's liking to use the mouse (and for the user in Figure 2, this is false).

A *hierarchical* representation allows some aspects of the user model to be regarded as higher level and more general than others. Hierarchy may allow inferences based on inheritance of properties within the hierarchy. A common hierarchical form is the *tree*. Other hierarchical forms include directed acyclic graphs [Rich 83]. Even more general graphs are supported by some systems [Kobsa 90a].

Once a user model has been constructed, it is possible that knowledge of the domain can permit extensions to the user model. This *knowledge based* reasoning is provided in some form by all user modelling systems. Moreover, there are a few classes of such reasoning that are common to many user modelling systems. These are discussed below.

Stereotypes are a natural way to generate initial or default values in a model. They permit the construction and extension of a rich user model on the basis of scant information about the user. So, for example, 2.4 could be used to conclude the user knows a range concepts commonly understood by **vi** users.

Another particularly useful form of knowledge based inference is that based on *preconditions* or *prerequisite* knowledge. This structure within the knowledge of a domain makes it possible to deduce more about what a user knows. So, in our example of Figure 2, the user's knowledge of the proper quit mechanism means that they also know how to select the command window (as that is necessary to use the quit command).

A critical aspect of the representation used is that it must be able to deal with noisy data about the user and the fact that the user is changing (as, for example, when she learns or forgets something). There is often considerable noise in the data available and many of the aspects we might like to model are difficult to assess from the type of data that is available to the system. For example, in Figure 2, several aspects in the second block of attributes are difficult to assess. Even the simpler aspects in the first block are uncertain if the dialogue with **sam** was the basis for this information and if there is a chance that the user has allowed other people to use her account.

Considerable user modelling work is devoted to developing approaches to model non-monotonically with noisy data about changing users. For example UMT [Brajnik et al. 90a, Brajnik & Tasso 92] uses a truth maintenance system and BGP-MS (Belief, Goal, and Plan Maintenance System) [Kobsa 90b, Kobsa 92] supports a partitioned reasoning system. By contrast **um** [Kay 90, Kay (forthcoming)] supports several approaches including a simple partial ordering based on the reliability of various types of information and the reliability of various forms of reasoning within the system. Some of the knowledge representation techniques include first order predicate calculus, modal logics, and possible worlds. Wahlster and Kobsa provide a careful analysis of each of these, including the inherent limitations of each for user modelling [Wahlster & Kobsa 86]. They conclude that there is no single approach that can fulfil all the requirements of user modelling.

5 ISSUES FOR PRAGMATIC USES

This section develops some of the issues that are relevant for the move from research prototypes to practical systems.

Firstly, there is the pragmatic need for tools that do the tasks involved in building and maintaining the user model. Reuse of these across several consumer systems reduces the cost of the modelling process for each. There has been a recent growth of interest in this area with work on strategies for implicit reasoning like Kass's [Kass 91] and the user modelling shells of [Kobsa 90b], [Kobsa 92], [Brajnik et al. 90b], and [Kay 90].

In addition to developing such tools for use in different systems, user models need to be reused. The motivation for this is straightforward. Modelling users is a costly business. If user modelling is to be practical, we have to amortise the costs over many systems. A user model will have various consumers rather like the series of examples introduced in section 2, all based on the same modelling information of Figure 2.

Then we need to address the issue of *granularity*, the detail of the level of modelling required. This has been a concern for ITS, for example, in the work of Greer and McCalla [Greer & McCalla 89]. Many existing research projects have been rather heavyweight and computationally expensive. This has been quite reasonable for the research prototypes that have developed theory and techniques.

However, for near-term pragmatic modelling, we probably need to develop light-weight models and modelling tools. This is especially so where the cost of building the consumer that takes account of even a few factors can be considerable. It seems likely that many useful consumers can achieve helpful levels of adaptability with quite small amounts of user modelling information. For example, [Neal 89] studied simple classifications of user knowledge, experience, learning style, and risk aversion. These improved the usability of an interface. If the model needed is modest, as in the case of Neal's system, its cost must be too.

An interface that is adaptive is also closely related to the more general work on *customization* of interfaces in operating systems and other software. Typically, it is not easy for an unsophisticated user to benefit from this flexibility: it requires the user to have considerable knowledge of the system and the particular means of customization. For example, a text editor could provide the level of customization that enables a user to either use a mouse or not, as he wishes. For the many users who lack the time, will, and knowledge needed to effect such a change, automatic adaptivity is the only practical option.

If the user model can provide information about the user's preferences, it may be feasible to provide tools which map this to the customization requirements of particular software. The essential distinction between a user model and customization primitives is that the user model holds information about the user and the latter information is program parameters and commands. The user model offers considerable portability benefits as it is tied to the user whereas the customization information is generally quite tightly linked to the particular software that can use it.

In the future, when we have pragmatic applications of user models for adaptation, we will have dealt with technical issues. Hence, we will have representations for user models that are flexible, giving low cost modelling for simpler modelling demands and yet with sufficient power for more sophisticated tasks. There will be agreed meanings for the information they hold so that different systems can use it. Then we will need to address issues related to the management of the user model. This includes the user's role in its creation and maintenance, the protection it provides for the user's privacy, and the access that the user is given to the system.

If a user model keeps information about an individual, one needs to consider her rights of *access* to it and the *privacy* of the information. If user models are to be of practical use, these issues are important and they have been raised elsewhere including, for example [Kobsa 90a].

There is considerable evidence that at least some users are keen to see their user model. For example, Zissos and Witten developed a system that used observation of the user to construct a user model [Zissos & Witten 85]. This enabled an advisor to give what should have been helpful and interesting pieces of information about EMACS. They reported that users wanted to know why the system selected particular advice. In much the same way, students using WEST [Burton & Brown 79] were reported to have played the game in ways that enabled them to explore the underlying mechanism controlling coaching advice.

These observations have important implications. From a technical point of view, we should note there are problems where a user tries odd behavior to see how it affects the system behavior. This is because the user's curiosity corrupts the user model if the odd behavior contributes to the system's model of the user.

Beyond this technical problem is the right of the user to know what his user model contains. More than this, the user should be able to really understand it. One solution to this is the approach taken in **um** [Kay 90, Cook & Kay 93]: a viewer is supplied with the user model. This provides an intuitive graphical interface that displays the structure and contents of the user model. In addition, it can justify the conclusions it makes about the user. These justifications are in terms of the sources of the data and how the data collection tools work. It also has a facility for tailored explanations of the meaning of components of the user model. In addition, the actual user model is stored in a form that the user can read directly and makes some sense. The motivation for this rather elaborate support for accessibility was the conviction that the users will only try to access their user model if they really can understand it without needing to learn technical details to get this understanding.

Such user access improves the accountability of the programmer. In our experience with the viewable models of **sam** [Cook & Kay 93], there were many times when we had to reconsider initial ideas because they would be hard to define to the user or they may have been unpalatable. This meant that we refined the user model and its construction until it was presentable.

A final benefit of user access to the user model is that the user can play an active role in constructing and verifying it. Since the user is the one affected by changes to their user model it is reasonable that he be allowed to alter it if he wishes. In the same way that we argued the need for easy access to the user model, so too should the user be supported in editing his model. This means providing an interface that makes the editing easy and provides recovery from accidental changes. This has the effect of shifting more of the responsibility for the correctness of the model onto the user, rather than the system (in fact, its programmers).

The discussion of user access to their model brings us to a critical observation about user model based adaptive systems: the fact that they do codify information about the user makes them fundamentally different from the humans that they are often built to emulate. For example, an advisory program may be intended to give advice about UNIX™ in the way that a good human advisor could. Now, the human advisor undoubtedly makes use of many assumptions about the user's knowledge and preferred style of interaction. However, this is not available for examination. By contrast, the user model in a program does exist in a well defined form and it is possible to make it accessible.

This difference offers considerable promise for adaptive systems to provide new forms of support for users. A user may never learn why he cannot understand some human advisors. However, a computer system should not be as opaque. Its basis for action is completely knowable by the user. It is possible to examine the underlying basis for the adaptation he is offered by a program. The user can alter it. As a side-benefit, he can even introspect on the basis of the model the system presents him! This aspect seems to open a new means of improving teaching systems [Crawford & Kay 92]. We have yet to explore the special potential of adaptive interfaces that is offered by such possibilities of changing our view of the operation of adaptive systems.

6   CONCLUSIONS

Current research work on user modelling for adaptive systems has a very diffuse literature. This is because it is spread across the various layers of goals and tasks that are needed to achieve adaptivity based on a user model:

- the top level of goals that the adaptive systems aim to achieve: advisory, filtering, tailoring of the output and the interaction, as well as ITS;

- the level of more elementary functions or tasks the user model supports in achieving the higher level goals: interpreting the user's actions, generating system actions, and attempting to cooperate with or to alter the user;

- the structure of the user modelling system in terms of its own subtasks: acquisition of modelling information, representation and dealing with conflict, as well as the interface between the user model and the consumer system.

In addition, there is a separate set of issues concerned with the construction of consumer systems so that they can exploit the user models.

If we are to move to pragmatic applications of user models, we need to establish approaches and tools for creating, maintaining, and exploiting user models. Also important are the issues of reusability, user control of adaptivity and the user model, accountability for system behavior, and the related issue of codification of assumptions about user.

User models represent a separation of this essential element of an adaptive system. They can be available for inspection. This opens the way to a new way of viewing interaction and responsibility.

REFERENCES

[Bender et al. 91]
>   Bender, W, H Lie, J Orwant, L Teodosio and N Abramson. *Newspace: Mass Media and Personal Computing.* USENIX Conference Proceedings, June 1991, pp 329-348.

[Benyon 93]
>   Benyon, D. *Accommodating Individual Differences through an Adaptive User Interface.* In: this book.

[Boy 91]
>   Boy, G. *On-line user model acquisition in hypertext documentation.* in Proc. IJCAI Workshop Agent Modelling for Intelligent Interaction, ed. J Kay and A Quilici. Sidney, Australia, 1991. pp34-42.

[Brajnik et al. 90a]
>   Brajnik, G, G Guida, and C Tasso. *User modeling in expert man-machine interfaces: a case study in intelligent information retrieval.* IEEE Trans on Systems, Man and Cybernetics, 20(1):166-185, 1990.

[Brajnik et al. 90b]
>   Brajnik, G C Tasso, and A Vaccher. *A shell for non-monotonic user modeling systems.* pp. 149-163 in Proc IJCAI Workshop W.4: Agent Modeling for Intelligent Interaction, ed. J Kay and A Quilici. IJCAI-91, Sydney, Australia, 1990.

[Brajnik & Tasso 92]
>   Brajnik, G and C Tasso. *A flexible tool for developing user modeling applications with nonmonotonic reasoning capabilities.* pp. 42-66 in Proc of UM92: Third International Workshop on User Modeling, ed. E Andre, R Cohen, W Graf, B Kass, C Paris and W Wahlster. Deutsches Forschungszentrum für Künstliche Intelligenz, 1992.

[Breuker 90]
>   Breuker, J. in *EUROHELP: developing intelligent help systems.* IOS, 1990.

[Burton & Brown 79]
>   Burton, R R and J S Brown. *An investigation of computer coaching for informal learning activities.* Intl J of Man-Machine Studies, 11:5-24, 1979.

[Carberry et al. 92]
>   Carberry, Sandra, Z Kazi, and L Lambert. *Modeling discourse, problem solving and domain goals incrementally in task-oriented dialogue.* pp. 192-204 in Proc of UM92: Third International Workshop on User Modeling, ed. E Andre, R Cohen, W Graf, B

Kass, C Paris and W Wahlster. Deutsches Forschungszentrum für Künstliche Intelligenz, 1992.

[Chin 89]
Chin, D. *KNOME: modeling what the user knows in UC.* pp. 74-107 in User models in dialog systems, ed. A Kobsa and W Wahlster. Springer-Verlag, Berlin, 1989.

[Cook & Kay 93]
Cook, R and K Kay. *Tools for viewing um user models.* SSRG Report 93/3/50.1, SSRG, Dept of Computer Science, University of Sydney, Australia, 1993.

[Crawford & Kay 92]
Crawford, K and J Kay. *Shaping learning approaches with intelligent learning systems.* Proc Intl Conf for Technology in Education. pp 1472-1476, France, 1992.

[Encarnacion & Boyle 90]
Encarnacion, A and C Boyle. *A user model based hypertext documentation system.* pp. 43-66 in Proc IJCAI Workshop W.4: Agent Modeling for Intelligent Interaction, ed. J Kay and A Quilici. IJCAI-91, Sydney, Australia, 1990.

[Goodman & Litman 92]
Goodman, B A and D J Litman. *On the interaction between plan recognition and intelligent interfaces.* User modeling and user-adapted interaction, 2(1- 2):83-116, 1992.

[Greer & McCalla 89]
Greer, J E and G I McCalla. *A computational framework for granularity and its application to educational diagnosis.* IJCAI, pp. 477-482, 1989.

[Haimowitz 90]
Haimowitz, I J. *Modeling all dialogue system participants to generate empathetic responses.* Second International Workshop on User Modelling, 1990.

[Huang et al. 91]
Huang, X, G I McCalla, J E Greer, and E Neufeld. *Revising deductive knowledge and stereotypical knowledge in a student model.* User Modeling and User-Adapted Interaction, 1(1):87-116, 1991.

[Jennings et al. 91]
Jennings, A, H Higuchi, and H Liu. *A personal news service using a user model neural network.* Proc IJCAI Workshop Agent Modelling for Intelligent Interaction, pp. 1-33, 1991.

[Kass 91]
Kass, R. *Building a user model implicitly from a cooperative advisory dialog.* User modeling and user-adapted interaction, 1(3):203- 258, 1991.

[Kay 90]
J. Kay (1990): *um: A Toolkit for User Modelling.* In Proc. of the Second International Workshop on User Modeling, pp. 1-11, Honolulu, HI.

[Kay (forthcoming)]
Kay, J. *Reusable, long term user models: issues and tools.* Intl J of user Modelling and User Adapted Interaction, to appear.

[Kobsa 90a]
Kobsa, A. *User modeling in dialog systems: potentials and hazards.* AI and Society, 4:214-231, Springer-Verlag, 1990.

[Kobsa 90b]
> Kobsa, A. *Modeling the user's conceptual knowledge in BGP-MS, a user modeling shell system.* Computational Intelligence, 6(4):193-208, 1990.

[Kobsa 92]
> Kobsa, A. *Towards inferences in BGP-MS: combining model logic and partition hierarchies for user modeling.* pp. 35-41 in Proc of UM92: Third International Workshop on User Modeling, ed. E Andre, R Cohen, W Graf, B Kass, C Paris, and W Wahlster. Deutsches Forschungszentrum für Künstliche Intelligenz, 1992.

[London 92]
> London, R V. *Student modeling to support multiple instructional approaches.* User modeling and user-adapted interaction, 2(1- 2):117-154, 1992.

[Malinowski et al. 92]
> Malinowski, U, T Kühme, H Dieterich, and M Schneider-Hufschmidt. *A Taxonomy of Adaptive User Interfaces.* pp. 391-414 in People and Computers VII, ed. A Monk, D Diaper, and M D Harrison. Cambridge University Press, 1992.

[Neal 89]
> Neal, L R. *The role of user models in systems design.* Technical Report-18-89, Center for research in computing technology, Harvard University, 1989.

[Norman 83]
> Norman, D A. *Some observations on mental models.* in Mental Models, ed D Gentner and A L Stevens. Lawrence Erlbaum.

[Nwana 91]
> Nwana, H S. *User modelling and user adapted interaction in an intelligent tutoring system.* User modeling and user-adapted interaction, 1(1): 1-33, 1991.

[Paris 88]
> Paris, C L. Tailoring *Object Descriptions to a User's Level of Expertise.* Computational Linguistics, 14(3):64-78, Assoc for Computational Linguistics, Sept, 1988.

[Paris 89]
> Paris, C L. *The user of explicit user models in a generation system for tailoring answers to the user's level of expertise.* pp. 200-232 in User models in dialog systems, ed. A Kobsa and W Wahlster. Springer-Verlag, Berlin, 1989.

[Pike 87]
> Pike, Rob. *The Text Editor sam.* Software Practice and Experience, 17:813-845, November 1987.

[Quilici 89]
> Quilici, A E. *Detecting and responding to plan-oriented misconceptions.* pp. 108 - 132 in User Models in Dialog Systems, ed. A Kobsa and W Wahlster. Springer-Verlag, 1989.

[Rich 83]
> Rich, E. *Users are individuals: individualizing user models.* Intl J of Man-Machine Studies, 18:199-214, 1983.

[Thomas et al. 91]
> Thomas, R, D Benyon, J Kay, and K Crawford. *Monitoring editor usage: the Basser data project.* Proc MNCC/IFIP Natl Conf on Information Technology, NCIT '91, pp.297-307, Penang, Malaysia, June 1991.

[Wahlster & Kobsa 86]
: Wahlster, W and A Kobsa. *Dialogue-based user models*. Proceedings of the IEEE, 74(7):948-960, July, 1986.

[Wenger 87]
: Wenger, E. *Artificial Intelligence and tutoring systems - computational and cognitive approaches to the communication of knowledge*. Morgan Kaufmann, Los Altos, 1987.

[Wilensky et al. 88]
: Wilensky, R, D N Chin, M Lurai, J Martin, J Mayfield, and D Wu. *The Berkeley UMX consultant project*. Computational Linguistics, 14(4):35-84, December, 1988.

[Zissos & Witten 85]
: Zissos, A and I Witten. *User modelling for a computer coach*. Intl J of Man Machine Studies, 23:729-750, 1985.

ZZ | **SINGLE Fr** | **S**

Customer:
Jim Demetriades

L TUE AM

Adaptive User Interfaces: Principles and Practice (Human Factors in Information Technology)

M. Schneider-Hufschmidt, T. K&uuml:hme. U. Malinowski

E2-S065-G6

UM-799-496

No CD
Used - Very Good
9780444815453

Picker Notes:
M _____ 2 _____
WT _____ 2 _____
CC _____

47580221

[Amazon] betterworldbooks_: 104-7838553-0490666

1 Item

1045137642

Friday Singles REG SHLV

Ship. Created: 9/29/2016 9:22:00 AM
Date Ordered: 9/29/2016 8:15:00 AM

Accommodating Individual Differences through an Adaptive User Interface

David Benyon

Open University
Milton Keynes, UK

ABSTRACT

Computer systems vary in their structure, functionality, purpose, size and the way in which they represent their internal workings. Humans differ in background, sex, education, personality, cognitive skills and preferences, motivation, goals and mood. There is a social context to HCI which involves organizational and political factors, the user support which is available and the pressures of a situation. The complexity of human-computer interaction must be dealt with. Computer systems are designed and built to be used. The question before us is to what extent can we improve the usability of systems.

One solution to problems of usability, which is unique to computer systems, is to supply the system with a suitable theory of interaction and how interaction can be improved. The computer can then adapt itself to the needs of individuals or groups of users. A theory of adaptivity should help us to decide when an adaptive system solution to usability problems is appropriate. This paper provides some suggestions as to how we should approach adaptive user interface development and some user characteristics which may prove to be useful.

1 INTRODUCTION

Human-Computer Interaction (HCI) is a complex activity. Computer systems vary in their structure, functionality, purpose, size and the way in which they represent their internal workings. Humans differ in background, sex, education, personality, cognitive skills and preferences. They also vary in motivation, goals and mood. There is a social context to HCI which involves organizational and political factors, the user support which is available and the pressures of a situation. When it comes to interpreting computer displays - even the use of command names or icons on the screen - users will infer different meanings depending on the connotations which they associate with the signs and behaviours of displayed objects. Users will attend to different aspects of the display in different ways.

On the one hand, attempting to tackle this complexity appears an impossible task but on the other hand it must be dealt with. Computer systems are designed and built to be used. The question before us is to what extent can we improve the usability of systems. How can we make them easier to learn, easier to use and more secure? How do we make the interaction more effective and more satisfying?

One way is to continue to improve the human-computer interaction design so that the average user is better able to understand and exploit the system. This approach assumes that there is a single design which will suit everyone. Another approach is to provide a variety of help and assistance for users so that they can obtain advice appropriate to their needs, when and where they need it. The problem with this approach is that the very complexity of the systems makes simple instruction inadequate. Many of the functions of a system are irrelevant for many of the users until some task arises in which they need to make use of it. By this time they may have forgotten the instruction. Unlike riding a bicycle, the skills of computer use are easily lost from memory.

There is another potential solution to problems of usability which is unique to computer systems. Computer systems can monitor the interaction at a level of detail unavailable to other artefacts. If the system is supplied with a suitable theory of interaction and how interaction can be improved, the computer is in a position to change its functioning, its structure or the representations provided at the interface to better match the preferences, needs and desires of the users. The computer can adapt itself to individuals or groups of users.

The mechanisms of adaptivity are not difficult. Alternative displays and functions can be programmed into the system and selected according to specific well-defined criteria. So, for example, if this user is a French-speaking person display messages in French. If this user is English use English language messages. The preferences of users can be elicited by a piece of the program which asks them to select a language from a list.

The mechanisms of adaptivity may be expensive, but they are programmable. It is the theory which needs attending to. The theory underlying the example above is that naturally French speaking people prefer French messages and English speakers prefer English. Of course this theory may be flawed and there are many situations in which it would make the system less usable. In particular a system which asked this question every time the system was started up would soon become annoying. The mechanisms of adaptivity must become more sophisticated to deal with this. They need to infer likely events. This may be based on their representations of users and applications and experience of previous interactions. For example, a system may have recorded that the person using this terminal is a natural French speaker, that the data in the system is in French or that the last fifty people to use this terminal were French so the probability is that the next one will be.

A theory of adaptivity should help us to decide when an adaptive system solution to usability problems is appropriate. There is little to be gained if expensive adaptivity mechanisms are used to achieve a minimal improvement in usability. There is no point in adapting to some user characteristic if that characteristic cannot be reliably and unobtrusively inferred from the interaction. This paper provides some suggestions as to how we should approach adaptive user interface development and some user characteristics which may prove to be useful.

2   INDIVIDUAL DIFFERENCES

It must be one of the few certain things in the world that people differ from one another. Two important questions arise from this observation. Firstly, how do people differ? We might agree that people differ in physical characteristics such as height, weight and girth, but beyond that we enter a potential minefield. People have different personalities, but what is personality? People have different cognitive skills and preferences, but what cognitive skills do people have and how do they vary? Secondly, for our pragmatic purposes of improving the usability of computer systems, we must ask what differences are useful, which ones are stable and which ones really have an impact on the interaction.

The study of individual differences is usually traced back to Galton, a half-cousin of Darwin, and Binet who published the first general intelligence scale in 1905 [Willerman 79]. Since then differential psychology, or the study of individual differences has gone through a number of phases. Some - such as the eugenics movement - now appear rather dubious. Attempting to selectively breed humans so that particular characteristics become dominant may be one way of improving usability, but one that would probably be deemed politically unacceptable.

Attempts to isolate characteristics have similarly foundered. Human activity is inevitably a social activity and so human characteristics interact with the social, environmental conditions in complex ways. Cronbach in [Cronbach 75] demonstrates this with a number of examples, highlighting the necessity of a science of aptitude-treatment *interactions*. We must consider both the characteristics of the individuals and the characteristics of the task and understand how these interact.

The lessons of the past suggest that individual differences are rather wayward, difficult to pin down and difficult to transfer from one situation to another. Yet the popularity of psychological tests, particularly for employment selection, suggests that many people do find such measures useful. The power offered by such methods is that a quick test of characteristics can lead to the avoidance of longer-term problems. It might take several months to discover that someone is not a good programmer unless something - tests, school grades, a performance at an interview - is used to assess the suitability of candidates before they start. The important point is to identify a stable and reliable correlation between the task and the tests.

Computer systems - along with may other artefacts - have to be used by a wide variety of people. A nomothetic approach to design excludes people who lie outside the norm. At a physical level, an increased awareness of this problem has led to better facilities for the physically less able; wider isles and ramps for wheel-chair users, larger handles for arthritics, speech input and output for the partially sighted. But computer systems have another dimension not shared by so many other artefacts. Using computer systems is to a large extent a cognitive activity. HCI is concerned with the acquisition, manipulation and expression of abstract symbols which signify something else. HCI involves information processing. Most other systems allow for some form of physical interaction which allows the user to look inside and see how it works. The user of such physical artefacts can employ a range of strategies which are unavailable to the computer user who must judge the system purely by its external displays. It is because of this that individual differences in cognitive abilities, preferences, methods and techniques become important in HCI.

2.1 Individual Differences in Cognition

Within what might loosely be labelled the Western tradition, attempts to isolate individual cognitive differences have been based around the production of various aptitude tests and other devices designed to isolate specific factors. Excellent reviews are provided in [Dillon & Schmeck 83], [Dillon 85] and [Sternberg 85].

Cognitive abilities, or cognitive skills seek to describe the methods by which humans process information. Cognitive abilities are relatively stable human characteristics which change very slowly over time (months or years) [Carroll 83]. Underlying the distinctions which are made is a general model of cognition which emphasizes how data from the world is perceived, or input to the brain (employing the individual's verbal abilities, reading abilities, visual abilities, etc.), how it is stored (in short-term memory, working memory or long-term memory), how it is processed (inductive and deductive reasoning, problem-solving abilities and strategies, the use of mental imagery) and how solutions and decisions are expressed (e.g. language ability). Many attempts have been made to collate a range of abilities into measures of 'general intelligence' and to produce an intelligence quotient (IQ). Other research focuses on specific domains of cognitive activity such as learning, mathematical reasoning or first or second language acquisition.

Although there is no single taxonomy of cognitive abilities, some broad differences have been repeatedly observed. Cooper and Mumaw's review of research on spatial ability [Cooper & Mumaw 85] concludes that 'the spatial aptitude literature is quite clear in showing that a broadly defined spatial factor exists independently of verbal and quantitative factors' (p.71). There is also good evidence for holistic and serialistic learning styles (e.g. [Pask 76, Entwhistle 78, Pask 80]), though an individual may be able utilize both (a versatile learner).

Cognitive abilities are measured or assessed by getting subjects to perform a cognitive task (i.e. one that involves information processing). Frequently these are 'paper and pencil' activities such as completing a sequence of numbers or abstract shapes, selecting synonyms for words or choosing which of several diagrams matches some criteria. On other occasions the cognitive task may be a 'real world' activity using some complex device.

Subjects are usually expected to try to complete the task to the best of their abilities and are assessed by how quickly or how accurately they perform the task.

One of the problems with studying cognitive abilities is that although differences may be observed and measured between individuals, it is difficult to judge exactly what the difference is. We cannot be sure precisely what caused the difference in performance. It may be that some subjects in an experiment did not understand the instructions sufficiently and this impaired their performance on the task. It may be that some subjects were less unfamiliar with the type of task, did not try as hard as other subjects or employed an inappropriate strategy for the particular task. Even if these problems can be controlled in an experiment, the interaction between cognitive factors presents further confounding factors. For example, do we see attention as a different function from perception or, as Neisser [Neisser 76] argues, as an integral part of perception? Johnson-Laird in [Johnson-Laird 85] has shown that deductive reasoning ability is more a function of the mental model of the task which the subject possesses, than it is an innate characteristic. If the experimenter gives the subject a problem situation with which he or she is familiar, the subject will demonstrate improved deductive reasoning powers than if presented with an unfamiliar problem. Our own work (see below) suggests that spatial ability and field dependence may be different aspects of the same cognitive aptitude.

Although the study of individual differences in cognitive abilities cannot present a rigorous theory, it should not be abandoned. A promising approach lies in identifying the components of complex tasks and the cognitive abilities which are required in order to perform them successfully. For example, the cognitive characteristic of spatial relations, one type of spatial ability, involves the mental rotation of objects to see which of a number of other objects it is a copy of. This can be decomposed into the components; encode the stimulus (create a mental representation), transform the representation, compare with other stimuli and respond. Each of these components may involve a particular cognitive skill on which individuals will differ. Understanding the components and the associated skills then becomes the focus of attention.

2.2 Individual Differences in Personality

An appeal to the notion of personality probably derives more from a general 'folk' psychology than from scientific rigour. We sum people up with statements such as 'she is rather introverted' or 'he is too temperamental'. As with cognitive characteristics, personality traits are difficult to pin down the more we examine them. The intuitive appeal of personality, however, and the reliance put on personality testing means that we should at least consider what role such differences between individuals have to play.

Personality would normally be considered to be a collection of enduring characteristics of people '...those individual, relatively enduring patterns of reacting and interacting with others and with the world...' ([Bee 81], p.295). Personality concerns characteristics which remain stable over time and across situations. We would assume that personality is changeable early in life, but that it settles down in adulthood. Unfortunately there is no simple measure of personality, nor general agreement on the traits which constitute personality. For example Cattell identifies sixteen personality traits [Cattell 71]. These are used as the basis of the most widely used personality test in the UK; the 16PF test. Eysenck in [Eysenick 67] on the other hand identifies three characteristics; psychoticism, extroversion-introversion and neuroticism, or emotionality. The discussion over personality traits continues unabated in Eysenck's *Journal of Personality and Individual Differences*.

The fact that cognition has been separated out from personality in this paper suggests that a view of personality which excludes cognitive characteristics is desirable. Thus personality would not include a measure of spatial or verbal ability. Personality is concerned with one's approach to the world in general and one's emotional and conative make-up. It is more to do with strategy than ability and, whilst it is controllable by most people to a large extent, it tends to dominate preferred approaches to specific tasks. Whilst there is no single definition of personality, the words employed by the 16PF scale give some idea as to its scope; sober v. enthusiastic, moralistic v. expedient, tough v. sensitive, zestful v. reflective, trusting v. suspecting, practical v. imaginative, self-assured v. apprehensive, conservative v. radical and so on.

2.3 Individual Differences and Human-Computer Interaction

The general theories of cognition and personality attempt to identify characteristics which are relatively stable across all domains. The concern of this paper is with human-computer interaction and an understanding of the application of these ideas to the demands of HCI.

Interacting with a computer is certainly in part a cognitive task and so we can expect individual differences in cognitive preferences and abilities to affect performance on computer tasks. Personality is assumed to affect all interactions and so it, too, should have an impact. Gerrit van der Veer's thesis ([Van der Veer 90]; see also [Van der Veer 89] and [Van der Veer et al. 85]) is one of the few attempts to consider what effects individual differences might have on HCI (Egan, in [Egan 88] gives a thorough review which is considered below). Van der Veer classifies some cognitive and personality factors along a 'resistance to change' dimension. He argues that personality factors (in which he includes intelligence, introversion-extroversion, fear of failure and (possibly) creativity) are most difficult for humans to change. When we provide a learning environment or design a human-computer interaction, we cannot expect the people to change. The environment must be flexible enough to cater for these personality differences. Cognitive styles and learning strategies (e.g. a preference for a holistic over a serialistic strategy) lie in the middle of the 'resistance to change' dimension. Humans may be able to alter their strategies, or develop their cognitive abilities given sufficient education, motivation and time. Personal knowledge, rules and skills are changeable by people (through education and practice).

His argument, then, and one which has been the motivation for much of our own work [Benyon et al. 87, Benyon et al. 87b, Benyon & Murray 88, Benyon & Murray 88] is that if people have characteristics which they can not easily change, or would prefer not to change, then the computer should change the way it appears or operates in order to better suit those user characteristics. It is worth putting effort in to changing aspects of systems where changing those aspects is likely to have the biggest effect.

Egan summarises the work on individual differences and human computer interaction [Egan 88]. He identifies three main areas where large differences have been observed; text editing, information retrieval and programming. Some of the experimental work shows up differences between individuals performing these tasks as high as 30:1! [Rosson 83]. That is to say, one individual takes thirty times as long to complete a computer-based task as another. For comparison he cites evidence from grocery checking where typical individual differences are less than 2:1 and illustrates the importance of the differences in computer tasks by pointing out that if grocery checking did demonstrate differences of 30:1, you could be waiting thirty times longer to get out of the supermarket than the person in the queue next to you!

He summarises the results from the literature by arguing that spatial ability is an important determinant of performance in evaluating detailed spatial patterns (e.g. in locating particular strings of characters) or other objects in a display and that reasoning ability underlies the development of appropriate searching and problem-solving strategies and in producing accurate symbolic expressions (e.g. formulating query statements or editing commands). Verbal ability did not seem to predict performance to any great degree. Nor was there much evidence that personality affected performance.

Egan is careful to point out that many of the studies which he cites involve relatively few subjects and there are also occluding factors such as different researchers presenting their results in different ways and in using different tests of cognitive and personality traits [Egan 88]. However, there is now a significant body of research which points to the importance of individual differences in HCI.

3 DEALING WITH INDIVIDUAL DIFFERENCES

The summary provided above indicates that, if possible, we should examine the extent of individual differences when designing computer systems and look at how they may be accommodated. In some cases, it is likely that redesigning the interface will be an effective method of dealing with differences. This was the approach adopted by [Vicente et al. 87] and [Vicente & Williges 88] who found that by introducing some additional commands, the poorer performance of those users with a low spatial ability could be overcome. In other cases, training and education and other 'meta-communication' can be used [Van der Veer 89, Van der Veer 90]. At other times, the differences may be small or insignificant and the system can be left alone. However, there are circumstances when these options will be inappropriate and when an adaptive solution will be the only viable answer. This was the focus of our research [Jennings et al. 91, Jennings & Benyon (in press)].

Database systems have exactly the characteristics through which to examine the importance of individual differences and HCI. In the first instance database systems are used by a wide variety of users, so we might expect a variety of cognitive and personality aptitudes to be demonstrated. Secondly the users have a variety of backgrounds in experience and of similar systems. Thirdly, we cannot expect people to be trained in using the system - *ad hoc* inquiries, by intermittent and discretionary users are exactly what databases are for. The interface to a database system has to support general goals (e.g. retrieve data) but it cannot be prescriptive about low level tasks. Flexibility is a key word in database use and users have to formulate specific queries. Help can be provided, but it is distracting from the main task and understanding the help may take much longer than expressing the problem. Discretionary users, such as departmental managers, senior clerks and the general public are precisely the users which we want to encourage to use the system.

In their work, Egan and Gomez suggest a three stage approach to dealing with individual differences [Egan & Gomez 85]. Firstly, it is necessary to 'assay', or assess the extent of the differences. This involves considering what to measure and how to measure it. Once differences have been observed, the essential differences have to be isolated from confounding factors. Thus there is a need to consider the features of the interaction, features of the users and the stability of the features. When the important features have been identified it is then necessary to accommodate these features.

Our experimental work with adaptive user interfaces embodies this philosophy. We want to assess, identify and isolate individual differences which have a significant impact on the human-computer interaction. Some of these differences can be accommodated through training, education and improvements to the interface. Others, however, will need to be accommodated through adaptive mechanisms built into the interface. It is those characteristics of users which are difficult for the users to change which will have the largest pay-off in respect of the usability of the computer system and it is those characteristics which we should concentrate on.

3.1 Assaying the Differences

In the first experiment (reported fully in [Jennings et al. 91]) we wanted to examine which characteristics - of both the user and the system - were important in determining performance on database retrieval. Five functionally similar interfaces to a database were designed and were each used by 24 subjects to perform comparable retrievals. Each subject was tested on five personality/cognitive variables; spatial ability, verbal ability, field dependence (the ability to distinguish an object from its environment), short term memory (STM) and a thinking/feeling personality test. Subjects were then assigned to a 'high' or 'low' group according to their score on the test. The time taken to complete the task was used as the measure of performance.

Significant differences ($p<0.05$) were observed between the high and low spatial ability and verbal ability groups on the menu interface, but the largest and most significant difference (p<0.01) was found between the performance of the high and low spatial ability groups on the command interface. Here the high spatial group achieved an average completion time for the 12 tasks of 278 seconds. The low group took 377 seconds. Thus the average task completion time for the low group was 35% greater than the high group. In comparison, there was only a difference of less than 1% between the two groups using the menu interface and 3% using the iconic (a pictorial) interface. No significant differences were found between the short-term memory groups and only small differences for the other groups and the other interfaces. However, a correlation was discovered between scores on the field dependence and spatial ability tests, with 18 out of the 24 subjects being in the same group for each. The probability of this occurring by chance is less than 0.05.

3.2 Isolating the Differences

There are clearly performance differences between users and between interfaces, some of which are highly significant and could not be put down to chance. Some of these are due to the characteristics of the particular interface (for example the iconic interface generally required less mouse clicks than the other interfaces) but the relative differences indicated something more fundamental.

In order to isolate these differences, we decided to concentrate on the level of spatial ability/field dependence and the characteristics of the command interface. This was were the most significant difference in performance had been observed. The command interface had an open and flexible dialogue; a user-determined dialogue [Thimbleby 90]. Users specified their query by typing the required item name and its attributes according to a particular syntax, in response to a simple prompt. Egan suggests that formulating such statements may be related to spatial ability [Egan 88]. If the users needed help in order to formulate the query, they had to leave the query mode and enter a help mode, returning to the query mode in order to specify the query. Intuitively there appeared to be some conceptual spatial activities concerned with moving around such a dialogue which was reliably measured by the spatial ability test we had used.

Other differences were clearly much less important. For example, there seemed to be no particular demands on short term memory by any of the interfaces. Other systems may make STM demands (e.g. [Benyon et al. 87b]). Also there were no significant differences between the different groups using the menu interface and only marginal differences using the button and the iconic interfaces.

A second database system was developed which we hoped would pin down the differences. This system had just two interfaces. One (a command interface based on SQL) was a user-determined dialogue, designed to be open and flexible and to require moving between modes to get help. The other, a system-determined dialogue, was a menu interface which was more constrained. It required users to respond to questions concerning the content of the query. From the answers, the system constructed the query.

The hypothesis we were testing was that users with a good spatial ability would perform better using the SQL-type interface. Being a command interface, we expected to observe a similar effect as that demonstrated by high spatial subjects on the first experiment. The SQL-type interface would be quicker for user who did not get 'lost' inbetween modes and who could formulate syntactically correct commands. By its nature the menu interface which provided a constrained dialogue was slower and more restrictive and so it would take longer for users to complete a task. However, poor spatial ability users were expected to perform better on the menu interface since they would make more mistakes and spend more time thinking when using the command interface.

Another controlled experiment was conducted in which 30 subjects performed similar retrieval tasks using both interfaces (reported fully in [Jennings & Benyon (in press)]). Initially only one half of the hypothesis was confirmed, namely that people with a high spatial ability would prefer the command interface. However, the results did not show a significant performance difference for those with low spatial ability. The results were re-examined and it was discovered that there was an additional factor involved - the level of experience with a command interface. When this was taken into account, the performance difference in the groups is significant (see Figure 1). Differences in performance could be explained by spatial ability *plus* previous command experience. The number of errors made shows this quite convincingly (Figure 2).

3.3 Accommodating the Differences

The experimental work described above should be seen as a part of the systems analysis, or evaluation, of possible interfaces to a database system. It may be hoped that over a period of time, some robust, general results concerning individual differences and interface characteristics may be determined. However, it may always be desirable for system developers to sample their expected user population in respect of particular interface designs. Let us assume that the designer has undertaken some experimental work along the lines described above. The system designer is now better equipped to produce a more usable system. Significant differences between members of the user population have been discerned. The differences have been identified as the spatial ability and experience of command languages. Experience will vary with frequency of computer use. The designer now has to decide how best to deal with the different aptitudes of the users.

One solution is to provide the database system with a menu interface. All users could then use this. However, this solution reduces the usability of the system for a significant majority of the user population who could perform their retrievals more quickly if a command interface was provided. If the command interface is the only interface to the system, it is likely that many users will be put off using the system. Discretionary users may decide not to use the system at all and hence will never develop experience with the command interface. Infrequent users may forget how to phrase their queries and again will have an impoverished interaction. Help and advice can be provided to compensate for these users, but this is then distracting from their primary task and may become annoying.

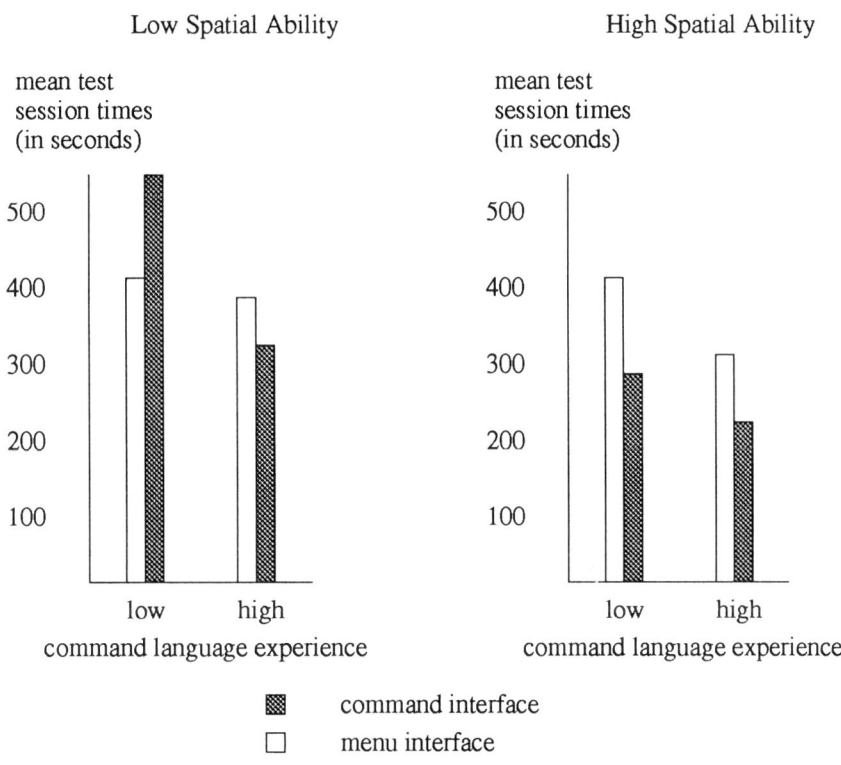

Figure 1: Mean test session times

The designer would weigh up these alternatives and possibly perform other analyses in order to evaluate other possible designs. Which ever way the designer decides to proceed, an adaptive system solution is one more option. Giving the system an adaptive user interface is one way to accommodate individual differences.

4 THE ADAPTIVE USER INTERFACE

In this case it was decided that an adaptive user interface would be appropriate. The database system was implemented with two interfaces - a command interface and a menu interface - and an adaptive mechanism. The purpose of the adaptive system was simply to select the more appropriate interface for the users. Hence the system was developed to achieve this purpose.

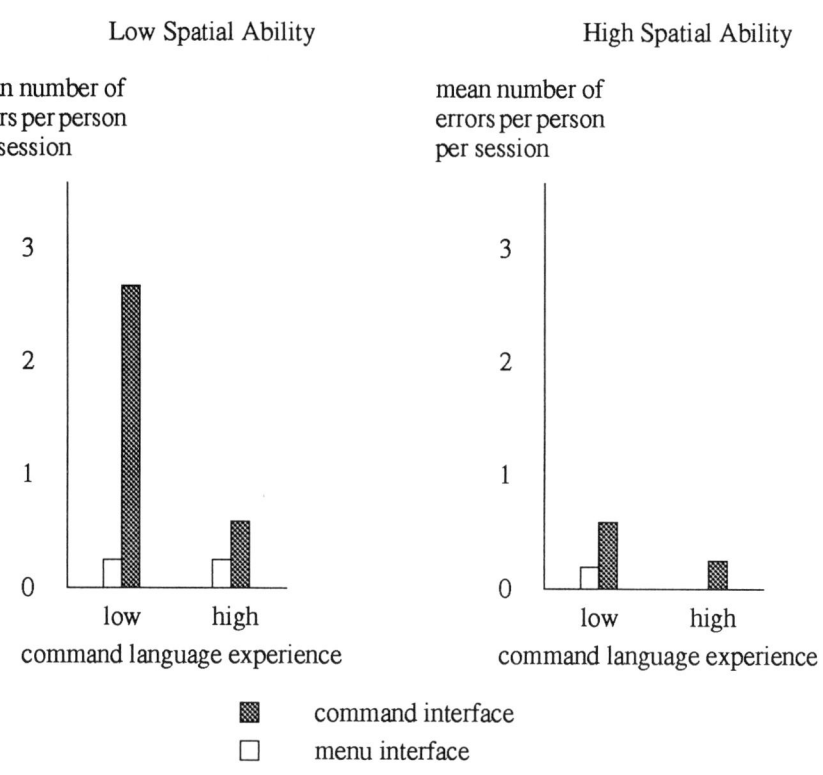

Figure 2: Mean number of errors per person per session

The adaptive system only needs to know enough about the domain in order to provide the required functionality. It therefore requires a definition of a task, an error, the average task completion time and an interface. The adaptive system needs to know enough about each user so that it can offer the most appropriate interface. From the experimental evidence, we know that the number of errors made by users using the command interface correlated significantly with the level of their spatial ability and command language experience. In turn, command language experience is affected by the frequency of computer use. Hence the adaptive system needs knowledge of the number of tasks the user has completed using the command language interface and the number of errors which they have made. The relevant user characteristics are spatial ability, command language experience and the frequency of system use.

The adaptive system needs to make some inferences from the interaction and requires an ability to alter the interface. In addition it must elicit the user's level of experience with command languages and the frequency of the user's usage of the system. These two facets can be obtained by asking the user when the user first uses the system. A record of the dialogue between user and system which records details of the number of errors made and the number of tasks completed is then sufficient to infer the users level of spatial ability using the simple rule:

        If   interface = command and
                 errors> 1 and
                 tasks = 12
        then spatial ability = low and command experience = none

Adaptations are accomplished using three rules:

        If   spatial ability = high
        then interface = command

        If   spatial ability = low and
                 command experience = none and
                 computing = frequent
        then interface = command

        If   spatial ability = low and
                 command experience = none and
                 frequency of computer use = occasional
        then interface = menu

5   DISCUSSION

This paper has illustrated a practical approach to the development of AUIs. Differences between individuals in a sample of the user population were analysed and their importance assessed. Spatial ability coupled with field dependency suggested a class of users who would have trouble with a command interface. However, the benefits of the command interface in terms of speed of task completion, was a significant one for a large proportion of the users. The problem stemmed from the openness and flexibility of the dialogue style which helped one group of users whilst hindering another. These differences could only be successfully accommodated by providing an adaptive interface. The feasibility of the proposed adaptations was considered and an error count seemed to offer an unobtrusive method of identifying the group of users. Frequency of computer use which would affect command language experience was included in the user model to allow for users improving their performance over time.

On its own, this work may be considered 'good practice' in the development of adaptive systems. The decision to have an adaptive capability arose from a consideration of the purpose of the system and the characteristics of the user population. Browne, Totterdell and Norman [Browne et al. 90] recommend the use of 'adaptivity metrics' to help the adaptive system designer evaluate the capabilities and extent of an adaptive system. The work presented here can be seen as complimentary to this approach. Their suggestion is that when developing adaptive systems, the designer should be quite clear as to the purpose of the adaptation, its generalisability, the recommendations and theory underlying the adaptivity and the trigger mechanisms which initiate the change. This is a vital part of adaptive systems development because without a measured and thoughtful approach to adaptive system development, the system may perform less effectively than a non-adaptive system. In this paper we have argued that the AUI arose in response to a particular set of circumstances.

The final implementation of the AUI described here used a co-operative approach to adaptation. Initially users were presented with the command interface since this was generally faster and most appropriate for three out of the four user groups (see Figure 1). When the system detected that a user was experiencing difficulties with the command interface (based on the number of errors made), the user was advised that a menu interface was available. At this point users could inspect their user model and amend it if required. For example, users could amend the value of the frequency of computer use attribute to 'frequent' and thus continue to be offered the command interface. Using this co-operative approach users were kept fully informed of the basis for the computer's recommendations.

Besides the AUI itself, the work presented here raises important considerations for HCI in general. In particular, the idea of navigation through information spaces is a large question concerning HCI and individual differences. Navigation, even in traditional applications of psychology such as moving around cities or across oceans is still poorly understood. We may appeal to the notion of mental models [Johnson-Laird 85] or cognitive maps [Neisser 76], but the question still arises as to how these are best constructed for particular environments. Hypertext systems and large networks demand a huge load from their users which may be related to their spatial ability, field dependence and personality factors such as an individual's propensity to explore, take risks and enjoy the sensation of discovery. The results of our experiments suggest that high and low spatial ability / field independent people may require very different help and guidance facilities for navigating the abstract spaces presented by large and distributed information systems.

ACKNOWLEDGEMENTS

Francis Jennings conducted the experimental work on which this paper draws. The National Physical Laboratory funded the project which led to the development of this system.

REFERENCES

[Bee 81]
   Bee, H. (1981): *The Developing Child*, (3rd edition). Harper and Row, New York

[Benyon et al. 87]
: Benyon D. R., Innocent P. R., Murray, D. M. (1987): *System Adaptivity and the modelling of Stereotypes*. In Bullinger, H.J. and Shackel, B. (Eds) *Human-computer Interaction INTERACT 1987*, North Holland 1987

[Benyon et al. 87b]
: Benyon, D., Milan, S. and Murray, D. (1987): *Modelling users cognitive abilities in an adaptive system*. Paper presented at 5th EFISS conference, Riso, Denmark

[Benyon & Murray 88]
: Benyon, D.R. and Murray, D. M. (1988): *Experiences with Adaptive Interfaces*. In The Computer Journal 33, no. 4, pp. 453 - 461

[Benyon & Murray 93]
: Benyon, D.R. and Murray, D. M. (1993): *Applying User Modelling to Human-Computer Interaction Design*. Artificial Intelligence Review 6, pp. 43 - 69

[Browne et al. 90]
: Browne, D.P., Totterdell, P. A. and Norman, M. A. (1990): *Adaptive User Interfaces*. Academic Press, London

[Carroll 83]
: Carroll, J. B. (1983): *Studying Individual Differences in Cognitive Abilities: Through and Beyond Factor Analysis*. In Dillon, R. F. and Schmeck, R. R. (1983) *Individual Differences in Cognition Volume 1*. Academic Press, London, pp. 1 - 33

[Cattell 71]
: Cattell, R. B. (1971): *Abilities: their structure, growth and action*. Houghton Mifflin, Boston.

[Cooper & Mumaw 85]
: Cooper, L. A. and Mumaw, R. J. (1985): *Spatial Aptitude*. In Dillon, R. F. (1985) *Individual Differences in Cognition Volume 2*. Academic Press, London, pp. 67 - 94

[Cronbach 75]
: Cronbach, L. J. (1975): *Beyond the two disciplines of scientific psychology*. American Psychologist 30, pp. 116 - 127

[Dillon 85]
: Dillon, R. F. (1985): *Individual Differences in Cognition Vol. 2*. Academic Press, London

[Dillon & Schmeck 83]
: Dillon, R. F. and Schmeck, R. R. (1983): *Individual Differences in Cognition Vol. 1*. Academic Press, London

[Egan 88]
: Egan, D. E. (1988): *Individual differences in Human-Computer Interaction*. In Helander, M. (Ed.) *Handbook of Human-Computer Interaction*. Elsevier-Science 1988

[Egan & Gomez 85]
: Egan, D. E. and Gomez, L. M. (1985): *Assaying, isolating and accommodating individual differences in learning a complex skill*. In R. Dillon (Ed.) *Individual differences in cognition*. Vol 2, New York: Academic press

[Entwhistle 78]
   Entwhistle, N. J. (1978). *Knowledge of structures and styles of learning: a summary of Pask's recent research.* British Journal of Educational Psychology, 48, pp. 255-265

[Eysenick 67]
   Eysenick, H. J. (1967): *The biological basis of personality.* Charles Thomas, Springfield, Ill.

[Jennings & Benyon (in press)]
   Jennings, F. and Benyon, D.R. (in press): *Database Systems: Different Interfaces for Different Users.*

[Jennings et al. 91]
   Jennings, F., Benyon, D. R. and Murray, D. M. (1991): *Adapting Systems to differences between individuals.* In *Acta Psychologica* 78, nos. 1-3, pp. 243 - 258

[Johnson-Laird 85]
   Johnson-Laird, P. N. (1985): *Deductive Reasoning Ability.* In Sternberg, R. J. (1985) *Human Abilities. An information processing approach.* Freeman and Co., New York, pp. 73 - 194

[Neisser 76]
   Neisser, U. (1976): *Cognition and Reality.* Freeman and Co., San Francisco

[Pask 76]
   Pask, G. (1976): *Styles and Strategies of Learning.* British Journal of Educational Psychology, 46, pp. 12 - 25

[Pask 80]
   Pask, G. (1980): *Developments in Conversation Theory - Part I.* International Journal of Man Machine Studies, 13, pp. 357 - 411

[Rosson 83]
   Rosson, M. B. (1983). *Patterns of experience in text editing.* Proceedings of the CHI '83 Human Factors in Computing Systems, pp. 171 - 175

[Sternberg 85]
   Sternberg, R. J. (1985): *Human Abilities. An information processing approach.* Freeman and Co., New York

[Thimbleby 90]
   Thimbleby, H. (1990): *User Interface Design.* ACM publications, Reading, Ma.

[Van der Veer et al. 85]
   Van der Veer, G.C., Tauber, M., Waern, Y. and van Muylwijk, B.(1985): *On the interaction between system and user characteristics*, Behaviour and Information Technology, Vol. 4(4), 1985

[Van der Veer 89]
   Van der Veer, G. C. (1989): *Individual Differences and the User Interface.* Ergonomics, 32, pp. 1431 - 1449

[Van der Veer 90]
   Van der Veer, G. C. (1990): *Human Computer Interaction: Learning, Individual Differences and Design Recommendations.* Offsetdrukkerij Haveka, B.V., Alblasserdam

[Vicente et al. 87]
Vicente, K. J. Hayes, B. C. and Williges, R. C. (1987): *Assaying and isolating individual difference in searching a hierarchical file system*. Human Factors, 29, pp. 349 - 359

[Vicente & Williges 88]
Vicente, K. J. and Williges, R. C. (1988): *Accommodating individual differences in searching a hierarchical file system*. International Journal of Man-Machine Studies 29, pp. 647 - 668

[Willerman 79]
Willerman, L. (1979): *The Psychology of Individual and Group Differences*. Freeman and Co, San Francisco

Intelligent User Support Based on Task Models

H. Ulrich Hoppe

GMD-IPSI
Darmstadt, Germany

ABSTRACT

This article reviews different aspects of representing and using task knowledge in intelligent user interfaces. Task knowledge determines the way in which users attain certain goals with the given system. Artificial Intelligence deals with related problems under the notion of plan recognition. These approaches will be discussed, but the general focus is on the traditions and practical requirements of human-computer interaction. Since general or multi-functional computer tools can be used for an unforeseeable variety of tasks, specific knowledge acquisition techniques have to be developed for providing user interfaces with task knowledge. Here, machine learning techniques have to be considered as a methodological background. Finally, general limitations of task-oriented support mechanisms will also be discussed.

1 INTRODUCTION

In the classical AI perspective, "machine intelligence" is based on a combination of knowledge representation techniques and inference mechanisms. Accordingly, in order to examine the possibilities of providing user interfaces with "intelligence" in terms of task knowledge, we have to deal with the problems of how task knowledge should be adequately represented, how it can be acquired automatically or semi-automatically, and how it is to be interpreted.

Task knowledge is only one ingredient of adaptive user interfaces, but an important one. As opposed to user models which typically capture individual characteristics (e.g. preferences or pre-knowledge of users), task models reflect the mapping of some set of meaningful external tasks onto the action primitives of a given device. Such a mapping may capture individual characteristics, i.e. idiosyncratic methods for attaining a certain goal, and may thus overlap with the content of the user model. It is a plausible observation that such idiosyncrasies are particularly important with erroneous or suboptimal procedures, but that optimal or "canonical" methods exist irrespective of individual differences.

The most prominent task-oriented inference mechanism used in intelligent user interfaces is plan recognition. Plan recognition and related techniques such as plan extrapolation form the basis for a variety of user support facilities in intelligent or adaptive user interfaces. In a recent study, Goodman & Litman have identified several such supportive functions [Goodman & Litman 92]. All coincide in using the recognition of partial or complete plans for assessing the user's current task context and for inferring potential user goals. For partially completed plans, task context and hypothesized goals may be used to constrain the interface in a way that facilitates plan completion. Tasks may also be automatically completed, usually after confirmation by the user. Techniques for constraining the interface range from dynamic menu defaulting to screen layout which anticipates certain likely next actions in graphical interfaces. The recognition of completed plans is particularly relevant for erroneous or suboptimal performance. Here, the system can correct the user's action sequence or suggest alternatives. Such mechanisms have been used in so-called active help systems [Finin 83, Fischer et al. 85, Hecking 87, Desmarais et al. 87, Hoppe 88]. In addition to this kind of instantaneous use, knowledge about completed plans is also an important source of information for dynamically updating a user model.

Much of the AI work on plan recognition is focused on natural language interfaces to advisory or consulting systems [Kobsa & Wahlster 89]. Although there is an obvious methodological overlap between plan recognition and goal inference in NL dialogues on the one side and the recognition of plans in concrete, non-linguistic action sequences on the other side, there are also strong indications that the latter problem may have simpler solutions. The main argument is that the user's input actions in command-driven interfaces have clearly defined operational semantics (in terms of their effects on the system environment), whereas the semantics of linguistic utterances is neither operational nor precisely defined. Therefore, in NL dialogues, plan recognition has to deal with an uncertainty in assigning a plausible or probable semantic interpretation even to single utterances [Raskutti & Zukerman 91]. The interpretation of concrete action primitives executed on a computer system is usually not ambiguous in this sense. This observation is not limited to command line systems but holds also for standard graphical interfaces. However, it is no longer true, e.g. for systems which have a flexible, context-dependent interpretation of reference by pointing as it is the case for certain multi-modal interfaces [Wahlster 91]. Of course, even if the operational semantics of actions are externally determined, there may be mismatches between the user's intention or goal and the actual effect of an action. A comprehensive treatment of this kind of erroneous performance may lead to difficulties similar to those with NL dialogues, but there are still simpler solutions for handling suboptimal performance or already known error patterns.

In the following, the problems of representing and acquiring task knowledge as well as recognizing task-related plans will be discussed from the point of view of human-computer interaction. Accordingly, it is assumed that the primitive elements of plans are effective user actions in the system environment. Thus the particular difficulties of conversational settings can be ignored. Also the subtle problems of mismatches between the intention and the effects of an action will only be covered in so far as they can be dealt with in the framework of the operational paradigm. But even in this "reduced problem space," we are far from having developed a sound and elaborate repertoire of modeling methods and implementation techniques. Even for the most prominent class of task-oriented support systems, namely active help systems or "intelligent coaches," there is little transferable methodology in spite of the relatively many example applications that have been presented. With this observation in mind, we will try to put together some potential mosaic pieces which could be relevant in a methodology for intelligent task-oriented interfaces which is yet to be developed.

2 THE REPRESENTATION OF TASK KNOWLEDGE

In accordance with the definition of a problem in a problem space, a task can be defined by an initial and a goal state. It is possible to define the initial state implicitly as the current state of the application environment. The goal can either be explicitly described as another state or as an incremental change to the current environment (a state difference). The description of the goal in terms of a state difference is preferable because it is not only more economical, but also more general in that it applies to a whole class of environments. In contrast to problem solving, the attainment of a task does not require the use of general "weak" methods such as backtracking searches. Instead, each task is associated with well-known specific solution procedures or methods. There may also be selection rules for choosing among different competing methods. A method is a procedural composition of subtasks or primitive operators.

So far, this is the typical HCI view in the sense of the GOMS model introduced by [Card et al. 83]. A task is defined as a particular goal associated with one or more solution methods. The term "method" in this sense is closely related to the notion of "plan" in AI, since both concepts represent procedural task knowledge. The difference is that the concept of a GOMS method is only indirectly recursive (it is the subtask which invokes another method), whereas plans can usually be directly nested [Sacerdoti 77]. Thus, a plan can be seen as a structure that merges the task and its associated method. This will also be called a task decomposition schema or simply task schema. In addition to its procedural decomposition, each task pattern is associated with a list of parameters (or "task features"). When applied to a concrete situation, a task schema or plan has to be instantiated. A concrete instantiation of a task schema can be represented as a task feature list, i.e. a list of parameter names and associated values.

An adequate description language for such procedural patterns should take account of different control structures as well as of the hierarchical (including recursive) composition of tasks. A set of such explicit control constructs, including sequential, order-independent, and parallel composition as well as alternatives and repetitions, has been suggested by Schwab [Schwab 89]. But tasks are not sufficiently described only by their control structure. It is also necessary to define certain parameter constraints between the components. Schwab allows for introducing global variables which are shared throughout the entire plan hierarchy [Schwab 89]. However, more flexibility is achieved by using local parameters or task features which can be connected to each other by certain primitive constraints. Accordingly, the notation has to reflect the possibility of passing parameters between tasks and subtasks.

Elementary tasks with attribute lists:

> conc_files [source_file1, source_file2, dest_file, dir]
> delete [name, dir]
> rename [name, new_name, dir]

Composite task:

> append_to_file [source_file, dest_file, temp_file, dir] ::=
> **sequence_of**
> (conc_files [source_file1 -> dest_file,
>   source_file2 -> source_file,
>   dest_file -> temp_file, dir],
> delete [name -> dest_file, dir],
> rename [name -> temp_file, new_name -> dest_file, dir],
> **option** (delete [name -> source_file2, dir]))

Figure 1: LEXITAS rule for an append-to-file task

·In our task representation language LEXITAS [Hoppe 88] these requirements are met by using an attribute grammar notation. Tasks correspond to the symbols of the grammar, and task parameters are represented as attributes which are associated with the symbols. The terminal symbols define elementary or "atomic" tasks that can be directly mapped onto primitive actions. The instantiation of attributes stems either from the syntactic appearance of the input tokens (e.g. commands) or from an operational definition with respect to effects in an external environment. The method only requires a sequential protocol of input tokens; operational definitions are not necessary. No additional assumptions about the nature of the application are made (i.e. also direct-manipulation systems can be modeled). Repetitive task structures are modeled by recursive rules, alternative methods by different rules for the same non-terminal. The current version of LEXITAS [Hoppe & Schiele 92] offers sequence-of, set-of (order-independent), and option as explicit control constructs. Figure 1 shows the LEXITAS representation of a specific method (rule) for an append-to-file task as it could appear with an operating system such as UNIX™[1]. Attribute con-

---

[1] The corresponding UNIX™ command sequence
  cat F1 F2 > F3 ; rm F1 ; mv F3 F1 [; rm F2]
  is not optimal in terms of a minimal number of commands.

straints are expressed by means of identical names. Arrows in the component patterns express that some internal attribute is identified with another attribute of the composite task (e.g. the "name" of the first delete is identified with "dest-file" of append-to-file). In this case, all the subtasks are elementary. But, of course, append-to-file could also appear as a subtask in a higher-level task schema.

Notational aspects are not only a technical issue with respect to internal requirements of user support mechanisms. The notation is a device for thinking about tasks and communicating task knowledge (e.g. it may have to be transformed into a user-oriented representation for explanation purposes), and it is the target representation for any kind of knowledge acquisition process. Also, certain representations are usually coupled with specific processing techniques. For instance, production rules which have been used for representing procedural task knowledge [Kieras & Polson 85] are typically processed by a forward-chaining rule interpreter. The production rule paradigm is well-suited for simulating user behavior, but not adequate for analytic purposes such as plan recognition, since it only lends itself to a "generate and test" approach which is clearly not efficient for analyzing unconstrained user performance. Anderson's model tracing strategy which uses production rules for analyzing student behavior in an intelligent tutoring environment [Anderson 84] avoids this problem by constraining the student's actions to what can be reconstructed by the model.

The initial definition of LEXITAS as a grammatical representation was inspired by the task-action grammar approach (TAG, [Payne & Green 86]). Accordingly, LEXITAS models can also be interpreted as partial generative models of user competence with respect to certain tasks and a given computer tool. However, differently from TAG, the focus of LEXITAS is on analyzing the user's actions by means of parsing.

3 THE INTERPRETATION OF TASK KNOWLEDGE

Given that the task model has the form of a grammar, plan recognition can be identified with parsing. In the area of intelligent tutoring, this view has already been characterized by Genesereth [Genesereth 82], although qualified as not sufficient:

Plan recognition can also be viewed as a parsing problem in which the student's actions are the "words" and his planning methods are the "rules of the grammar." This is an overly simplistic view, since the dataflow among the commands must also be taken into account.

Evidently, attribute or feature grammars together with a unification mechanism invalidate the negative argument put forward by Genesereth. It is also clear that a grammar may be used bidirectionally for parsing as well as for generation purposes. Plan extrapolation is a mixture of both, in that hypotheses about potentially following actions or subtasks are derived from a partial parse which is completed as far as possible by means of using the interpreter as a generator. Not only can the type of following actions be inferred, but also parameters can be (partially) instantiated by a forward/downward propagation of attribute constraints.

Although the grammar-oriented approach is now also common in the AI view of plan recognition, the problem of efficiently implementing powerful parsing techniques for this special purpose has gained relatively little attention as compared to fundamental problems of knowledge representation and "reasoning about plans" [Allen et al. 91]. The dominating formal approach to plan recognition is based on the logic of circumscription and has been developed by [Kautz 87]. However, Vilain could show that Kautz's method can be transformed into parsing with a context-free grammar without essential loss of generality [Vilain 90].

From an HCI point of view, providing both powerful and efficient implementations of task parsing and generation techniques is absolutely crucial. What are the essential requirements for such a task interpreter?

- To allow for flexible combinations of parsing and generation (e.g. extrapolation) the interpreter should be bidirectional. This implies that it should also be possible to propagate attribute values and constraints through the derivation tree in different directions.

- The interpretation should not only be syntactic. Desmarais et al. discuss different levels of semantics in plan recognition mechanisms and give empirical evidence that operational semantics are particularly necessary for treating non-canonical (sub-optimal, erroneous) methods of task performance [Desmarais et al. 91].

- For efficiency reasons, the parser should be incremental (e.g. similar to a chart parser).

The method of task-oriented parsing [Hoppe 88] partially complies with these requirements. It is based on the attribute grammar representation (LEXITAS) and supports parsing, generation, and extrapolation by means of a bidirectional interpreter written in Prolog. Parameter dependencies are directly handled by means of Prolog unification so that constraint propagation in different directions is possible. The primitive actions (or elementary tasks) are specified in three dimensions: (i) syntax, expressed in terms of an input pattern, (ii) operational semantics in terms of effects in the application environment, (iii) a description of how associated attributes are instantiated with parameters taken from the input pattern or from the environment. The interpreter derives the operational semantics and the surface syntax of composite tasks by composition from the primitive specifications. The specification of operational semantics can also be "empty", i.e. no effects are modeled. This option is important since the inclusion of operational semantics can be costly in complex environments. In its present form, the interpreter does not support incremental parsing, but an incremental interpreter is currently being implemented. The new interpreter will also extend the set of constraint relations which can be evaluated. As yet, these relation are either identity constraints between attributes or restrictions of certain attribute values to constants.

It may seem that one's position in the debate on adaptive vs. adaptable systems or user interfaces ([Fischer 93], in this volume) should have a strong impact on the task processing mechanisms needed for the envisaged kind of systems. However, intelligent task-support such as suggestions that extrapolate the assumed current task or corrections of previous sub-optimal or erroneous performance can usually be implemented by active, as well as by passive, mechanisms. Active mechanisms are usually classified as adaptive components since they provide context-dependent, system-initiated reactions to certain patterns of user behavior. But the same information could also only be given in a passive way, i.e. on demand, which would rather be seen as an instance of adaptability. Nevertheless, in both cases the underlying "intelligent" mechanism is essentially the same, namely an analysis of the procedural context of input actions. Based on the active/passive dichotomy, it has been argued that adaptive mechanisms should not be intrusive. Designing non-intrusive strategies for active help and advice-giving does probably not require novel methods of representing and processing task knowledge. The problem lies rather in externalizing or "reifying" good intuitive coaching or teaching strategies of humans.

4 THE ACQUISITION OF TASK KNOWLEDGE

Multi-functional software tools such as document editors or operating systems can be used for a huge variety of tasks. It is usually impossible to anticipate a sufficiently complete set of canonical tasks and even less so to anticipate all the possibly relevant sub-optimal or erroneous action patterns. Automatic or semi-automatic knowledge acquisition techniques are necessary to make task-oriented support mechanisms responsive to the potential variety of task schemata.

At a first glance, the technical problem is similar to the one of macro learning in problem solving environments. But the respective techniques are based on the existence of distance measures (an evaluation function) with respect to an explicitly known final goal (e.g. [Minton 85, Iba 89]). In open task environments, users may pursue many different goals which can usually not be anticipated. The assessment of a goal state would require task knowledge which, on the other hand, is to be acquired. Since this situation forbids the use of an evaluation function, a first order approach to macro learning for intelligent interactive systems has to be based on syntactic criteria.

In general, any macro learning mechanism has to provide solutions to the following three sub-problems:

- assessment of candidate sequences in the dialogue transcript,
- generalization of the examples in terms of task schemata, and
- evaluation of the newly acquired rules.

A viable criterion for selecting candidate sequences for macro learning in the absence of knowledge about goals is the frequency of certain patterns in a given transcript. Such an approach has been suggested and implemented by Hoppe & Ploetzner [Hoppe & Ploetzner 91]. Task protocols are used as the source of learning and the target representation is LEXITAS. The method is inductive and exploits syntactic similarities in the concrete examples in order to define attribute constraints in the generalized schemata. In the first step of selecting candidate sequences from a given task protocol, only the task types (names) and not the specific attribute values are considered. Candidate sequences of task types have to appear with a certain frequency in the transcript. The required frequency can be specified either as an absolute value or relative to the length of the protocol. The selection algorithm is parsimonious in that it only extracts maximal sequences which comply with the frequency criterion. Maximal sequences are those which cannot be enlarged without violating the frequency criterion.

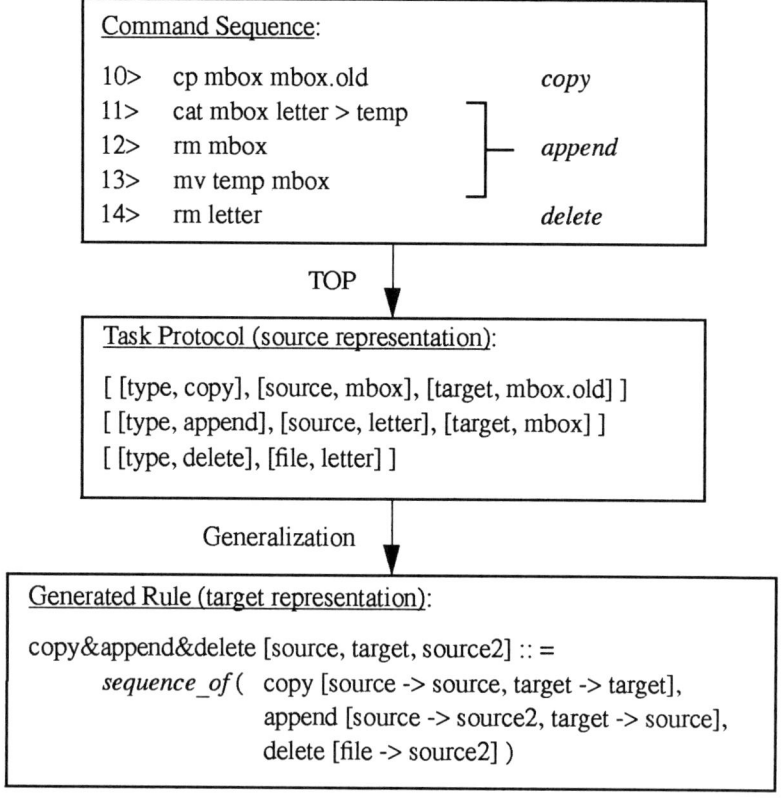

Figure 2: An example of the generalization mechanism

In the generalization step, new task schemata are constructed as abstractions from the example sequences by means of replacing constants with variables and determining the constraints on these variables. Constraints are expressed as attribute identities. In order to avoid undesired identities between different subtasks, it may be necessary to introduce new attribute names. The generalization mechanism in its current form cannot assess order-independences between the different constituents of a plan, so that the type of new rules is always sequence-of. Order-independences or optional components could be detected by ex-post analyses (e.g. an analysis of pre and post conditions of the constituents).

Figure 2 shows an example taken from the domain of file handling with the UNIX ™operating system. The initial command sequence is interpreted as a sequential composition of the tasks copy, append, and delete. (Here, the task parser has interpreted commands 11-13 as an append task, based on a known task composition rule.) The composite task copy&-append&delete inherits the internal attributes source and target from the copy subtask, and a new attribute source2 is introduced to avoid unification of the source of append with the source of copy. Identity constraints are established, e.g. between the source of the copy and the target of the append and between the source of append and the file which is deleted.

After the generalization step, different instances of sequences of identical task types may produce rules with different attribute constraints. To avoid the acquisition of many similar rules of the same type, each class of rules with identical type sequences is "thinned out" by keeping only the most general representatives. The notion of generality is defined as follows: For two rules R and R' with identical sequences of subtask types, R is said to be more general than R' (or: R subsumes R') if the constraints of R form a subset of the constraints of R'. This relation 'subsumes' induces a partial ordering within each class. Only local maxima with respect to this ordering are further considered. A similar subsumption analysis on substructures of tasks is performed when hierarchically nested task-subtask structures are introduced. This process of restructuring serves as a filter which reduces the number of new rules. For each of the rules which passes this filter, the frequency criterion is again checked through a comparison with the entire set of initially constructed rules. Here, attribute constraints are taken into account.

The method as described so far is generally applicable to any protocol comprising task descriptions in the required format of lists of attribute/value pairs. Its implementation in Prolog on Sun workstations is efficient enough to be used for interactive applications. The most costly step involved is the selection of maximal sequences from the task protocol according to the frequency criterion. It involves comparisons of single task instances with respect to the identity of the type attribute. If we assume the maximum length of potential sequences to be independent of the protocol length L, the number of comparisons required is at most quadratic in L.

The relative ease with which the acquisition problem could be solved is at least partly due to the underlying grammatical representation which facilitates syntactic processing without too drastic shifts of representation (see Figure 2). Although the operational semantics of tasks are not used in the acquisition process, the newly acquired rules inherit operational semantics by composition in the same sense as predefined tasks, given there is an operational definition of the primitives.

Still, the results of the inductive learning of task schemata do not all form reasonable patterns of coherent and meaningful user behavior. Schiele & Hoppe formulate certain heuristics for deciding whether or not a given task rule is plausible [Schiele & Hoppe 90]. The decision is based on operational definitions of "coherence" (in terms of parameters shared between component tasks) and "degrees of freedom" (the number of unconstrained attributes). Plausible task patterns should show a certain amount of coherence and the degrees of freedom of the final subtask should be largely reduced by constraints with preceding components. It could be shown that the effect of these merely syntactic heuristics coincides with selection based on a semantic relevance criterion.

5 LIMITATIONS AND EXTENSIONS OF TASK-ORIENTED SUPPORT MECHANISMS

The perhaps most relevant argument against the usefulness of intelligent task-oriented user support mechanisms stems from the situated action paradigm [Suchman 87]. User support based on task models is based on the assumption that the user's actions follow certain stable schemata and are not just responsive to changes in the external environment. Browsing activities and other more explorative forms of system use seem to fall under the situationist paradigm. However, even for browsing and retrieval activities, certain procedural dependencies can be identified in the user's behavior.

In a recent study, Peck & John present a GOMS-like model[2] of using a help browser [Peck & John 92]. The model accounts for iterative procedures in terms of what could be called select-evaluate-modify cycles. When matched against interaction transcripts, the model is reported to account for 90% of the observed behavior (although a precise definition of "accounts for" is missing). However, taking this figure as an indicator for the appropriateness of procedural-hierarchical task models even under typically "situated" conditions would be too simple. The problem is that this browsing model is highly underdetermined, i.e. it has many degrees of freedom in terms of alternative actions, possible iterations, and it is completely unrestricted with respect to lexico-semantic decisions concerning menu items or terms to be looked for. Thus, it can hardly provide detailed and selective information for predictive purposes. For the purpose of recognition, i.e. when "looking back," it can only associate the current activity globally with a certain phase in the iterative browsing process. Certainly this information alone is not enough to substantially support the user.

---

[2] The implementation of the model is based on the SOAR architecture, but on a descriptive level it can be viewed as a GOMS-like task decomposition.

A similar situation is encountered with information retrieval tasks in which a given database is consulted using a query language. In the incremental retrieval process it is mostly impossible to plan or anticipate longer sequences of actions because the semantic evaluation of intermediate results (co-)determines the selection of the next action. Nevertheless, several lower level "moves" or tactics as well as more global strategies have been identified in the behavior of professional searchers [Bates 79, Fidel 85]. These strategies are in turn highly iterative, flexible, and underdetermined. They impose only weak constraints on the relation between the actions in a sequence and can thus hardly be used as a knowledge base for the generation of help and advice. The situation changes, however, if the retrieval process is seen as embedded into some external task context with specific semantics such as travel planning. In this case of embedded information retrieval, [Hoppe & Schiele 92] identified and modeled certain stable procedural dependencies in the users' action patterns. In such models, we find two essentially different classes of tasks; on the higher levels, we have tasks whose semantics are defined in terms of the external context. For example, the overall task of travel planning is broken down into different separate retrieval tasks such as find-destination or find-accommodation. The retrieval subtasks may use heterogeneous information sources, and also non-retrieval tasks appear which have the function of combining information from different sources (like calculate-travel-cost). On the lower levels of the hierarchical decomposition of the overall task, we typically have iterative subtasks for query reformulation which may still have task-specific semantics or may even be general-purpose retrieval tactics or strategies.

Elementary tasks:

>specify_attribute [attr, value]
>evaluate_query [no_of_hits]
>delete_attr_value [attr, value]

Composite task:

>specify_and_broaden_attr [attr, val1, val2] ::=
>   **sequence_of**
>   (specify_attribute [attr, value -> val1],
>   evaluate_query [no_of_hits = 0],
>   delete_attr_value [attr, value -> val1],
>   specify_attribute [attr, value -> val2]),
>   **where** broader_term (val2, val1)

Figure 3: LEXITAS rule for a retrieval subtask

Figure 3 shows a LEXITAS rule for a general-purpose retrieval subtask, e.g. for formulating queries with a form-based interface where the field names in a form correspond to database attributes, and the user input into a field specifies the attribute value. The rule models a sequence of two successive queries where the initial query yields zero hits and the user replaces the previously specified attribute value (a term) by a broader term. Notably, the rule makes use of an extension of the grammar representation in that the broader term constraint between val2 and val1 is specified in a separate "where" clause[3] (and not in the feature lists of the subtasks). Given this extension, interesting transitions between the task-syntactic and the lexico-semantic levels are possible, for example, if the user has issued an initial query on an attribute and got zero hits, the task-oriented support mechanism can not only suggest replacing the term by a broader term, but can also consult a thesaurus and directly offer appropriate substitute terms.

Presumably, the retrieval example is only a representative of a much wider class of hybrid mechanisms where task-oriented support mechanisms interact with other intelligent modules. Typically the task model reflects "procedural syntax" and potentially operational semantics, whereas other types of semantics or even pragmatic knowledge have to be added. Nevertheless, we should not underestimate the value of task knowledge since it provides an important clue to analyzing user behavior in intelligent systems. Task knowledge is the primary resource for any action-oriented communication, be it implicit or explicit, between the system and the user.

6 CONCLUSIONS

There is an obvious need for developing a sound methodological basis for intelligent task-oriented user support mechanisms from both a computer science and cognitive science point of view. In the HCI community, the discussion of adaptive interfaces has been centered around example systems and very general non-operational principles. In the future, we should concentrate on using scientific prototypes primarily as vehicles to communicate methods. The focus of this article was on implementation methodology. Accordingly, general computer science and AI serve as reference fields from which notations as well as knowledge representation and interpretation techniques are "borrowed." The approach presented here favors an enriched grammatical representation which enables the treatment of plan recognition as parsing, and facilitates macro learning from interaction histories.

However, the assessment of methodological limitations and the evaluation of implemented mechanisms also requires ingredients from cognitive science, including empirical studies. In general, cognitive science can contribute relevance criteria and validation paradigms to the field of intelligent or adaptive user interfaces. For example, the heuristic evaluation principles for automatically acquired macros are closely related to a cognitive model of analysis-based generalization of procedures developed by Lewis [Lewis 88]. Also vice

---

[3] Our interpreter is currently being extended to cope with such constraints.

versa, work on adaptive systems can be relevant for cognitive science, such as the study of the limitations of plan-based support mechanisms, which is highly relevant to the debate about situated versus goal-driven cognition.

REFERENCES

[Allen et al. 91]
Allen, J.A, Kautz, H.A., Pelavin, R.N., & Tenenberg, J.D. (Eds.) (1991). *Reasoning About Plans*, Morgan Kaufmann, San Mateo.

[Anderson 84]
Anderson, J.R. (1984). *Cognitive psychology and intelligent tutoring*, Proceedings of the Cognitive Science Conference, Boulder (Colorado), pp. 37-43.

[Bates 79]
Bates, M.J. (1979). *Information search tactic*, Journal of the American Society for Information Science, vol. 30, pp. 205-214.

[Card et al. 83]
Card, S.K.; Moran, T.P. & Newell, A. (1983). *The Psychology of Human-Computer Interaction*, Erlbaum, Hillsdale (NJ).

[Desmarais et al. 87]
Desmarais, M.C., Larochelle, S., & Giroux, L. (1987). *The diagnosis of user strategies*, Proceedings of Interact '87, Stuttgart, pp. 185-189.

[Desmarais et al. 91]
Desmarais, M.C., Giroux, L., & Larochelle, S. (1991). *Plan recognition in HCI: the parsing of user actions*, in Tauber, M.J. & Ackermann, D. (Eds.), *Mental Models and Human-Computer Interaction 2*, Elsevier, Amsterdam, pp. 291-311.

[Fidel 85]
Fidel, R. (1985). *Moves in online searching*, Online Review, vol. 9, pp. 61-74.

[Finin 83]
Finin, T. (1983). *Providing help and advice in task-oriented systems*, Proceedings of the 5th Int. Joint Conference on Artificial Intelligence, Karlsruhe, pp. 176-178.

[Fischer et al. 85]
Fischer, G., Lemke, A., & Schwab, T. (1985). *Knowledge-based help systems*, Proceedings of the ACM SIGCHI Conference on Human Factors in Computing Systems, San Francisco (CA), pp. 155-169.

[Fischer 93]
G. Fischer: *Shared Knowledge in Cooperative Problem-solving Systems - Integrating Adaptive and Adaptable Components*. In: this book.

[Genesereth 82]
Genesereth, M. R. (1982). *The role of plans in intelligent teaching systems*, in Sleeman & Brown (Eds.). *Intelligent Tutoring Systems*. London: Academic Press. pp. 137-155.

[Goodman & Litman 92]
: Goodman, B.A. & Litman, D.J. (1992). *On the interaction between plan recognition and intelligent interfaces*, User Modeling and User-Adapted Interaction, vol. 2, pp. 83-115.

[Hecking 87]
: Hecking, M. (1987). *How to use plan recognition to improve the abilities of the intelligent help system SINIX Consultant*, Proceedings of Interact '87, Stuttgart, pp. 657-662.

[Hoppe 88]
: Hoppe, H.U. (1988). *Task-oriented parsing - a diagnostic method to be used by adaptive systems*, Proceedings of the ACM SIGCHI Conference on Human Factors in Computing Systems, Washington D.C., pp. 241-247.

[Hoppe & Ploetzner 91]
: Hoppe, H. U. & Ploetzner, R. (1991). *Inductive knowledge acquisition for a UNIX coach*, in Tauber, M.J. & Ackermann, D. (Eds.), Mental Models and Human-Computer Interaction 2, Elsevier, Amsterdam, pp. 313-335.

[Hoppe & Schiele 92]
: Hoppe, H.U. & Schiele, F. (1992). *Task models for embedded Information Retrieval*, Proceedings of the ACM SIGCHI Conference on Human Factors in Computing Systems, Monterey (CA), pp. 173-180.

[Iba 89]
: Iba, G. (1989). *A heuristic approach to the discovery of macro operators*, Machine Learning, vol. 3, pp. 285-317.

[Kautz 87]
: Kautz, H.A. (1987). *A Formal Theory of Plan Recognition*, PhD Thesis, Rochester University, Rochester (N.Y.).

[Kieras & Polson 85]
: Kieras, D.E. & Polson, P. (1985). *An approach to the formal analysis of user complexity*, Int. J. Man-Machine Studies, vol. 22, pp. 365-394.

[Kobsa & Wahlster 89]
: Kobsa, A & Wahlster, W. (Eds.) (1989). *User Models in Dialogue Systems*, Springer, Berlin.

[Lewis 88]
: Lewis, C. (1988). *Why and how to learn why: Analysis-based generalization of procedures*, Cognitive Science, vol. 12, pp. 211-256.

[Minton 85]
: Minton, S. (1985). *Selectively generalizing plans for problem solving*, Proceedings of the 9th Int. Joint Conference on Artificial Intelligence, Los Angeles (CA), pp. 596-599.

[Payne & Green 86]
: Payne, S.J. & Green, T.R.G. (1986). *Task-action grammars - a model of the mental representation of task languages*, Human-Computer Interaction, vol. 2, pp. 93-133.

[Peck & John 92]
: Peck, V.A. & John, B.E. (1992). *Browser-Soar: a computational model of a highly interactive task*, Proceedings of the ACM SIGCHI Conference on Human Factors in Computing Systems, Monterey (CA), pp. 165-172.

[Raskutti & Zukerman 91]
: Raskutti, B. & Zukerman, I. (1991). *Generation and selection of likely interpretations during plan recognition in task-oriented consultation systems*, User Modeling and User-Adapted Interaction, vol. 1, pp. 323-353.

[Sacerdoti 77]
: Sacerdoti, E.D. (1977). *A Structure for Plans and Behavior*, Elsevier, New York.

[Schiele & Hoppe 90]
: Schiele, F. & Hoppe, H.U. (1990). *Inferring task structures from interaction protocols*, Proceedings of the 3rd IFIP Conference on Human-Computer Interaction, Cambridge (UK), pp. 567-572.

[Schwab 89]
: Schwab, T. (1989). *Methoden zur Dialog- und Benutzermodellierung in adaptiven Computersystemen*, Doctoral Dissertation, University of Stuttgart, Inst. f. Informatik, Stuttgart.

[Suchman 87]
: Suchman, L. (1987). *Plans and Situated Actions*, Cambridge University Press, Cambridge (MA).

[Vilain 90]
: Vilain, M. (1990). *Getting serious about parsing plans: a grammatical analysis of plan recognition*, Proceedings of the 8th National Conference on Artificial Intelligence, Cambridge (MA), pp. 190-197.

[Wahlster 91]
: Wahlster, W. (1991). *User and discourse models for multimodal communication*, in Sullivan, J.W. & Tyler, S.W. (Eds.), *Intelligent User Interfaces*, Addison-Wesley, Reading (MA).

A Demonstrator Based Investigation of Adaptability

Franz Koller

Fraunhofer Institut für Arbeitswirtschaft und Organisation
Stuttgart, Germany

ABSTRACT

This paper presents the results of the ESPRIT II explanatory action AURA (Adaptable User Interfaces for Reusable Applications, Project 5634). The project AURA has been aiming towards a general architecture for adaptable systems. Therefore, a review of current research into user models and their state of development has been carried out and the possible role of user models has been investigated in the context of three different application domains by means of demonstrators.

Furthermore, this paper describes a prototypical implementation of dialogue nets, as well as an event-driven dialogue definition language (EDDDL) with post- and preconditions. Dialogue nets allow the specification of adaptable dialogue behaviour by means of graphical representation. This graphical representation can be transformed into the notation of EDDDL. The language EDDDL is tool independent but can be used for dialogue specification of user interface management systems (UIMS), and has been realized for the dialogue specification of the UIMS "ISA Dialogmanager."

1 INTRODUCTION

The project AURA was an ESPRIT explanatory action which had a preparatory function. Within the project a review of current research in the area of adaptable interfaces was carried out and prototypes of adaptable systems for three different application domains were developed to evaluate concepts and demonstrate the benefits of adaptability.

The three application domains and prototypes were:

- In the CNC area, ASSYST, an adaptable support system has been developed to support different people working at a CNC-machine tool.

- In the medical area, PRACSYS, an adaptable primary health care administration system, was designed to serve the needs of all personnel employed within the practice.

- In the area of software development, an adaptable tutoring system for the SPIRITS prototyping and system development environment has been developed.

Chapter two describes the common understanding of user models in the project. In chapter three, the adaptable support system (ASSYST) is described in more detail.

Chapter four introduces dialogue nets as a method for specifying dialogues and a prototypical implementation of dialogue nets used to specify dialogue behavior together with a commercial user interface management system (UIMS).

2 USER MODELS

Users interacting with a system have different levels of knowledge about the system and the application domain as well as different goals or tasks. The system should acknowledge these differences among the individual users and respond accordingly in order to effectively communicate with the users. To achieve this, the system should contain knowledge about users which might include information on expertise levels, goals, preferences and plans. Such information is usually contained within the user model component of a system.

As a common basis within the project, we used the following definition of a user model (adapted from [Wahlster & Kobsa 86]):

> A user model is the knowledge about a user that a system stores which contains explicit assumptions on all aspects that may be relevant for the dialogue behaviour of the system and its presentation.

In AURA [AURA 91] we were interested in user models which are designed along the lines of a knowledge base. In order to be reusable, the user model should be independent of the domain. Thus, the information about the user must be stored in a separate module rather than distributed throughout the system. The function of this module is to acquire information about the user, store and represent that information, and respond to queries about the user from the application. Additionally, the language in which the knowledge is encoded within the user model must be sufficiently expressive to allow inferencing to take place.

The Purpose of Adaptation

In AURA, the purpose of adapting the interface varies from domain to domain but it covers most of the possible reasons for wanting to adapt:

- Variety of users
- Efficient use
- Effective use
- Optimization of use
- Acceptability

3 THE APPLICATIONS

The three applications (a CNC support system, a tutorial system for an advanced interface builder and an appointment system for a primary health care administration) within AURA demonstrated the range of complexity and intervention required by user models. Having identified the user variables which could influence the dialogue of a system, we examined:

- what is required from the user model for each application,
- which of these variables the system designers thought were important in their model of the user, and
- who were the prospective users in each system

This was extracted initially from the original domain analysis which was carried out by the partners responsible for the different application domains. For each application area the requirements were outlined and consequently the system designers' models of the user was produced. These are summarised under the application requirements and include the classification of the user characteristics which would cause a change in the system interaction. The assignment of user-model characteristics to the different applications are shown in Table 1.

The CNC Support System (ASSYST)

The intention was to supply efficient and innovative training on CNC machines providing high quality and usable support. The user model only acts on the training and help system for CNC machines, namely the Adaptive Support System (ASSYST). ASSYST will be used both in the office as a pure training tool and in the factory as a support system to prevent erroneous operations by the operators. ASSYST demonstrates the facilities of an adaptable training and support system for the interface of a CNC machine. A complete prototypical implementation for all tasks of the CNC machine was not possible according to the resource limitations of the project. Therefore, a single task (called Load Tools) has been selected to demonstrate the advantages of adaptability along with the benefits of multimedia support in such a system.

The main purpose in adapting the CNC system is to tailor the explanation provided to the user's level of expertise, and make it appropriate to what was previously learned and understood. It also allows the user to turn off repeated explanations or selectively obtain either reminders or full explanations of previously seen material.

The main stereotypes identified for the CNC-application were: novices, NC experts, CNC experts of other CNC machines, and CNC experts of the current machine's predecessor. The assignment of users to different stereotypes take place by means of a questionnaire after the login. A stereotypical profile has been developed for each actor in terms of the goals, sub-goals, and tasks relevant to their particular role. The analysis has been used to

	PRACSYS	SPIRITS	CNC
Specialization			
Individual Profile	No[1]	Critical	Yes
User Stereotypes:	Yes	Yes	Yes
- Expertise			
- Domain	No	Yes	Yes
- System	Yes	Critical	Critical
- Job/Role	Critical	Yes	No
Modifiability			
Static elements			
System Designer / Manager	Yes	Yes	Yes
First Session	Yes	Yes	Yes
New Session	No	Yes	Yes
Dynamic elements	No	Yes	No
Adaptive	No	Yes	No
Temporal Extent			
Long Term	Critical	Critical	Critical
Short Term	No	Yes	No
Acquisition			
Explicitly			
System Designer / Manager	Yes	Yes	Critical
Users	Yes	Yes	Yes
Implicitly	No	Yes	No

[1] Except for the familiarisation period

Table 1: The assignment of user model characteristics to the different domains

determine what information and what facilities should be made available in a convenient way to a user with respect to their use of the system.

The main difference in the use of the system with the addition of the user model is in the initiative of ASSYST and the presentation techniques used. The two stereotypes chosen to demonstrate this difference are novice and CNC expert. In the case of the novice, ASSYST takes the initiative and guides the user through the system explaining the way one works with the control and the machine. ASSYST presents an "ideal pathway" (default path) through the system and points out which commands the novice must carry out in order to achieve the individual goals/subgoals. In the case of the expert, ASSYST works on demand giving maximum flexibility for navigation.

A CNC interface of a milling machine, as used on the shop floor, has been integrated in ASSYST which has not been modified. For the demonstrator, it is not connected to a CNC machine.

For user guidance, ASSYST provides a dialogue and a navigation window. The user mainly interacts within the dialogue window whereby the navigation window shows the current location in the dialogue tree. The ideal path for the actual user will be taken through the system by pressing the "next" button. The user is always able to go back to a previous dialogue or navigation window by selecting the "back" button. If a task should be performed directly at the CNC, it is possible by simply clicking a button to go to the corresponding CNC interface display. For a novice user this is only possible after reading the respective explanations of the subgoal which is obtainable by selecting the help button. The user then fulfils the task as described by the explanations. The CNC expert is not constrained to read the explanations, for the expert it is also possible to start the CNC task directly.

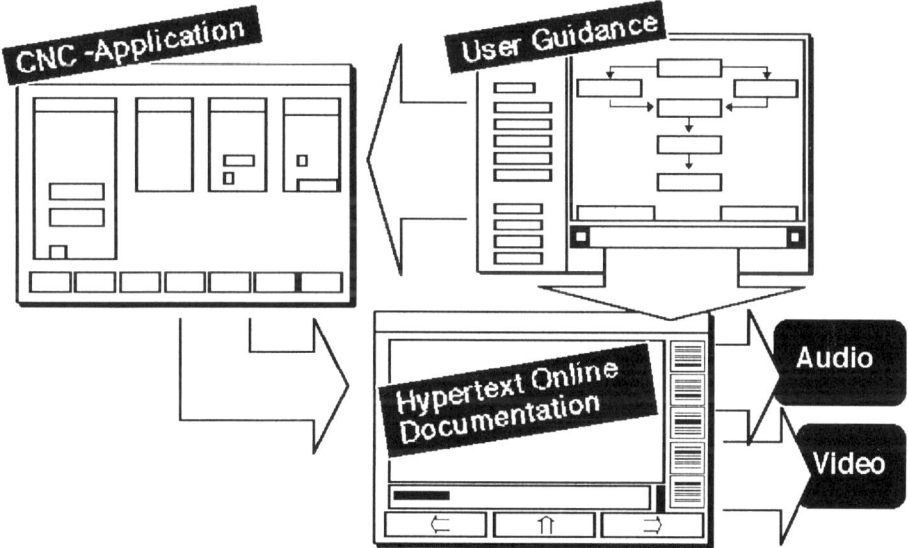

Figure 1:   Layout of the Interface of ASSYST

The experience with the prototype in the CNC area, as well as the two other prototypes, have shown that adaptable user interfaces effectively meet the needs of the different users in the three application domains.

The prototypes ASSYST and PRACSYS were realized with the User Interface Management System (UIMS) "ISA Dialogmanager" on top of the X Window System. The ISA Dialogmanager provides an event driven language. By means of this language, adaptable behavior of the prototype was manually realized. What we were actually aiming at were easier and more comfortable ways to implement adaptable user interfaces. The concept described in chapter four could be a basis for such a project.

4 SPECIFICATION OF ADAPTABLE DIALOGUES

Currently there are no commercial tools available which support the easy generation of a user model and its use for dialogue control and information presentation. At the moment there are some UIMS (e.g. ISA-Dialogmanager, OpenUI, SNI-Dialog Builder, TeleUse, etc.) available on the market which support the graphical specification of the user interface and the specification of the dialogue behavior by means of a dialogue description language. These dialogue description languages normally do not support the specification of dialogues which are adaptable, e.g., to certain stereotypes. Therefore, it was an intention to provide tools which allow the extension of existing UIMS for better support of adaptability by means of a graphical description of dialogues.

4.1 Dialogue Nets for the Specification of User Interfaces

Different graphical representation methods have been investigated with regard to their applicability in describing dialogues. Especially Petri Net based techniques like RFA-Nets [Oberquelle 87], Event Graphs [Roudaud et al. 90], Petri Net Objects [Bastide et al. 90], and dialogue nets [Janssen 91] were examined (An actual comparison of the approaches can be found in [Janssen 93]). The concept of dialogue nets [Janssen 93] has been considered as most suitable for dialogue representation.

Dialogue nets consist of places, transitions, and flow relations like Petri Nets. Every dialogue flow is specified through a dialogue net. Dialogue steps carried out by the user are realized by transitions. As for the event graphs from [Roudaud et al. 90], conditions and actions may be connected to a transition. A condition consists of an input event and other conditions. Actions may modify attributes of interface objects or activate application functions. The rules for transitions in a dialogue net are defined as follows:

> (T1) A transition will only fire when all input and side places are marked (filled with a token) and no output place is marked (every output place is empty). When firing, all tokens from input places will be removed and each output place will be marked (filled with a token) (see Figure 2).

> (T2) A transition can only fire if the input event and the conditions of a transition are true. When the transition is fired, its actions are executed.

If a modal dialogue window is opened, all other dialogues are blocked until the modal dialogue window is closed (that means the modal sub-dialogue is finished). A modal place (a place belonging to a modal sub-dialogue) is represented with a fat border. A transition without modal places as input places are called non-modal transitions. The others are called modal transitions. To enable the easy description of modal dialogue behaviour in multi-threaded dialogues, for example, a confirmation box, the following rule is provided by dialogue nets.

> (T3) A non-modal transition can only fire if no modal places are marked in the entire system.

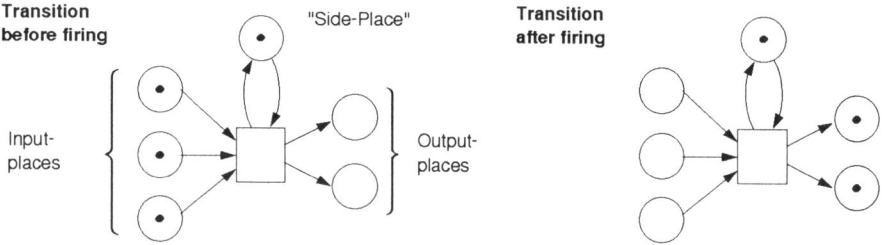

Figure 2: Transition before and after firing

Also to simplify the representation of dialogue nets, optional places are supported by the supplement rule:

(T1a) Optional input-, side- and output-places do not affect the firing of a transition. When firing a transition, existing tokens of optional input places will be removed and optional output places will be marked.

Normally, it is not possible to describe the entire dialog flow within one dialogue net. Therefore dialogue nets provide complex places which support a hierarchical structuring of the dialogue. Complex places are displayed with a double border and represent one or more sub-dialogue nets (see Figure 3).

The relation between a complex place and a sub-dialogue net is as follows:

(C1) If a complex place gets marked, the start event of the subnet is activated.

(C2) of the token of a complex place is removed, all tokens from the sub-net are removed deactivating it.

(C3) If all tokens in a sub-net are removed, the token of the complex place will be removed.

4.2 An Event Driven Dialogue Definition Language (EDDDL)

The dialogue nets have been implemented by means of the Editor EDIANE (Editor for DIAlogue NEts) [Eisenmann 92]. EDIANE allows the specification of dialogues using the symbols and mechanisms of the dialogue nets. To enable the user of EDIANE to use the specified dialogue flow for application development, the dialogue flow can be translated into event driven dialogue definition language (EDDDL). EDDDL is a tool-independent event driven language which supports the definition of pre- and post-conditions [Eisenmann 92]. (For description of the syntax of EDDDL see Figure 4.)

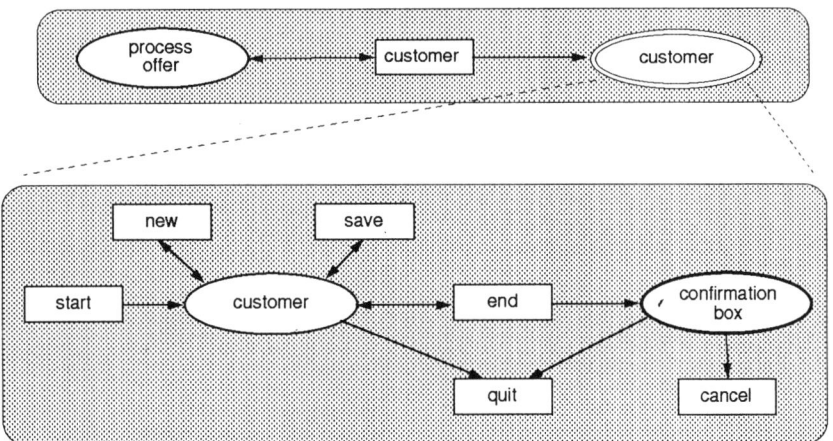

Figure 3: Refinement of a complex place. (Confirm box is a modal place)

EDDDL supports the following features:

- Rules can be combined in groups for better structuring. These rules can be activated or deactivated by activating or deactivating the corresponding group.

- Graphical models by means of groups (PLACE) are supported. PLACEs in EDDDL are similar to places of Petri Nets. The dialogue-net model can be easily expressed within EDDDL.

- EDDDL can be easily transformed into other dialogue languages, e.g., that of an UIMS.

- By means of the conditions in EDDDL, adaptable dialogue behavior can be expressed.

By means of a simulation module, it is possible to check whether all rules and states are achievable, how many dialogue steps are necessary to reach a certain state/rule, and its liveliness. An element of uncertainty is the results of possible function calls. In the simulation module of EDDDL, it is possible to choose between best case and worst case behaviour of function calls during simulation.

The language is tool independent but can be translated into other languages which has been realized for the commercially available UIMS "ISA Dialogmanager."

EDDDL	=	declaration {declaration} { action } rule_group { rule_group }
declaration	=	functionname "(" [type {"," type}] ")" type | eventclass (eventclass { eventtype })
rule_group	=	"WHEN" event [condition] "THEN" action { ";" action} | "PLACE" name[condition] ["THEN" action { ";" action}] rule_group {rule_group} "END" name [condition] ["THEN" action { ";" action }]
action	=	function | variable "=" expression | "OPEN" name | "CLOSE" name | "CHANGE" name
expression	=	expression math_operator expression | "(" expression ")" | function | variablename | constant
condition	=	condition logic_operator condition | "!" condition | expression comp_operator expression
math_operator	=	"+" | "-" | "*" | "/"
logic_operator	=	"&&" | "||"
comp_operator	=	"==" | ">=" | "<=" | "!=" | ">" | "<"
event	=	eventclass eventobject eventtype
function	=	functionname "(" [expression { "," expression }] ")"
constant	=	number | name | "true" | "false"
type	=	"char*" | "int" | "boolean" | "void"
name eventclass eventobject eventtype functionname		
variablename	=	("a" - "z" | "A" - "Z") {"a" - "z" | "A" - "Z" | "0" - "9" | "_" }
number	=	["+" | "-"] "0" - "9" { "0" - "9" }

Figure 4: Syntax of EDDDL

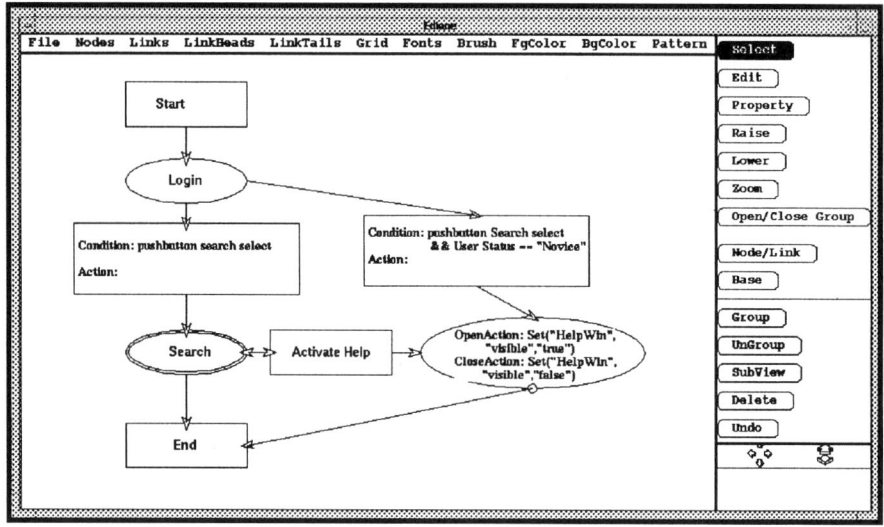

Figure 5: Dialogue net for search with opened transaction and opened place

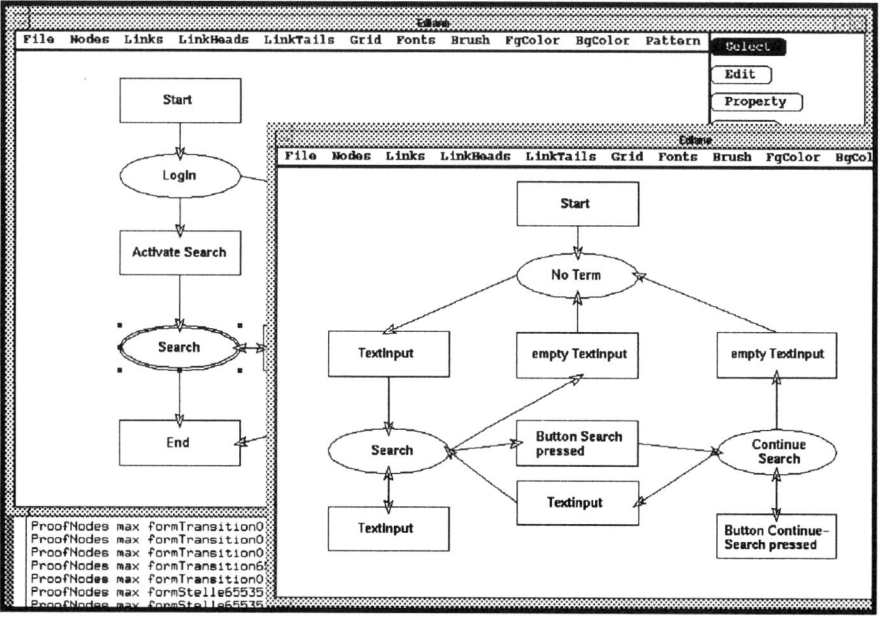

Figure 6: Dialogue net for search with opened complex place

4.3 Application of Dialogue Nets and EDDDL

Figures 5 to 7 show a simple example of how dialogue nets can be used to specify dialogue behavior. A window is specified for searching. Depending on the user type, a help window is opened automatically or is not.

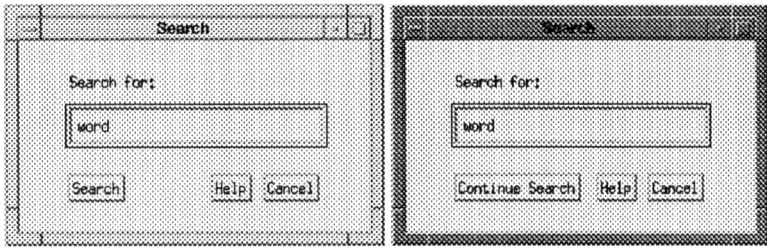

Figure 7:   Screen dump of the specified dialogue

4.4 Relation of Dialogue Nets with Adaptability

By means of post- and preconditions which are supported by the dialogue nets it is easily possible to describe dialogues which behave differently with respect to, for instance, certain user types. The actual implementation of dialogue nets are considered a basis for further developments in the direction of adaptable interfaces. The implementation supports different views of the system by means of the following features:

- display of parts of the dialogue in different colours, with respect to definable conditions,
- tracing facilities, and
- fading out of dialogue parts with respect to definable conditions

An integration of a component handling the user model is still missing. Whether it is a feasible approach to integrate a user model component with the dialogue net approach to ease the specification of dependencies in the dialogue, combined with the automatic generation of dialogues based on such a user model component has yet to be evaluated.

5   DISCUSSION

The graphical representation of dialogue nets can be transformed into the event driven dialogue definition language EDDDL and with some restrictions vice versa. The advantages of EDDDL in combination with the dialogue nets are as follows:

- Independence from the tools used can be achieved.
- The dialogue flow for different user types can be tested and visualized early.
- It is possible to present different views of the same dialogue.
- The dialogue behavior can be tested very early.
- The usage of predefined dialogue parts is possible.

For the future, an evaluation of the approach of dialogue nets and event driven language for adaptable, multimedia interfaces is foreseen.

Currently, the dialogue nets are loosely coupled with an UIMS which causes problems concerning the naming and keeping the description of a dialogue and the corresponding user interface objects consistent. Therefore, an integration of the dialogue net approach with an UIMS is desirable.

The strength of the described approach is mainly expected in the design phase of an adaptable user interface/system because of the early visibility and testability of dialogues.

REFERENCES

[AURA 91]
Parker-Jones, C., Howes, M.: *User Modelling*, ESPRIT 5634 AURA Adaptable User Interfaces for Reusable Applications, Deliverable D2, July 1991

[Bastide et al. 90]
Bastide, R. and Palanque, P.: *Petri Net Objects for the Design, Validation and Prototyping of User-Driven Interfaces*, In: Diaper et al. (Eds.) Human-Computer Interaction - INTERACT`90, North-Holland Amsterdam, 625-631, 1990

[Eisenmann 92]
Eisenmann, G.: *Ein Konzept zur Definition und Darstellung von Dialogabläufen*, Diplomarbeit Nr. 842, Universität Stuttgart, Institut für Informatik, Januar 1992

[Janssen 91]
Janssen, C.: *Dialognetze als neue Beschreibungsmethode für Dialogabläufe*, Zwischenbericht des Projektes TASK 01 HK 849 A2 Projektträger AuT, 49-60, Juli 1991

[Janssen 93]
Janssen, C.: *Dialognetze zur Beschreibung von Dialogabläufen in graphisch-interaktiven Systemen*, to appear in Proceedings of the Software-Ergonomie Tagung 1993, Teubner Stuttgart, 1993

[Oberquelle 87]
Oberquelle, H.: *Benutzerorientierte Beschreibung von interaktiven Systemen mit RFA-Netzen*. In: Schönpflug, W., Wittstock, M. (Eds.): Software-Ergonomie`87, Teubner Stuttgart, 271-284, 1987

[Roudaud et al. 90]
Roudaud, B., Lavigne, V., Lagneau, O., Minor, E.: *SCENARIOO: A New Generation UIMS* In: Diaper et al. (Eds.): Human-Computer Interaction - INTERACT'90, North-Holland Amsterdam, 607-612, 1990

[Wahlster & Kobsa 86]
Wahlster, W., Kobsa, A.: *Dialog-based user models*, Proceedings of the IEEE-74 (Special Issue on Natural Language Processing), 948-960, 1986

A Built-in Provision for Collecting Individual Task Usage Information in UIDE: the User Interface Design Environment

Piyawadee "Noi" Sukaviriya and James D. Foley

Georgia Institute of Technology
Atlanta, USA

ABSTRACT

Developing an adaptive interface requires a user interface which can be adapted, a user model, and an adaptation strategy. Research on adaptive interfaces in the past lacks support from user interface tools which allow designers to easily create and modify an interface. Also, current user interface tools provide no support for user models which can collect task-oriented information about users.

In this paper, we present the User Interface Design Environment (UIDE) which provides an automatic support for collecting task-oriented information about users. UIDE uses its high-level specifications in its application model as a basic construct for a user model. By using this model, UIDE will be able to provide a number of adaptive features as interface design options 1) adapting menu and dialog box layouts; 2) suggesting macros to users; and 3) adaptive help.

1 INTRODUCTION

Developing an adaptive interface requires a user interface which can be adapted, a user model, and an adaptation strategy. In simple cases, the user explicitly defines his or her own model and adaptation strategy. For example, an experienced user may be aware of her expertise level and request full menus and brief prompts. A novice, on the contrary, may request short menus and lengthy prompts. In more interesting cases, the adaptive interface infers information about the user based on some aspects of how the user works with the application. A novice user who requests help on more advanced features and manages to use them should be asked whether she wants full menus and less elaborated prompts. A repetitive sequence of actions may be made into a single step by the system or the system perhaps can infer these actions automatically. Regardless of how sophisticated an adaptation is, its purpose is to make computer interfaces faster to use and match the skills acquired by users over a period of time. In order to achieve these goals, computers need to maintain information about each individual user.

A *user model* is a collection of processable information about a user of a computer application. The model may vary in its simplicity, from an individual screen configuration file such as that of Apple Macintosh™ desktop or OpenWindows' .xinit file, to a more sophisticated novice/expert distinction [Rich 89], device and interaction technique preferences [Sanderson 91], and screen layout preferences. More sophisticated user models often require information to be collected dynamically as the user operates an application. More sophisticated user models can be cognitively-oriented, representing, for example, how much the user knows about each application command, how the user currently conceptualizes the application, and how the user maps tasks onto command sequences. In general, the model can change over time as the user works with the application and learns (or forgets) various aspects of the application. Our interest is in modeling the user's procedural knowledge of how to use the application to carry out tasks.

However, collecting information about users requires additional tedious programming work to produce information which is needed. We have been working for some time with **UIDE**, the **U**ser **I**nterface **D**esign **E**nvironment [Foley et al. 88, Foley et al. 91]. The focus of UIDE is to create a comprehensive user interface environment which supports user interfaces, from the design process to the execution of these interfaces. UIDE uses knowledge of an application to help automate the user interface design of an application, to control the execution of the interface designed, and to provide various forms of run-time help. The UIDE knowledge model is declarative and object-oriented, dealing with objects, attributes of objects, actions on objects, pre- and post-conditions of those actions, and interaction objects and interaction techniques through which the user interacts with the application. The model partially represents application semantics and semantic constraints imposed upon interface mechanisms used to access application functionality. Essentially, the UIDE application model represents the procedural requirements of an application, and uses such information to control run-time dialog sequencing. We see an advantage in our representation model that it already represents relevant information needed in a user model which could be related to users' procedural knowledge. We propose that our representation model can be used as a basis to construct a task-oriented user model.

The advent of free information collected as part of executing an application interface in UIDE will allow us to explore several forms of adaptive behavior. For example, with respect to on-line help, we are able to provide explanations of how to carry out various tasks. For example, given that there may be several ways to carry out a task, we can utilize information in the user model to choose the one which best maps onto the user's current knowledge of the application. Similarly, the amount of explanation detail, and extent to which detail is repeated in an explanation, can be adapted. With respect to improving an interface, by combining the application model with a command trace, UIDE will be able to reorganize menus and dialog boxes and suggest new macro commands to make an interface more "convenient" to use.

The UIDE adaptive interface project is in its first year. Our short-term goal is to provide some adaptive interface and adaptive help behavior as optional features to the user interface designer. A more desirable end is to allow the designer to specify adaptive behavior and relationships between data collected in the user model and the adaptive behavior without having to program. This paper only reports the core representations of the UIDE application knowledge, and how task-oriented user information can be collected based on this model. We also discuss possible adaptive behavior which can utilize the information collected in the user model.

We first provide a big picture of UIDE in Section 2, followed by discussions on related work in Section 3. In Section 4, we give detailed descriptions of the UIDE application knowledge model, its user interface functional components, and how these components are semantically linked. Section 5 discusses some of the components from the application knowledge which are used in UIDE's user model and semantics of the information in the user model. Sections 6 and 7 provide summaries of user interface and help adaptive behavior which can be supported in UIDE, and which we are currently developing. Section 8 discusses our current status and future work and Section 9 concludes the paper.

2 UIDE: THE USER INTERFACE DESIGN ENVIRONMENT

UIDE is designed to support interface designers to easily create, modify, and generate an interface to an application through high-level specifications. Our purpose is to support the interface design process through its life cycle – from its inception to the actual execution stage. This support has been made possible using high-level specification, referred to as an *application knowledge base*, which describes various details of an application interface including related application semantics. In the past, our emphasis has been on the design support. Within the past few years, we have expanded our research to strengthen the quality of both design aides and run-time support which can be automatically provided from the same common knowledge base. Design aides include automatic layout of menus and dialog boxes [Kim & Foley 90, de Baar et al. 92], and design transformation aides using a compositional model of interface components [Kovacevic 92]. Run-time support includes controlling interface objects using pre- and post-conditions [Gieskens & Foley 92], automatic generation of animated procedural help [Sukaviriya & Foley 90, Sukaviriya 91], automatic generation of textual explanation on why a widget is disabled [de Graaf 92], and coordination of textual and animated help [Sukaviriya & de Graaff 92]. Should the specifications in the knowledge base change, the generated interface and help at run-time will change accordingly.

Through UIDE, a designer designs an interface by putting in the knowledge base information about the application for which the interface is designed. This is done by creating entities in the knowledge base which capture application actions and objects. The designer then chooses various user interface functional components which best fit the application and link them to the application entities. User interface functional components include user interface actions, user interface objects (commonly known as widgets), presentation objects for representing application objects, and interaction techniques to be used with both application objects and interface widgets. In fact, various design tools have been developed to aid this process.

Kim, in his DON system, analyzed the knowledge representations of an application and logically grouped various actions into menus and dialog boxes [Kim & Foley 90]. He also used graphics design principles to improve the visual design of dialog box contents. [Gray et al. 92] used OpenLook style guides [OpenLook 90] to enforce the generation of dialog box contents from the data model of an application. [Kovacevic 92] automatically formed the internal representations for UIDE to map application entities to interaction techniques, and allowed the designer to easily navigate through alternative designs.

Once application representations are mapped to user interface functional components, either by using the tools mentioned above or manually and piecemeal if the designer wishes, the UIDE run-time environment depends on these specifications to generate a desired interface.

Though we use the OpenLook Intrinsic Toolkit [SunSoft 92] to create an interface in C++, UIDE does not generate code with a conventional program structure as one might expect. The designer-given application representations and associated interface components are used for controlling user interactions and status of user interface widgets at run-time. UIDE also provides automatic support such as help from the same representations. For example, textual and animated help on how to perform actions is constructed from the specifications upon user request [Sukaviriya & de Graaff 92]. Current context is used in the help construction process to map the help content to the current status of the user's work context. Help on why a widget is disabled at a particular time can be generated when requested using pre-conditions information associated with actions and interaction techniques related to the disabled widget [Gieskens & Foley 92].

3 RELATED WORK

Our work on the general UIDE framework and now adaptive interfaces touches upon multiple research areas within the user interface field – high-level user interface representations, automatic generation of help, adaptive interfaces, and user models. The following discussions will walk you through these related areas.

High-Level User Interface Representations

UIDE's knowledge representations center around describing commands and parameters of a user interface. These commands are called *actions* in our knowledge base and they are means for users to communicate with an application. Using descriptions of commands and parameters to generate interfaces was also the approach used in Cousin [Hayes et al. 85], MIKE [Olsen 86], MICKEY [Olsen 89], UofA* UIMS [Singh & Green 89], HUMANOID

[Szekeley et al. 92], and MASTERMIND [Neches et al. 93]. Except for HUMANOID, these systems parsed textual descriptions of commands and parameters, either embedded in a program structure or stored in a file, and used them as inputs to interface generators in their systems. UIDE and HUMANOID, however, created a knowledge base with entities corresponding to commands and parameters and used these entities actively at run-time. In UIDE, these entities also contained additional information which facilitated automated design aides [Kim & Foley 90] and manipulation of the interface being designed by the designer [Kovacevic 92].

Unlike these systems, UIDE's knowledge base captures more information about an interface beyond commands and parameters. It has declarative representations of application-independent components of an interface having to do with interaction techniques and manipulations of interface objects. By allowing an interface designer to manipulate the interaction level of representations, the designer has more control over the kind of interfaces to be generated for an application. Also, unlike other systems, UIDE captures action semantics through pre- and post-conditions of actions. Pre- and post-conditions are used to determine when an action can be invoked by the user, and the effects of an action to the user interface context. HUMANOID used guards, which are similar to our pre-conditions, to prevent an action from being invoked in an inappropriate context. However, HUMANOID did not represent or use post-conditions.

Automatic Generation of Help & Adaptive Help

On the automatic generation of help side, there is a little body of research on automatic generation of help from user interface representations. Tuck & Olsen used the interface descriptions (commands and parameters) in MICKEY, which were used to generate interfaces, to generate guided tasks [Tuck & Olsen 90]. Their guided tasks prompted users on what to do, step by step, to complete a task, and the user could follow these steps. If the user wished not to follow these steps, their system used pre-defined parameter values to demonstrate the steps. His help system was tightly integrated with MICKEY, which is the user interface management system for the generated interface. The help system had access to menu item and dialog box objects designed for each step. Taking advantage of this access, the system displayed help by pointing at these objects on the screen to context-sensitively show what needed to be done. Tuck's help was not designed to systematically handle all interface objects and interaction techniques. The system would require re-coding should interactions with interface objects change. Also, Tuck and Olsen's help system did not provide help on objects other than menu and dialog boxes. These other objects are mostly application objects, which are created dynamically at run-time. Tuck and Olsen's system, though was automatically generated, was not adaptive.

Neiman in his system GAK [Neiman 82] generated animated help for a CAD system from natural language representations. His animation was mostly canned and would have to be re-implemented if the interface changed, yet it was adaptive to certain run-time information such as the current extent of an object. Feiner, in the APEX system, generated illustrations to depict procedural tasks using descriptions of actions, pre-conditions, post-conditions, and objects [Feiner 85]. His emphasis was on synthesizing the illustrations such that relevant parts stood out for each procedure. APEX is adaptive to the current illustration context and the operational procedure context being shown.

Cartoonist [Sukaviriya & Foley 90, Sukaviriya 91] generated context-sensitive animated help from UIDE representations. That is, when a user requested help on an action, Cartoonist showed an icon of a mouse moving on the screen with a mouse button pressed before pulling down a menu, selecting a menu item, and so forth. Cartoonist then proceeded to show all steps which were required to complete an action. Keyboard typing was shown with a keyboard icon and characters flowing to an appropriate dialog box entry. Each animated help scenario was dynamically generated at run-time taking advantage of descriptions of actions, parameters, pre-conditions, interface actions, and detailed lexical descriptions of interaction techniques. Similarly to APEX, Cartoonist adapted its help demonstration based on the operational procedure context on which help was requested. Unlike APEX, Cartoonist adapted to the current user working context as opposed to the illustration context, which was determined solely by APEX itself.

SINIX Help [Hecking 87] was also help about user interfaces; it provided help on UNIX™-like operations in the SINIX operating system. SINIX's help knowledge base [Kemke 87] represented commands, parameters, and objects which these commands operated on (such as files, directories). However, these representations were created only for help purposes, and were not shared by the user interface mechanism in SINIX. UC [Chin 86] also used representations which were generated only for help purposes. Both SINIX help and UC were adaptive. Their help contents adjusted based on previous actions which users had performed. SINIX help suggested a shorter way to achieve the same goal. UC also provided explanations of failures caused by previous actions.

Another interesting work on automatic help generation is by Feiner and McKeown in their COMET system [Feiner & McKeown 91]. Unlike these previous systems mentioned which generated help for on-line applications, COMET generated help for operations which were to be performed in the real world. The system used representations of physical objects and their surroundings in the real world to help human operators proceed through their required tasks. Help presentations for a task resulted from an intelligent synthesis which highlighted objects in the scene related to the task at hand. The natural language generator then generated explanations which complemented the graphical depiction of the task. Though COMET only dealt with a rather static environment of fixed objects and scenes, its help presentation was dynamically created and adaptive to the tasks being depicted.

User Models

Research on user models have been around for quite some time and a large body of research exists as documented in [Wahlster & Kobsa 89]. We too will support adaptive interfaces and adaptive help by modeling users and use information about each user to guide adaptations. Since user models vary from one system to another depending on what they are for, the application they concern, and how they are used, there are no two user models which are alike. In this section, we merely attempt to clarify the characteristics of what we claim to be our "user model."

According to the compiled list of user model features by Sanderson, UIDE's user model falls in the same category as that of his N-CHIME system [Sanderson 91]. N-CHIME's user model is explicitly represented for each individual user, dynamic over an interactive session, persistent throughout non-consecutive sessions, and its information is inferred from interacting with users. Interestingly, a number of elements in N-CHIME's user model such as number of times an action has been selected, user experience with various interaction techniques, etc., are similar to UIDE's user model. The user model in UIDE is derived from a model that is used primarily to construct interfaces, be they adaptive or not. Our work is quite different from other research where user models are usually built totally separately from the underlying user interface support.

Adaptive Interfaces

In addition to using information in the UIDE user model for adaptive help presentation, we aim at demonstrating how the user model can be used to support two other kinds of adaptive interfaces – re-organization of menus and dialog boxes, and automatic suggestions for macros. [Dieterich et al. 93] in this book already provided a comprehensive survey and a taxonomy of adaptive interfaces. For this chapter, we will only mention research work which is more closely related to the types of adaptations we are pursuing.

Re-organization of menu is often used to reduce menu access time. Browne, Totterdell, and Norman reported a self-regulating system which changed a menu tree for a telephone directory [Browne et al. 90]. The system constantly placed items the user accessed frequently higher in the menu tree. A self-monitoring system was implemented to monitor how the average depth of menu selection changed over time. This allowed the system to evaluate whether the adapted menu tree indeed helped users reduce menu access time. Another example cited in [Browne et al. 90] was a system which reorganized a menu of word choices suggested by the system for spelling corrections. The words were organized based on the types of error most frequently made by users. Notice in these two applications that the adaptation in each application was based on the same task over time. The user selected data for the same operation – searching for a phone number or correcting a word. The user operated the systems knowing beforehand that they would have to search for their data choice in the menu to complete the repeated task.

Reorganizing a menu of commands (so a frequently used command is moved to the top of the menu, for example) changes user perception of how to perform tasks. Re-organizing menus in this sense will result in user having to relearn a motor distance for invoking a familiar command, therefore should not be done dynamically at will. We only intend to explicitly suggest modifications to menu layouts to users and users can reject or accept the suggestions. Even under this assumption, reorganization of menus and dialog boxes should be done at an early stage when an application has just been launched.

Recent work by Sears analyzed the frequency of widget-level action sequences to improve layouts of dialog boxes [Sears 92]. His *Layout Appropriateness* metric took into account task descriptions, and also designer's criterion factors such as distance and size of targets, the number of eye fixations needed to extract the necessary information for a task, and other factors of choice into the analysis process. Through the analysis, Sears' system computed an optimal layout which the designer could take and implement. The analysis such as Sears' can be incorporated into the UIDE environment. UIDE can take an advantage of its task-oriented representations to collect user performance information at run-time related to these tasks, and suggest a better dialog box layout to the user. Again, the user should be able to accept or reject UIDE's suggestions.

As for related work in automatic macro suggestions, Cote in his dissertation [Cote 90] aided users in extending system functionality by helping them easily create macros. His system AIDA utilized object-drawing command representations to extract common parameters among commands programmed by the user for a macro, and used them as parameters for the macro. AIDA in fact did not automatically suggest macro to users. A more intelligent system, EAGER [Cypher 91], recorded the history of user's command invocations, detected a repetitive pattern when one occurred, and took the initiative to suggest a macro to the user. UIDE has action representations which could be used for recording history of user actions, hence a pattern recognition mechanism like that of EAGER could be added for macro suggestion.

As for related work in adaptive help, we have already mentioned some adaptive help systems [Feiner 85, Hecking 87, Chin 86] which are relevant to our work. A number of adaptive help research efforts clustered in the area of intelligent tutoring systems as documented rather extensively in [Sleeman & Brown 82]. Many of the systems mentioned in Sleeman and Brown aided users in solving problems. Our scope is not as broad; we only look at adaptive help which uses history of previous interactions as user models. UC [Chin 86] and SINIX Help [Hecking 87] fall under this category. One other related system is by Senay [Senay 87]. Senay's help system recorded the statistics of command access by users of IBM VM/CMS operating system and used it to suggest new commands related to those already familiar to users. All these systems shared a common objective; they were designed to enrich user knowledge of the interface of the systems in which they were embedded.

In this section, we have mentioned a number of both past and ongoing research efforts which are related to adaptive UIDE. In the next section, we will discuss the knowledge representations of UIDE that are used to generate application interfaces. This section should give readers a background on the kind of information captured in UIDE. The following section will then show how a subset of this information can be used to construct a user model.

4 THE KNOWLEDGE BASE MODEL

The UIDE knowledge model is object-oriented. The model defines generic classes of various representation entities in the model. The knowledge base for an application consists of instances of these classes; each instance contains information specific to an application aspect it represents or a particular interface feature chosen for the application. In addition to these instances, the knowledge base is also formed by semantic connections among components.

We view the knowledge model as consisting of three layers of representations which describe application interface functionality at different levels of abstraction. At the highest level, representations capture more abstract components and are designed to capture semantics of application actions. The mid-level representations capture actions which exist in various interface paradigms but are independent of any specific application. The lowest level representations describe mouse and keyboard interactions and are designed to capture lexical groupings which define related lexical input and output. Through these layers of representation, a designer has different granularity of interface features which he can choose for an application. Ideally, changing an interface style is a matter of manipulating connections between these layers.

Section 4.1 and 4.2 elaborate on various types of representations in these layers. In Section 4.3, we discuss pre-defined types of connections among these layers which bind application semantics to specific interface aspects.

4.1 Describing an Application

An application is described in the knowledge base as a set of actions which the user can perform within the application, and objects on which these actions operate. All the functionality which is available to the users is described as actions. The knowledge model defines *action*, *parameter*, *parameter constraint*, *pre-condition*, and *post-condition* classes to capture user operations in an application, and *object*, *attribute*, and *attribute type* classes to capture objects on which users will operate in the application.

An action is a unit of activity which is meaningful to an application. Executing an action may affect objects, attribute values of objects, or object classes. An action may require parameters, hence the *parameter* class is defined to describe a parameter of an action. Constraints on parameter types and parameter values are defined as instances of the *parameter constraint* class. More detailed information about parameter constraint classes can be found in [Sukaviriya 91]. The *pre-condition* class is defined to capture what needs to be true before an action can be executed and the *post-condition* class is defined to capture what will be true after an action is executed. Both pre- and post-conditions in fact use first order predicate logic[1], and their class definitions capture such a representation. An action which requires parameters has pointers to its parameter instances. Each parameter points to the constraint instances associated with it. An action also points to pre- and post-condition instances associated with it.

To give a better picture of what application descriptions involve, let's use a digital circuit layout as an application. In this application, end-users create different kinds of gates and connect them to form a functional digital circuit. This application will be used throughout this section. Examples of application actions in this application are

> *create-gate*   (gate-type, location)
> *delete-gate*   (gate)
> *move-gate*   (gate, new-location)
> *rotate-gate*   (gate, angle-of-rotation)
> *connect*   (gate-1, gate-2)

In addition to action descriptions, objects or classes of objects which are manipulated within an application must also be defined in the knowledge base. For example, objects in the digital circuit layout application are of types gates, circuit boards, or designs. A GATE class would have subclasses of various gate types such as AND, NAND, OR, NOR, etc.

Figure 1 depicts a view of an action. In the UIDE model, an action is linked to its parameters, pre-conditions, and post-conditions. Each parameter is linked to its constraints. Figure 2 gives an example of the "connect" action in the circuit layout application. The "connect" action has 2 pre-conditions which altogether state that two gates must exist in the context. Both "gate-1" and "gate-2" have constraints stating that they must be of type GATE, and "gate-1" and "gate-2" must not be the same gate.

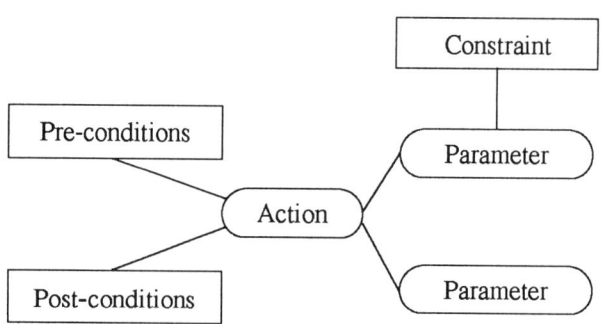

Figure 1:   A View of an Action Representation and its Associated Components.

---

[1] We currently do not handle universal and existential qualifiers.

A Built-in Provision for Collecting Individual Task Usage Information in UIDE

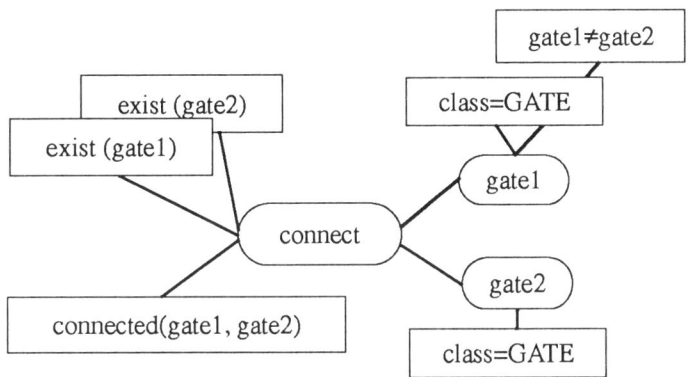

Figure 2: The Representation of a *connect* action from a digital circuit layout application.

4.2 User Interface Descriptions

The designer, after describing application actions, has to commit to an interface. Mapping from application components – actions and their parameters – to an interface is specified in the knowledge base as links from these application components to *interface actions*. Various types of interface actions can be linked to application components; this is primarily based on what the designer sees fit as interfaces to enter different parameter values or to indicate selecting different actions. For example, the designer may choose a graphical interface for the "rotate" action from the action list above. To do so, the "rotate" action is linked to the "select-action-from-pulldown-menu" interface action. Its parameters, objects and angle of rotation, are linked to the "select-graphical-object" and "enter-integer-in-dialog-box" interface actions respectively.

Similarly to application actions, each interface action has pre-conditions, which state what must be true in the interface context before it can be invoked. For example, the dialog box, which contains the numeric input widget for entering an angle of rotation, must be visible before a number can be entered. In this case, *visible(box)* is defined as the pre-condition where *box* is the name (pointer) of the dialog box which is the parent of the numeric input widget. Pre-conditions for interface actions also include those which indicate the sequencing of these actions [Kovacevic 92]. For instance, an angle of rotation cannot be entered unless an object has been selected, and an object cannot be selected unless the rotate action has been selected. Each interface action also has post-conditions, which state what will be true in the interface context after it is invoked successfully.

Interface actions are linked to yet another lower level representation – interaction techniques. Interaction techniques specify how interface actions are to be carried out by the user. For example, the "select-graphical-object" interface action can be carried out by using the mouse to click on an object. "Mouse-click-object" is the interaction technique chosen for this example. More than one interaction technique can be linked to an interface action to designate possible alternative interactions. Typing in an object name can be used to select an object, for instance. In this case, we link the "type-in-string" technique to the "select-graphical-object" action.

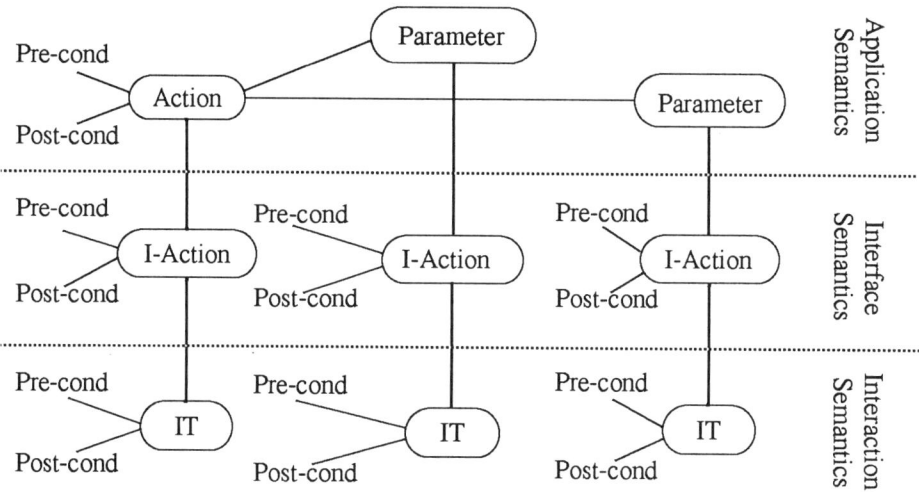

Figure 3: UIDE Knowledge Base's Relational hierarchy

Figure 3 depicts the representation layers in the UIDE knowledge model. The top level is what we sometimes refer to as the *conceptual design* of an application. A conceptual design ideally serves as a starting point in the design process and should be independent of what the end-user interface would be like. The same conceptual design can be mapped to multiple sets of interface action and techniques targeted for different environments.

Figure 4 shows the representation of the *Rotate* action from the example above. Some details are elided. For example, we did not show that the "Object" parameter of the "Rotate" action has a constraint stating that it has to be of type GATE. The "Angle-of-Rotation" parameter has constraints stating that its value must be of an integer type and must be within the range of 0 to 360. Details on the interface actions' parameters are also left out. The "Select-Action-from-Pulldown-Menu" has two parameters – the menu item "ROTATE" and the menu which contains the menu item. "Select-Graphical-Object" has an object as a parameter, and so forth. Interaction techniques have parameters as well; the

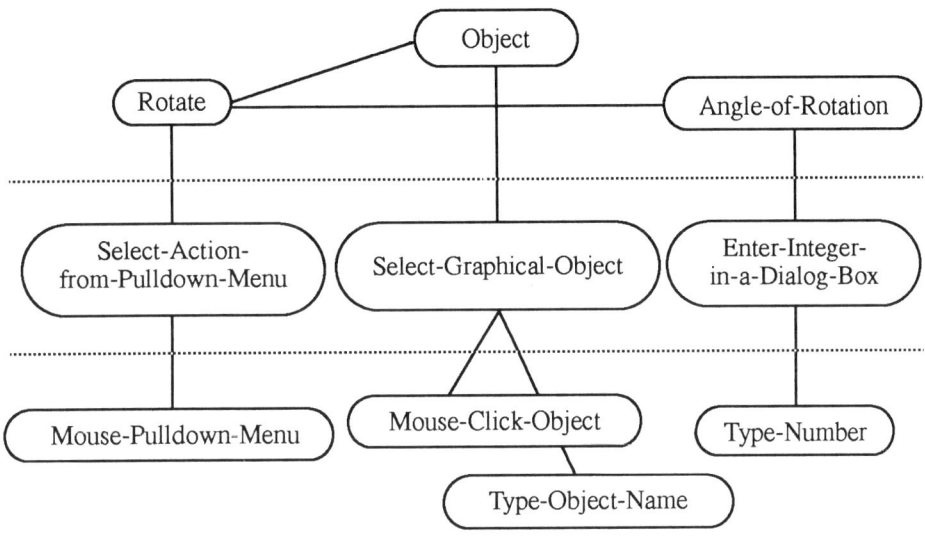

Figure 4: A Representation of Rotate Action

"Mouse-Pulldown-Menu" technique has a menu and a menu item as parameters. Pre- and post-conditions are also left out completely in this figure.

Interaction techniques could also have pre- and post-conditions. Their pre- and post-conditions tie closely to the screen context, i.e. the numeric input widget must be enabled for a type-in-number technique, and will be disabled after a number is entered. Interface objects such as dialog boxes, menus, buttons, etc., must be created and named during the design process so they can be referenced in the knowledge base.

In summary, once an application is described in the knowledge base as actions, parameters, objects, and so forth, interface actions can be chosen and linked to actions and parameters to specify the interactions which will interface with each application function. As mentioned in Section 2, intelligent tools have been developed to automate the process of linking these components. This is done by using semantic information about actions and parameter types. In the same fashion, interaction techniques can be linked to interface actions to specify the actual interactions which will carry out these interface actions. More details on this automatic process can be found in [Kovacevic 92].

4.3 Controlling the Interface Through the Knowledge Base

Remember that each component in the UIDE knowledge model is an instance of a C++ class. These instances have multi-facet behaviors – one of the facets is to control user interactions at run time[2]. The UIDE run-time architecture is designed such that the UI representations are used to guide the dialog sequencing. This means that UIDE does not hard-wire the dialog sequence and bindings to interaction techniques in the run-time code. When the specification changes, the corresponding connections in the knowledge model change and hence the interface behaviors change accordingly.

At run time, UIDE always knows which application actions have all their pre-conditions satisfied and are thus available to users. The interface actions and interaction techniques associated with these enabled actions are enabled. Interface objects and widgets associated with these interaction techniques are also enabled, the results of which are reflected in the status of objects in the interface, i.e., a dialog box is popped up, a corresponding text entry widget is enabled, etc. UIDE only accepts interaction techniques which are enabled at any point in time and sequence the dialog accordingly.

UIDE uses the three levels of specifications to control an interface. After the user selects an action from a pulldown menu, for example, the run-time environment checks in the knowledge base to see which parameters the action requires, which interface actions are assigned to them, and which interaction techniques are expected next. UIDE then enables appropriate dialog boxes, menu items, and other interaction objects. For instance, if a parameter must be entered through a dialog box, UIDE displays the dialog box. User interactions with the interface are always recognized by UIDE as the action or part of an action that the user is performing. When the user successfully enters all the parameters required for an action, UIDE invokes the corresponding application routine for that action. UIDE is then ready for the user to start another action. Since the knowledge model is constantly consulted by UIDE, specification changes initiated by designers become immediately effective in the generated interface.

4.4 Automatic Generation of How and Why Help

By using the relational hierarchy of information, procedural steps designed for completing each single application action can be inferred. For example, from the representations, rotating an object can be done by first selecting the "rotate" action, selecting an "object" to be rotated, and then entering the angle for rotation. An object of type GATE is chosen from the current context for the animated help to demonstrate selecting an object. This is derived from the constraint for the "object" parameter, which states that the object has to be of type GATE. An integer number between 0 to 360 is chosen for the "angle-of-rotation" parameter according to its constraints. The "rotate" procedure is animated by showing clicking the left mouse button while pulling down the menu where the "rotate" action is located, releasing the mouse button at the "rotate" menu item to select the action. The animation then proceeds with clicking on the chosen object, and typing the chosen number in the dialog box which pops up after the object is chosen.

---

[2] The other two facets are 1) to maintain the knowledge model, and 2) to cooperate with the run time help system.

Pre- and post-conditions are used to evaluate whether a context is ready for animating an action. For example, to rotate an object, the pre-condition of the "rotate" action states that an object must exist. If there is no object of type GATE in the current context, a planner is invoked to search for an action in the knowledge base which will create a gate. Animated help will include animating how to create a gate first, and then how to rotate a gate. Artificial intelligence planning techniques are used for action searches using pre- and post-conditions of actions. Currently, we are working on generating text to accompany animation. Research on task representations is also under way.

UIDE can also generate explanations of why a widget is disabled if the user inquires. A widget is disabled if the interaction techniques for it are disabled. The pre-conditions which are not satisfied are used as the basis for textual explanation generation, as discussed in [Sukaviriya & de Graaff 92]. The explanations also include which actions must be performed to enable the widget. Currently, we are integrating animation with this type of explanation.

Our recent research efforts have considerably refined UIDE's knowledge model and its architecture, resulting in much finer control over features of a desired interface. Indeed, UIDE removes interface programming from the application design process. What is more exciting is that the UIDE knowledge model opened the way to automatic support for user models, adaptive interfaces, and adaptive help. In fact, adaptive behaviors that are plausible in the UIDE framework are extensions of our previous automatic generation research such as automatic organization of menus and dialog box layouts and automatic generation of animated and textual help.

5 USER MODELS AS A SUBSET OF THE KNOWLEDGE BASE MODEL

The benefit of our representation-based user interface architectural approach is twofold. One is the previously mentioned run-time generation of user interfaces and help. The other is to provide the basis for recording information about user interactions. User models can be created using a subset of entities in the knowledge base. Since the knowledge model consists of layers of information at different levels of abstraction, user data can be captured in these units of information at any layer.

Taking advantage of the fact that UIDE constantly traverses application representations to control the run-time environment, UIDE always knows which action is being interacted with, which parameter of which action is being entered, and which interaction techniques can be used and which is being used by the user. UIDE constantly visits different parts of the representations for various types of information. This makes it possible to select the already existing components of the UIDE knowledge model as a start for constructing a user model.

The UIDE knowledge components are instances of actions, parameters of actions, interface actions, and interaction techniques. One basic approach is to infer user knowledge about each instance based on how the user has employed the instance. For example, several successful invocations of an action implies that the user knows about the action, its parameters, at least a set of interface actions which are used for the action, and at least one set of interaction techniques for interacting with the action. Multiple successful uses of an interaction technique implies that, when providing help on an unfamiliar action which employs the same technique, elaboration on the technique is not required. Hence animated details may not be needed. The user should have no difficulties executing the technique, but only needs to know that the technique could be used with the new unfamiliar action. Currently, we are not at a stage where we know how many successful uses of different components actually mean that the user has understood these components. This is part of our adaptive interface research and can only be confirmed by testing. Our current research emphasis is constructing a framework wherein statistics can be collected.

Our approach is to use an overlay of the UIDE knowledge model as a user model to record information pertaining to user history of interactions. However, much of UIDE representations deal with links among semantically related components. These links are not necessary in the user model since they can be inferred from the UIDE knowledge base. Those links hence are dropped from the user model. Each user has a copy of her own user model.

In most cases, there is an entity in the user model corresponding to an entity in the knowledge base. For example, each application action has a corresponding "shadow" object in the user model. Each of the action's parameters also has a "shadow" parameter object in the user model. These shadow objects are place holders where statistics of usage of the entities they represent is kept.

Following are the categories of information which UIDE can collect for the user model using the current knowledge base structure.

5.1 Statistical History of Interactions

Upon a successful completion of each application action, its shadow in the user model has one count added to a slot marked "completed by the user." The shadows of all parameters of the action also get one count for completion. All interface actions and interaction techniques which are chosen for invoking the action also get one count each as being completed by the user.

It may prove useful to record situations such as the user requests help on an action right after cancelling it or right in the middle of performing it, the state of user interaction when an action is cancelled (for example, action A is cancelled after the action is selected and its first parameter is entered), and so forth. Such a recording can be easily done in the UIDE framework, even if the parameter values need to be recorded. Uses of interface actions and their parameters can also be recorded in the same fashion.

Two kinds of statistics related to interface actions and interaction techniques can be recorded. One is the local statistics, per application action, of how many times each interface action and interaction technique has been chosen to invoke the action. That is assuming that many application actions have alternative interface actions and interaction techniques associated with them. The other kind of statistics is global statistics for each interface action or interaction technique, regardless of for which application action it is used. This is to provide a global view, for each application, of each user's skill. This global view ideally could be transferred to a different application which employs some common interface actions and techniques.

5.2 Chronological History of Interactions

Chronological history can be recorded rather straightforwardly in UIDE. Taking advantage of UIDE's layers of representations, the history of user actions can be recorded at various levels of detail. For example, upon completing an application action, UIDE can write to its history file that the application action has been invoked, with user's choice of parameter values recorded. UIDE can also record the interface actions and interaction techniques chosen to invoke the action. For chronological recording, it is important to record timestamps for each unit of recording.

To emphasize the benefit of UIDE recording, we have to emphasize that recording the actual keystroke and mouse events the user generates while interacting with an application can be easily done, with or without the UIDE framework. However, recording events consumes much more disk space, and yet their related semantics are not captured in the data. By recording application actions and specific parameter values the user chooses, the kind of semantic information, which is often needed by those who analyze and evaluate interface designs, is readily captured. Recording information at a high-level of abstraction and storing specific parameter values makes low-level event recording unnecessary. In addition to providing the recording for analysis purposes, UIDE will use the chronological recording to detect action usage repeated patterns which can be suggested to users as macros.

5.3 History of Help Requests

We believe that recording the kind of help requests the user made in the past could be useful if used intelligently. For example, the history of help requests for each topic could be used to predict how much of the same help to present the next time it is requested by the same user.

Since UIDE automatically generates help on actions, each application action is considered a help topic. We at first will focus on recording help requests on actions. That is, an action gets one count on help when help on the action is requested. In fact, the history of help requests is recorded both statistically and chronologically with timestamps.

The chronological recording is merely a list of help on actions in the order in which they are requested, and timestamps when these requests occur.

6 UIDE SUPPORT FOR ADAPTIVE INTERFACES

We discuss in this section examples of adaptive interfaces, and in the next section adaptive help which takes advantage of the statistical and chronological recordings in the UIDE user model.

Adaptive systems have sometimes adapted the user interface without any user control, leading to user confusion and lack of acceptance [Browne et al. 90]. In essence, the user has seen the interface changing without knowing exactly what changes were made (exploration being the only means of discovery), why the changes were made, and without consenting to the changes. We will give the user control over the adaptive behavior at three levels.

At the first level, the user will be able to completely disable user interface adaptation, either globally or with respect to different types of adaptation (our hope, of course, is that most users will not do so). This is analogous to turning prompts on or off in keyboard-oriented interfaces, or to choosing short versus long menus in contemporary interfaces.

At the second level, the user will be asked to confirm changes. Adaptation suggestions *and their rationale* will be presented to the user, who will be free to accept, reject, or defer the adaptation. That is, the user will be able to ignore the suggestion and work on a project with a deadline that might be 10 minutes away, in which case there won't be time to consider even the most worthy suggestion. Also, suggestions will be able to be deferred to a later time.

A third level of user control is the frequency with which adaptation suggestions are made. Because an adaptation requires relearning, and at least a temporary loss of productivity, reorganizations which have a low benefit in terms of productivity increases and a high cost in terms of relearning should perhaps never be made. Adaptations with high benefit and low relearning cost should be made quickly, while those "in between" are more problematical. We will allow the user to be involved in determining thresholds used in deciding when and if adaptations should be suggested.

Our initial focus is on two types of interface adaptation reorganization of menus and dialog boxes, and addition of new commands (macros). A simple power-law learning model [Card et al. 83] will be used to predict how rapidly the user will return to the pre-reorganization level of performance, and a keystroke model [Card et al. 83] is used to predict performance using the reorganized interface.

The power law learning model is of the form

$$T_n = T_1 \, n^{-\alpha}$$

where T_1 is the time taken to perform a task the first time, T_n is the time taken to perform the task the n-th time, and α indicates how much performance improves from one trial to the next. The power law is quite robust, covering a wide range of activities from typing to carrying out sequences of operations.

The system will periodically examine a trace of user actions and consider alternative menu structures and dialog box designs, evaluating each of them against the keystroke performance model applied to the trace and redesign. If the best reorganization found is predicted to improve user performance within a reasonable number of uses, then the reorganization will be suggested to the user, who will be free to accept or reject the suggestion.

To suggest command macros, the chronological history of interactions will be periodically examined to find repeated sequences of commands. The records of the sequence and timing of actions, parameter values specified by the user, and the interaction technique used for each action or parameter are considered. It will be necessary to identify which command parameter values are literals of the macro, and which are to be variables specified by the user when the macro is invoked. Also, variable-length repeating sequences of commands might take as a variable the number of iterations. In general, identifying macros faces the same challenges as does programming tasks by example, such as discussed in [Cypher 91].

7 UIDE SUPPORT FOR ADAPTIVE HELP

UIDE currently supports context-sensitive animated help which is automatically generated using the knowledge of an application. UIDE also supports textual help explanations of why an interface object is disabled, and how to enable it. The textual and animated help are being integrated to provide a more complete, yet automatically generated help for users by showing and explaining procedural information.

Within the scope of the kind of help UIDE can currently generate automatically, we are developing 2 types of help adaptation selection of preferred procedural steps and variation of help contents. For the first type of help adaptation, given that there is more than one way to achieve a task, we would present procedural help using methods assumed familiar to the user. For the second type of help, we assume that the user who revisits a help topic in a short period of time must seek more or different kinds of information from that she could assimilate the first time. We plan to research user's help request patterns and usage of relevant help information. By analyzing both statistical and chronological recordings in the user model, we hope to be able to help users get at required information effectively.

Selection of Preferred Procedural Steps

The statistical history of interactions allows UIDE to assume that a technique used frequently by a user is a preferred technique, or at least a technique which the user has already mastered. When help on an action which can be performed by multiple interaction techniques is requested, help can demonstrate how to perform the action based on the techniques which are used more often by the user. This is assuming that the focus of the user is to get the task at hand done without having to learn new techniques. However, if the purpose of help is to introduce alternatives to the user, alternative but less familiar interaction techniques should be demonstrated. A more thorough help in fact should present alternative techniques as well. Adaptive help would present more familiar techniques as a primary method to perform an action, while less familiar techniques are presented as alternatives.

Varying interaction techniques for an action is one level of adaptation in UIDE. Another level of adaptation is at the application action level where a series of actions to perform a task is presented in help. For example, when the user asks how to make a widget enabled, UIDE presents a series of actions which needs to be performed. Planning techniques are applied to derive this series of actions using pre- and post-conditions of actions as the search mechanism. Another time when a series of actions is presented is when animated help cannot demonstrate a procedure within the current context (because not all pre-conditions of the action for which help is requested are true). A planner is then invoked to search for actions which will satisfy the pre-conditions. In essence, the planner derives a path which accomplishes a goal, and a goal is to make certain conditions true. During the planning process, the planning algorithm may find that a condition can be satisfied by several paths of actions. Heuristics are needed to determine which path is the most appropriate. Using the statistical history of interactions collected in the model for each user, a path with more actions already familiar to the user is assumed to be the easiest to learn. The statistics in the user model can be used to choose among alternative actions, and planning can proceed based on the chosen action. Different users have their own statistics and therefore may see the same procedure delivered differently.

Variations of Help Contents

When the user revisits a help topic in a short period of time, we propose that the system should adapt to assist users in getting the needed information. Help contents can be adapted between sessions using the chronological recording of help requests. For example, the first time help on an action is requested by a user, UIDE would elaborate how to perform the action in detail using both textual and animated help. Textual help explains the underlying concepts of the action and animated help demonstrates how the action can be carried out. This is based on our assumption that textual help is brief and quickly presents the overall process while animated help is direct, visual, but time-consuming. After one (or more) requests on the same action, animation can be faster and briefer leaving out continuity of animation. Repeated requests on the same action over a period of time should result in animation being left out altogether, unless requested by the user. On the contrary, if the user fails to select an appropriate interaction technique or to accurately locate related interface objects on the screen, help should start using animated demonstrations again. Ideally, we should also predict, from the types of errors the user makes when performing an action, which parts of help contents the system should further elaborate and which media to use. Error types are not currently represented in the UIDE representations.

Unlike adaptive interfaces, adaptive help which varies help contents does not require relearning and can be presented without users being aware of it. This is similar to the case of human-to-human communication in which speakers often adjust their conversations to fit current contexts and listeners. We are interested in how varying help contents, and which variation strategies, would be more effective in getting users to achieve their tasks. What we have presented in this section is adaptive help capability which UIDE can support; using them effectively depends on our future research on relationships between information collected in the user model and individual adaptation strategies used.

8 CURRENT STATUS AND FUTURE WORK

UIDE was developed in ART and Smalltalk-80 in the past. UIDE is currently being developed in C++ running on Sun Workstations and X server. Interfaces are created using OLIT widgets [SunSoft 92] as well as our own object sets supporting visual presentations of application objects. Major development work has been on representing knowledge entities in the model to represent aspects of interfaces we need to control, and supporting the automatic sequencing control using the specifications in the knowledge model to reason which actions are enabled and how the interface context should change to accommodate the next step in an action. The work on animated help was implemented in Smalltalk-80 and is now being ported to the C++ platform. The work on textual help generation of why a widget is disabled, and how to enable it, was previously developed separately in C++ using only partially the UIDE model. The work is being integrated with the C++ platform to utilize the full application knowledge model. The work on adaptive interfaces and adaptive help behavior has not been implemented, though changing menu and dialog box layouts can be done fairly easily in UIDE.

Our short term plan is to integrate the core UIDE environment with the automatic help generation mechanisms, and to widen the support base for various kinds of OLIT widgets and presentation objects. Currently the digital circuit layout program is the only application we have modeled. We plan to model an industrial process control application to include more interesting cases for adaptive interfaces and adaptive help.

Our future work includes developing task representations which capture a longer sequence of interactions beyond the action level. We hope to use task representations to intelligently guide users in a more task-oriented fashion, and to apply adaptivity at this level.

As you may notice, we are still focusing at low-level concerns about adapting an interface – how is one supported by our user models, and how user models can be supported automatically in a user interface tool. The next challenging research issues would be to create interfaces for those who design and those who benefit from adaptive behavior. For example, for an interface designer, how should an interface to the designer look? How do we allow the designer to instruct UIDE to collect additional information in the user model? How does one create a new adaptive feature and how does one relate information in the user model to the new interface feature? As for the user, how does one understand and realize adaptations and how can one customize adaptive interfaces?

9   CONCLUSIONS

In this paper, we have described UIDE, a user interface design environment which supports the interface design process from creating an interface to executing one. The environment centers around the knowledge model of an application to which an interface is being designed and supported. Various tools which are developed to aid in the design process and at run-time are mentioned in the overview of UIDE in Section 2. We elaborated the knowledge model in great details in Section 4 and described how the various entities and their semantic links in the knowledge model are used at run-time. By elaborating on the knowledge model and how UIDE operates at run-time, we hope that the readers can easily see how a user model can be constructed automatically, and how information is collected at run-time. Section 4 should give a parallel view of information represented in UIDE's knowledge model and information frequently needed in the user model. We then described the statistical and chronological recordings in the UIDE user model in more detail. Finally, we discussed possible adaptive interfaces – reorganization of menus and dialog boxes and macro suggestion – and adaptive help which can be supported in UIDE utilizing the user model.

ACKNOWLEDGEMENTS

This work has been supported by the Siemens Corporate R&D System Ergonomics and Interaction group of Siemens Corporate Research Laboratory, Munich, Germany, and the Human Interface Technology Group of Sun Microsystems through their Collaborative Research Program. The work builds on earlier UIDE research supported by the National Science Foundation grants IRI-88-131-79 and DMC-84-205-29, and by the Software Productivity Consortium. We thank the members of the Graphics, Visualization, and Usability Center for their contributions to various aspects of the UIDE project J.J. "Hans" de Graaff, Martin Frank, Mark Gray, Srdjan Kovacevic, Ray Johnson, and Krishna Bharat. We also thank colleagues and former students at the George Washington University who contributed to UIDE Hikmet Senay, Christina Gibbs, Won Chul Kim, Lucy Moran, and Kevin Murray.

REFERENCES

[Browne et al. 90]

    Browne, D.; P. Totterdell; and M. Norman. (1990) *Adaptive User Interfaces*. London: Academic Press.

[Card et al. 83]
   Card, S.K.; T.P.Moran; and A. Newell. *The Psychology of Human-Computer Interaction*. NJ: Lawrence Erlbaum Associates Publishers. 1983.

[Chin 86]
   Chin, D.N. (1986) *User Modeling in UC, the UNIX Consultant*. In Proceedings of Proceedings of Human Factors in Computing Systems, CHI'86, 24-28.

[Cote 90]
   Cote, J. (1990) *AIDA - Ein an den Benutzer angepaßtes Graphisch-Interaktives System*. A Dr.-Ing. Dissertation, Fachbereich Informatik der Technischen Hochschule Darmstadt.

[Cypher 91]
   Cypher, A. (1991) *Eager: Programming Repetitive Tasks by Example*. In Proceedings of Human Factors in Computing Systems, CHI'91, 33-39.

[de Baar et al. 92]
   de Baar, D.; J.D. Foley; and K.E. Mullet. (1992) *Coupling Application Design and User Interface Design*. In Proceedings of Human Factors in Computing Systems, CHI'92. May, 259-266.

[de Graaf 92]
   de Graaf. (1992) *Context-sensitive Help as an Integral Part of a User Interface Design Environment*. A Master's Thesis, Delft University of Technology.

[Dieterich et al. 93]
   Dieterich, H., Malinowski, U., Kühme, T., Schneider-Hufschmidt, M. (1993). *State of the Art in Adaptive User Interfaces*. In this book

[Feiner 85]
   Feiner, Steve. (1985) *APEX: An Experiment in the Automated Creation of Pictorial Explanations*. IEEE Transactions on Computer Graphics and Applications, 5, 29-37, November.

[Feiner & McKeown 91]
   Feiner, S.K. and McKeown, K.R. (1991) *Automating the Generation of Coordinated Multimedia Explanations*. IEEE Computer. 24, 10: 290-303.

[Foley et al. 88]
   Foley, J.D.; C. Gibbs; W.C. Kim; and S. Kovacevic. (1988) *A Knowledge-based User Interface Management System*. In Proceedings of Human Factors in Computing Systems, CHI'88. May, 67-72.

[Foley et al. 91]
   Foley, J.D.; W.C. Kim; S. Kovacevic; and K. Murray. (1991) *UIDE-An Intelligent User Interface Design Environment*. In *Architectures for Intelligent Interfaces: Elements and Prototypes*. Eds. J. Sullivan and S. Tyler, Reading, MA: Addison-Wesley.

[Gieskens & Foley 92]
   Gieskens, D. and J.D. Foley. (1992) *Controlling User Interface Objects Through Pre- and Post-conditions*. In Proceedings of Human Factors in Computing Systems, CHI'92. May, 189-194.

[Gray et al. 92]
   Gray, M.; D. de Baar; and J.D. Foley. (1992) *Coupling Application with User Interface Design*. SIGCHI Video, 1992.

[Hayes et al. 85]
> Hayes, P.J.; P. A. Szekeley; and R.A. Lerner. (1985) *Design Alternatives for User Interface Management Systems Based on Experience with COUSIN.* In Proceedings of Human Factors in Computing Systems, CHI'85. April, 169-175.

[Hecking 87]
> Hecking, M. (1987) *How to Use Plan Recognition to Improve the Abilities of the Intelligent Help System SINIX Consultant.* In Proceedings INTERACT'87, 2nd IFIP Conference on Human-Computer Interaction, 657-662.

[Kemke 87]
> Kemke, C. (1987) *Representation of Domain Knowledge in an Intelligent Help System.* Proceedings INTERACT'87, 2nd IFIP Conference on Human-Computer Interaction, pp. 215-220.

[Kim & Foley 90]
> Kim, W.C., and J.D. Foley. (1990) *DON: User Interface Presentation Design Assistant.* In Proceedings of the ACM SIGGRAPH Symposium on User Interface Software and Technology, October, 10-20.

[Kovacevic 92]
> Kovacevic, S. (1992) *A Compositional Model of Human-Computer Dialogues.* In *Multimedia Interface Design.* Eds. M.M. Blattner and R.B. Dannenberg, New York, New York: ACM Press.

[Neches et al. 93]
> Neches, R.; J.D. Foley; P. Szekeley; P. Sukaviriya; P. Luo; S. Kovacevic; and S. Hudson. (1993) *Knowledgeable Development Environments Using Shared Design Models.* To appear in Proceedings of Intelligent Interfaces Workshop, Orlando, Florida, January 4-7.

[Neiman 82]
> Neiman, D. (1982) *Graphical Animation from Knowledge.* In Proceedings of AAAI'82, 373-376.

[Olsen 86]
> Olsen, D. (1986) *MIKE: The Menu Interaction Kontrol Environment.* ACM Transactions on Graphics 5,4: 318-344.

[Olsen 89]
> Olsen, D. (1989) *A Programming Language Basis for User Interface Management.* In Proceedings of Human Factors in Computing Systems, CHI'89. May, 171-176.

[OpenLook 90]
> *OPEN LOOK™ Graphical User Interface Application Style Guidelines.* (1990) Reading, MA: Addison-Wesley Publishing Company, Inc., 1990.

[Rich 89]
> Rich, E. (1989) *Stereotypes and User Modeling.* In *User Models in Dialog Systems.* Eds. A. Kobsa and W. Wahlster. Berlin Springer-Verlag.

[Sanderson 91]
> Sanderson, P. (1991) *Structure Design if an Adaptive Human-Computer Interface.* A Ph.D. Dissertation, University of Pittsburgh.

[Sears 92]

Sears, A. (1992) *Layout Appropriateness: A Metric for Widget-level User Interface Layout Evaluation*. To appear in SIGCHI Bulletin.

[Senay 87]

Senay, H. (1987) *A Knowledge-based Approach to Designing Interfaces*. A Ph.D. Dissertation. Syracuse University.

[Singh & Green 89]

Singh, G. and Green, M. (1989) *A High-Level User Interface Management System*. In Proceedings of Human Factors in Computing Systems, CHI'89. May, 133-138.

[Sleeman & Brown 82]

Sleeman, D. and Brown, J.S. Eds. (1982) *Intelligent Tutoring Systems*, London: Academic Press.

[Sukaviriya & Foley 90]

Sukaviriya, P., and J.D. Foley. (1990) *Coupling a UI Framework with Automatic Generation of Context-Sensitive Animated Help*. In Proceedings of the ACM SIGGRAPH Symposium on User Interface Software and Technology. October, 152-166.

[Sukaviriya 91]

Sukaviriya, P. (1991) *Automatic Generation of Context-sensitive Animated Help*. A Ds.C. Dissertation, George Washington University.

[Sukaviriya & de Graaff 92]

Sukaviriya, P. and de Graaff, J. (1992) *Automatic Generation of Context-sensitive "Show & Tell" Help*. Technical Report GIT-GVU-92-18. Atlanta, Georgia: Graphics, Visualization, and Usability Center, Georgia Institute of Technology.

[SunSoft 92]

SunSoft. (1992) *OLIT 3.0.1 Reference Manual*. Sun Microsystems, Inc. Part-No: 800-6391-10, Revision A, June.

[Szekeley et al. 92]

Szekeley, P.; P. Luo; and R. Neches. (1992) *Facilitating the Exploration of Interface Design Alternatives: the HUMANOID Model of Interface Design*. In Proceedings of Human Factors in Computing Systems, CHI'92. May, 507-515.

[Tuck & Olsen 90]

Tuck, R., and D. Olsen. (1990) *Help by Guided Tasks: Utilizing UIMS Knowledge*. In Proceedings of Human Factors in Computing Systems, CHI'90, pp. 71-78.

[Wahlster & Kobsa 89]

Wahlster, W. and A. Kobsa. (1989) *User Models in Dialog Systems*. In *User Models in Dialog Systems*. Eds. A. Kobsa and W. Wahlster. Berlin: Springer-Verlag.

Part III

Prototypes and Systems

Adaptive User Interfaces
M. Schneider-Hufschmidt, T. Kühme & U. Malinowski (Editors)
© 1993 Elsevier Science Publishers B.V. All rights reserved.

AIDA – An Adaptive System for Interactive Drafting and CAD Applications

Jairo A. Cote-Muñoz

Honeywell Regelsysteme GmbH
Maintal, Germany

Abstract

AIDA is a tool to make CAD systems adapt their functionality to the user's skills and learn from the user's method of working. AIDA is based on a User Model, Application Model, and monitor. The User Model is based on the user's knowledge; the Application Model, which describes the application and its functionality, is based on the results of the user's actions; the monitor module records the user's actions and analyzes them. With this system, we pursue the goal to explore the possibilities of giving the user a system that is better tailored to his capabilities, with mechanisms to adapt itself to the user's skills and method of working.

1 INTRODUCTION

This paper describes a model to allow a software system to adapt to the user. It starts by developing a schema that regards user assistance as the central aspect of an interactive system. User assistance is regarded as the support provided to the user in order to increase his performance of task completion. Next, a frame is fixed to assist the user, focussing the adaptation of the system on the user. The intention in giving the user a system that adapts itself to him, is to show new approaches for improving human-computer interaction. The spread of graphical user interfaces has improved human-computer communication considerably; nevertheless, users still feel the need for, and seek, improvements in communication.

One reason for this lies in the lack of regard for user assistance as a main aspect of the system design, and also the lack of any method to easily and actively tailor the system to the user's needs.

As quoted from [Browne et al. 90], "*The raison d'être of adaptive computer systems is primarily the acknowledgment that end-users are heterogeneous.*" They also mentioned that another reason for adaptivity is that "*building tailorability into any one product increases its potential market....*" Furthermore, we see that one of the problems that dialogue designers designing a system have is that the users are always changing their expectations of the system due to their increases in experience and skills. Very soon they start asking for new, more efficient ways to solve their problems [Clowes et al. 85]. Edmonds argues for the necessity of adaptive systems [Edmonds 81]: *"The user's wishes and needs are constantly changing and consequently cannot be fixed."* In [Benyon et al. 87] it is observed that *"users change behavior from problem solving through learning to routine cognitive skill as their experience with a system develops. It may be expected that there will be a need for different interfaces for the same user and task at different stages."* Therefore, changes in the application or the way it behaves have to be taken into account to assist the user. This can happen when the user requests a better way to solve his problems, or the system can advise him with a more efficient way to solve the problem. The system should grow along with the skill level of the user and, if possible, with his expectations. Empirical data shows systems that take individual differences of the users into account perform better [Carrol & Carrithers 84] for the same task than fixed systems.

2 USER ASSISTANCE AS THE CENTRAL ASPECT OF SYSTEM DEVELOPMENT

The goal of user assistance is to minimize the load on the user [Elkerton 88]. User assistance includes all the possibilities to make the user's interaction with the computer more efficient. It can start with the design of a simple conceptual model for the application. The consistency and simplicity of the application can be taken into account during the definition of the conceptual model. Putting the user as the central aspect of the system design requires a new classification of user assistance [Cote 90]. It gives up the artificially created separation [Campbell et al. 88] of user assistance in help, tutorials, and on-line manuals [Shneiderman 87], and sees user assistance as the main goal.

User assistance can be characterized depending on the purpose as long-term or short-term assistance (Figure 1). Short-term assistance covers the solution of a problem without trying to teach new concepts. This may happen due to a loss of orientation, lack of knowledge of a specific syntax, lack of knowledge of the correct command name, etc. Long-term assistance covers the understanding of the software system. It can be reached through a simple, consistent conceptual model or through theoretical instructions. Short-term assistance can be seen as problem-solving mode, and long-term assistance as a learning mode.

Within long-term and short-term assistance, you can also differentiate between whether the assistance occurs off-line or on-line.

The user assistance we find in this schema represents the assistance we can offer the user. User assistance is a combination of the assistance given both off-line and on-line. In order to achieve a certain level of user assistance, we have to clarify where to concentrate the efforts. Since the variables involved are not independent (e.g., the on-line assistance can

	user assistance			
	offline		online	
long-term	before and during implementation	• conceptual model • UI design	• tutoring systems	
	after implementation	• system instructions • written material	• user-dependent system's adaptation	
short-term	system consultant		• situation-related trouble assistance • situation-dependent adaptive mechanisms	

Figure 1: User Assistance

be fixed during the design of the conceptual model), we can not simply disregard any of them, but we can define them in a manner in which they fit into our goal of user assistance.

Long-Term Off-line Assistance

Long-term off-line assistance has two main aspects. The first is the written material to instruct the user or explain the system. Today, the written material is still an important element within user assistance. Tests show that reading rates decrease considerably when text has to be read from the screen [Shneiderman 87]. The importance of handbooks can be seen from [Campbell et al. 88]. Campbell regards the design and development of handbooks as one of the most important components of user assistance. The second part concerns the base for the quality of the on-line assistance. It starts with the system design. Here, there are possibilities for controlling the complexity and consistency of the system, those aspects that concern the building of the mental model. Depending on the conceptual model, the user can easily (or roughly) predict the behavior of the system. By the mental model, we mean the model in the user's mind of how the software system works; and as the conceptual model, the technical description of the system.

Short-Term Off-line Assistance

The assistance given by a consultant is the most effective available. A consultant makes a better analysis of the problem than the user can, and he can also make better assumptions about the goals the user is pursuing. He can confirm or discard his assumptions very quickly by asking questions or through discussion with the user. He is able to give the user mixed assistance, i.e., he helps the user to solve problems, gives him more references, and teaches him to better understand the system.

Long-term On-line Assistance

Long-term on-line assistance follows two goals:

(1) To allow a better understanding of the system. This ensures a better performance in goal achievement and problem solving. A common tool to instruct the user is the on-line tutorial.

(2) To tailor the system to the user's needs. This can be achieved with an adaptation of the system to the user wherein the system infers the changes from the user's knowledge, or the system learns from the user's method of working.

Short-term On-line Assistance

In the short-term, the system can assist the user with a mechanism that helps him overcome problems quickly. It can be a mechanism to correct errors automatically or a mechanism to increase the efficiency of tasks that do not appear to be worth the time to explicitly construct a macro. When they do appear, however, the task has to be repeated several times.

3 ADAPTIVE SYSTEMS

Adaptivity is a behavior of systems that we all know from daily life. We all operate on adaptive devices every day, e.g., the devices that control the air conditioning of a room. We are all familiar with the situation when someone asks a question and the answer he gets depends on his skills and/or knowledge. An expert in operating systems will react to the question of how an operating system works differently depending on whether the question is asked by a child or by a computer-science student.

Short-Term Adaptation

Short-term changes of the system turn out to be disadvantageous if the user does not understand the concept or the purpose lying behind the changes. This leads to an unstable mental model. Short-term adaptation is sensible in simple situation-related troubles and in tasks that either differ little from an existing command or do not occur very often but have to be repeated successively. These macros do not have to be saved because of the rarity of occurrence. For situation-related troubles, the user can be assisted with automatic error correction, supplemented with explanations that depend on the kind of error, context, and user. The explanation is derived from the information from the Application Model and the User Model; the information from the Application Model determines the type of error and the context; the information from the User Model provides the required explanation level.

Long-Term Adaptation

For the user, long-term adaptation means that the system, or the system behavior, changes because of new requirements. Two constraints have to be taken into account when adapting the system to the user. First, cognitive changes of users are difficult to measure, and the conclusions that can be drawn from this measurement are inexact. Second, fast changes of the system can confuse the user; therefore the changes have to occur very slowly. They have to occur just as if the user were to get a new upgrade of the software with every change, and this upgrade took him and his tasks into account.

Consequences of Using Adaptive Systems

The use of adaptive interactive systems can have at least four consequences. These are discussed in the following sections.

The first consequence will be that the user will better master the complexity of software systems. The complexity of software systems is constantly increasing. The user will find in an adaptive interactive system, a system tailored to his skills and task needs; as his task and skills change, the user will receive the proper functionality.

The second consequence will be better user performance. Investigations show that there is a relation between the performance and the individual differences of the users; furthermore, these relations are predictable. A summary of these investigations can be found in [Egan 88]. He compared the results in three areas: text editing, information retrieval, and programming. He noted: *"For moderately small samples (typically 10 to 30 subjects) and completion time measures that include the time to deal with errors, completion times for text editing had a range of approximately 5:1, information search approximately 9:1 and programming approximately 22:1."* If the software system provides for individual differences, it looks as though the bigger the complexity of the task is, the bigger the gain in performance.

The third consequence will be to gain and maintain the attention of the user. The fourth will be to avoid underloading or overloading the user. The third and the fourth consequences are discussed together. We all know of software systems that work with user models: computer games. E.g. chess. Most chess games have different options or levels of play. They represent the depth of the search and they are, on the other hand, also a representation of the competence of the player (the User Model). The purpose of User Models in computer games is clear: to gain and maintain the attention of the user and to avoid overloading or underloading the user.

Although the attention and the load on the user are not the main goals of multifunctional applications; they play a key role in the user's performance in completing tasks. The appropriate load and attention can be reached through an appropriate selection of functionality, "gradual challenge" [Neal 89]. For example, an interface that offers the user a menu with only functionality pertinent to his skills and needs will be less difficult to use than an interface that offers concepts that the user does not understand or need. The dynamic behavior of user interfaces is one way to gain the attention of the user. Mechanisms to change or increase the functionality will enhance the engagement of the user.

short-term adaptation (considers the user, the context, the application)	**long-term adaptation** (considers the user, user's method of working, user's changes, application, context, and task

• for syntactical error assistance (problem solving mode)
 	
 • dynamical fixing of default values
 	
 • creating macros for situations that will not easily return
 	
 • automatic error correction
	• changing the system behavior
	 • changing the extension of the applications' functionality
	 • for semantic error assistance (learn mode)
	 • user - and task-dependent selection of the interactions
	 • user-dependent selection of default values
	 • automatic error correction
	 • learning from the users' method of working
	  - controlled by the user
	  - automatically

Figure 2: Summary of Forms of Adaptation

3.1 Architecture of an Adaptive Interactive System

An adaptive interactive system should track the user's changes and accommodate the application to those changes. In order to track the user's status, the system needs knowledge about the user. Furthermore, the system needs knowledge about the application in order to be able to accommodate it to the user's changes.

A system that adapts to the user needs knowledge about the user and about the application, as well as a module that makes assumptions about the user. Knowledge about the user means an explicit representation of the user (User Model). Knowledge about the application means an explicit representation of the application that allows runtime modifications of the application. In order to be able to make assumptions about the user, one needs information about him. This takes the form of a file that records the interactions between the user and the system. The system can then change according to the assumptions of how the user is changing.

Therefore, AIDA separates its functionality into three modules: the User Model, the Application Model, and monitoring. The monitoring module records the user's interactions and evaluates them. From this evaluation, the system will generate new commands or macros. This module connects the User Model with the Application Model. The Application Model module provides the application's knowledge and the mechanisms to allow adaptability.

The User Model module controls the explicit representation of the user and provides the mechanism to create new user classes. Figure 3 shows the relations and control flow of the described modules.

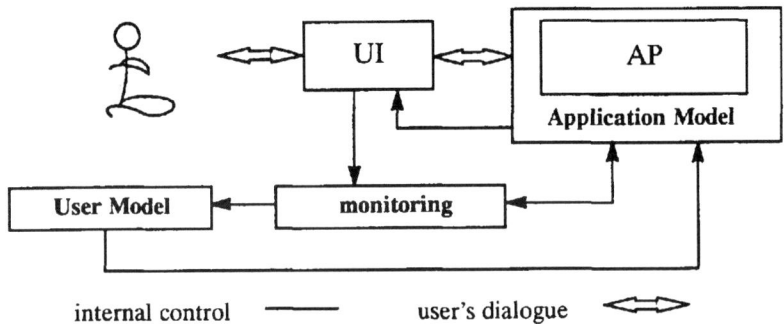

Figure 3: Adaptive Interactive System Architecture [Cote 90]

3.2 User Model

As already mentioned, the system needs a user representation that supports users individually, a model that recognizes the user as an individual or as a member of a class of users. In the context of this work, we define the User Model as a concept to make a differentiated and explicit description of users or classes of users to improve the user's interaction with the software system.

To classify characteristic differences between users or classes of users, it seems to be sensible to consider human ways of acting, communicating, and thinking. These characteristics should be relevant to the performance and the task the user performs with the system.

Shneiderman [Shneiderman 87] mentioned as relevant factors: cognitive and problem solving style, background knowledge, ergonomic factors such as fatigue, perceptual load, monotony, boredom, anxiety, or fear of doing something wrong, and motivation. Bösser [Bösser 87] classified the user based on the knowledge the user has about the task, and the tools to perform the task. Foley [Foley 87] characterized the user by his personality, knowledge, working environment, attitude to the task, and flexibility. In [Browne et al. 90] there is an overview of characteristics of individual differences that can affect user-computer interaction: psycho-motor skills, capability, learning ability, understanding, expectations, motives, cognitive strategies, cognitive abilities, preferences, temporal changes, and situation specificity. These characteristics are very far-reaching and general for an explicit dynamic representation of the user. One of the most important aspects for performance in a multifunctional system is the understanding the user has about the system. Furthermore, the knowledge of the user about the whole system plays a relevant role for the building of a stable mental model. An interactive system gives very limited possibilities to measure the user's changes. We gather user's knowledge of similar complexity to generate user's classes [Rich 89]. These classes represent a rough grouping. Due to the inaccuracy of the predictions of the user's knowledge, the classes will not differentiate specific details.

AIDA considers three types of the user's knowledge to classify a user class:

- The user's knowledge about an specific system. This covers the practice and experience the user has about using a specific software system. This knowledge is usually very specific and can seldom be transferred.

- The user's knowledge about computer concepts and terms. This covers the general computer concepts that the user needs to use when working with computers, e.g., file, file create, and delete. Users with more background knowledge about computers, such as programmers, learn to operate a new system more easily than mere beginners in the computer area.

- The user's knowledge about the task domain.

This covers the theoretical background knowledge the user needs to perform his task. For some applications, the domain is very complicated and the user needs a lot of knowledge to achieve the expected results. This knowledge does not concern the knowledge about dialogue forms or interaction styles, but rather the concepts of the domain.

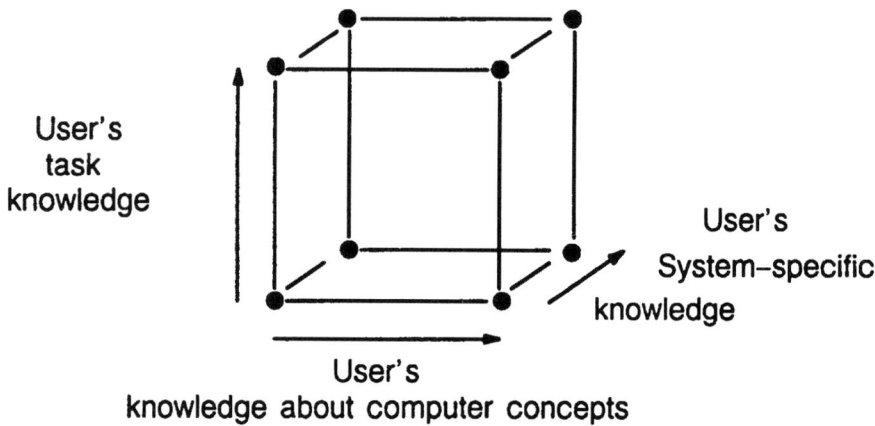

Figure 4: A User Model Based on the User's Knowledge

If a user knows a lot about the task, e.g., engineering design, and does not know anything about computers, he needs completely different assistance than an expert in computer systems who knows nothing about CAD.

3.3 Application Model

Although the necessity to involve the user in the design process is a recognized goal [Shneiderman 87, Foley 87], there is no model that explicitly includes the user during the design and specification of an interactive system. To assist the user at more than one logical level, the representation has to cover several logical levels of the application. For that reason, we use a layered model. Such a model can be found in [Foley et al. 90] and [Moran 81]. Besides user assistance at different logical levels, we pursue the goal of including adaptive mechanisms within the layered model. Using a layered model, one finds that after defining a specific layer (e.g., semantic layer) one must then define the next layer top-down (e.g., syntax layer).

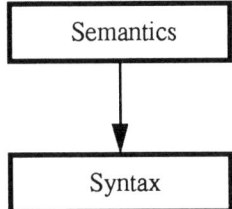

Figure 5: Semantics - Syntax Transformation without an Explicit User's Specification

In this example of defining the syntax, the kind of user has not explicitly been taken into account. Defining the syntax this way means that the user has been considered in an implicit way, and all the users have been assumed as similar. This procedure is repeated for every involved layer. One can imagine that the definition of the syntax (from the semantics) could be different depending on the type of user. For example, users who seldom work with a computer and without any knowledge about computers consider natural language as the proper dialogue form to formulate a command. Computer experts, on the contrary, love shortcuts; they will search for the possibility of doing the task with the least effort possible (e.g., key strokes). Between these extremes, there are several types of users that can be considered in order to give the proper user definition.

Application models based on layers offer good possibilities for structuring the whole system, and they allow the application to be seen from different points of view (the layers). One of the weaknesses of the layered model is that the application has to be represented several times, one representation for every layer. A compromise has to be found between a detailed description and a low complexity; therefore, AIDA considers four layers: the task, semantics, syntax, and interaction layers (Figure 6).

The task level handles and describes the tasks that can be performed with the system. Tasks can be built from several functions and can concern several objects.

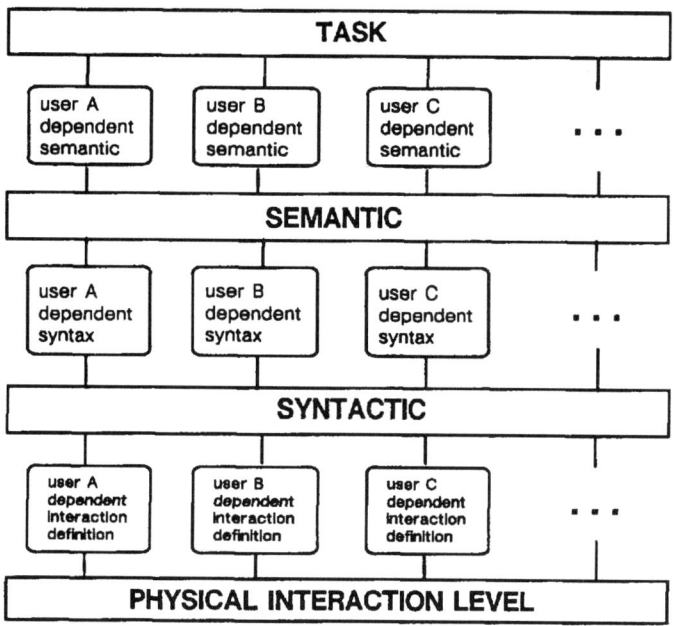

Figure 6: A layered model that explicitly includes the user

The semantic level handles and describes the meaning of the functions and objects that the system offers the user to accomplish his tasks. The semantics are described through the result of the actions and they are linked to the functions. For that reason the semantics are constraint to an operational semantics. This representation has to account for the relation between the user's actions and the result of these actions. A representation of the results and the link to the user's actions allows the comparison of different steps that reach the same result. The ability to represent the results of the user's actions means knowing how to extend the application from the user's way of working. AIDA was designed for a CAD environment. The results of the user's actions in a CAD environment are mainly drawings. Geometrical concepts are a proper way to describe drawings. Because of the necessity of comparing drawings, the semantic representation has to allow analogies to be inferred between them.

In order to gain flexibility the syntax level is divided into two parts:

- the user syntax, which is managed by the Application Model, and
- the syntax of the application, which is the interface to call the functions.

The interaction level handles the input devices and manages the definitions within the input devices; for example, the definition of function keys in a keyboard.

3.4 Monitoring

The monitoring module is informed of every interaction of the user, and then analyzes and records them in a logfile. To analyze the user interactions it uses the Application Model and the User Model.

The monitoring module covers three main tasks:

- Analysis of the logfile's content in order to get an indication of the user's knowledge level. From this analysis the user is classified in the User Model.

- Analysis of the user's interactions in order to recognize operational semantics. The results of this analysis are used to generate new commands/macros and also to identify the results of user's actions that are already covered by existing functionality.

- Construction of the relation between the User Model and the Application Model to enable individual assistance.

In our use of the term knowledge within a monitoring environment, we constrain the term to an operational definition. A user has knowledge about a command if the user has theoretical information about the underlying concept and he has the capability to use it. As already mentioned, these concepts are comprised of only geometrical concepts (e.g. orthogonality, parallelism, quadrilateral, etc.) in AIDA's case.

In order to compare concepts, we use their complexity. The complexity of a concept is determined with the help of the cognitive complexity theory [Polson 87].

The number of production rules that describe a concept (based on primitive geometric elements) is the basis for calculating the complexity of the concept.

In the context of knowledge recognition, the knowledge of the user is inferred from the command vocabulary and the complexity of the commands.

The monitor module of AIDA is restricted to the definition of the operational semantics of geometrical objects. This module analyzes the results of the user's actions, taking these restrictions into account. The generation of new commands/macros is restricted to geometrical objects as well as the recognition of discarding commands/macros that are less complex than the one the user has used.

AIDA reacts to user's errors using the knowledge that the system has about the application and about the user. The Application Model provides information if the application layer is where the error occurred; the User Model provides information on the knowledge level of the user.

3.5 AIDA notation

In the following, a notation to represent the application is presented. AIDA is divided into four levels. Between the levels there is a structure similar to production systems in the form of a list which we define as the Methods, with rules of choices. A Method describes how to represent one level in the next higher level. This representation is only valid for pre-described classes of users or for an individual user. A rule of choice in a Method determines the conditions under they are applicable. The representation as mentioned here is dynamic throughout the runtime manipulation of the Methods.

A Method consists of the entity to be represented as the head, followed by a separator "<-", the rule of choice, and the instruction. For example, to define the syntax of a function to delete objects, the dialogue designer has to define the command, the possibilities of the command, and the reaction of the system, all in relation to a user or a class of users.

>   delete objects <- (CoKn == 0; ApKn == 0; TaKn == 0)
>   [layer & user's feedback] del x_1
>   delete objects <-(CoKn == 1; ApKn == 1; TaKn == 1)
>   del $x_1...x_k$
>   delete objects <- (User == Smith) del $x_1...x_k$

where CoKn, ApKn, TaKn are defined as:

> CoKn := user's knowledge about computer concepts
> ApKn := user's knowledge about a specific application
> TaKn := user's knowledge about the task domain
> X_i := objects
> Smith := the name of a user
> [0 ... 1] := the range to map the concepts of the application

One of the key aspects of representing an application is the representation of the meaning of a command: the semantics. One way to represent the semantics of a command is to use the results of the command. It has been already mentioned that AIDA was designed primarily for CAD-Applications; therefore, the results of the user's actions are graphic objects. The graphic objects are represented through nodes and the geometrical relations between them. The kind of geometric relations taken into account depend on the knowledge of the user. In the User Model, the concepts that the user already knows are stored. Only these concepts are considered in the analysis of the graphic object. To clarify how the representation works, consider the following example. Let us suppose there is an application that draws lines and that the user understands both the concept of a line and the concept that a line can be parallel to the x-, y-, and z-axes. Define the following symbols:

> lx: a line parallel to x-axis
> ly: a line parallel to y-axis
> lz: a line parallel to z-axis
> la: any line that does not apply in the other cases

Each node will have a list of the connections that originate there, e.g., n(K, [list of connections]). In this list of connections the connected nodes are labeled with their type of connection. For instance, n(K, [v(B, lx)]) indicates that node K is connected with node B with a line parallel to the x-axis.

Furthermore, let us say the user draws the object depicted in Figure 7.

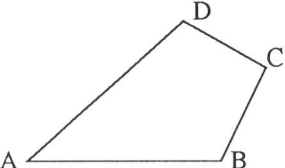

Figure 7: Result of a sequence of user actions

The AIDA system will produce the following representation of the object in this case:

Graphic object := [n(A, [v(B, lx), v(D, la)]), n(B, [v(A, lx), v(C, la)]),
n(C, [v(B, la), v(D, la)]), n(D, [v(A, la), v(C, la)])]

From this situation it is possible to recognize that either:

(1) The command to draw a such quadrilateral already exits (The produced representation by the user matched an existing one).

If the user does not use it, the system will react with feedback informing the user of the existence of such a command.

(2) The command to draw this figure does not exist.

If the user repeatedly draws this object, the system will react with an offer to make a new command automatically.

If the user knows that he is going to need such an object often, it is possible to tell the system to analyze the object and to make a new command from it.

4 CONCLUSIONS AND FUTURE WORK

All the modules and the notation were implemented. The AIDA prototype was programmed in PROLOG. To create and manage the user interface, SIEMCAD [Bittner et al. 88] was used. SIEMCAD was based on a mixed control architecture. As a consequence of the monitoring module needing all the events that the user interface gets, and of the control architecture being mixed, we had to change SIEMCAD internally to an external control architecture. Although the application had more functionality than a simple drawing program (Figure 8), the performance was acceptable.

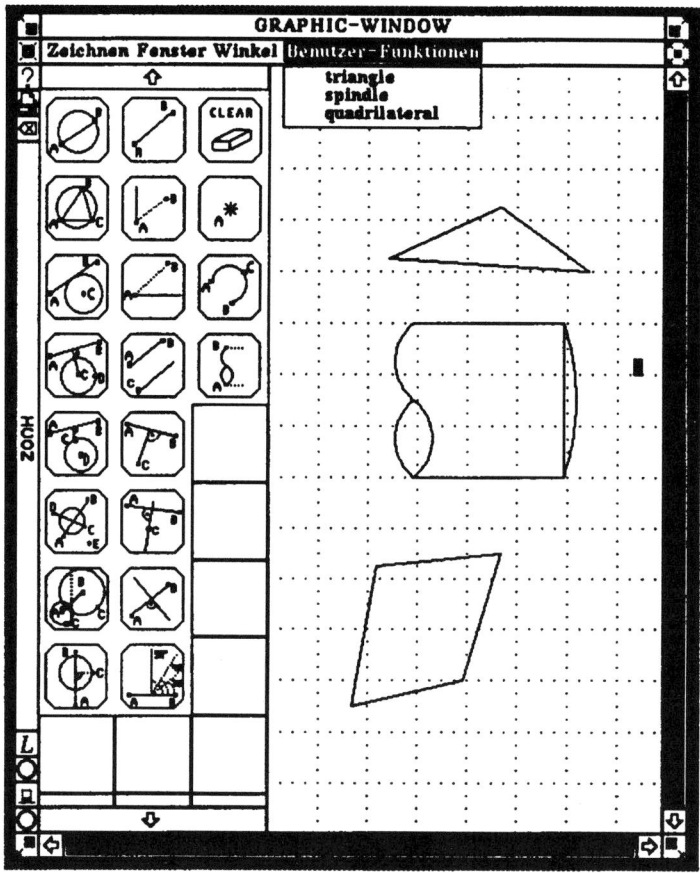

Figure 8: Printout of the AIDA User Interface

The user has access to the application's functionality through icons, menus, and commands. The amount of functionality offered by the icons and menus is restricted to the classification of the user in the User Model. In order to allow exploratory learning the user has access to the full system's functionality through a command line. The error and assistance messages appear in an extra window. AIDA offers two possibilities to create new commands/macros. First, AIDA will react by asking the user if he wants to create a new command/macro for a graphic object which he repeatedly accesses.

Second, the user has the possibility to initiate the process of creating a new command/macro. The user interface has a button for this purpose on the left side of the window, marked with the letter "L". In Figure 8 the user has already created three new commands/macros: triangle, spindle, and quadrilateral.

To assure that the adaptive system will be always better, or at least equal to, the non-adaptive system, we decided to:

(1) fix the amount of functionality based on the user's knowledge.

(2) expand the application through new commands/macros introduced by the user.

(3) create the error messages from both the logical level of the error and the user's knowledge.

To accomplish this functionality AIDA analyses the operational semantics, errors, command vocabulary, and complexity of the commands. There are more factors that could be measured and will be considered in the next version of AIDA in order to make better assumptions about the user; e.g., help requests, the link between a help request and a successful command, and the link between errors and the lack of knowledge of a concept.

Another major goal that needs to be pursued is to expand AIDA to other application domains, e.g., Computer Based Training in CAD, Layout systems, and industrial control.

REFERENCES

[Bittner et al. 88]
Bittner, H.; Cote Munoz, J.; Eser, F.; Frantz, D.(1988), *SIEMCAD - A User Interface Management System for Integrating Electronical and Mechanical CAD*, In: *Man-Machine Systems, Analysis, Design and Evaluation*, The IFAC/IFIP/IEA/IFORS Conference, Oulu, Finland.

[Benyon et al. 87]
Benyon, D.; Innocent, P.; Murray, D.(1987), *System Adaptivity and the Modelling of Stereotypes*. In: Human-Computer Interaction - INTERACT'87 / Bullinger, H.-J.; Shackel, B. (Eds.). Amsterdam: Elsevier Science Publishers B.V. (North-Holland), 245-253.

[Bösser 87]
Bösser, T.(1987), *Learning in Man-Computer-Interaction*. Berlin, Heidelberg, New York, London: Springer-Verlag.

[Browne et al. 90]
Browne, D.; Norman, M.; Riches, D.(1990), *Why Build Adaptive Systems?* In: *Adaptive User Interfaces* / Browne, D.; Totterdell, P.; Norman, M. (Eds.). London: Academic Press.

[Campbell et al. 88]
Campbell, G.; Elkerton, J.; Judd, W.; Walker, J. (1988), *Online Help Systems: Design and Implementation Issues (Panel)*. In: Proceedings of the CHI 88 Conference on Human Factors in Computing Systems, Washington, D.C. / Soloway, E.; Frye, D.; Sheppard, S. B. (Eds.). New York: ACM, 287-288.

[Carrol & Carrithers 84]
Carrol, J. M.; Carrithers, C.(1984), *Training Wheels in a User Interface*. In: Communications of the ACM 27, 8, 800-806.

[Clowes et al. 85]
Clowes, I.; Cole, I.; Arshad, F.; Hopkins, C.; Hockley, A.(1985), *User Modelling Techniques for Interactive Systems.* In *People and Computers: Designing the Interface* / Johnson, P.; Cook, S. (Eds.). Cambridge: Cambridge University Press, 35-45.

[Cote 90]
Cote M., J.A.(1990): *AIDA - Ein an den Benutzer angepaßtes Graphisch-Interaktives System.* PhD. thesis, Department of Computer Science, Technical University of Darmstadt. D17.

[Edmonds 81]
Edmonds, E.A.(1988), *Adaptive Man-Computer Interfaces.* In: *Computing Skills and the User Interface* / Coomb, M.J.; Alty, J.L. (Eds.). London, Orlando: Academic Press, 387-426.

[Egan 88]
Egan, Dennis E.(1988), *Individual Differences in Human-Computer Interaction.* In: *Handbook of Human-Computer Interaction* / Helander, M. (Ed.). Amsterdam: Elsevier Science Publishers B.V. (North Holland), 543-568.

[Elkerton 88]
Elkerton, J.(1988), *Online Aiding for Computer Interfaces.* In: *Handbook of Human-Computer Interaction* / Helander, M. (Ed.). Amsterdam: Elsevier Science Publisher B.V. (North-Holland), 345-364.

[Foley 87]
Foley, J.(1987), *Tutorial on Designing User-Computer Interfaces.* In: CHI + GI 1987, Human Factors in Computing Systems and Graphic Interfaces, 4/6/87, Toronto, Canada.

[Foley et al. 90]
Foley, J.; Van Dam, A.; Feiner, S.K.; Hughes, J.H.(1990): *Computer Graphics: principles and practice.* Reading, Massachusetts: Addison Wesley Publishing Company.

[Moran 81]
Moran, Th.P.(1981), *The Command Language Grammar: a representation for the user interface of interactive Computer systems.* In: IJMMS 15 (1981), 3-50.

[Neal 89]
Neal, L.R.(1989), *The Role of User Models in System Design.* PhD. thesis, Center for Research in Computing Technology, Harvard University. TR-18-89.

[Polson 87]
Polson, P.G.(1987), *A Quantitative Theory of Human-Computer Interaction.* In: *Interfacing Thought, Cognitive Aspects of Human-Computer Interaction* / Carroll, J.M (Ed.). Cambridge, MA, London, England: MIT Press.

[Rich 89]
Rich, E.(1989), *Stereotypes and User Modeling.* In: *User Models in Dialog Systems* / Kobsa, A.; Wahlster, W. (Eds.). Berlin, Heidelberg, New York, London, Paris, Tokyo: Springer-Verlag, 35-51.

[Shneiderman 87]
Shneiderman, B.(1987), *Designing the User Interface, Strategies for Effective Human-Computer Interaction.* Reading, Massachusetts: Addison Wesley Publishing Company.

Adaptive User Interface Design and Its Dependence on Structure

D. Peter Sanderson and Siegfried Treu

Southwest Missouri State University
Springfield, USA

University of Pittsburgh
Pittsburgh, USA

ABSTRACT

Users exhibit wide ranges of knowledge, experience, skills, objectives, and preferences in their dealings with computers. Especially for inexperienced, learning users, the interface system should be designed to adapt to and compensate for individual user differences. But, creating an adaptive interface is much more easily prescribed than carried out. The designer needs a lot of methodological help. This paper is based on experiences gained from the design of an adaptive interface system (prototype) called N-CHIME (NCR-sponsored Cohesive, HSL-oriented, Interactive Modeling Environment). HSL is the Hierarchical Simulation Language. A brief overview of N-CHIME and its capabilities is presented in the introduction. That is followed by description of a profile of conditions, under which interface adaptation to the user becomes appropriate, possible, and effective. The different kinds of structure, which were utilized in support of rendering the interface adaptive, are discussed. Structure was pervasive in this entire interface design effort: 1) in the high-level, three-pronged design methodology, 2) in the composite, modular interface system, 3) in the object-oriented software architecture, and 4) in the context-specific knowledge base organization. In addition, the user's interaction with the system is carefully structured to provide goal-oriented guidance in the application domain (modeling and simulation). Adaptation decisions affect the user within the context of a "user state scenario graph", which is a high-level graph of user-visible states encapsulating the functionality available to the user at each point of an interactive session. An example is included to illustrate the adaptations. The paper ends in discussion of observations and conclusions.

1 INTRODUCTION

As is evident from the distinctions between "adaptive" and "adaptable" interfaces [Fischer 93] and from the relevant framework of taxonomic parameters [Dieterich et al. 93], the designer of an adaptive human-computer interface (HCI) is faced with a myriad of decisions on why, where, when, and how to provide for adaptation. The task of HCI design is thereby complicated considerably beyond the normal task of creating non-adaptive interfaces. Further, based on the limited literature thus far available, much room exists for differences in design emphases, approaches, styles, and overall design philosophy. It is therefore incumbent on those who report on their work in this area to justify their design perspectives and relevant methodological considerations as clearly as possible.

Accordingly, this paper presents our view and approach to designing the adaptive component of an interface system named N-CHIME (NCR-sponsored, Cohesive, HSL-oriented, Interactive Modeling Environment). The overall design methodology for N-CHIME was reported at length [Treu et al. 91], prior to the addition of an adaptive capability [Sanderson 91, Sanderson & Treu 91]. Only a brief overview of the N-CHIME design is given below. However, it is important to point out that the design methodology, which is itself very structured, was formulated in anticipation of later introjection of adaptation. That fact is relevant to the purpose of this paper.

Our experience with N-CHIME suggests that the comprehensive design of an adaptive interface requires a very systematic, highly structured approach. In other words, the objective of causing the system to successfully adapt to the user is dependent on meaningful definition and effective utilization of several important structures. The structures are representative of each of the methodology, the user, and the system. This structure dependency is the theme of this paper. In our view, it is especially significant for:

(1) users who are novices in an application area, trying to learn more about it and improve their skills in using it, or who perhaps are individuals without any expectation (or aspiration) of becoming experts; in either case, the users are in need of, and likely to be receptive to, being carefully guided or directed in the use of the interface system and the application domain;

(2) applications that are "structurable," that is, that are conducive to having organizational paradigms superimposed, in a manner that will enable the designer to provide the user with assistance (in various localities and contexts) and goal-oriented guidance (e.g. according to various task plans).

Thus, our perspective on adaptive interface design is significantly influenced by wanting to serve certain types of users who have need for structure-contingent, adaptive support, in conjunction with certain kinds of structurable applications. The major categories of supportive structures are described in Section 3. But, toward taking proper advantage of them, the designer must first know the conditions under which adaptation is to take place. It is necessary to understand in advance the answers to questions like: why adapt? to whom? where? when? how? and with what?

These questions are addressed in Section 2. Once they are adequately understood by the designer, and once they are suitably mapped into the modules and nodes of the supportive structures (Section 3), the framework for adaptive interface design becomes established.

Overview of N-CHIME

In 1987-88, our research group designed and implemented in prototype form a new, Hierarchical Simulation programming Language, HSL [Sanderson et al. 91]. That language was expected to become the basis for interactive modeling and simulation of systems. The prospective users of this application were to include non-experts in modeling & simulation methodology, such as salespersons. They were to be able to illustrate potential system performance for their customers, by carrying out dynamic modeling (using a graphics editor) and simulation (programmed in HSL) of selected system configurations. The hardware and software platform was to be PC-based.

To that end, it was clear that a very supportive interface system, namely N-CHIME, was essential. Our group developed the design methodology for it, as well as implemented and tested a prototype version, over the 1989-90 time frame [Treu et al. 91]. N-CHIME basically is an intermediary software package, situated between the user and the HSL-based application domain. It is prepared to present the user with a variety of widgets, techniques, and tools, all intended to

(1) Facilitate,

(2) Provide Context, and

(3) NOT Constrain

the user in carrying out tasks in modeling and simulating a system of interest. These three goals were stipulated as user-oriented design principles. The fourth goal, specified from the outset of the project but purposely delayed until late 1990 and 1991 [Sanderson 91], was to

(4) Adapt to Individual User Needs

with respect to satisfying each of the other three principles. As a result of this work, we identified the conditions for rendering an interface adaptive from the standpoint of the designer. They are outlined below.

2 ADAPTATION CONDITIONS

It is not appropriate to talk about adaptive interface design as if it were some kind of singular or homogeneous result to be achieved. Too many variables are involved; too many different versions of adaptation are possible. To provide guidance to the designer on how to proceed toward selecting and developing the version desired, it is essential to ask and answer questions about why adapt? to whom? where? when? how? and with what? We call these the "conditions" for adaptation. They are to be distinguished from the "criteria" for adapting and the "rule conditions" of the expert system (Section 3.3), which are used in actually making adaptation decisions. Adaptation conditions are discussed in the following subsections, with reference to the framework shown in Figure 1.

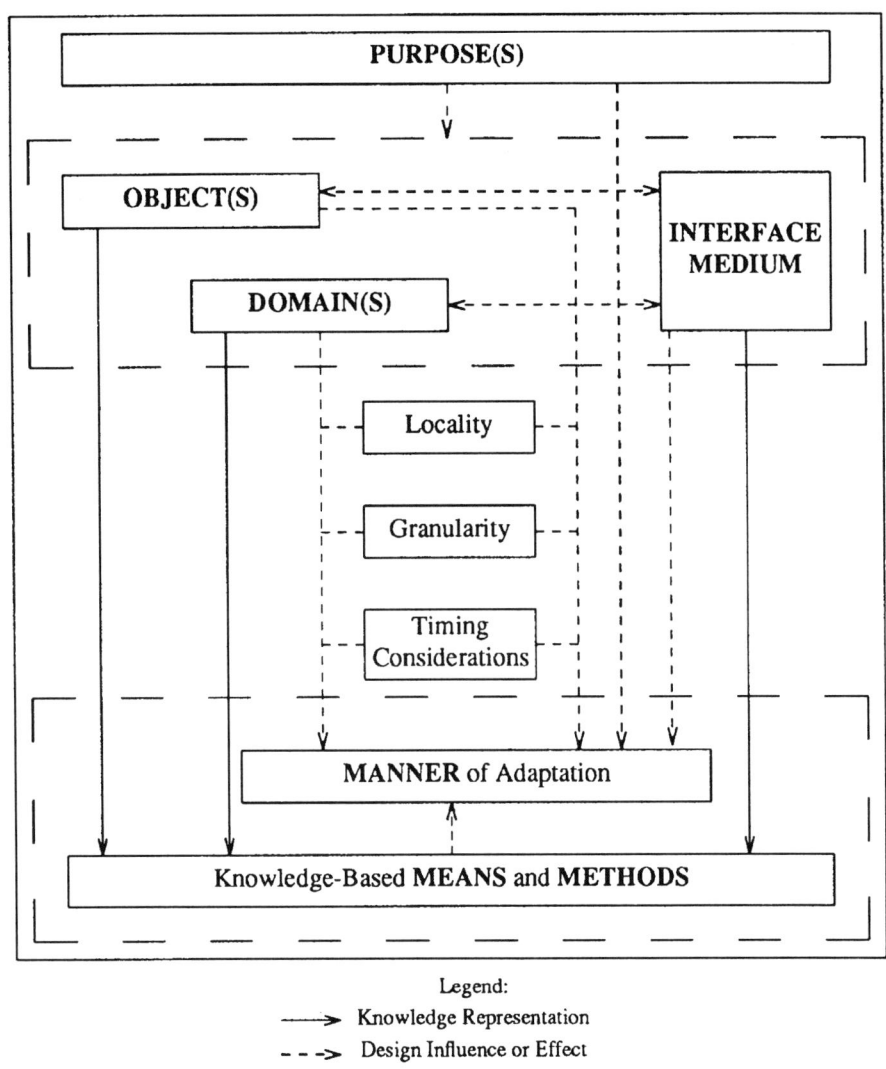

Figure 1: Framework for adaptation conditions

2.1 Purpose

Why adapt? Indeed, there may be good reasons not to have the system adapt dynamically to the user. For example, expert users working in very familiar application domains may wish to have direct, explicit control over certain system functionality and initiate shortcuts on their own, subject to whatever limits (in being "adaptable") the system imposes. This is somewhat analogous to an automobile driver who insists on changing gears, using a manual transmission. On the other hand, for the novice user, such as envisioned for N-CHIME, automatic transmission is a very desirable option.

Actually we have thus far only asked whether to adapt. Once it is determined that adaptation is really needed or desired, the more detailed purpose(s) must be prescribed. They can be couched within the design principles, or goals, to which the interface is to adhere. For example, if a stated principle in HCI design is to cause the interface to be "facilitative" of the user's interaction with the system, then any adaptation decisions should be consistent with that goal. That is, depending on the needs of a particular user to whom the interface is to adapt, the adaptation behavior should be facilitative, such as by enabling the user to complete tasks more quickly or with less knowledge and effort.

2.2 Object

Adapt to whom? The object of adaptation, not to be confused with the objective, is the intended beneficiary of adaptive behavior. In a more general, symmetric model for adaptation [Tyler & Treu 86], the object of adaptation could be either the computer (to which the user adapts) or the user (to whom the computer adapts). Our interest here is only in the latter alternative, that is, the user being the object, or the adaptee, while the computer is the adapter.

Having decided that, it then becomes important for the designer to thoroughly analyze the user and develop a user model (Section 3.3) which can be utilized in making adaptation decisions.

2.3 Domain

Knowing who is to benefit from adaptation does not yet identify what is to be adapted within the environment of a computer system. In other words, where or in which domain(s) does the adaptation take effect?

Several potential domains are subject to being dynamically changed for the benefit of the user:

(1) the way the chosen application software appears to work, at a low (command-specific) level of interaction with the user;

(2) the way the interface software/hardware appear(s) to work in terms of functional capabilities, not necessarily dependent on the application;

(3) the way the interface appears to work in terms of guiding, directing, and explaining objects and tasks to a user at a high level of interaction with the application.

For the N-CHIME prototype, our interests were primarily focused on the third domain. However, the system can be extended to encompass the other domains also.

As shown in Figure 1, the objects of adaptation, namely the users, and the adaptation domains are necessarily associated with the interface medium. The general result is the three-module composite: the user, the interface, and the application. Knowledge about each of them must be represented in conjunction with the expert system (Section 3.3) that renders the adaptation decisions for N-CHIME. This is suggested by the solid, downward arrows in Figure 1.

But, as also shown in Figure 1, identifying the domain that is subject to being changed is not enough. The designer must analyze and structure the domain toward meeting the conditions of

> *Locality*: exactly where, in which states in the user-domain interaction should changes be made?
>
> *Granularity*: at what level of generality (e.g. high-level goal-oriented decisions) or specificity (e.g. low-level commands) within a locality should changes be made?

The adaptation domain and the locality and granularity within it all relate to the question: adapt where? One more related condition deals with when to adapt, under what circumstances, or the timing for making changes.

2.4 Timing Considerations

If a user while interacting with a particular application domain encounters a certain locality and level of granularity, the interface can be designed to trigger a form of adaptation at that time. This represents one kind of timing. But, other kinds exist. For example, the timing can be triggered by current circumstances, such as how well the user seems to be prepared for performing the task at hand, as reflected by the stored user model (which may just have changed); or some real-time consideration about the critical nature of the application, the completion of which has become more urgent today (than it was yesterday). This means that adaptation does not necessarily take place consistently, in a particular context (e.g. locality, granularity); it may instead be affected by circumstances involving other factors including how well the user seems to be doing. The user is, after all, the object of adaptation.

Hence, conditions for designing an adaptive interface, as they are depicted by Figure 1, become components of the criteria for making adaptation decisions. That is, when the current context (locality, granularity) and circumstances (various timing considerations) meet the requirements for an adaptive action, that action is invoked. This is basically the format of a production rule, as discussed in Section 3.3.

2.5 Manner

Adapt how? In what ways? After determining why, when, where, and for whom to adapt, the really difficult task arises: selecting the ways or forms of adaptation that are possible and useful. These are of course dependent on answers to the previous questions. As indicated by dashed arrows in Figure 1, the purpose, object, interface, and domain conditions collectively influence the manner of adaptation. The manner is also contingent on available means and methods designed to carry out the adaptation.

Adaptation actions, their ranges of values for variables, and options must be clearly defined. For example, under certain conditions, two or more alternative forms of assistance might be available. Or, in certain states of interaction, a complex decision point might be bypassed because the current knowledge about the user suggests that it is advisable to do so.

2.6 Means and Methods

Finally, the different available ways or forms of adaptation must be implementable. That is, the designer must decide: with what?

In general, the means and methods can be based on

(1) Knowledge bases that represent each of the adaptation object, domain, and interface medium, and

(2) Rule-based expert system techniques that utilize the knowledge bases, according to stipulated conditions, and then invoke changes.

The changes are either visible to the user in the interface, and/or in the knowledge bases themselves thereby further affecting future adaptation decisions. Accordingly, the designer of an adaptive interface must carefully formulate condition-action rules for an expert system and then incorporate the latter within the architecture of the interface system. All of this must be done with the hope of meeting the purpose(s) for adaptation that were originally prescribed.

Such a design process is very complex. In our experience, it is therefore very useful to have supportive structures available, both for purposes of guiding the designer and for representation of the required modules, conditions, criteria, and forms of adaptation. In the next section, we describe the major kinds of supportive structures and illustrate them by means of examples.

3 SUPPORTIVE STRUCTURES

For any particular HCI design, the adaptation conditions that are generically defined in Section 2 must be systematically considered and specified in detail. Based on our experience with N-CHIME, the designer and, later on, the user of an adaptive user interface (AUI) can obtain useful assistance from certain supportive structures. With reference to Figure 2, the categories of such structures are outlined as follows. In each case, the applicable adaptation conditions are highlighted in capital letters:

(1) *Structured Design Methodology*: by virtue of the structured process, ensuring that the designer attend carefully to the adaptation PURPOSE and to the analysis of the adaptation OBJECT(S) and DOMAIN(S), to ensure that the appropriate forms of adaptation (MANNER) are provided through the available INTERFACE MEDIUM.

(2) *Structured Interaction* (Between User and Application): with the assumption that a "structurable" application is involved, the designer must analyze the adaptation DOMAIN and OBJECT, both separately and in conjunction. The result should include (a) representational schemes (structures) that are user-recognizable and that can guide and direct the user during operational interaction with the AUI, and (b) decisions based on interaction context (LOCALITY, GRANULARITY) and TIMING CONSIDERATIONS, and of course on the appropriate MANNER of adaptation at any point of the interaction.

(3) *Structured Knowledge Representation*: as it reflects the major modules (OBJECT, DOMAIN, INTERFACE) and provides the MEANS and METHODS, using suitable expert system techniques, for making and carrying out the adaptation decisions at various places of the interaction.

(4) *Interface Software Architecture*: which must provide the INTERFACE MEDIUM capable of accommodating the adaptation MEANS and METHODS, within the structured interaction, in a way that will support adaptation performance as desired.

These four categories of supportive structures are described in the following subsections. The first two are summarized relatively briefly, with reference to already published papers. The last two are treated in more detail, thereby giving an overview of the design features of the expert system and its place in the modular software architecture of N-CHIME. To illustrate the structures and the relevant adaptation conditions, an application-specific example of the use of N-CHIME is developed.

3.1 Structured Design Methodology

Just as is true of structured programming and other techniques representative of good software engineering, adaptive interface design benefits from suitably structured methodology. For N-CHIME we developed a three-pronged approach [Treu et al. 91]. It is broadly modeled by Figure 3.

The three prongs accentuate early attention to the individual capabilities and limitations of each of the three modules involved in AUI design. For example, the designer is first expected to consider the needs of the target user, independent of the application domain, and, likewise, the nature of the application, regardless of the limits of the particular type of user to be served. Then, it becomes necessary to try to match them up, that is to analyze them in combination. We feel that the designer becomes better prepared to decide when

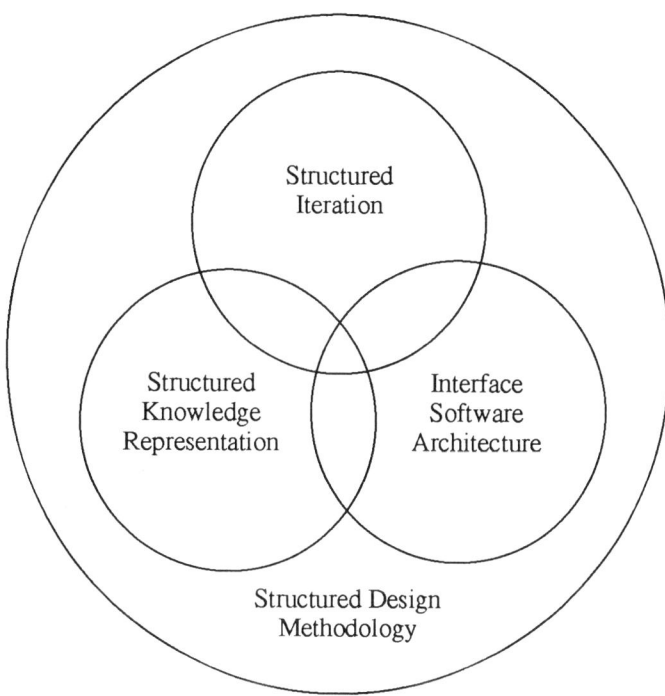

Figure 2: Categories of supportive structures

and where and how adaptation should take place, after the interacting parties have been analyzed first individually and then in conjunction.

Very early in the AUI design methodology, the designer should be required to determine the PURPOSE, OBJECT, and DOMAIN of adaptation. As suggested in Section 2.1, adaptation purpose can be linked directly to the principles specified as design goals for the interface. For the N-CHIME project, this meant that the interface was to adapt to the objects of adaptation, namely its users, in a manner that would variously 1) facilitate, 2) provide context in, and 3) not constrain (i.e. not preclude user learning) during interaction. These are the user-oriented principles mentioned in Section 1.

The emphasis on adapting "variously," or differently, clearly pertains to the fact that users exhibit an amazing range of individual differences. In general, they need or want very different kinds of context-specific help, guidance, or instruction. The AUI design methodology must, therefore, insist on early analysis of intended users and their needs. This is part of Prong 1 in Figure 3. For N-CHIME, we categorized the intended users into novices,

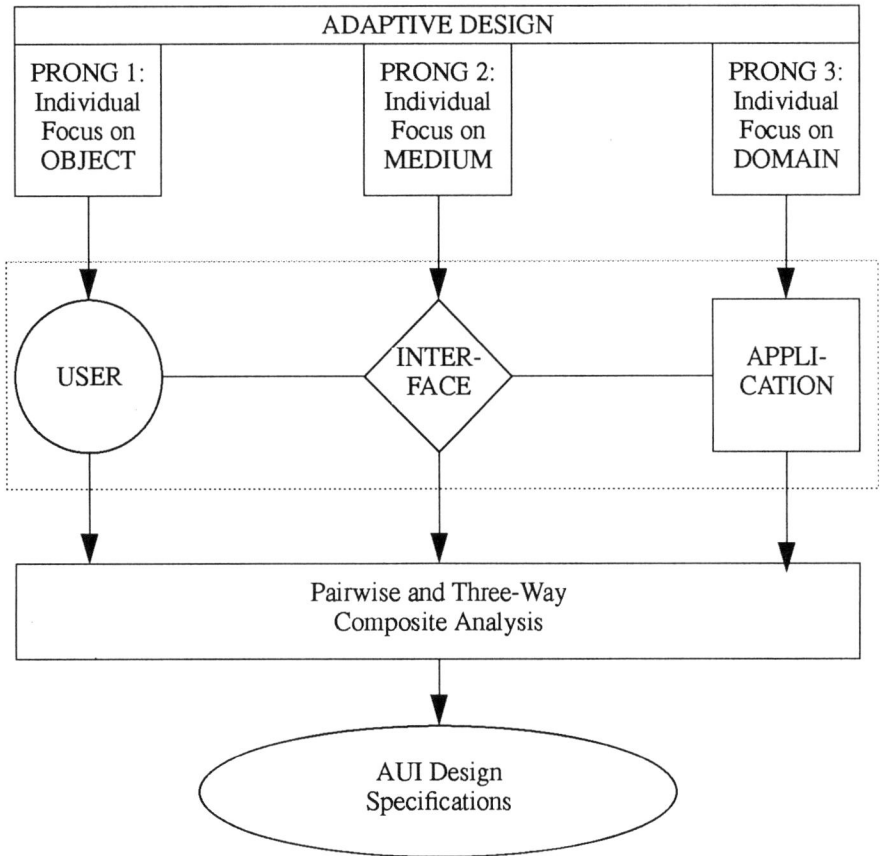

Figure 3: Three-pronged design

apprentices, and experts. The adaptive capability was to treat each user, in part, according to the needs implied by his/her assigned user category.

In addition to the purpose and objects of adaptation, the adaptation domain must be formulated early in the methodology. This is subsumed by Prong 3 of Figure 3. For N-CHIME, this domain was limited to high-level guidance, direction, and explanation, as the user follows a selected path toward reaching his/her modeling and simulation goal. An example to illustrate the high-level state scenarios involved is presented in following sections.

It confirms how a structured design methodology should lead the designer to create user-oriented structures for the interaction itself (Section 3.2). Also, the knowledge-based MEANS and METHODS (Section 3.3) for implementing the adaptation must be determined, along with the exact MANNER of adaptation (Section 3.4) prescribed to serve the previously specified purpose and objects in the target domain. Finally, the INTERFACE MEDIUM (Prong 2, Figure 3) must be developed, as described in Section 3.5.

3.2 Structured Interaction

A user generally wants or needs guidance and direction. User performance and satisfaction are likely to improve as a result [Tyler & Treu 89]. This is especially true for a novice who is interacting with an application domain that is structured into clearly defined states, each with a limited number of available functions and actions that can ultimately enable task completion. Totally free-form interaction is neither realistic nor desirable for many users.

The application of interest in N-CHIME is modeling systems and then simulating them using HSL-programmed versions of resulting models. Detailed analysis of that application led to creation of a user-visible state scenario graph [Treu et al. 91]. This is a directed graph that consists of high-level states or nodes (H-nodes) and transitions (arcs) between them. A sequence of such state transitions constitutes a scenario (or path) through the graph. As is described in Sections 3.3 and 3.4 below, each H-node, in turn, provides context for lower-level support nodes, including special nodes that reflect the expert system rules designed to trigger adaptation actions whenever specified criteria are satisfied. The user can, therefore, follow high-level paths of H-nodes, with adaptive support provided whenever invoked, in order to reach his/her objectives within the application domain.

To illustrate, we have extracted a subgraph from the above-mentioned user state scenario graph and display it in Figure 4. The high-level states and the scenarios running through them are labeled. This enables referencing in the following sections. They describe the means, methods, and manner of adaptation experienced by different N-CHIME users as they proceed on different paths.

3.3 Structured Knowledge Representation

The MEANS and METHODS for making and carrying out N-CHIME adaptation decisions are provided by a rule-based expert system. This interface component is dependent on suitably structured knowledge bases. Most expert systems are designed to carry out either analysis, to analyze and interpret situations, or synthesis, to construct goal-oriented solutions [Buchanan & Duda 83]. Our N-CHIME situation called for a combination of the two. It is analytic because the interface interprets interaction activity for the purpose of classifying individual users. It is synthetic because interaction techniques and advice must be tailored to individual users and situations. Further, the expert system chosen for N-CHIME is of the control type [Hayes-Roth et al. 83], because it generally addresses the problem of interpreting, predicting, repairing and monitoring system behaviors. Finally, the expert system is a production system [Buchanan & Shortliffe 84], consisting of a set of production rules, which specify the expert system semantics; a working memory to dynamically maintain the system state; and a rule interpreter to control rule evaluation and firing.

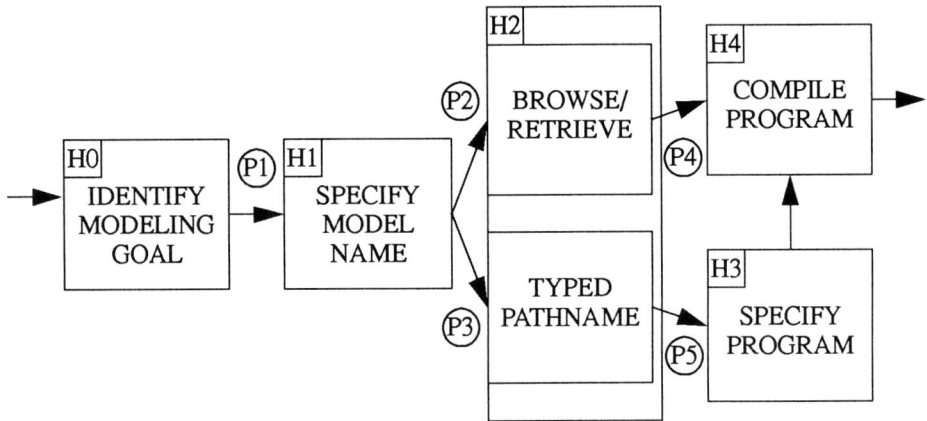

Figure 4: Subgraph of high-level state scenario graph

Several important considerations apply to how the expert system must be embedded in the interface. It must act on the user's behalf without the user necessarily being aware of its activities. Most information needed for consultation is contained in a knowledge model of the individual user, thus minimizing manual input. Also, the expert system's run-time performance must be very efficient, if the user is to remain unaware of its existence. A third consideration is the multifaceted domain that the expert system must utilize. It is outlined below.

The expert system developed for N-CHIME is modeled in Figure 5. It features the modular partitioning of production rules for computational efficiency and use of individual user models as working memory. The high-level state scenario graph, although external to the expert system, helps determine which production rules are evaluated.

The essential steps in developing an expert system are to define the problem, identify the types of relevant knowledge, and determine how to represent the knowledge [Rolston 88]. The problem in N-CHIME was to control user interaction through dynamic modification of the visible user interface. The other two steps are discussed below.

Expert systems simulate human expertise and reasoning processes by applying domain-specific knowledge and inferences, rather than trying to model generic expert behavior. Consistent with the three-pronged N-CHIME design methodology, the stored knowledge must be multifaceted in nature. The user, interface, and application are all represented in Figure 5. The user is hypothesized to hold some subset of knowledge about the interface and application. The expert system likewise contains knowledge about the interface and application, as well as knowledge about the user and what the user knows. The user model

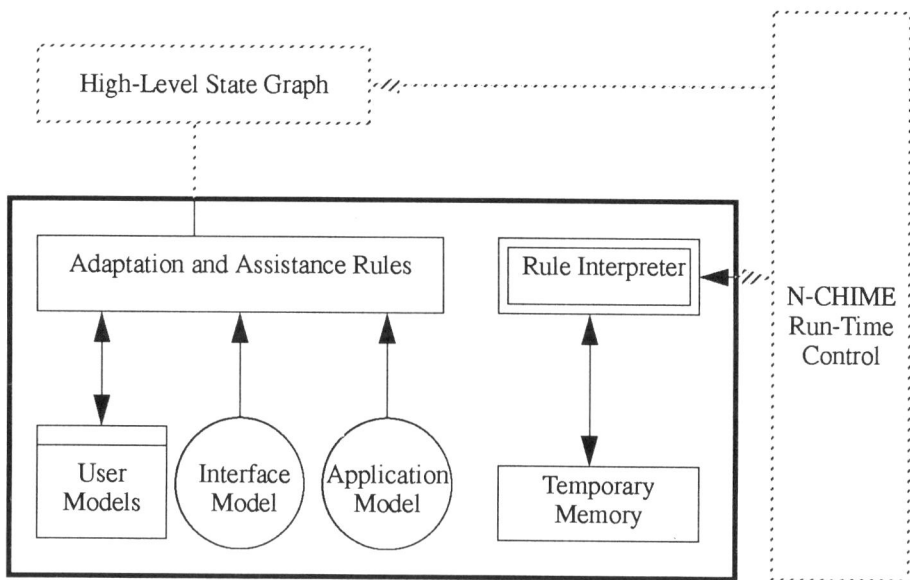

Figure 5: Embedded N-CHIME expert system with connections to outside modules [Sanderson 91]

is distinguished from the others because it is modified dynamically to reflect the user's expanding knowledge and experience gained through N-CHIME use.

Knowledge in a production system is represented primarily through rules. However, the production system can be augmented with other schemes for knowledge representation to serve a particular purpose [Aikins 83]. For N-CHIME the set of production rules was partitioned into modular subsets, each associated with a high-level interaction state [Mahling & Lefkowitz 89]. This enhances rule maintenance as well as performance efficiency. In addition, the user, interface and application models provide supporting knowledge for the production rules. This combined representation scheme resembles that developed for the CENTAUR expert system [Aikins 84], in which rule-based structures were linked into a network representing their relationships.

Each of the three components of the resulting N-CHIME knowledge representation scheme, shown in Figure 6, is further described below.

3.3.1 Knowledge Representation: States

One approach to providing guidance and direction to computer users is to surround the user's current focus and activity with suitable, high-level structural patterns. This approach

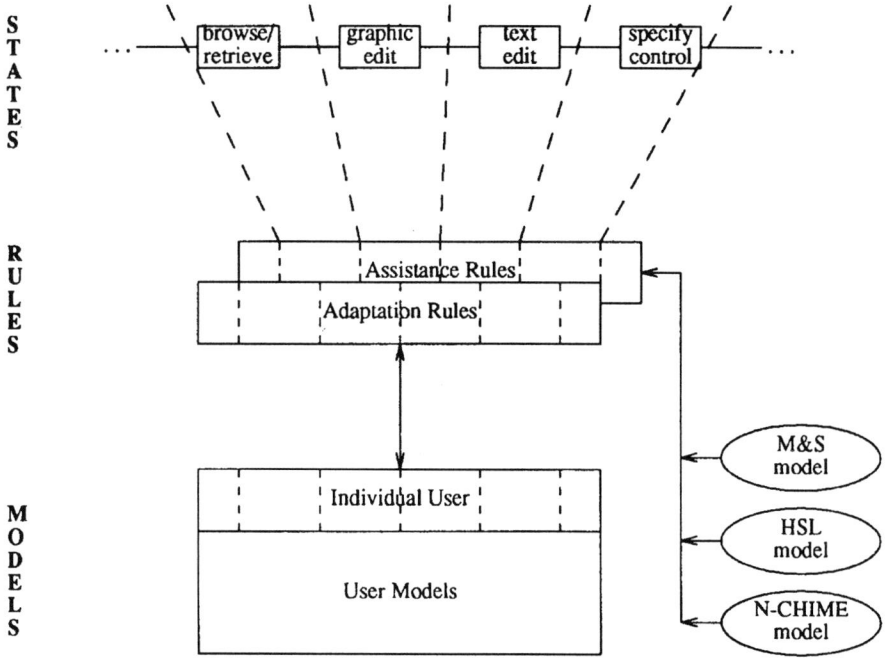

Figure 6: N-CHIME three-layer knowledge representation scheme

is realized in N-CHIME through its high-level user state scenario graph. Task plans, which are pre-defined paths through the graph, serve to guide the user toward achieving his/her specified goals. Referring to the subgraph in Figure 4, the high-level states are indicated by the boxes labeled H0 through H4. Each is represented by an H-node in the interface.

The explicit representation of goal- and plan-oriented knowledge [Black et al. 87] provides several benefits for the expert system designer. The state graph serves as the basis for organizing and linking other knowledge, as can be observed by inspection of Figure 6. The dashed lines in that figure illustrate the partitioning of knowledge by state. This organization facilitates knowledge maintenance, including possible extensions to include new and novel task plans. The state graph also directs rule selection, allowing only those rules relevant to the current situation to be evaluated. This improves run-time efficiency.

3.3.2 Knowledge Representation: Rules

The second component of the N-CHIME knowledge representation scheme consists of production rules to control the adaptation and assistance features. An adaptation decision made by N-CHIME is based on one or more criteria, such as timing considerations and user characteristics. Several are listed below. Each MANNER of adaptation to be applied as the result of such a decision must be implemented by a programmed method. Several N-CHIME adaptation methods are listed below. Not all adaptation criteria are pertinent to all methods.

Adaptation criteria and methods are applied directly in the formulation of expert system rules. The term "criterion" is defined to be "a standard on which a judgement or decision may be based" [Gove 63]. Therefore, adaptation criteria may be utilized as rule conditions. Adaptation methods, because they specify system behavior, correspond to the rule actions.

Rule Conditions

Several adaptation criteria may be included in the condition of an N-CHIME rule. Each represents one dimension of the current state of the system or the user. Expert system knowledge about the user, together with contextual information (e.g., current high-level state and task plan), form the basis for specifying N-CHIME rule conditions. The criteria considered in N-CHIME rule conditions include:

1. Position in user state scenario graph.
2. Session goal, as stated at the beginning of the session.
3. user's level of expertise in use of: N-CHIME, HSL, M&S, etc.
4. Command selection.
5. Stated preferences.
6. Past behavior in same high-level state.
7. Frequency of use and time lapse since previous use of tools.
8. Recent command history.

Rule Actions

The action part of a rule "fires" when all the rule conditions are met. The actions listed below implement several different N-CHIME adaptation methods. For instance, the action part of assistance rules produce explanations. Other rules serve to record user behavior as evidence for some future adaptation decision. Actions considered by N-CHIME include:

1. Tailor the output in a certain way.
2. Act on a stated preference.
3. By-pass a choice point.
4. Provide guidance/feedback supportive of a declared goal.
5. Produce an explanation.
6. Enable interaction modes (e.g. command shortcuts)
7. Update user model parameter.
8. Accumulate evidence of user behavior.

Organization of Rules

Several factors motivate the need to impose structure on the body of N-CHIME production rules through a logical grouping scheme. One is the diverse nature of N-CHIME rule conditions, which can be quite confusing to the rule base administrator. Modularity also makes good software engineering sense. In addition, grouping the rules so that only a subset need be evaluated at a given time reduces system response time, critical for an embedded expert system such as this.

The highest-level partitioning of rules is into those responsible for adaptation based on user command activity, and those responsible for presenting assistance when the user requests it. At the next level, rules are grouped into sets and each set is attached to the H-node representing the relevant high-level user state. Thus a rule set is evaluated only at runtime only when its H-node represents the current state of interaction. There is no reason to restrict the attachment of rules only to H-nodes. For example, when the user selects an operation and begins using the software tool that has been defined for it, he/she enters a local interaction context which may have its own set of states and plans. Although adaptation at this local level was not a focus of this project, the same principles apply.

3.3.3 Knowledge Representation: Models

A thorough analysis of the goals of N-CHIME users, the features of the N-CHIME interface, the structures of the HSL language, and the concepts of the modeling and simulation domain was conducted. This is consistent with the 3-pronged design approach illustrated in Figure 3. The third component of the knowledge representation scheme, Models, followed directly from the analysis [Sanderson 91]. Its four models are shown in Figure 6 and explained below.

Three Static Knowledge Models

The Interface (Prong 2) and Application (Prong 3) were analyzed to define three knowledge models. Interface analysis was centered on N-CHIME, while application analysis encompassed both the HSL language and the modeling and simulation domain.

Analysis of N-CHIME knowledge considers global visible features such as windows, local visible features such as the various supportive tools, and logical features such as how display methods are determined. Since these features directly relate to the visible adaptive interface, it is essential to identify those objects which can be manipulated and to recognize how to do so for the user's benefit.

HSL knowledge analysis is guided by user goals. This is a hierarchical analysis of HSL, with general concepts at the top of the hierarchy, supported by specific language syntax and semantics [Mayer 87]. Three levels of knowledge are distinguished; each level provides additional detail relevant to language concepts and constructs. The knowledge level necessary for an individual may depend on his/her stated role in a simulation study.

Analysis of knowledge about modeling and simulation methodology is directed toward expert system support of various user goals. A composite analysis method was applied. Its vertical component considers the level of knowledge detail. Three levels are defined. This can depend on the level at which the user relates to the system as a specific type of user, or as a member of a particular organizational group. Its lateral component imposes structures onto the process of developing and using simulation models, without regard to user expertise. The high-level user state scenario graph is the major such structure. The essence of the composite analysis method is that different modeling and simulation concepts are applicable in different interaction states, and different levels of knowledge for these concepts are applicable for different task plans and types of users.

The factual knowledge gained through the above-described analysis was applied to N-CHIME in the form of three knowledge models to support the assistance feature. These models are static in nature; once their contents are specified, they remain intact during interactive use. Each piece of knowledge is represented by a frame which is linked to other frames containing related knowledge. The network of frames forms the model. Of the three, only the N-CHIME knowledge model was implemented in the prototype system.

The Dynamic User Model

The user model is distinguished from the other knowledge sources both because it is dynamic in nature and because it is utilized by the production rules which control the adaptive features of N-CHIME. Considerations for user modeling include who is to be modeled, what is to be modeled, how the information is to be acquired and how the information is to be maintained [Finin 89, Sparck-Jones 89]. Within those general guidelines, researchers have classified user models along several dimensions [Brajnik et al. 90, Rich 83]. In N-CHIME, *individual* users are *explicitly* modeled. Each user model is persistent across interactive sessions, and its values can change *dynamically*. The N-CHIME prototype maintains a database of individual user models.

The model uses a combination of techniques for acquiring its values. When an individual uses adaptive N-CHIME for the first time, he/she engages in a short question-and-answer session to determine experience and knowledge in certain areas. Once these initial values are obtained, the model is maintained through the application of production rules by the expert system. In addition, the user may specify preferences and modify certain user model parameters using special software tools.

Specific user model attributes fall into the general categories of goals, plans, preferences, domain knowledge, and beliefs. The decision of what to model directly affects the choice of knowledge representation scheme. There are many schemes for representing user knowledge. N-CHIME combines the *template* method, which maintains a number of expertise ratings relevant to domain knowledge, with a variation of the *overlay* scheme. Overlays [Carr & Goldstein 77, Clancey 84, Mastoglio 90] are frequently employed in intelligent tutoring systems. The student knowledge is modeled as an overlay of the expert (tutor's) knowledge so that areas of deficiency become readily apparent. The overlay portion contains parameters for user expertise ratings and activity counts for each high-level interaction state.

3.4 Illustrative Interaction Scenario

The previous sections focus on the interface software structures that support adaptation. Here, we concentrate on the MANNER of adaptation. Several types of adaptation are illustrated through the detailed presentation of an N-CHIME interaction scenario. The scenario is one of several developed for demonstration and informal evaluation of the N-CHIME prototype [Sanderson 91].

The goal of this interactive session is for a novice user to run an existing HSL simulation program. The scenario follows the user as he/she transitions from one high-level state to the next. The states are shown in boldface type. Adaptation is illustrated at each state through annotated rules selected from the N-CHIME rule base and presented in English-like form. The high-level states and transitions in this scenario are those included in the subgraph shown in Figure 4; the high-level states are denoted by the labels H0 through H4 and the transition paths by the labels P1 through P5. These labels are referenced in the following discussion. The specific transition that occurs at any point in an interactive session is determined by either an adaptation decision or the operation the user selects.

(1) *Session Login.* Each user has an I.D. because the system maintains individual user models. Until the user is identified, no adaptation can occur. The user model contains the fact that this user is an N-CHIME novice.

(2) *Identify Modeling Goal (H0).* Several goals have been pre-defined and are found in the *goals* menu. Goal selection activates the corresponding task plan, which defines an idealized path through the high-level state graph. The only adaptation at this point concerns the appearance of the visible interface, which may vary depending on previously-specified user preferences. Selection of *run stored model* as the goal for this session results in a state transition along path P1 to state H1.

(3) *Specify Model Name (H1).* The first step is to specify the name of the HSL program. Two means are available: a browse/retrieval tool or a dialog box into which the name is typed. Sample adaptation rules for this state are:

       IF   user is Novice AND goal is RunStoredModel
       THEN message "Browser is invoked automatically";
            invoke BrowserTool;

       IF   user is Apprentice AND goal is RunStoredModel
       THEN message "Unless you know the pathname, use the Browser";

Since the conditions of the first rule are met, it is fired and its actions carried out. In this case, N-CHIME automatically selects the means for name specification. This is an example of *decision* by-passing. The rationale is that use of the browse/retrieval tool, which allows selection from a list of HSL programs, is easier for the novice than use of the dialog box. The novice is automatically transitioned along path P2 to state H2. The apprentice user (next expertise level up from novice) in a similar situation is able to select the file specification method, but is given *advice* regarding that decision. The apprentice who chooses to use the dialog box will also be transitioned to state H2, but via path P3. Notice that all three components of the knowledge representation scheme are involved in adaptive decision making. The high-level state determines which set of rules to evaluate. The rules themselves determine under what conditions adaptation occurs and what form it takes, and the user model provides information utilized in rule conditions.

(4) *Conceptualize (H2)*. Once the novice has selected an HSL program using the browse/retrieval tool, N-CHIME effects the transition to this high-level state. Several new operations are now available, including the ability to edit the textual version of the program. Sample adaptation rules for this state are:

>   IF   user is Novice AND goal is RunStoredModel
>   THEN   message "Compiler is invoked automatically";
>   invoke CompileTool;
>
>   IF   user is Apprentice AND goal is RunStoredModel
>   THEN   message "Based on your goal, Compile is the best choice";
>
>   IF   CheckStateExpertise(Conceptualize)
>   THEN   SetStateExpertise(Conceptualize)

The first two rules demonstrate the same types of adaptation as those in the previous state. The next logical step toward the novice's goal is to compile the selected HSL program, so that choice is made by the system. The novice is thus transitioned along path P4 to state H4. The apprentice user is advised to select *Compile* but is free to choose. Other choices available include those to invoke the text editor tool or the graphic editor tool.

The third rule checks the user's history in using this high-level state, which is stored in the user model. If the history indicates that the user's state-specific expertise rating should be updated (i.e., CheckStateExpertise returns *true*), then that will occur. This rating reflects only the user's experience in this high-level state and must be distinguished from the N-CHIME expertise rating which appears in the rule conditions of this example.

(5) *Compile Program* (H4). The novice user was transitioned here by N-CHIME as a consequence of the previous automatic action and successful compilation. Adaptation in this state for the novice running a stored HSL model takes the same form as before; the decision to run the program is made for the user.

Thus, once the user specified the HSL program in step 3, all subsequent decisions were made by N-CHIME based on the stated session goal.

(6) *Specify Program* (H3). Suppose the N-CHIME apprentice elected in step 4 to invoke the text editor, and after its use was transitioned here via path P5. Examine one of the rules defined for this state.

> IF   user is Apprentice AND goal is RunStoredModel AND previous selection was TextualEdit
> THEN message "Use of the Text Editor was inconsistent with your goal";

This rule applies to a very specific situation. An apprentice user who has stated *run stored model* as the session goal decided, once the stored model was retrieved, to invoke the text editor. Since the action most consistent with the stated goal would have been to compile it instead, N-CHIME provides *feedback* concerning that decision.

The scenario continues in this fashion until the stated goal has hopefully been achieved. The remainder of the scenario is omitted since it demonstrates no new types of adaptation.

3.5 Interface Software Architecture

The structured interaction (Section 3.2), the expert system with its associated structured knowledge (Section 3.3), and the resulting manner of adaptation (Section 3.4) must be properly accommodated by the architecture of the adaptive interface software system. Two design approaches, one general and one specific to user interface design, have been applied to N-CHIME. In the object-oriented design approach, the software system is viewed by focusing on objects rather than on processes [Booch 91]. Object-oriented software does not magically result from the shoehorning of preliminary analysis and design results into an object model; the object-oriented approach needs to be consistently followed throughout the development process. This is apparent in N-CHIME by its underlying interface model which is based on various types of nodes exhibiting specific behaviors.

The second design approach applies specifically to user interface design. It utilizes the user interface management system, or UIMS, which is a software organization model for managing user-computer interaction dynamically. It is characterized by having an identity largely separate from the underlying application functionality.

3.5.1 Interface System Design Structures

With N-CHIME, the object-oriented specification technique is based on nodes as descriptors of N-CHIME components. The abstract interface model consists of a network of these nodes, the types of which are summarized in Table 1.

node type	what it represents
H-node	high-level interaction state
L-node	low-level interaction technique
F-node	family of related operations
O-node	operation
T-node	supportive software tool
R-node	rule to control adaptation
K-node	knowledge to support rules

Table 1: Summary of abstract interface model structures

The H-, R- and K-nodes are most relevant to the expert system. These correspond to the state, rule, and model components, respectively, of the three-layer knowledge representation scheme described previously and depicted in Figure 6.

The interface system design includes two special object types, the *help* object and the *user model*. Both are refinements of the K-node. Any object in the N-CHIME design may have a help object attached. The help object contains information about the attached object which can be presented to the user upon request. The user model contains the interface system's description of the current user, which is crucial for rendering adaptation decisions. Its attributes fall into three general categories: global, state-specific and operation-specific. Each global attribute is a single variable representing either a preference or an expertise rating (novice, apprentice, expert). State-specific expertise consists of a rating of N-CHIME expertise for each high-level state. Each rating is calculated based on state- and operation-specific monitored values, which are collected upon state transition or operation selection.

The N-CHIME interface specification itself consists of networks of objects created from the classes shown in the table. These networks are complex; the H-node network alone is similar in structure and complexity to the user state scenario graph. The upper portion of Figure 7 shows the node subnetwork associated with a single high-level interaction state. Certain nodes, such as help objects, have been omitted to simplify the figure.

3.5.2 Design Structures to Visible Interface

One notable feature of the interface specification method developed for N-CHIME is that the node network can be mapped to the visible interface in a straightforward manner. In the design specification, this is accomplished by associating node classes with widget classes. A widget is an object which can be displayed on the terminal. At run-time, a wid-

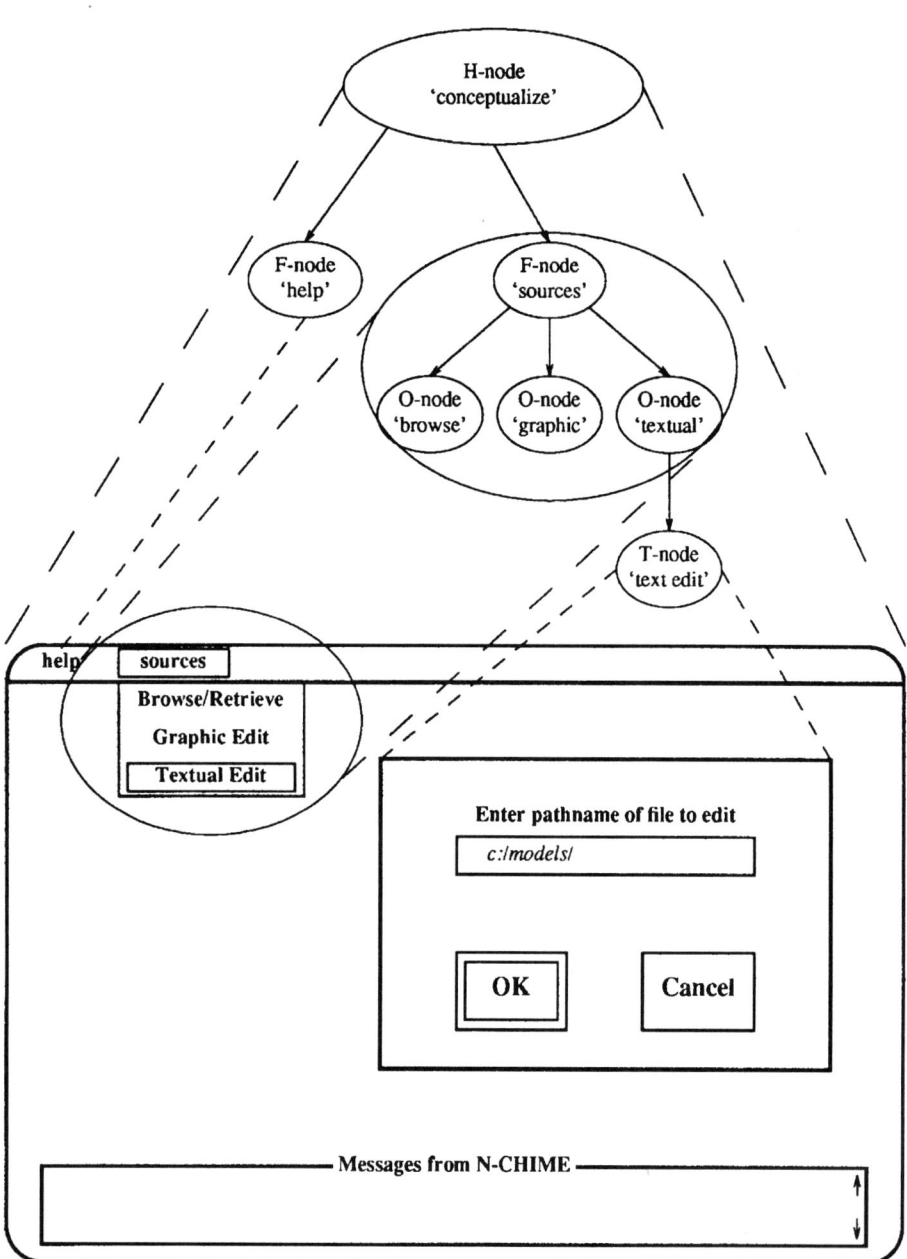

Figure 7: Correspondence of interface objects to visible interface [Sanderson 91]

get is bound to a node so that the results of widget manipulations by the user can be communicated to the node, and changes to nodes reflected on the visible interface.

Figure 7 illustrates the mapping from the N-CHIME interface specification to the display terminal for a number of nodes. In this figure, an H-node and the rich assortment of contextual structures centered around it are mapped directly onto the display to surround the user with information supportive to the subtask at hand. The upper half of the diagram shows a portion of the node network. At any given instant during the interactive session, only one H-node is active. In this figure, the high-level state "conceptualize" is active, along with the lower-level nodes attached to it. The lower half of the diagram shows a sample display image that reflects the subgraph that conceptually lies in the background. The dashed lines relate each node or group of nodes to the corresponding widgets or groups of widgets on the display. When the user progresses to a different high-level state, the image is remapped.

The H-node maps to the outline of the display, and in particular to the menu bar that stretches horizontally along the top of the display. Each attached F-node corresponds to a menu. In this example, the menu "sources" has been highlighted with the mouse, causing its items to be revealed. Each of the menu items can be seen to correspond to an O-node in the subgraph.

The menu item "Textual Edit" is highlighted, which indicates that the user has dragged the mouse down the menu to this item, and furthermore, that the item has been enabled for selection. After the selection is made, the corresponding T-node invokes its software tool, which displays a dialog box on the screen to solicit parameter information from the user. The scrolling window at the bottom of the display, labeled "Messages from N-CHIME," displays textual messages from the system to the user. This is used by the expert system for dispensing advice, suggestions and feedback to the user upon firing of adaptation rules.

The mapping shown in Figure 7 is only one example among many that are possible. Different interaction styles reveal different amounts of contextual information, and the need of the user for this information should be a determining factor in the user interface designer's selection of styles. It is also possible for an adaptive interface to determine this selection dynamically. N-CHIME currently does not dynamically alter the mapping from nodes to the widgets through which the user interacts with the node network. Nor does it provide multiple simultaneous views of the underlying network. When considered in conjunction with user interface adaptability, both capabilities provide much potential for future research.

3.5.3 Software Modules

The design components introduced up to now, their attributes and their relationships combine to specify the N-CHIME software architecture. Specific details of that architecture can be found in [Sanderson 91]. In general, software engineering practices conducive to good user interface design [Draper & Norman 85, Foley et al. 90] also facilitate the integration of adaptive capabilities into the interface. Several examples are:

(1) *Modular design.* If the user interface is highly modular, the design of adaptation methods that modify inter-module connections (either dynamically or at design time) is simplified.

(2) *Separation of physical and logical devices.* This allows alternate physical I/O devices to be mapped to the same logical device and vice versa. Device-specific operations are limited to software modules that interact directly with I/O devices.

(3) *Separation of interaction techniques from dialog control.* If the (high-level) dialog specification is independent of the interaction techniques used to carry on dialog, then the same dialog specification can serve multiple interaction techniques.

(4) *Separation of dialog control from application software.* The separation of dialog, and of the user interface in general, from the application software enables multiple interfaces to the same system functionality.

In addition to these general practices, the interface must exhibit flexible dialog control. To accommodate adaptable dialog control, the dialog control module must either have integrated adaptive control or be interfaceable to an external adaptive control module which can overrule its decisions. N-CHIME implements all the above listed practices to varying degrees.

4 OBSERVATIONS AND CONCLUSIONS

This paper is intended to make the case that designers of adaptive interfaces have a special need for better methodological assistance. An interface can be designed to adapt in many different ways, which are dependent on many different variables. To be successful in such a complex design situation, a variety of supportive structures is necessary. These structures should not only be inherent to the design process, including the formulation of a framework of relevant adaptation conditions; they should also apply to organization of the adaptive interface and the way in which the user interacts with it according to well-defined paradigms.

Results of this work with the N-CHIME interface system appear to have reinforced our views. It has not as yet been feasible to carry out a formal evaluation of the adaptive component of N-CHIME. However, informal assessment of its performance, involving a group of graduate students in computer science, has generally led to positive feedback [Sanderson 91]. The students especially liked the adaptively provided guidance and suggestions. On the other hand, some of them, as N-CHIME novices but computer science experts, expressed concern about certain adaptively made decisions about what to do next, thereby taking away their feeling of control. Such reservations are not unexpected. They illustrate the importance of clearly understanding the intended beneficiary of the adaptation, as well as the other relevant conditions.

Indeed, a lot of room exists for differences in opinion on adaptive interface design. Yet, we are convinced that its potential is great. At the same time, the designer's task is extremely complex. As illustrated in Section 3.4, we implemented only selected forms of adaptation within the highly structured N-CHIME environment. Nevertheless, it took a substantial amount of time and effort to do so. We hope that other specialists in this area will continue to push forward to improve the state-of-the-art of adaptive interfaces. Undoubtedly much more research and development in adaptive interface design is necessary before it will become more of an accepted and attractive alternative in human-computer interaction.

REFERENCES

[Aikins 83]
    J. S. Aikins (1983): *Prototypical Knowledge for Expert Systems*, Artificial Intelligence 20, pp 163-210.

[Aikins 84]
    J. S. Aikins (1984): *A Representation Scheme Using Both Frames and Rules*, in *Rule-Based Expert Systems*, B. G. Buchanan, E. H. Shortliffe (Eds.), Addison-Wesley, Reading, Mass, pp 424-440.

[Black et al. 87]
    J. B. Black, D. S. Kay, E. M. Soloway (1987): *Goal and Plan Knowledge Representations*, in *Interfacing Thought: Cognitive Aspects of Human-Computer Interaction*, J. M. Carroll (Ed.), MIT Press, Cambridge, Mass.

[Booch 91]
    G. Booch (1991): *Object Oriented Design With Applications*, Benjamin/Cummings, Redwood City, CA.

[Brajnik et al. 90]
    G. Brajnik, G. Guida, C. Tasso (1990): *User Modeling in Expert Man-Machine Interfaces: A Case Study in Intelligent Information Retrieval*, IEEE Transactions on Systems, Man and Cybernetics 20 (1), pp. 166-185.

[Buchanan & Duda 83]
    B. G. Buchanan, R. O. Duda (1983): *Principles of Rule-Based Expert Systems*, in *Advances in Computers 22*, M. C. Yovits (Ed.), Academic Press, New York, pp 163-216.

[Buchanan & Shortliffe 84]
    B. G. Buchanan, E. H. Shortliffe (1984) (Eds.): *Rule-Based Expert Systems*, Addison Wesley, Reading, Mass.

[Carr & Goldstein 77]
    B. Carr, I. P. Goldstein (1977): *Overlays: A Theory of Modeling for CAI*, Report 406, MIT Artificial Intelligence Lab.

[Clancey 84]
W. J. Clancey (1984): *Use of MYCIN's Rules for Tutoring*, in *Rule-Based Expert Systems*, B. G. Buchanan, E. H. Shortliffe (Eds.), Addison-Wesley, Reading, Mass, p 464-489.

[Dieterich et al. 93]
Dieterich, H., Malinowski, U., Kühme, T., Schneider-Hufschmidt, M. (1993). *State of the Art in Adaptive User Interfaces*. In this book

[Draper & Norman 85]
S. W. Draper, D. A. Norman (1985): *Software Engineering for User Interfaces*, IEEE Transactions on Software Engineering 11 (3), pp 252-258.

[Finin 89]
T. W. Finin (1989): *GUMS - A General User Modeling Shell*, in User Models in Dialog Systems, A. Kobsa, W. Wahlster (Eds.), Springer-Verlag, New York, pp. 411-430.

[Fischer 93]
G. Fischer (1993): *Shared Knowledge in Cooperative Problem-Solving Systems - Integrating Adaptive and Adaptable Components*. In this book.

[Foley et al. 90]
J. D. Foley, A. Van Dam, S. K. Feiner, J. F. Hughes (1990): *Computer Graphics: Principles and Practice*, 2nd Edition,

[Gove 63]
P. B. Gove (1963) (Ed.): *Websters Seventh New Collegiate Dictionary*, G & C Merriam, Springfield, Mass.

[Hayes-Roth et al. 83]
F. Hayes-Roth, D. A. Waterman, D. B. Lenat (1983) (Eds.): *Building Expert Systems*, Addison-Wesley, Reading, Mass.

[Mahling & Lefkowitz 89]
D. E. Mahling, L. S. Lefkowitz (1989): *Using Task Context to Support an Adaptable Interface*, in *Designing and Using Human-Computer Interfaces and Knowledge Based Systems*, G. Salvendy, M. J. Smith (Eds.), Elsevier Science, New York, pp 565-573.

[Mastoglio 90]
T. W. Mastaglio (1990): *A User Modelling Approach to Support Cooperative Problem Solving*, PhD Dissertation, University of Colorado.

[Mayer 87]
R. E. Mayer (1987): *Cognitive Aspects of Learning Using a Programming Language*, in *Interfacing Thought: Cognitive Aspects of Human-Computer Interaction*, J. M. Carroll (Ed.), MIT Press, Cambridge, Mass.

[Rich 83]
E. Rich (1983): *Users Are Individuals: Individualizing User Models*, International Journal of Man-Machine Studies 18, pp 199-214.

[Rolston 88]
D. W. Rolston (1988): *Principles of Artificial Intelligence and Expert System Development*, McGraw-Hill, New York.

[Sanderson 91]
D. P. Sanderson (1991): *Structured Design of an Adaptive Human-Computer Interface*, PhD Dissertation, University of Pittsburgh.

[Sanderson & Treu 91]
D. P. Sanderson, S. Treu (1991): *Designing the Intelligent Component of a User Interface for Modeling and Simulation*, Proceedings of the Artificial Intelligence and Simulation Conference, New Orleans, LA, April 1-5, pp 47-52.

[Sanderson et al. 91]
D. P. Sanderson, R. Rozin, R. Sharma, S. Treu (1991): *The Hierarchical Simulation Language (HSL): A Versatile Tool for Process-Oriented Simulation*, ACM Transactions on Modeling and Computer Simulation 1 (2), pp. 113-153.

[Sparck-Jones 89]
K. Sparck-Jones (1989): *Realism About User Modeling*, in *User Models in Dialog Systems*, A. Kobsa, W. Wahlster (Eds.), Springer-Verlag, New York, pp 341-363.

[Treu et al. 91]
S. Treu, D. P. Sanderson, R. Rozin, R. Sharma (1991): *High-Level, Three-Pronged Design Methodology for the N-CHIME Interface System Software*, Information and Software Technology 33 (5), pp 306-320.

[Tyler & Treu 86]
S. W. Tyler, S. Treu (1986): *Adaptive Interface Design: A Symmetric Model and a Knowledge-Based Implementation*, ACM SIGOIS Bulletin 7 (2-3), pp 53-60.

[Tyler & Treu 89]
S. W. Tyler, S. Treu (1989): *An Interface Architecture to Provide Adaptive Task-Specific Context for the User*, International Journal of Man-Machine Studies 30, pp. 303-327.

Adaptive Hypermedia for Support Systems

Gernoth Grunst

German National Research Center for Computer Science (GMD)
St. Augustin, Germany

1 INTRODUCTION

The paper introduces the system HyPLAN[1]. It consists of two modules forming an adaptive hypermedia help system supporting spreadsheet calculations. The support environment is related to ExcelinExcel[2], an Excel™ based spreadsheet application.

HyTASK (Hypermedia TASK support) is a hypermedia tutorial and help system. This includes a network of hypertexts and animations explaining characteristic tasks for knowledge workers using spreadsheet calculation.

PLANET (PLAn recognition through activated task NETs) is a knowledge based plan recognition system evaluating recordings of Excel™ / ExcelinExcel operations. PLANET [Quast 91] identifies performed work steps and infers the actual aims of the user on various task levels. An access to the HyTASK help environment is performed according to the inference results.

The system is realized on a Macintosh MacIvory. ExcelinExcel and HyTASK are implemented on the Macintosh whereas PLANET runs on a Symbolics Lisp board installed in the machine. A file exchange utility handles the communication between the modules.

HyPLAN allows the system to answer unspecific help requests with focused support. The plan recognition, and thereby the initiation of focused help, is limited to tasks represented in the knowledge base of the system. This restriction corresponds to a fixed set of tutorials and help themes in HyTASK. The usefulness of the entire system depends on the relevance of the plans considered. Thus, empirical detection of crucial and recurrent problems in the use of spreadsheet calculations has been a basic development requirement. The contents

---

[1] The developments were embedded in the research project SAGA which was supported by a grant from the "Work and Technology" fund of the Ministry of Science and Technology of the Federal Republic of Germany.

[2] ExcelinExcel is a duplication of Excel™ utilizing its macro facilities. It offers an interface identical to the short menu version of Excel™ supplemented by the "series" function. For the user, it is not different from the normal Excel™. ExcelinExcel generates a protocol of usage sequences that is used by PLANET.

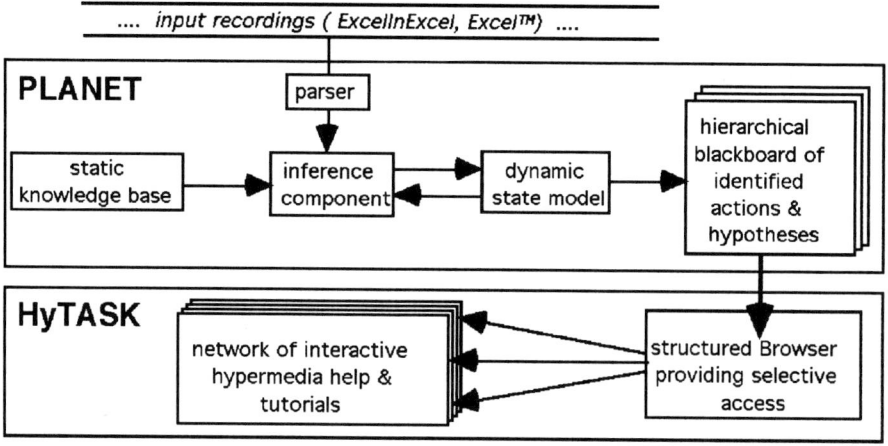

Figure 1: The architecture of the adaptive hypermedia support system HyPLAN

covered are derived from the work domain of knowledge workers casually using spreadsheet calculation.

2 THE DEVELOPMENT OF THE HYPERMEDIA SUPPORT SYSTEM HYTASK

We developed the hypermedia help system HyTASK in design-evaluation-redesign cycles beginning with analysis of human tutorial strategies. In these empirical studies we applied video recordings of computer related interactions in order to identify efficient human patterns of correcting, criticizing, and helping with crucial Excel™ features. Successful ways to correlate how user aims could be matched with spreadsheet concepts were scrutinized as potential models of technical support.

2.1 Empirical identification and modelling of adequate support

In the final version of HyPLAN, help is given through multiple means of orientation: texts, graphics, interactive animations, and spoken comments. Suitable scopes of application for the different communicative media were identified and evaluated in empirical studies. Cognitive reconstructions of the orientation effects were based on audiovisual recordings of system use supporting actual work with Excel™ / ExcelnExcel.

The design cycles started with experiments disclosing the processing of actual tasks taken from the real work domain of our target users. Although these test users had learned the suited operations, as casual users of Excel™, they had mostly forgotten pertinent function-

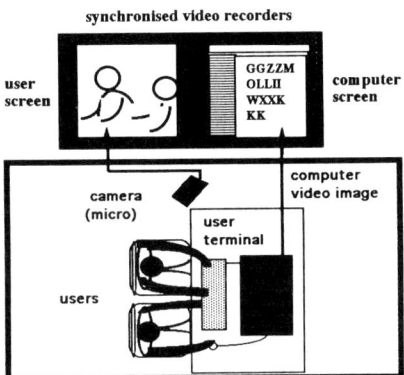

Figure 2: A test design disclosing use problems and pertinent human help

alities. In order to impart efficient concepts appropriate to the test tasks, they received introductory tutorials from a human expert. After this preparatory phase the users had to solve similar tasks applying the newly learned or refreshed Excel™ concepts. In these situations the accompanying expert changed from a guiding tutor into a consultant, helping with difficulties as they occurred.

These video recordings of the interactions can be seen as a means of knowledge acquisition. They are a variant of more traditional forms of protocol studies relying on the think-aloud utterances of a single user [O'Malley et al. 85]. In think-aloud situations the test subject is usually missing a natural purpose for the utterances. On the other hand, two subjects of related experience and motivation, dealing with a complex matter quite naturally, communicate hypotheses, questions, answers, critiques, and justifications, thereby displaying their actual mental models.

Behavioral items were interpreted and scrutinized as potential models of efficient technical support concepts. Methodologically we applied discourse analytical means [van Dijk 85, Sinclair & Coulthard 75]. Selected interaction sequences were analyzed in depth through transcripts, segmentations, classifications, and comprehensive interpretations. Thus, probable mental models guiding the users' observable behavior could be reconstructed and used as an "epistemological horizon," guiding the design of cognitively adequate technical tutorials.

Besides invisible mental inferences, the interactions naturally involved four overt modes of task related behavior:

- processing the task (test subjects)
- indicating trouble (test subjects)

- suggesting pending support or critique (expert)
- conveying orientations (expert).

These behavioral units usually constituted patterns of interactions which corrected misconceptions or elicited appropriate ideas of how to solve the problem at hand [Rehbein 80]. Once problems had been mutually recognized and pending support was admitted, the tutor typically clarified the issue by using example demonstrations. The task steps were accompanied by short verbal comments illustrating their relevance to the users' aims.

After having conveyed a graphic conception of how to solve a task, the expert sometimes tried to impart a deeper understanding of how the spreadsheet program worked in the actual case. Instead of demonstrations, utterances now gained a high rank. These detailed verbal explanations often described the system metaphorically as someone taking input information, transforming the contents into desired results, and presenting them at the interface. Crucial functional principles of Excel™ such as the difference between copying cells with relative or absolute relations to other cells were sometimes illustrated through graphic metaphors such as "moving rubber band connections," as contrasted with "rigid pointers." These types of metaphorical expressions were well received by the users and uttered in analogous contexts.

2.2 Technical transformations of findings and evaluations of the help system HyTASK

The identified human success models of adequate support patterns and the most efficient means of explanation were taken as detailed target explications guiding the development of functionally equivalent technical orientation concepts. In designing the hypermedia help system HyTASK, we did not try to mimic human behavior. Rather, we tried to exploit specific strengths of computer based techniques such as graphics, animations, voice, hypertext links, and click-sensitive buttons in order to compensate for the crucial weakness of computers to simulate human contextual understanding and behavior. Conceiving the user as the primary decision instance, we mainly focussed on ways to support self-judgements of actual help demand. In terms of D. Schoen [Schoen 90], we tried to design a support environment that presents a situation which gives continuous and explicit feedback concerning conditions and consequences of specific actions. The inquisitive user who is invited to move actively through the demonstrations receives multilevel references to task relevant details she may or may not have noticed. Thus, in order to compensate for spontaneous human ad hoc interactions used for clarifying actual problems, we prepared a set of related scenarios dealing with foreseeable and crucial items.

As a stand-alone help system HyTASK can be accessed through a static click-sensitive index list of tutorial and help themes. The final version consists of help demonstrations including click- and touch-sensitive hot spots. The system is realized in HyperCard™ and MediaTracks™. The system provides specific task contexts as film-like sequences of work progressing in Excel™. Therefore, help accesses leading to deepening information can be selectively prepared for different system states according to assessable demand. To make potentially troublesome points further inspectable, HyTASK presents graphically emphasized click buttons leading to additional information about relevant system functions.

Having entered the support environment analogous to the identified human explanations via demonstration, contents are mainly imparted through interactive hypermedia presentations showing how to perform certain types of tasks. In order to stimulate an immediate understanding of misconceived details, a presentation of relevant operations accompanied by verbal comments about reasons and pitfalls turned out to be an efficient analogue to human didactic habits. Demonstration based teaching concepts applying hypermedia usually show faster learning but worse transfer effects [Palmiter & Elkerton]. Therefore, as suggested by identified strategies of human tutors, the "how to do" animations were supplemented by "how it works" illustrations of crucial features of Excel™. In this sense the tests confirmed the applicability of the human didactic models identified in pilot studies. Adding metaphorical descriptions and animations of the system's operating methods could evidently further activate use of the learned concepts. Analogous to pertinent moves of human tutors, the transfer of imparted concepts to similar task contexts was efficiently backed through visualizations and metaphorical descriptions of the application's functioning.

Consecutive HyTASK versions passed evolutionary debugging processes. Shortcomings identified were fixed, and reasonable improvements were integrated into the system. Follow up tests passed the newly improved versions. Usually subtle faults uncovered in subsequent evaluations could be seen after the usage of the system had been cleared from masking impediments. In order to identify fine grained cognitive adjustments of the support system, coarse problems had to be corrected. For example, before one is sure that relevant information is not overseen, there is no way to evaluate and modify intelligibility. Moreover, to make certain that hints are graspable for users coming from different contexts of work and understanding, the design of a support module in this sense first has to be cleared of generally counterintuitive features.

A reasonable modularisation of help items could only be achieved after clusters of information relevant to a specific task context were put together and checked against demands in a spectrum of analogous problem situations. Very often problems of complex spreadsheet operations are quite context specific, and related explanations have to take into account the relevant aspects. Therefore, the support environment in its final design includes a mixture of high level demonstrations illustrating particularly intricate tasks and short explanations of smaller concepts applicable in different types of spreadsheet calculations.

HyTASK transformed into a smoothly usable system after about one year of test and modification cycles resulting in three major and a lot of minor changes. The tests had the same experimental design as the tutorial prestudies. Instead of an expert aiding a novice, two equally skilled users now had to solve test tasks by discussing their different conceptions of it. The users could use HyTASK for support. They had experienced a guided tour illustrating the use of the system.

Four main flaws of the hypermedia system could be identified and three of them were fixed during the test redesign cycles of HyTASK:

(1) One of the most clear-cut results of the tests was that written text should be avoided if possible. In preliminary tests we recognized that a text based precursor of HyTASK was inappropriate. Long texts offered on help cards were refused as onerous. In addition, the first graphical realization of the support environment realized in HyperCard™ presented touch-sensitive hot-spots within animations leading to further (textual) information. Even this second test system confused the users when text popped up. The textual information mode apparently disturbed the users watching the demonstration of a task and taking up graphical information.

- Thus, in the first redesign cycles, the help card texts were significantly reduced and we increased the number of buttons leading to demos illustrating the contents instead. Now, written information primarily functions as a kind of "door inscription," inviting the user to start pertinent demonstrations. In contrast to the textual explanations, the users now readily accept the demos even if they impart complex contents. They have no problems in matching demonstrated work steps with their own intentions or uncertainties.

(2) A further shortcoming of the HyperCard™ based support environment was its confusing dynamics and control concept. In this HyTASK version, a series of screen shots of work progressing in Excel™ was presented either in a step-by-step or in a self running mode. Users from different starting points required different modes of presentation when addressing the support system. Since it could not be foreseen if an actual user wanted to see a presentation of a whole task or just specific details, the user had to determine the desired mode of a presentation. Though the users usually had an intuitive idea of what they wanted to see, they were often not able to understand the request to specify whether a demonstration should be presented step-by-step or in a self running mode.

- We therefore replaced the HyperCard™ sequences by realistic demonstrations of the Excel™ operations recorded in MediaTracks™. Integrating MediaTracks™ as a development tool facilitated the production of animations decisively. The execution of a task could, moreover, be shown more realistically. Even subsemantic levels of work such as movements of the mouse are now displayed. The user sees how every state changes into the next and can thus remember the execution of task elements even as (perceptual) motor programs [Wright 90] corresponding the trajectories of mouse movements.

The user now is only offered continuously running "films." The animations are controlled through the MediaTracks™ command facilities. A simple control panel resembling a cassette recorder intuitively allows to stop, step-back and forward a running animation without effecting extra cognitive load. The presentation can easily be influenced in any desired form.

(3) On some cards the HyperCard™ version of HyTASK presented touch and click-sensitive icons and areas leading to further information. These "buttons" were visually marked as framed graphical elements which were highlighted when touched with the mouse cursor. As the demonstrations presented a lot of unknown information the users frequently overlooked the specific function of these graphical buttons and pertinent hints were missed.

- In the MediaTracks™ redesign we therefore implemented contextual access for further information through temporary text buttons previously realized as icons. The demonstration pauses if such "doors" leading to other demonstrations are offered. The user can decide if he should continue to watch the current explanation or switch to suggested side films by clicking the appropriate button. Later, as the HyTASK information space became more and more complex, this "doorway" concept turned out to be a useful idea. The decomposition into films linked by salient doors whose relevance could be intuitively assessed turned out to be a useful orientation concept.

The shortcomings described so far could be fixed by modifying the hypermedia presentation and interaction concepts. A serious limitation, however, was related to the fact that the system often was not used at all. All HyTASK versions can be entered through a click-sensitive index list of tutorial and help topics. The most significant use problem of HyTASK is related to this initial access feature. Without advice from a supervisor, the system was used as little and ineffectively as written handbooks applying the same entry concept. The analysis showed that real problems arising in actual tasks blocked entering the help environment via the index list. Matching vaguely understood problems to a broad spectrum of help themes turned out to be a cognitive load incompatible with the processing of real tasks. Quite normal intuitions seemed to be blocked by stress. Users indicated that the search for possible help through long index lists was seen as diverting from the scope of duties and was therefore refused. The smooth access of pertinent information therefore was seen to be just as important for the efficiency of the support system as intuitive explanations.

In order to facilitate entering the support environment we decided to develop a plan recognition system (PLANET) offering contextually relevant choices of relevant help themes briefly illustrating expectable information. The system should identify probable user intentions by evaluating elementary Excel™ operations and maintain a picture of the actual help demand by adaptively taking into account changes of the work in progress.

3 THE DEVELOPMENT OF THE KNOWLEDGE BASED PLAN RECOGNITION SYSTEM PLANET

Analogous to the empirical analyses of human behavior preceding the design of HyTASK, we started the developments with studies of human strategies to identify actual help demand. Additionally, we specified the intended basic features of the module related to the HyTASK orientation concepts. PLANET should support self-assessments of help demand on the entry level. Once having entered the HyTASK presentations, the user receives multilevel orientations guiding self-assessments of further help demand.

3.1 Modelling human plan recognition

We started the discovery experiments as so called "Wizard of Oz" tests [Hill & Miller 88]. Applying HyTASK as the actual help offered we simulated context-sensitive selections of pertinent items.

In these experiments human experts controlled the test subjects through a terminal. Pairs of test users (novices or low level experts) tried to solve actual tasks beyond their routine competence together. Two Excel™ specialists followed the course of actions via a control terminal in an adjacent room. The prevention of nonverbal and verbal exchanges forced the experts to rely on observable computer operations. They displayed patterns of plan/problem recognition based entirely on cues available via computer. This data was seen as a source of information which could be technically exploited by plan recognition modules. The connection between the two Macintosh terminals was provided by Timbuktu™. The experts could answer recognized difficulties through topically configuring and prompting access cards suggesting pertinent support in HyTASK. Thus features of the conceived recognition and help proposal module could be evaluated before really implementing it.

The setting effectively allowed modelling of human plan and failure recognition. The experts, not knowing the actual tasks, expressed and mutually criticized their assumptions following the input sequences. In the analytic reconstructions, every judgment could be evaluated against ad rem discussions of the user group. On both sides of the wall related constructive interactions [Miyake 82] took place.

Active help offers were rejected surprisingly often by the test users. Especially when they were still following a (possibly false) idea of how to solve actual task steps, they were really annoyed by interruptions. On the other hand, three different types of successful identification processes could be determined on the expert side:

> (1) The experts utilized semantic information such as the contents of column heads. From these cues the intentions of the users could often be adequately estimated.
>
>> - In order to interpret these terms the experts had to apply complex semantic knowledge. They had to differentiate between names of people, departments, products, time-spans, and costs. Furthermore, they needed domain specific

Adaptive Hypermedia for Support Systems

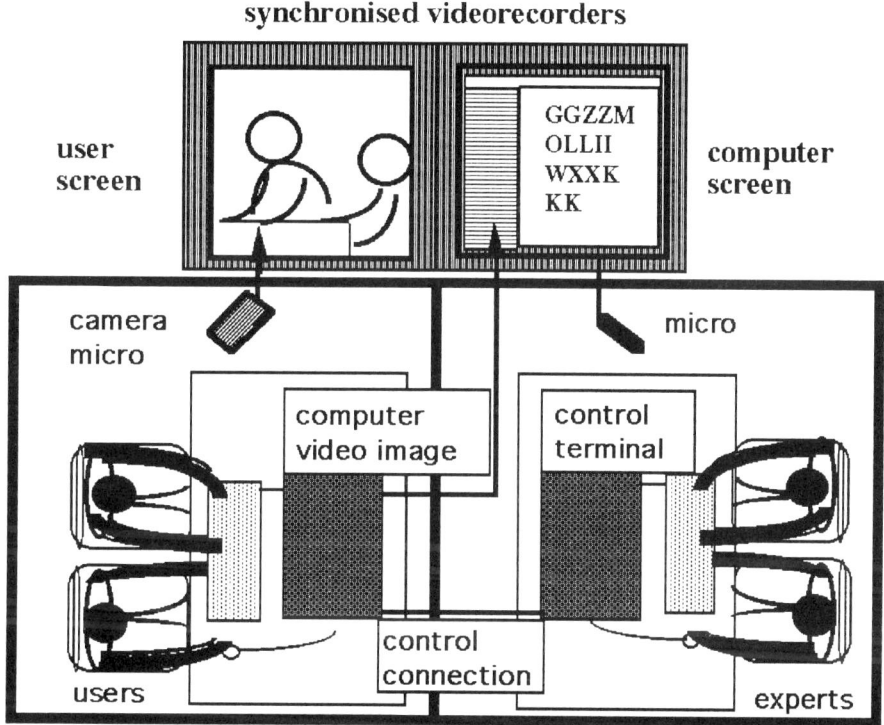

Figure 3: A test design disclosing indices for plans and use problems

knowledge about the relevance of certain relations between the denoted concepts. A technical equivalent of this aspect of human expertise was therefore rated as unrealistic.

(2) The Excel™ specialists matched input sequences to task patterns. Taking into account the whole spreadsheet after few steps, they usually were rather sure, although sometimes incorrectly, as to whether the users had trouble or to what aim they were pursuing.

 - This kind of competence was taken as a feasible model to design the intended plan recognition module.

(3) The use of single significant functions as a "set database" let the experts immediately infer quite complex aims. Certain error messages caused by inadequate input indicated particular, sometimes extensive, gaps of knowledge. This type of cue turned out to be rather reliable.

- Since these cues can be technically handled, we rated this human basis of assessment as a valuable feature of the intended plan recognition module.

Thus, if the human experts were not actively coordinated with users solving a task, they were only able to identify actual aims and problems, not the appropriate "time windows" in which to suggest pending support.

3.2 Technical transformations of human plan recognition

The knowledge based plan recognition system PLANET reflects compositional features of human plan recognition (finding 2) through a hierarchical network of linked actions.

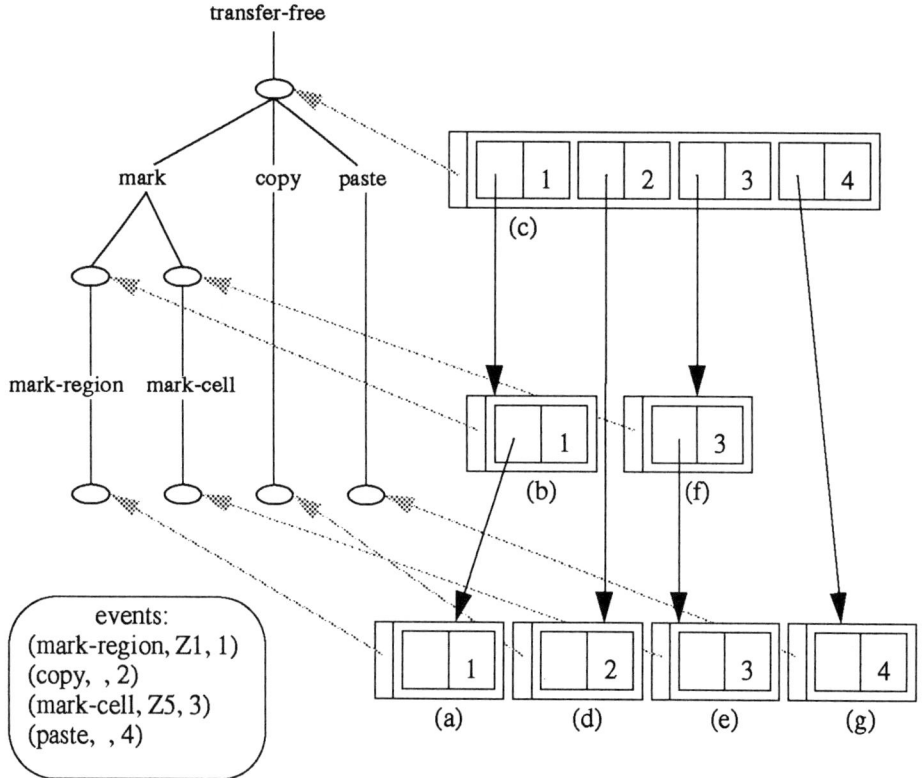

Figure 4: An example model of the PLANET task objects

Applying a simplifying closed world assumption, the task domain is modelled as an ascending network of elementary, intermediate, and complex task nodes covering seven levels of complexity. The task objects contain placeholders for constituents in a temporal order and associated constraints. Alternative solutions are included, and suboptimal ways can be marked.

Elementary actions correspond to basic operations recorded by the Excel™/ ExcelinExcel protocols. In order to receive this basic information about the actual spreadsheet use, the plan recognition module had to be fed with a recording of the elementary operations. ExcelinExcel is a simulation of Excel™'s short menu state utilizing its macro facilities as interface tools. Commands are indirectly triggered via macro calls simultaneously sending messages to a recording file. The user faces no differences from the original Excel™. In contrast with the recording file set up by Excel™ in its macro mode, here cancelled operations and error messages can be handled. As an experimental device ExcelinExcel integrates two important advantages: the familiarity and smoothness of a perfected application and the openness to generate informative recordings of its use.

The recordings are parsed and the events are evaluated according to the knowledge base of task patterns. All plan types including a recorded operation are instantiated. Further protocol elements are filled into these frames forming complex actions if specific conditions are matched. In a spreading activation process, confirmed complex actions, just as the elementary recording events, trigger all patterns including the identified units as elements. This ascending identification process spans seven task levels. The results are recorded on seven corresponding blackboard layers. A history component allows tracing back every inferred complex task unit to the elementary operations that actually constituted the identified item. PLANET is able to identify different plans realized through parallel action sequences and to relate disconnected task elements.

Besides completed actions, PLANET can identify hypotheses of probable plans. The identification of not yet or falsely executed plans is mainly achieved through a specific handling of cue functions such as "extract," evidently indicating certain intentions. In PLANET the human "key indicator" strategy (empirical finding 3) was transformed into different weights attached to pertinent elementary or intermediate operations. The knowledge base reflects the status of cue elements through marked links. During system use, the identification of these items in the recording triggers high level hypotheses which are kept on a particular blackboard.

If help is requested, PLANET updates the evaluation of the recording. A heuristic then maximally selects five of the current inference results (primarily high level hypotheses) noted on the blackboards. They are sent to HyperCard and filled in as items of the access card leading to pertinent help in HyTASK. This card is designed as a structured browser allowing intuitive switching between different levels of complexity within a thematic frame. Related help items of more elementary or complex character are presented in side columns and can be accessed immediately. Touching an item with the mouse displays a brief informal description of the expectable content. The selection formed does not exceed five items so that they are easily surveyed by the user and related to his actual problem.

Thanks to the multiple choice and browsing facility of the help access card, the requirements concerning granularity and precision of the inference results can be kept moderate.

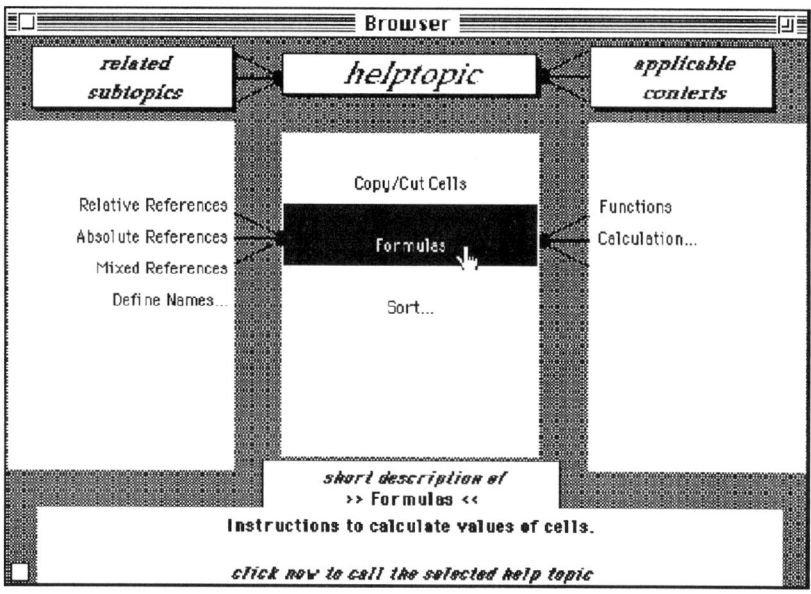

Figure 5: An example configuration of the structured browser

4 GENERAL FEATURES OF THE INTEGRATED SYSTEM HYPLAN

In all tests human experts very seldom were able to spot difficulties according to the content and level of (mis)understanding without clarification dialogues about the problem at hand. Even less often could they see appropriate "time windows" to interrupt the user in order to make help suggestions when they merely recognized the course of actions. Taking the human model as the most advanced example of cognitive estimation competence, attempts to provide active one shot presentation of support by means of a plan recognition module seems to be inappropriate [Moore 89]. As the "Wizard of Oz" studies showed, everything that can be achieved by analyzing a recording of user actions narrows the probable intentions and problems. Every reasonable recommendation of help was therefore, at best, seen as a cautious selection of themes matching the identified user actions. Compared to help access via index lists, the selection has to make a spontaneous self-estimation by the user possible.

The fact that most cues for certain help demands have a vague character rules out active offers. Passive conceptions of context-sensitive help are more consistent with these restrictions of conceivable technical help access. On the other hand, to come into play at all, such systems require appropriate expectations of the user. In our tests users were likely to address the HyPLAN system via help key after they had been made familiar with the concept. They became more and more confident when its value had been accepted. Using the support environment, the users developed rather realistic expectations and attitudes. This is an important feature of long time usability. Though it could not really be shown by way of (single session) "Wizard of Oz" tests, there is good reason to assume that active systems in this sense are likely to be quite inconsistent. Otherwise, they may be restricted to a spectrum of trivial performances. Without the option of clarifying feedback, active dialogue suggestions were often marked as confusing and rejected by the supported user. This held more so if she was still following a (possibly wrong) conception how to solve a task. Error messages alone provided a context triggering consistent expectations and a motivation to receive related instructions. In other situations, deviations from task patterns, as they were represented in the knowledge base, sometimes turned out to be unforeseen but reasonable solutions.

The domain of spreadsheet calculations is heterogeneous and open-ended. It therefore seems to be poorly suited for a general critiquing approach [Fischer et al. 88]. Supporting self-estimation, therefore, is a basic requirement with respect to entering, as well as continuing, help search [Grunst et al. 91].

As opposed to brief help illustrations, complex tutorials have to be decomposed into distributed information units. Starting a tutorial, the user of HyTASK is shown a basic level illustration of a chosen item. Though continuing or deepening information is sometimes necessary in a factual sense, it is left out on the entry level of a help demonstration in order to impart a coherent first impression of a complex operation. Rather than this, HyTASK presents salient accesses to deepening explanations, possibly corresponding to actual problems of the user. In HyTASK, "doors" leading to related animations are realized as temporary click buttons. They are placed at those points in sequential presentations of task contexts where violations of pertinent requirements may cause trouble. Some of these presentation points are related to possible error messages. Thoroughly placed and speaking buttons act as cues which invite the user to match actual vague (mis)understandings of task elements with the items indicated. Like real world situations, presented scenes support subconscious preprocessing of possibly relevant details [Suchman 87]. Thus, cues may not distract the user´s concentration from thinking about actual task steps, but rather should come into focus if the impression of something unexpected is realized. Often potential relevance of continuing information is not generally determinable but depends on courses of task realizations. Therefore, adaptive presentations according to recognized actual work of a user would further improve this scene based orientation concept.

In order to provide a broad spectrum of valuable (multilevel) orientations, a lot of mostly domain related acquisition and design effort is necessary. This is amplified if the information presented should be made to adapt to different contexts of work. To select appropriate suggestions using a plan recognition module requires the identification and operationalization of pertinent criteria. As that their relevance is highly context dependent, there is always a trade off between breadth of validity and degree of sophistication. Unforeseen work contexts may turn intelligent inferences into confusing absurdities. The design of HyPLAN therefore started with provisions for generally relevant and definitely identifiable support situations. Few examples of more sophisticated types of support access applying deeper and contextually stable reasoning could be added.

Support environments raised by external developers may turn out to be fragmentary or mostly irrelevant for specific target domains. To guarantee contextual validity of support and help access, users in the actual target domains should be responsible for the selection and treatment of crucial problems. A maintenance and extension concept shifting the design of help modules into the stage of system use seems to be a reasonable attempt to cope with the otherwise conflicting claims to be contextually informative, exhaustive, and valid. Besides capabilities to identify domain specific difficulties, this process requires competence in hypermedia and plan recognition design as well as in didactics. Considering the recognition of help demand in a domain and the effective impartment of pertinent information it can be assumed that the necessary competence can most often be found or developed within a target group. This holds especially true if these users participated in the development of help units by design experts. Transparent tools and examples can further enable nonspecialists to design help modules. In HyPLAN "copy and modify" attempts are rather intuitive considering the multi-media items of HyTASK.

Complementing the knowledge base of PLANET, on the other hand, requires furthermore, a detailed and abstract metalevel understanding of an application. A designer of adaptivity has to evaluate alternative clusters of possible input operations as cues indicating aims or difficulties considered. Patterns valid in one type of task can most often not be applied in analogous contexts. Moreover, each plan added to the knowledge base has to be thoroughly checked for potential contradictions. Thus, even providing a smooth interface does not guarantee that plan recognition techniques can be usefully applied by end users.

References

[van Dijk 85]
van Dijk, T. (1985): *Semantic Discourse Analysis*. In: van Dijk, T. (ed.): *Handbook of Discourse Analysis*. Vol.2: Dimensions of Discourse. London: Academic Press, pp. 103-136.

[Fischer et al. 88]
Fischer, G., A., Morch, Ch. Hair, A. Lemke, B. Bernstein, C. Stevens (1988): *Explorations in the Design of Intelligent Support Systems and Innovative User Interfaces*, Department of Computer Science Report, University of Colorado, Boulder.

[Grunst et al. 91]
    Grunst, G., R. Oppermann, Ch. Thomas (1991): *Intelligente Benutzerschnittstellen*, in: Handbuch der modernen Datenverarbeitung, Heft 160, Wiesbaden, pp. 35 -47.

[Hill & Miller 88]
    Hill, W.C. and J.R. Miller (1988):*Justified Advice: A Seminaturalistic Study of Advisory Strategies*, in: Soloway, E., D. Frye and S.B. Sheppard (eds.), CHI '88 Conference Proceedings, Human Factors in Computing Systems, Washington, pp. 185-190.

[Miyake 82]
    Miyake, N. (1982):*Constructive Interaction*, CHIP Report 113, San Diego.

[Moore 89]
    Moore, J.D. (1989): *Responding to "Huh?" : Answering Vaguely Articulated Follow-up Questions*, in: CHI '89 proceedings, pp. 91 - 96.

[O'Malley et al. 85]
    O'Malley, C.E.O., S.W. Draper, M.S. Riley (1985): *Constructive Interaction: A Method for Studying Human - Computer - Human Interaction.* Proceedings of INTERACT '84, London, Amsterdam, pp. 269-274.

[Palmiter & Elkerton]
    Palmiter, S., J. Elkerton (1991): *An Evaluation of Animated Demonstrations for Learning Computer-based Tasks*, in: Robertson, S. P., G. M. Olson, and J. S. Olson (eds.), Reaching Through Technology, CHI '91, Conference Proceedings, pp. 257-263.

[Quast 91]
    Quast, K. J. (1991): *PLANET, Planerkennung mit aktivierten Handlungsnetzen*, GMD-Studie 195, St. Augustin.

[Rehbein 80]
    Rehbein, J. (1980): *Hervorlocken, Verbessern, Aneignen. Diskursanalytische Studien des Fremdsprachenunterrichts.* Bochum: mimeo.

[Schoen 90]
    Schoen, D.A. (1990): *Educating the Reflective Practitioner*, Jossey-Bass Publishers, San Francisco/Oxford.

[Sinclair & Coulthard 75]
    Sinclair, J. McH. & R.M. Coulthard (1975): *Towards an Analysis of Discourse*, University Press, London.

[Suchman 87]
    Suchman, L. (1987): *Plans and Situated Actions*, Cambridge University Press, Cambridge, UK.

[Wright 90]
    Wright, Ch. E. (1990): *Controlling Sequential Motor Activity*, in: Osherson, D. N., St. M. Kosslyn, J. M. Hollerbach (eds.), *Visual Cognition and Action, An Invitation to Cognitive Science*, Volume 2, Cambridge, Massachusetts, pp. 285-316.

A User-Adaptable Interface to Predict Users' Needs

Eric H. Sherman and Edward H. Shortliffe

Columbia University
New York, USA

Stanford University
Stanford, USA

ABSTRACT

User modeling has become an important and common approach for designing user interfaces (UIs). Many different types of user models, both quantitative and qualitative, have been proposed. Some of these models have been integrated into guidelines, and some have become the basis of standard techniques for UI design. But using these techniques can be both time consuming and costly, particularly if an application is expected to be used by multiple user communities, with different patterns of use. A UI designer must choose between spending a great deal of time and money designing an interface for each distinct user community, and designing a less ideal, single, generalized UI for all user communities.

User-interface management systems (UIMSs), a set of tools to support UI design and implementation, have been used to speed and improve the process of UI design. They were originally built to assist the traditional UI designers, computer scientists. They also have been used to make it easier to adopt user models in the design of UIs and to automate the integration of user models into UIs. UIMSs have allowed experts in human-factors design, without experience in computer programming, to create UIs. More recently, UIMSs have been created to incorporate user knowledge into the design of a UI automatically.

We have created a UIMS called PODIUM (personalized designer: an intelligent user-interface manager). The purpose of PODIUM is to show that a UIMS that is supplied with a UI automatically designed for a large and diverse user community can tailor that UI automatically for each of many subgroups of a large user community. The only knowledge that the system uses to complete this task is the user characteristics that divide the community into subgroups and its experience with users who have tailored UIs previously.

PODIUM was built for the domain of the physician's clinic chart and was tested on physicians from two specialties. The physicians were given the opportunity to edit their UI interactively, and these experiences were used by PODIUM to guide the building of UIs for other physicians of the same specialty. Two different UIs resulted from this procedure, one for each specialty. The physician users evaluated the feasibility and usefulness of the process, revealing that UIs built by PODIUM when it used more experience were indeed preferred to those PODIUM built using less experience.

1 INTRODUCTION

During the 1980s, computers were moved into the home, resulting in an explosion in the number of computer applications designed to be used by people who had little knowledge about computers and little energy to learn. Therefore, pressure has mounted on computer designers to create applications that are simple to use and easy to learn.

The functions of a computer application and the user's conceptualization of an application's functions meet at the *user interface* (UI). A UI translates between functionality and appearance. The ideal UI is clear and easy to use, but is simultaneously powerful. Its design determines how the information and actions of the application are displayed on the screen (or other input–output devices) and how the user can interact with the system to produce a desired result. Therefore, the ultimate goal of a designer of UIs is to provide the user both with a means to translate her desired goals into actions and with a consistently clear portrayal of the current state of the application. The latter function includes the important task of symbolizing (usually on the screen) the application's response to each user action.

The study of the design of UIs has become known as the field of human–computer interaction. A recurrent problem in this field is how to provide enough flexibility to satisfy a variety of users without incurring high costs. The developers of an application typically must expend a great deal of time, effort, and money to produce a UI. Bobrow and Topping have reported that up to one-half of the code [Bobrow et al. 86] and between 10 and 40 percent of the overall cost [Topping et al. 87] of a system is dedicated to the UI. Yet, there are multiple examples in the literature of useful and clever applications that have failed due to UIs that users have refused to accept.

Numerous approaches have been suggested for developing appropriate UIs. The original and a still frequently used technique of UI design consists of building the UI using only the application builder's preconceived notions of what the user wants and needs, based on intuition or on a minimal study of the user. This method has the benefit of being uncomplicated and inexpensive, but it has not always led to successful UIs.

One of the first and most important attempts to produce a methodology of UI design has been the development of *user models*. As the term is currently used, a user model represents characteristics of the user in a form that helps to define how to tailor a product for that person. For example, a list of actions that a secretary performs, and the order in which they are performed, can help define the optimal appearance of a workstation designed for her. Many theories on what a user model is and how it should be created have been proposed (see Section 2.1).

The modeling of users has not been used routinely by most designers of UIs, largely because of the impression that it demands an extraordinary effort. In light of this impression, much of the research on human–computer interaction has concentrated on enhancing some aspect of the user-model methodology for building UIs, in the hope that this will encourage application builders to use user modeling.

One approach has been to improve the tools used for UI development. There are two major categories of tools: *user-interface toolkits* and *user-interface management systems* (UIMSs).[1] A user interface toolkit is a library of interaction techniques such as pop-up menus, and scroll bars, that application programs can use. A UIMS is a set of tools to support UI design and implementation. In addition, a UIMS helps the UI designer to do easy prototyping, maintenance, and, in some cases, evaluation.

We have created a UIMS called PODIUM (Personalized Designer: an Intelligent User-Interface Manager). The purpose of PODIUM is to show that a UIMS that is supplied with a "generic" UI (i.e., a UI designed for a large and diverse user community), can with experience custom-tailor that UI for each of many subgroups of the user community. The only knowledge that the system uses to complete this task is the user characteristic(s) that divide the community into subgroups and PODIUM's experience with users who have previously custom-tailored UIs.

2 BACKGROUND

Research in the design of UIs has progressed from ad hoc techniques to formalized techniques for understanding human–computer interaction, and from a need to build each new UI from scratch to automated approaches for building UIs. There has also been an evolution in deciding who should be using these automated tools. New technology notwithstanding, designers can build better UIs only by understanding both the users' needs and their impressions of how the system works. This insight has led to studies that attempt to formalize the user's knowledge either qualitatively and quantitatively (some of these studies will be reviewed in Section 2.1). The results raised questions about whether tailoring the UI through the use of user modeling made better UIs. Researchers responded to these questions by developing UI design tools that automatically incorporate knowledge and experience about users, and tools that make it easier for a designer to incorporate this knowledge and experience into the UI as it is being built.

2.1 User Modeling

In 1971, Hansen proposed his first principle of user engineering: know the user [Hansen 71]. Since that date, many models of human–computer interaction have been developed. Researchers have gained a greater appreciation of the importance of expending time and

---

[1] Some people feel the term *user-interface development systems* is more descriptive.

money to build good UIs. The result has been applications that are easier to learn and to use.

The General Problem Solver [Newell and Simon 72] was a system designed both to produce a machine that solves problems requiring intelligence and to help develop a theory of how humans solve such problems. They applied it in the development of the task-oriented goals, operators, methods, and selection rules (GOMS) model. They used this performance model to specify a prototype of a user's cognitive structure, to predict the time and effort a user would expend to accomplish specific tasks.

Foley and van Dam [Foley & Van Dam 82] proposed a model of human–computer interaction that divided the process into four levels of understanding: the user's conceptual model, the semantic level, the syntactic level, and the lexical level.

Norman and coworkers [Norman 84, Norman 85, Norman & Draper 86] identified three views of an application to be considered by a UI designer: the user's model, the designer's model, and the actual system behavior – the system image. They also developed a "theory of action" that depicts human–computer interaction in terms of several steps and identified two communication gaps between the application and the user: the *gulf of execution* (a gap between what the user wants to do and how a task can be accomplished) and the *gulf of evaluation* (a gap between how the system has changed and what the user believes has occurred).

Another frequently cited model of human–computer interaction, *syntactic–semantic model of user knowledge*, was developed by Shneiderman. First described in 1979 [Shneiderman & Mayer 79] to portray computer programming, the theory distinguishes the *syntactic* and *semantic* knowledge that a user, when faced with a new application, requires if she is to understand how to complete a task. Syntactic knowledge is device-dependent and is difficult to obtain or retain (e.g., typing "quit," or "e," or command-Q are all ways to leave an application). Semantic knowledge is divided into computer concepts (e.g., files and directories) and task concepts (e.g., a spreadsheet) both of which can be subdivided into actions for the user to undertake (e.g., find results of laboratory test) and objects on which to act (e.g., a laboratory database).

The information used to model individuals or groups of users can be obtained through observation of the workplace, and can be collected in either a structured (e.g., recording each action and the times at which they occur) or an unstructured (e.g., taking notes of important events) fashion. Information can also be obtained through listening. Listening can be subdivided into open-ended listening (e.g., unstructured interviews) and structured analysis (e.g., directed questioning, taking inventory of tasks used, or diagramming actions). A third method for collecting this knowledge is experimenting (e.g., testing UI mockups or prototypes and role playing with the user). Automated tools for obtaining information have been based on those methods that lend themselves easily to automation (e.g., the directed interview), while other information is are still gathered only by hand (e.g., unstructured interviews). Any attempt to automate the construction of user models, in the hope of speeding production of UIs, must deal with not only the automation of these knowledge-gathering techniques, but also the automation of new techniques and the creation of syntactics for understanding the acquired knowledge.

2.2 Direct Uses for User Models

The development of user models has had a greater benefit than simply providing a better understanding of the psychology of human–computer interaction. These pioneering works have been the inspiration for research in user understanding, for new approaches to the design of UIs, and for new tools for building UIs. Over the past decade, numerous books have appeared that are filled with advice on how to design a UI. Many papers and books have been written that lay out basic design principles, most of which use one or more of these psychological user models as their foundation.

Examples of systems and theories that use modeling theory to mold the design of UIs include the Consul system for knowledge-based UI design [Mark 86], and the *Naive Theory of Computation* [Owen 86] for understanding how a user thinks about computers, among others [Reilly 86] which attempted to close Norman's gulfs of execution and evaluation. The GOMS model was extended by Gong, John, and Young [Gong & Ellerton 90, John 90, Young & Whittington 90]. The work of Card, Simon, and Newell [Card et al. 83] has led them to assert that, before the syntactics of a UI are created, the UI designer should formally define both the task and computer concepts that must be represented – a process called the *task analysis* – and she should also define the user who will use the system. The mark of Shneiderman's ideas can also be seen in other work done in human–computer interaction [Fisher & Joy 87].

We have used the framework of Shneiderman's syntactic–semantic model of user knowledge to help define the areas in which PODIUM acts independently, and those in which it interacts with the user (see Section 2.5).

2.3 Problems with the User-Model Approach

Despite the usefulness of user models, recent work has raised doubts about the flexibility and feasibility of user modeling. Even if the guidelines and techniques of user modeling are followed carefully, an "ideal" match of application and user through a UI is impossible to achieve. A few factors have been identified that limit the designer's capacity to create an ideal UI.

First, the term "user modeling" denotes a nebulous concept. Any technique that claims to model the user must require generalization. Models generally reflect the community, not the individual. Yet individual differences remain large, even within well-defined user communities (e.g., the physicians of a single medical subspecialty). The designer can recognize and deal with inter-user variation only by further subdividing communities, until he is dealing with individuals. Norman has stated that, even when the tasks and users are restricted, an optimal design is often not possible [Norman 83]. And Shneiderman has proclaimed that "there can be no 'average' user, and that compromises must be made or multiple versions of a system must be constructed" [Shneiderman 87].

Even if it were possible to produce models that accurately reflected a user's knowledge at a given moment about the application and its domain, that knowledge is not static, as user modeling assumes it is. A typical user may start using a system while she is a novice, gain experience over time, and eventually become an expert. As she grows more experienced in the use of an application, the techniques that she prefers to use in manipulating the application will change.

In addition to, and partially as a result of these weaknesses in user modeling, other researchers have noted their inability to create sufficiently accurate models. (In this context, *accuracy* is defined as the degree to which a model or interface matches the desires, needs, and skills of a user.) Baecker and Buxton [Baecker & Buxton 87] have asserted that the effort to develop formal models has so far contributed little to our understanding of deeper cognitive issues that are the basis for important design decisions. And, in the Computer Human Interaction Conference Proceedings of 1989, two of the articles [Lewis et al. 89, Young et al. 89] noted the inability of psychologists and philosophers to translate their theories and models into usable solutions for interface design. Young also stated that it is unrealistic to expect UI designers to engage in user modeling with the tools currently available, due to the inadequacy of those tools and the lack of constraints on typical user models.

Finally, user modeling is not a practical approach when an application has a large number of significantly different user communities. One of the purposes and perhaps the greatest strength of user modeling is its ability to create relatively accurate UIs for a typical user. In practice, however, when the user community is large and is composed of many distinct subcommunities, it is impossible to define the typical user. A clever UI design for one segment of that community may be inappropriate for another. The tasks that have been selected for inclusion in the UI for one group may prove to be insufficient for another. But defining a user model and UI for each small user community would be very difficult and time consuming.

A UI for an automated medical clinic chart (the outpatient record for a physician's patient) is an application with many user communities (physician specialties and subspecialties). Furthermore, each type of subspecialty uses tailored charts with attributes specific to the discipline. For example, an examination of the paper clinic charts currently in use at the Stanford University Medical Center reveals numerous similarities across subspecialties, but also significant differences. These differences include data (or tasks) which are required by users of one subspecialty, but are felt to be unimportant by the users of another.

In business, the problem of multiple small user communities has typically been faced from a perspective different from that of users in an academic setting. If a new application is successful, the owner has an incentive to deliver it to a greater number of users. When originally conceived, however, UIs are often tailored for a only one small community of users.

An attempt to transfer the interface to a different group of users can be difficult and expensive. When a new user community is targeted, the user model (implicit or explicit) on which the UI was based is no longer accurate. If the builder of the application is to maintain the usefulness and ease of use of the system, he must adjust the user model such that the UI that it supports accurately reflects the desires, needs, and skills of the new user community. Both the user model and the UI must be accordingly redesigned.

Some application builders deal with this problem by providing a UI that can satisfy the needs all of its potential user communities; that is, they create a generalized UI. This saves significant time and money whenever an application is transferred. But generalized UIs, although less costly, are also less efficient. They contain more features and provide more ways to manipulate those features than any single user or user community needs. An analogous tradeoff occurs in database-management systems. For example, access to the data and the functions of a university grading system is not offered to all users. Faculty must be able to access, add, and change grades for students in the classes that they teach. Workers in the registrar's office must be able to read and print the grades of all students, but should not be able to change the grade of any student. Individual students should only have the capability to read their own grades. Not only does the university not want students to be able to change their own grades, or to look at the grades of other students, but giving a student access to the entire database and all of its functions also will confuse him and make it less likely that he will be able to accomplish his original task (i.e. to look up his grade for English 101). The same confusion is likely to occur to users using any UI overloaded with capabilities.

The theoretical limitations of user modeling and the practical tradeoff of generalization versus cost have demonstrated how difficult it is to employ user modeling to represent users in detail. These problems have proven to be the impetus for much of the research of the past 5 years. The goals of this work have been to reduce the effort and cost of the process of UI design (see Section 2.4.1), to transfer some of the work into the hands of designers with more knowledge about human factors (Section 2.4.2), and to place some of the responsibility for defining the user's requirements into the hands of the user, through her interaction with the application (see section 2.4.3). These new approaches free application builders to spend more time custom-tailoring and testing UIs for multiple user communities.

2.4 Refinement of the User-Model Approach – User-Interface Management Systems

Because of the weaknesses in user modeling, researchers have attempted to refine this technique. The approaches that have been taken include speeding the process of building a UI, thus allowing more time to be spent on modeling and testing. This goal has been accomplished by easing the process of building a UI, allowing human-factors experts (who have more knowledge about appropriate design techniques) to be the designer, and involving the user in the design of portions of the UI, thus obtaining the modeling information from the most logical source.

2.4.1 Speeding UI Design

One of the first and most successful steps toward reducing the cost and effort involved in the design of UIs was to improve the tools used for UI development. There are two major categories of tools: user-interface toolkits and UIMSs. The goal of both these tools is to allow designers to build UIs that are more accurate and to simplify the creation and maintenance of interface code. The ways in which this goal has be accomplished were reviewed by Myers [Myers 89].

The early UIMSs were language-based. A special-purpose language is used to specify the UI. Many languages (including context-free grammars, state-transition diagrams, menu networks, and event languages) have been used. These systems require that the designer be a programmer, and that he learn a new language. Three of the better known examples in this category are HYPERTEXT [Shafer 88], Rapid/USE [Wasserman & Shewmake 82] and Sassafras [Hill 86]. Recently, the development of UIMSs based on object-oriented languages has made such tools easier to use because they can easily handle highly interactive, direct manipulation interfaces [Sibert et al. 86].

2.4.2 Easing the Process of UI Design

The next class of UIMSs is known as the *graphical-specification UIMS*. These UIMSs provide graphical tools to the designer, allowing him to place objects on the screen with various input–output tools. Many of these UIMSs require the user to have little or no computer programming. Examples are Trillium [Henderson 83] and Menulay [Buxton et al. 83]. Also, HyperCard and the NeXT™ Interface Builder partially fit this classification, although they require the designer to write program code. An interesting example in this class is the more flexible Peridot [Myers & Buxton 87], which allows designers to build their own interaction techniques from primitive structures (such as lines, circles, and text). In addition, the system simplifies the process by using inference to assist Peridot in understanding what the user wants to build, shortening what would otherwise be a tedious process. For example, when building a pop-up menu, a designer can specify that clicking on a line of the menu with a mouse will cause that line to become highlighted. When two lines of the menu are so designated, the system uses inference to guess that every line that the user selects should be highlighted, and asks the user to corroborate this supposition. The code that implements the result of this interaction is produced automatically by Peridot.

A third class of UIMSs comprises those that allow for automatic creation. Typically, these tools allow the designer to specify the application semantics (both actions and objects), and then automatically to build the UI by associating each procedure with an appropriate graphic representation. For example, the Control Panel Interface [Fisher & Joy 87] associates Boolean operators with buttons and integers with knobs or bars. Some of these systems allow the designer to edit the results by overriding the representation that the system has chosen.

One of the most important advances that has resulted from the emergence of UIMS tools has been the slow evolution toward placing these tools into the hands of designers who are not computer programmers (The Trillium, Menulay and Peridot systems, the object-oriented language-based tools, and the Control Panel accomplish this task to varying degrees). This trend has allowed greater involvement of human-factors experts in the design process, with the potential benefit of the development of more efficient and accurate UIs, that are more closely based on user models.

2.4.3 Involving the User

Another recent trend in the field of UI design has been to place some of the control into the hands of the user, that is, to allow the user to custom-tailor some portion of his UI. Perhaps the most important decision that UI designers must make when creating a UI or UIMS is what parts of the UI, if any, will be available for users to adapt. A useful way to divide the UI into parts is the syntactic–semantic model of user knowledge, which a UI designer can use to divide the UI into syntactic and semantic components, semantics being divisible into computer and task concepts [Shneiderman 87].

The UI designer initially involves the user in the design process by allowing her to have input into the syntactics of a UI. Some systems allow the user to choose the type of dialogue mode she wishes to use, prior to the start of a session. Among these systems is Workspaces [Enderle 85], which has partial adaptability. The most significant example in this group, reported by Kanotorowitz and Sudarsky [Kantorowitz & Sudarski 89], is an adaptable UI named GUIDE that allows the user to switch between different dialogue modes at any time, even in the middle of multistep commands. Other investigators have had the user help to define the command-language syntactics of their system [Wixon et al. 83].

Walton and Shortliffe created Tailor, an adaptable UI for a physician's workstation [Walton & Shortliffe 89]. The part of the UI that is adaptable is not the syntactics or even the computer concepts, but rather is the task concepts. Each new user is interviewed, and is asked to fill out checklists that determine what tasks will be included in the UI. Tailor uses an expert system, with knowledge in the form of design heuristics (at least some of which are based on [Shneiderman 87]), and the knowledge obtained from the user, to build the UI. A weakness of Tailor is that the user must specify each task that eventually appears in the UI, a lengthy process.

2.4.4 The PODIUM approach

PODIUM fits into the category of user adaptable UIMSs, although only some of the UI design responsibility is in the hands of its users. In addition, PODIUM stores the knowledge obtained from each user to build a model of each user community. These models are used to create new UIs, custom-tailored for each particular user community. Although there has been speculation about UIs that are adaptable based upon user characteristics, none has yet been shown to work [Eberts & Eberts 89].

User characteristics, which are obtained directly from users, can be used to divide a large user community into numerous smaller groups. Users are supplied with simple UI editing tools with which they can simultaneously custom-tailor their own UI and provide the system with knowledge that can be used to help model their user subcommunity. The models are used to build UIs that predict the needs and desires of users from the same user subcommunity (members of which have the same user characteristics). When a new user is introduced to the system, she is presented with a UI that has been custom-tailored for her by incorporation of the system's knowledge of past users.

Although we agree with Walton and Shortliffe that it is appropriate to provide users of physicians' workstation with control over only the task concepts included in their UIs [Walton & Shortliffe 89], since this is the only part of the UI in which they are expected to have expertise, we believe that such a system must be flexible enough to allow a novice or busy user to do an absolute minimum of work (in PODIUM, the user is required only to type her name, to select her specialty or subspecialty, and to quit the application), while allowing the more interested user to custom-tailor her UI extensively. Even the novice user should walk away having created a UI that is custom-tailored for her.

3 PODIUM

The purpose of PODIUM is to show that a UIMS that is supplied with a generic UI, designed for a large and diverse user community, can automatically tailor that UI for each of many user subcommunities. The only knowledge that the system needs to complete this task is the user characteristics that divide the community into subgroups and its experience with users who have custom-tailored their UIs previously.

3.1 Domain

The domain chosen for PODIUM is the clinic chart for a physician's workstation. Physicians fit the criteria set out for a user community for PODIUM, and there is a need for friendly UIs in the field. Physicians constitute a large diverse community of users, including novice and experienced computer users. Their user community is easily divisible. Specialties and subspecialties provide a natural grouping for subcommunities of physicians, and it is simple for users to identify to which group they belong during their interaction with the system.

PODIUM's full functionality cannot be demonstrated unless the division of users into subcommunities corresponds to a need for significant differences in the product of the system, the UI map. As noted in Section 2.3, paper clinic charts currently in use reveal differences that are found across physicians' subspecialties. Therefore, the design of UIs for a computer-based clinic chart should allow for differences in the UI of different subspecialties.

The paper clinic chart is the display of the clinic records of one patient. It contains patient data collected previously and blanks where new data can be entered. Likewise it contains old notes and orders as well as places to insert new ones. Some paper clinic charts contain predesigned flowsheets for the data that are frequently collected in that subspecialty. Any other data required for a particular patient must be entered either on blank flowsheets or in handwritten notes. Some clinic charts even contain assorted test-report slips that have been pasted in.

If she needs data that are not in the clinic chart, the physician must examine the complete medical record of the patient (that includes hospital admission data and information from other clinics). This kind of comprehensive data repository is represented in PODIUM by a complete generic chart that is always available to a user.

The UI model of a clinic chart needs to contain a representation of only those parts of the UI that the system allows the user to custom-tailor. In which parts of the UI design process should a user be included, and in which parts should the responsibility be left to the UI designer? Although a definitive answer is outside the scope of this project, it is reasonable to start by allowing users to custom-tailor those parts of the UI about which they have expertise and about which they are therefore likely to have an opinion.

The users in the domain of the physician's clinic chart can be expected to be experts only in the area of task concepts (as defined by Shneiderman [Shneiderman 87]). In PODIUM, task concepts are depicted as graphics that display data, or that allow the physician to add data or to order tests. Physicians understand the elements of the clinic chart, since they use charts daily and we can expect them to have opinions regarding how charts should be arranged and what elements should be included. Therefore, the user map needs to represent the graphical depiction of the tasks only: which are included, how they are organized, and, if there is a choice, how they are represented. All other design decisions (representing the computer concepts and the syntactics) are integrated into the permanent part of the generic UI and thus are in all UIs created by the system.

The user map is a representation of the organization, and a record of the tasks (or information) included in the chart, not a record of the appearance and interaction techniques (the *look and feel*) of the chart. Also included in the model and therefore available for custom-tailoring are the display-mode decisions about which users have expertise, such as using graphs versus tables to display certain types of data.

3.2 Scenario

Each new user of PODIUM is asked two questions. First, the user supplies his name. Second, he summarizes his user characteristics by identifying his specialty or subspecialty. PODIUM uses this information to identify the user's community, and thus the appropriate "ideal" user map, and proceeds to build the initial UI. The user can then use PODIUM's editing tools to custom-tailor the default UI that is provided for him. Finally, he is offered the opportunity to include in his final version of the UI the most recent edits performed by other users who have the same specialty (see Section 3.3.3). These edits are UI design changes from users of the same community that have not been included in the ideal user map (the edits are offered to new users to identify those UI design changes that are desired by most users of the community). The completed UI is then added to the cumulative user map that corresponds to the community delineated by the user's specialty.

3.3 Design

The structure of PODIUM is based on that of the typical UIMS. The most basic UIMS is the two-module system shown in Figure 1. In PODIUM, the UI Generator is used to design and implement the UI. It contains the data structures used to describe the UIs – the UI Definition. The Interaction Handler arbitrates all interaction between the user and PODIUM (which includes allowing the user to custom-tailor the UI.

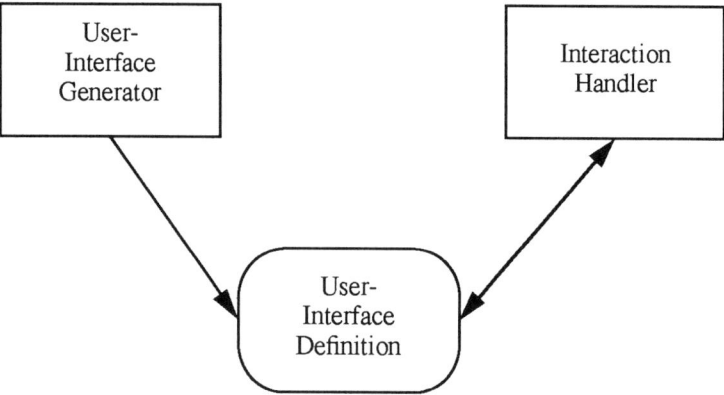

Figure 1: The two-module model of a user-interface management system. During run time, all interaction between the user-interface and PODIUM is arbitrated by the Interaction Handler. This interaction occurs through the UI, as defined by the UI Definition. This definition is generated and translated into a UI by the UI Generator.

3.3.1 User maps

The UI Generator can be thought of as a user-map center. It stores a representation of each UI built through user interaction with the system, as well as a representation of PODIUM's cumulative experience within each user community. These are user maps in the sense that the data contained within them constitute the task information of the UI: what tasks have been included in the user's UI, what the organization of the UI is (the UI consists of multiple pages, each filled with tasks and buttons to access other pages), and, for any specific task, what design mode has been chosen to represent it visually. It is these and only these data that can be edited by the user.

The single-user data structure for mapping the UI (the single-user map) is a *directed acyclic graph*. Each node on the graph represents either a UI page name or a single task or data group (e.g., the patient's chief complaint, or the electrolytes laboratory test). The arcs represent page-to-page connections (a button on the parent page that provides direct access to the child page) or the inclusion of a task on a particular page of the UI. A page may be accessible from more than one other page (it may have multiple parents), and any task may appear on any number of pages (it also may have multiple parents). Therefore, if a task is particularly important to a user, it can be included on multiple pages of the UI, and a page that the user perceives as important can be accessible from multiple locations in the UI. Thus, the user can redesign the tasks of his UI. Finally, each task in the data structure is associated with a pointer to PODIUM's database, where the graphics and code associated with each task are stored. Some tasks can be displayed in more than one way (e.g., both tables and graphs for the same data elements); this pointer defines which display mode has been selected.

The user-community data structure is also a directed acyclic graph that has been modified to represent a cumulative user map. Each arc is labeled with the percentage of users belonging to that community who have included that particular parent–child arc in their UIs. The UI Generator translates a cumulative user map into a new ideal (single) user map by using a simple thresholding technique: Any arc of the cumulative user map that has been included by a preselected percentage of individual users is included in the new ideal UI.

The benefit of using a high number for this threshold is that only the additions made by the first one or two users of a community are automatically included in the next ideal UI (e.g., if the third user out of three adds a new arc, only a threshold over 34 percent will not automatically include that arc in the user map). In contrast, low thresholds make it more likely that a good new idea (represented as an arc between two nodes) will be included in future ideal UIs. We chose a high threshold of 49 percent for our initial evaluation of PODIUM because of the limited number of users tested (five physicians from each of two specialties). If a lower threshold had been used (e.g., 25 percent), any addition that one of the first three users had made would have been included in the ideal UI for the fourth user in that specialty. Ideally, the quantity of this threshold should be obtained experimentally.

3.3.2 UI Building Tools

The UI Generator builds the UI from a single user map. It can be subdivided into individual modules, including a glue system, which physically builds the UI; the libraries, which contain the data used to build the UI; and two elements (the Task Builder and the Module Builder) that build new data and graphics for inclusion in the libraries, as shown in Figure 2. The libraries are stored as relations in PODIUM's relational database. The other relations in the database are the collections of single user maps and cumulative user maps.

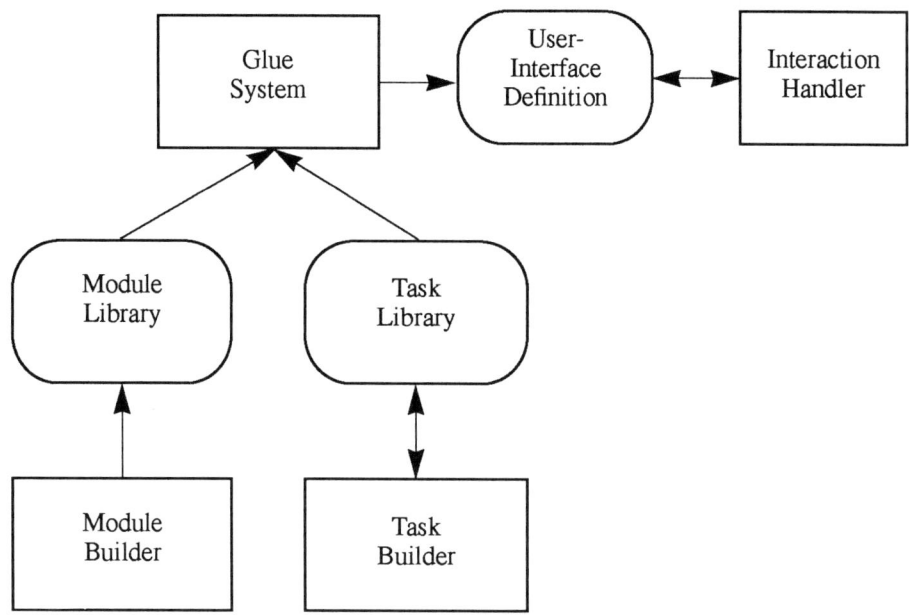

Figure 2: The user-interface management system with detailed UI Generator. The UI is built by the glue system, typically from existing components drawn from the task library (e.g. Chief Complaint). The elements of the task library are generated using the task builder from existing components of the module library (e.g. an empty scrolling field or a title field). And the modules from the module library are built from scratch using the module builder.

The library relations are divided among the UI Task Library and the UI Module Library. The UI Task Library contains all the tasks in the complete generic UI, including the code and graphics required to insert the task into the UI. The UI Module Library contains templates that were used to build some of the tasks in the task library. These templates are generic structures, such as tables, that can be filled with any combination of test results known to PODIUM and to the hospital database. These templates are available to the more sophisticated users who want to create new tasks. The UI Module Builder and the UI Task Builder both use the SuperCard graphics and script-building tools [Gookin 89] to create their respective libraries. SuperCard provides a multiple-window environment in which a UI can be represented as a single window with a consistent look and feel and still have multiple pages. In SuperCard, this window consisting of pages is known as a stack. Other windows are used for the graphical database relations and other functions. Ideally, the quantity of this threshold should be obtained experimentally.

3.3.3 Editing Tools

The UI Generator (Figures 1 and 2) calculates the single-user map or ideal UI from the cumulative user map. This cumulative model is supplied to the UI Generator from the relational database at the start of a session with a new user, so that the glue system can build and display the new UI. Figure 3 shows a sample page of a typical UI. The user can browse through this custom-tailored UI and, if she wishes, can further custom-tailor it using the simple tools of the Interaction Handler.

The screen shown in Figure 4 is displayed when the user wishes to add a button to provide direct access to another page of the UI. She must first use the mouse to select the name of the page to be added (or she can select "Define New Page" if she wants to create a new page), and then must select "Add Item" to complete the change. She can continue to add buttons that provide access to other pages, or she can quit by selecting the button at the bottom of the form, labeled "Done – Show Changes." After she quits, the system transfers control to the UI Generator, which revises both the user's single-user map and the user's current UI. Figure 5 shows the screen that is displayed when the user wants to remove a task from the current page. In addition to removing the task, she can simultaneously add that task (using the "Move To" button) to another page.

The final function of PODIUM is designed to help solve the problem of how to recognize the importance of a new idea. A demonstration of this dilemma could occur when the tenth user of a particular user community creates a new UI. If he makes a change to the UI that moves the cumulative user map closer to the theoretically ideal UI, (i.e., the change would be agreed to by the average user of that user community), then it would be best if the importance of this change were recognized immediately and the change were included as part of the initial UI offered to the next new user belonging to that user community. But because this change has appeared in the user map of only one of the first 10 users, it will not be offered to the next user.

In an attempt to recognize important new ideas and to include them in future UIs, PODIUM maintains a record of the most recent changes made by the users of each user community. Any subsequent user who does not make a minimum number of edits (arbitrarily set at eight) will be offered the opportunity to include the changes recorded in this list (where the total of current user changes and offered past user changes is eight). PODIUM proposes the change as a "Yes" or "No" question (Figure 6), a form with which even the most novice of users can deal.

Thus, a change made by a previous user will be offered to the next user unless the latter makes numerous (at least eight) changes. This technique will increase the likelihood that an important new idea will be included in subsequent UIs. If the second user selects a change from the list, that change remains on (and is moved to the front) of the list. Eventually, if the change is offered to and accepted by enough subsequent users so that it passes the specified threshold, it will be incorporated into the next ideal UI model.

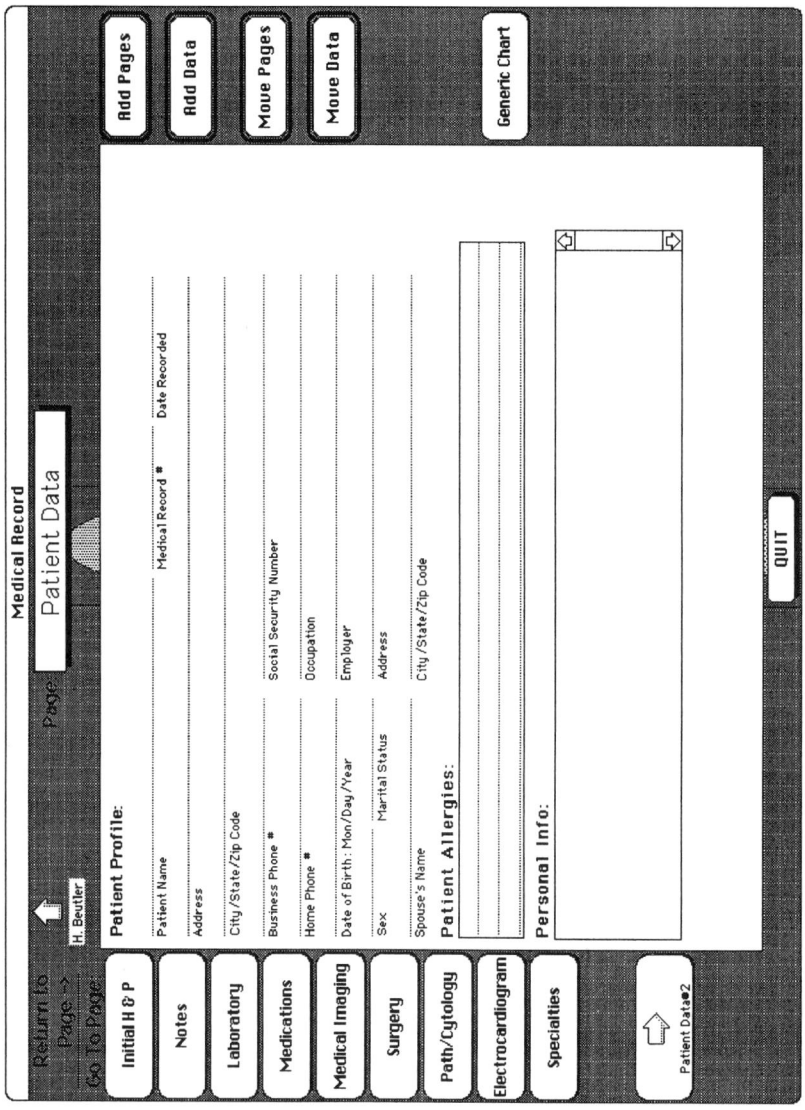

Figure 3: A sample page of PODIUM's clinic chart. The name of the page appears at the top. When the user selects the buttons on the left side of the page, the display changes to show the corresponding page. The four buttons on the top right provide access to the editing tools

A User-Adaptable Interface to Predict Users' Needs

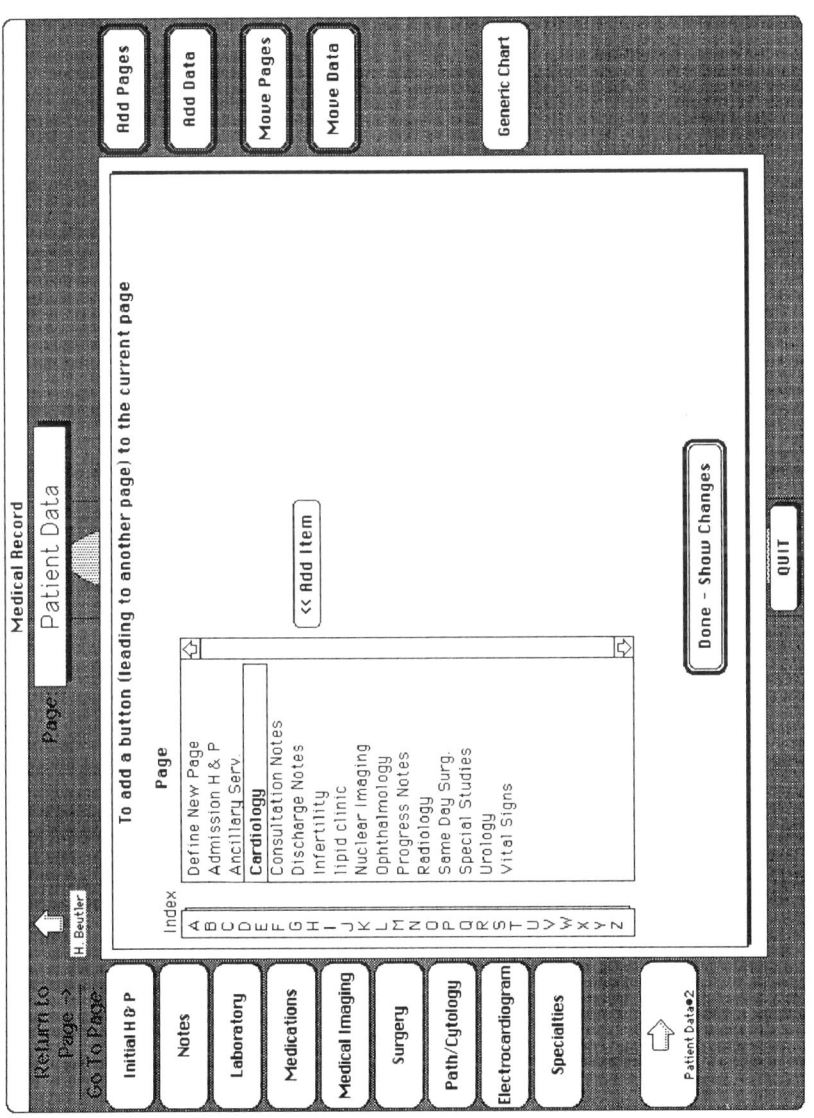

Figure 4: Add a page. A user can go directly from this page to another by clicking on the buttons on the left. To add a new button, allowing direct access to a page of choice, the user (1) selects the page to be added (Cadiology in this example), then (2) selects the "Add Item" Button.

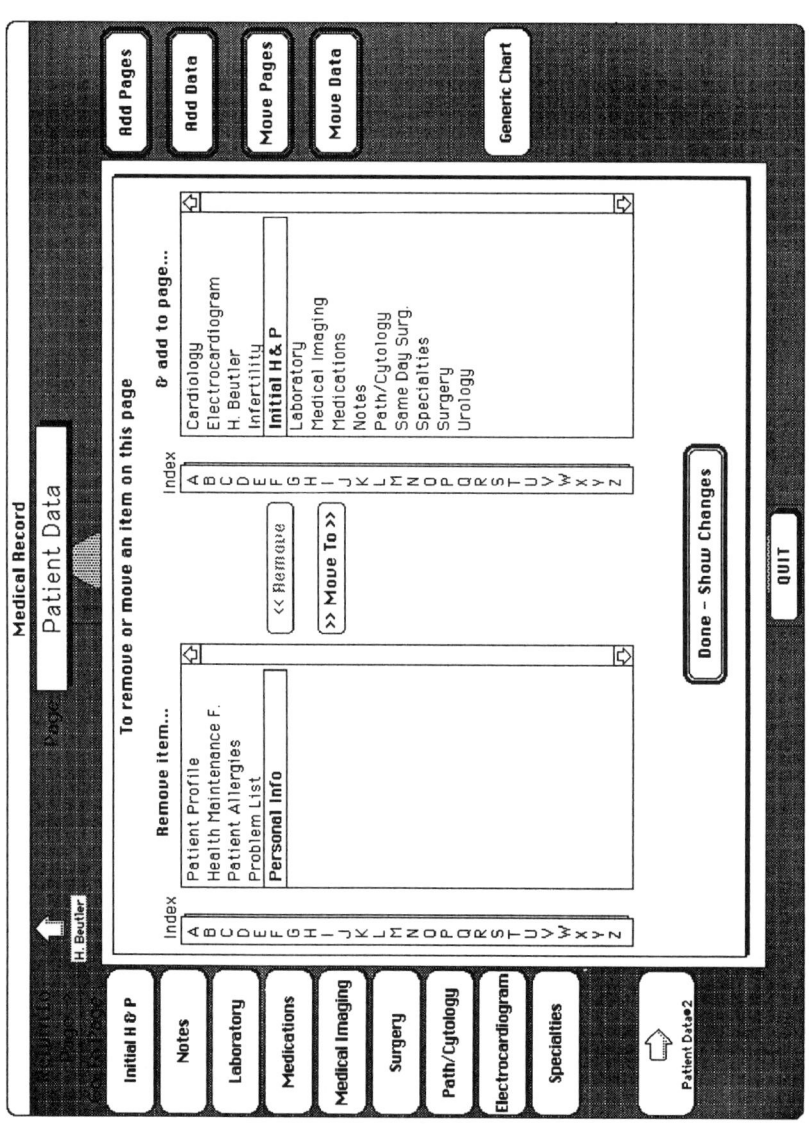

Figure 5: Move a task. To remove "Personal Info" from this page ("Patient Data") and to add it to the page labeled "Initial H&P", the user (1) selects the item to be moved ("Personal Info"), (2) selects the page the item is to be moved ("Initial H&P"), then (3) selects the "Move To" button.

A User-Adaptable Interface to Predict Users' Needs

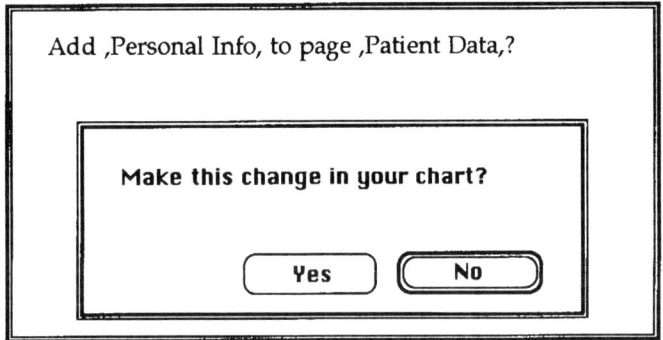

Figure 6: Forced Learning.
Old ideas that have not been included in the user map are tested on new users by asking simple "Yes" or "No" questions

4 EXPERIMENTAL DESIGN

To demonstrate that user characteristics can be used to model users, and that experience with these users can be used to custom-tailor a chart for a user community, we set out to show that physicians could use PODIUM to produce and custom-tailor accurate UIs.

4.1 Issues to Assess

The first requirement for the success of PODIUM was a demonstration that users (many of them novices) can designate their user characteristics and can use PODIUM's editing tools to alter the user map and custom-tailor their UIs. Second, we had to show that PODIUM could represent the UI such that it can use the information obtained through its experience to refine the initial, generic UI. Finally, we needed to show that the results of the interaction of PODIUM and its users produce UIs that are improvements over what would exist without PODIUM.

To assess the last point, we had to show that the UIs created by PODIUM directly from its experience were perceived by users to be a better representation of their needs than the original generic chart, and that the UIs that were custom-tailored by users were in turn perceived by those users to be a better representation of their needs than the UI with which they started.

To avoid the bias inherent in basing our evaluation on people who have used PODIUM and who may be attached to their own ideas (although, if it exists, this attachment is a positive prognosticator of the usefulness of the system), we also need to show that independent judges (physicians who have not used PODIUM, but are members of the same community), find that the final UI created from PODIUM's experience is more accurate for the users of their specialty than are both the generic UI and the UIs developed for other specialities. We shall ask users from each community that has been studied, who have not used PODIUM, to choose from among the UIs represented by the final cumulative user maps.

4.2 Methods

Eight physicians volunteered to test PODIUM, four from each of two specialties of general internal medicine and urology. These two groups were chosen because they were judged in advance to have different information needs. The study was designed to show that many individuals from a single group can together produce a tailored UI, and that the physicians from different specialties do have different information needs that can be represented in PODIUM.

Each physician was given a brief (5-minute) explanation of the purpose of PODIUM, and then was allowed to make edits to the clinic chart with no time limit. For a user to interact with PODIUM, the typical paper chart must translate easily into the electronic chart (or UI) of PODIUM. Also, the user must be able to understand what is meant by editing the chart, and how to accomplish that task. The physicians were told that they could make any changes to the UI or, if they were satisfied with its appearance, they could leave the UI as it was. Interactive instructions are part of PODIUM, but we often offered additional explanations as we observed the session and discussed with the users' their impressions of PODIUM's strengths and weaknesses. Upon completion of their interactions with the system, the physicians were asked several questions relating to the experience and the adequacy of the UI they had created with PODIUM.

The two groups of physicians had different levels of experience with computers. The physicians in the general-internal-medicine group all had had experience with computers; the urologists all had had little or no experience. Yet, as we shall show, there was great similarity in the way these two groups used PODIUM and in their opinions of the system.

5 RESULTS

Responses to the series of questions asked immediately after the users finished testing PODIUM are summarized in Figures 7 through 8. The first two questions pertained to the representation of the chart in electronic form. The users agreed that PODIUM created a close but not direct translation of the paper chart (Figure 7, question 1), and that this representation of the chart was easy to understand (Figure 7, question 2).

Whether the user understand the concept of editing PODIUM's UI, and the task of using its editing tools, is not as clear. The concept of editing the UI was introduced during the 5-minute explanation at the beginning of each session with a new user. Yet the users often needed further assistance to complete an action, as is reflected by their responses to the questionnaire. Question 3 asked the users to rate the ease with which they understood the

A User-Adaptable Interface to Predict Users' Needs

Question 1. Was the computer chart similar (analogous) to the typical clinic paper chart?

Similar ___ ___ ___ ___ ___ Dissimilar
            1   2   3   4   5

All users $2\,^{1}/_{2}$ General internists $2\,^{3}/_{4}$ Urologists $2\,^{3}/_{4}$

Question 2. Was it easy or difficult to understand how to use the computer chart (e.g., did you understand how to move from one page to another and back again)?

Easy ___ ___ ___ ___ ___ Difficult
       1   2   3   4   5

All users $1\,^{5}/_{6}$ General internists 2 Urologists $1\,^{3}/_{4}$

Figure 7: Questions pertaining to the style of the clinic chart.

concept of editing the UI (this does not include actually using the editing tools to perform the edit). The responses indicated that they had some difficulty (Figure 8). Similarly, when the physicians were asked whether they had difficulty understanding how to use the tools to execute an edit once they had thought of it, their reactions were mixed (Figure 8, question 4).

The users were give the freedom to change anything in their UI or to change nothing at all. The session ended when the user expressed satisfaction with the current state of his UI. The average number of edits completed successfully by the users from both of the specialties was 4.5 (5.0 for the general internists, and 4.0 for the urologists). The number of additional edits accepted by each user when offered at the end of the session (forced learning; see Section 3.3.3) was 1.75 (1.5 for the general internists, and 2.0 for the urologists). This number does not include the first user for each group, who of course was not offered this opportunity. The use of forced learning caused 4 edits to be included in the final charts (1 for the general internists, and 3 for the urologists) that otherwise would not have been included. An example of this phenomenon occurred in the development of the urologist chart (Figure 9). The second urologist removed the page "Infertility" from the page "Specialties" and added it to the page "Patient Data." This change had the effect of allowing the urologist rapid access to data contained within the page "Infertility"; that is, the urologist no longer needed to go through the page "Specialties" to get to the page "Infertility." The next two urologists did not independently make this same change in the UI, but when the edit was offered to them at the end of their sessions, they both chose to accept it. Therefore, the arc created (page "Patient Data" to page "Infertility") broke the 49 percent threshold and is included in the final urologist UI. Similarly, the arc removed (page "Specialties" to page "Infertility") fell below threshold and was eliminated from the final urologist UI.

The UIs that resulted from the cumulative work of the two groups are represented graphically in figures 9 and 10. The differences between these and the generic chart shown in figure 11 can be observed. Numerically, there are a total of 6 differences between the generic chart and the general internist's chart, 7 differences between the generic chart and the urologist's chart, and 10 differences between the general internist's chart and the urologist's chart.

In addition to establishing numeric evidence of PODIUM's ability to incorporate its users' knowledge and opinions into UI design decisions, this study attempted to demonstrate that, as PODIUM accumulates user input, its users prefer a chart that it builds using that experience (with users of the same group) over a chart it builds based on less experience. The users were asked to compare their final UI (the UI that resulted from their completed interaction with PODIUM) with both the generic UI, and the UI that they were offered initially, prior to making any changes. They were also asked to compare the chart that they were initially offered to the generic UI (except for the first user in each group, for which these two UIs were the same).

Question 3. How easy or difficult was it to understand the concept of editing (changing or rearranging) the computer chart?

Easy   1   2   3   4   5   Difficult

All users $2\frac{7}{8}$ General internists $2\frac{3}{4}$ Urologists 3

Did you make any changes to the chart?   All "Yes"

Question 4. How easy or difficult was it to edit (change or rearrange) the computer chart once you had decided what change you wanted to make?

Easy   1   2   3   4   5   Difficult

All users $3\frac{1}{8}$ General internists $3\frac{1}{2}$ Urologists $2\frac{3}{4}$

Figure 8:   Questions pertaining to editing of the clinic chart.

A User-Adaptable Interface to Predict Users' Needs 307

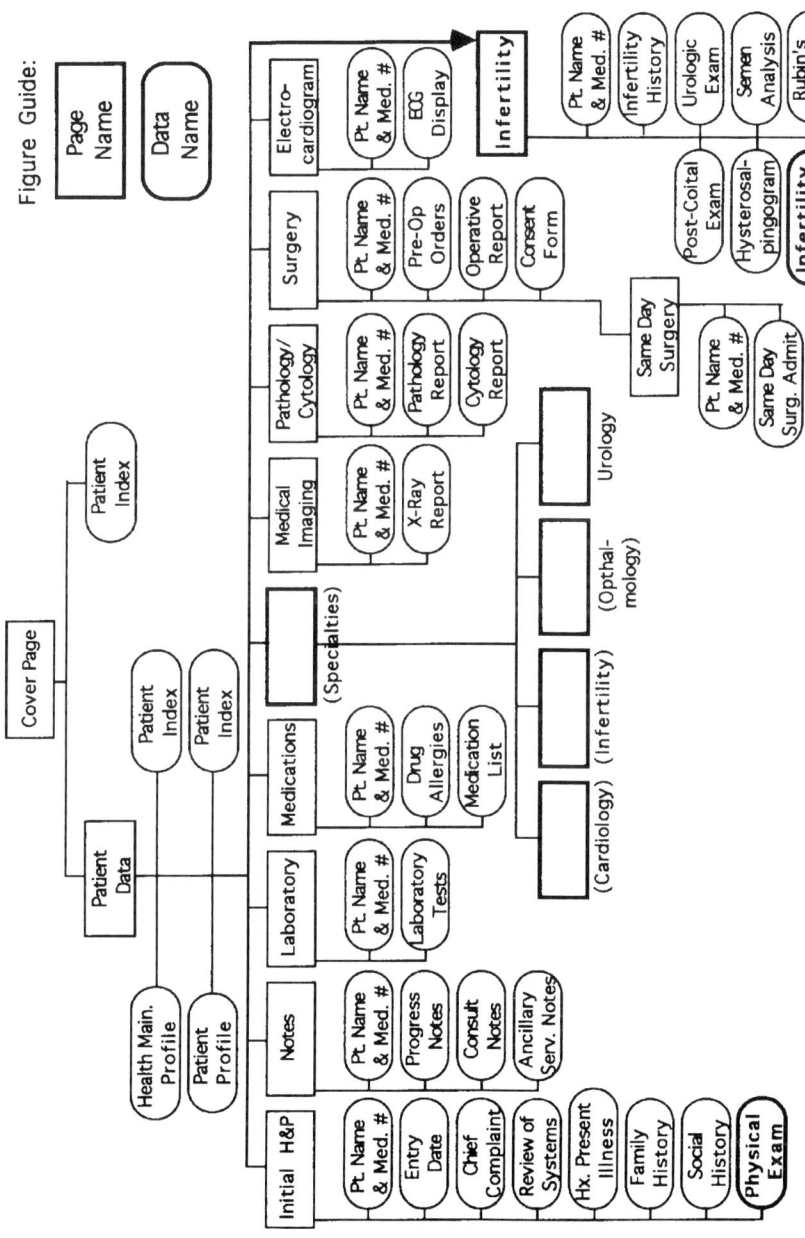

Figure 9: The urologist's final chart. The entries and arrows in boldface type were not found in the generic chart. The empty boxes outlined in boldface are entries that were eliminated. Note that the ovals indicate data elements on a page, whereas the rectangles indicate page names.

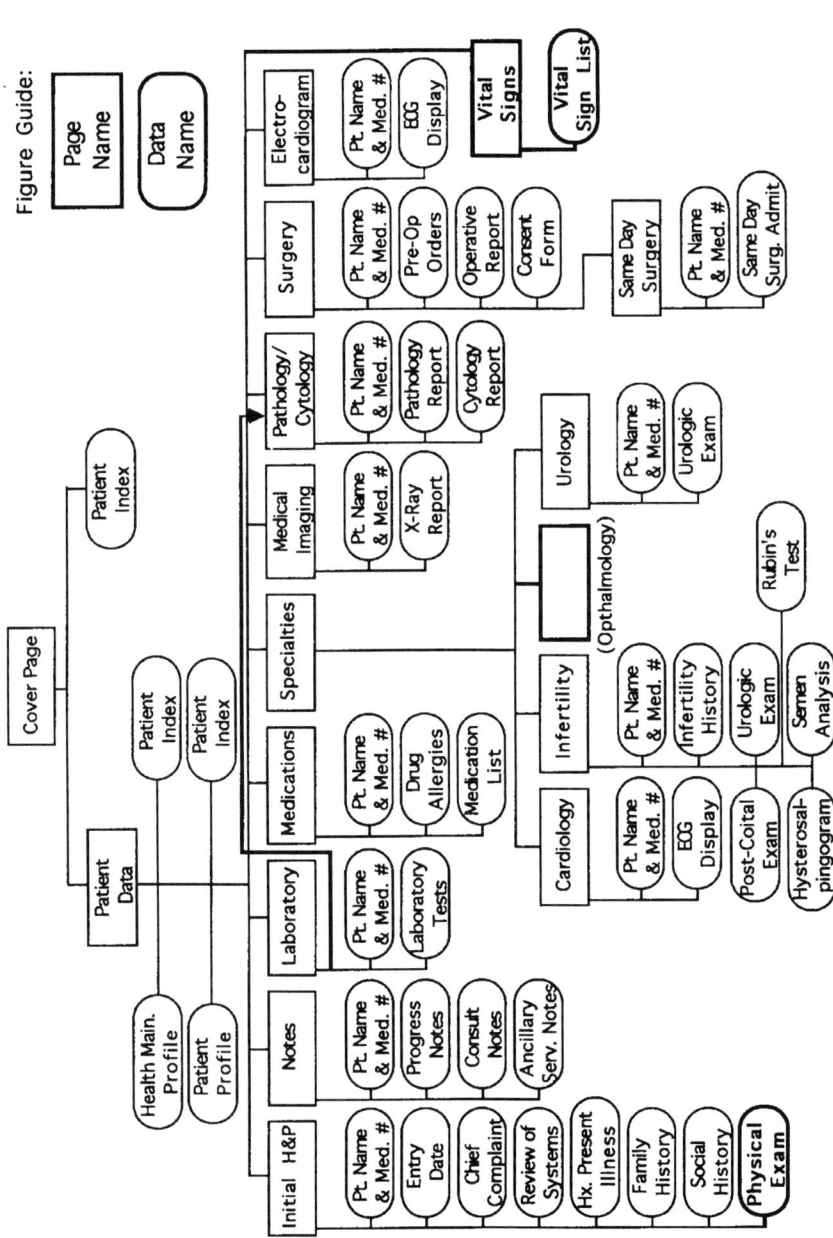

Figure 10: The general internist's final chart. The entries and arrows in boldface type were not found in the generic chart. The empty boxes outlined in boldface are entries that were eliminated.

A User-Adaptable Interface to Predict Users' Needs 309

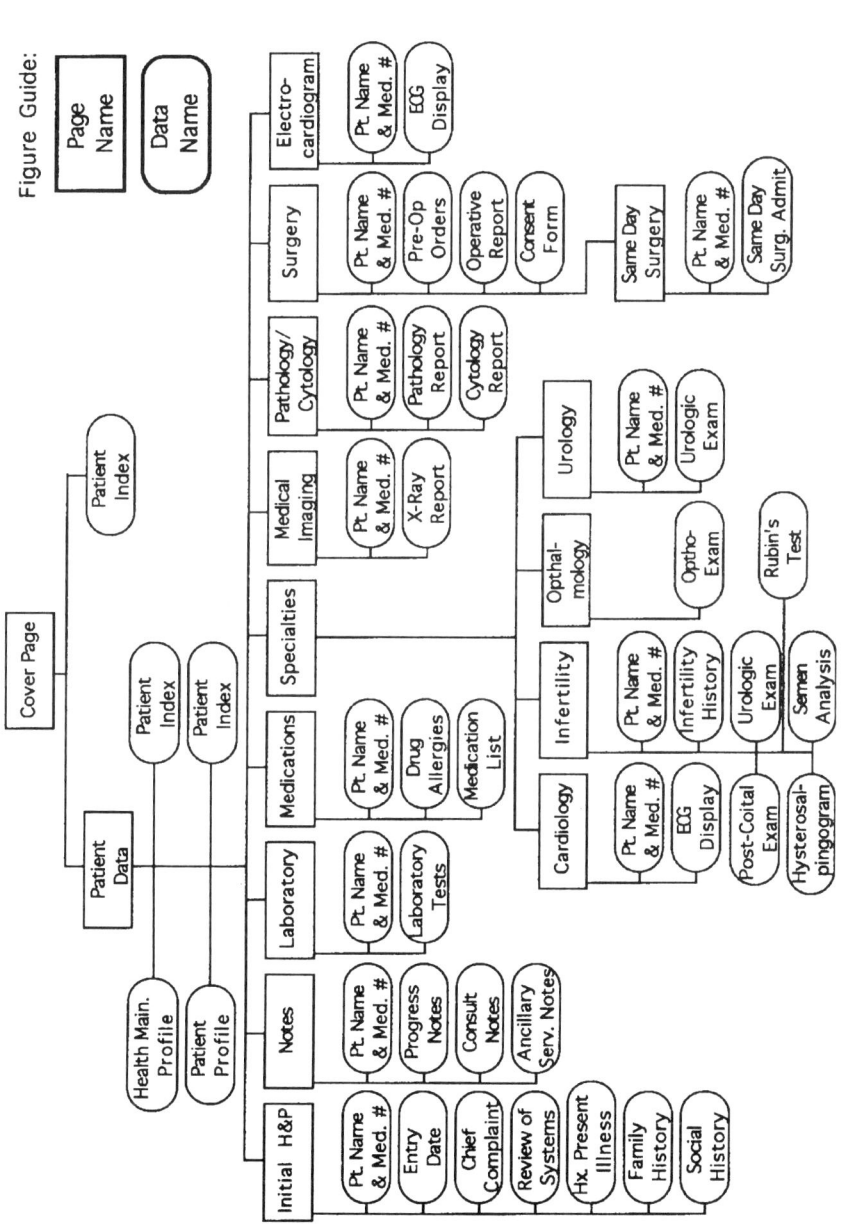

Figure 11: The generic chart. This chart was created by the authors and provided to the users as a starting point for the process of custom-tailoring.

These three UIs represent (1) the UI built with the complete past experience of users of the same specialty, plus the personal preferences of the current user, (2) the UI built using all previous experience with users of the specialty prior to obtaining the personal preferences of the current user, and (3) the UI built using no experience.

When asked whether their final version of the UI would be easier to use than the one with which they had started (the difference being edits they asked for during the session), the users all expressed a preference for the former (Figure 12, question 5). When asked whether their final version of the UI would be easier to use than the generic chart (built using no experience with users), the users again preferred the former UI, although not as strongly (Figure 12, question 6). Finally, when asked to compare the UI which they were initially offered, prior to their own edits, to the generic UI, they again chose the former (Figure 12, question 7). In each of these cases, the users preferred the UI that PODIUM had built based on the most experience with its users.

Question 5. Is your final computer chart easier (more pleasant) or more difficult to use than is the one you were given originally?

Easier   1   2   3   4   5   More Difficult

All users $1\,3/8$ General internists $1\,1/2$ Urologists $1\,1/4$

Question 6. Is your final computer chart easier (more pleasant) or more difficult to use than is the generic computer chart?

Easier   1   2   3   4   5   More Difficult

All users $1\,7/8$ General internists $1\,3/4$ Urologists 2

Question 7. Is the computer chart you were given originally easier (more pleasant) or more difficult to use than is the generic computer chart?

Easier   1   2   3   4   5   More Difficult

All users $1\,3/4$ General internists $1\,3/4$ Urologists $1\,3/4$

Figure 12: Questions pertaining to evaluation of the changes made to the clinic chart.

Finally, three physicians for each of the two specialties who had no prior experience using PODIUM were asked to choose from amongst the final urology UI, the final general-internal-medicine UI, and the original generic UI. All six physicians preferred the UI that PODIUM had built using the experience with their fellow specialists.

6 CONCLUSION

The building of a UI has been recognized as an important part of the creation of successful computer applications. Yet creating a custom-designed UI for a target user community has become a lengthy and complicated process.

One of the reasons that UI development has become more time consuming is that potential users must be assessed. Any attempt to define user abilities and needs requires study of individual users. These individuals are usually grouped as a single user community, for whom it is assumed there exists a best UI, representing the needs of the average user. The more diverse the group for whom the UI is being designed, the more difficult finding a compromise solution will be. Some UI designers, when confronted with a diverse group of users, try to minimize the compromises they need to make by dividing the community into subgroups and designing a UI for each subgroup.

PODIUM, a UIMS that allows users to design UIs interactively, is a new prototype solution that avoids the dilemma of whether to take the time to create multiple UIs for a single application or to use a single UI that may not be satisfactory to many of its users. More important, PODIUM employs user expertise to organize UIs (e.g., what information appears where) and to make final design decisions (e.g., whether to display information as a chart or as a table). PODIUM accomplishes these tasks by identifying the area in which the users have expertise and then extracting user input within that area in the form of edits to the UI, which determine how the UI should be organized and how the information should appear. Those areas in which the users are not expected to have expertise are designed as permanent features of the UI, so as not to confuse the users with too many editing options, many of which they would be unlikely to understand.

The information obtained by recording to what group a user belongs and how that user edits his chart provides the basis for producing a UI design for future users of the same group and for predicting their UI needs. The assumption leading to (and tested by) the experiment reported in this paper is that UI design choices are influenced by membership in a particular user subcommunity if the domain and subcommunities are chosen carefully.

The experimental results obtained using a physician's clinic chart as the UI, physicians as the users, and physician specialty as the user characteristic have demonstrated the ability of PODIUM to create different UIs interactively for easily distinguished subcommunities of users. Despite the small number of users tested in each group, the final UIs (representing the average final UI for each individual in a group) revealed numerous differences from the original (generic) UI and from that of the other group tested.

In addition, when the users examined the chart that was the result of their efforts, which included the efforts of those who used PODIUM before them, they thought that their UIs were superior to the original (generic) UI from which PODIUM began. In addition, they concluded that the changes that they made in the UI represented an improvement in UI design, and that the changes that previous user had made prior to their own changes also represented an improvement in UI design over that of the original (generic) UI.

Another study that further solidifies the usefulness of PODIUM involved offering the three completed UIs, one developed by group 1 (general internist), one developed by group 2 (urologists), and a control (the generic chart – which does not contain input from either group) to users who belong to groups 1 and 2 but have not used PODIUM. The study showed that the UI produced by each group is preferred by users of that group.

What these studies do not address is the importance that the users accord these changes. Are the differences critical to the usefulness of the underlying application or are they simply nuisances that have been fixed? A more complex and expanded study would be required to answer this critical question.

A failing of PODIUM is that its own interface fails to communicate clearly what it means to edit a UI. In addition to the ratings reported in Section 5.0, physicians told me that they had difficulty understanding what a UI was, how to divide it into supplements that they could move or remove, and how to accomplish the feat of editing the UI. Yet, with an assistant helping them, they were all capable of understanding and accomplishing each of these tasks.

For the ideas presented in the PODIUM prototype to be feasible in a routine (non-research) setting, more work needs to be done on the UI to this UI builder. An inventive technique for presenting these concepts visually would be helpful.

The PODIUM experiment does demonstrate that user input can be used directly to make UI design decisions, through interaction with a UIMS. If the system is designed appropriately, and if the areas in which user input is obtained are chosen carefully to reflect user knowledge, user input in the form of edits to a UI can be used not only to design better UIs, which will be more acceptable to their users, but also to create a greater variety of UIs without requiring that UI designers study each individual subgroup of users. The ability to extract user opinions while classifying them into groups produces the impression that the computer can predict the UI design needs of its users.

REFERENCES

[Baecker & Buxton 87]
    Baecker, R., & Buxton, W. (1987). *Readings In Human-Computer Interaction: A Multidisciplinary Approach*. Los Altos, CA: Morgan Kaufmann Publishers, Inc.

[Bobrow et al. 86]
   Bobrow, D., Mittal, S., & Stefik, M. (1986). *Expert Systems: Perils and promise.* Communications of the ACM, 29(9), 880-894.

[Buxton et al. 83]
   Buxton, W., Lamb, M.R., Sherman, D., & Smith, K.C. (1983). *Towards a Comprehensive User-Interface Management System.* Computer Graphics, 17(3), 35-42.

[Card et al. 83]
   Card, S., Moran, T., & Newell, A. (1983). *The Psychology of Human-Computer Interaction.* Hillsdale, NJ: Lawrence Erlbaum Associates, Pub.

[Eberts & Eberts 89]
   Eberts, R., & Eberts, C. (1989). *Four Approaches to Human Computer Interaction.* In P. Hancock, & M. Chignell (Ed.), *Intelligent Interfaces: Theory, Research and Design* (pp. 69-127). Amsterdam: North-Holland.

[Enderle 85]
   Enderle, G. (1985). *The Flexible Configuration of Interaction Environments Using GKS and Workspaces.* In G. Pfaff (Ed.), *User Interface Management Systems* (pp. 161-170). Berlin: Springer-Verlag.

[Fisher & Joy 87]
   Fisher, G., & Joy, K. (1987). *A Control Panel Interface for Graphics and Image Processing Applications.* Proceedings of SIG-CHI+CHI 1987, New York: American Association for Computing Machinery, 285-290.

[Foley & Van Dam 82]
   Foley, J., & Van Dam, A. (1982). *Fundamentals of Interactive Computer Graphics.* Reading, Mass.: Addison-Wesley Publishing Co.

[Gong & Elkerton 90]
   Gong, R., & Elkerton, J. (1990). *Designing Minimal Documentation Using GOMS Model: A Usability Evaluation of an Engineering Approach.* Proceedings of the Conference on Human Factors in Computer Systems, CHI '90, Seattle, Washington: American Association for Computing Machinery, 99-106.

[Gookin 89]
   Gookin, D. (1989). *The Complete SuperCard Handbook.* Radnor, PA: Compute! Books.

[Hansen 71]
   Hansen, W. (1971). *User Engineering Principles for Interactive Systems.* Montavale, NJ: AFIPS Press, 523-532.

[Henderson 83]
   Henderson, D. (1983). *The Trillium User Interface Design Environment.* Proceedings of the Conference on Human Factors in Computer Systems, CHI '83, Boston, Mass.: American Association for Computing Machinery, 221-224.

[Hill 86]
   Hill, R. (1986). *Supporting Concurrency, Communication, and Synchronization in Human-Computer Interaction - The Sassafras UIMS.* ACM Transactions on Graphics, 3(3), 179-210.

[John 90]
> John, B. (1990). *Extensions of GOMS Analyses to Expert Performance Requiring Perception of Dynamic Visual and Auditory Information.* Proceedings of the Conference on Human Factors in Computer Systems, CHI '90, Seattle, Washington: American Association for Computing Machinery, 107-115.

[Kantorowitz & Sudarski 89]
> Kantorowitz, E., & Sudarsky, O. (1989). *The Adaptable User Interface.* Communications of the ACM, 32(11), 1352-1358.

[Lewis et al. 89]
> Lewis, C., Hair, C., & Schoenberg, V. (1989). *Generalization, Consistency and Control.* Austin, Proceedings of the Conference on Human Factors in Computer Systems, CHI '90, Austin, TX: American Association for Computing Machinery, 1-5.

[Mark 86]
> Mark, W. (1986). *Knowledge-Based Interface Design.* In D. Norman, & S. Draper (Ed.), *User Centered System Design: New Perspectives on Human-Computer Interaction* (pp. 219-238). Hillsdale, NJ: Lawrence Erlbaum Associates, Pub.

[Myers 89]
> Myers, B. (1989). *User-Interface Tools: Introduction and Survey.* IEEE Software, (Jan.), 15-23.d

[Myers & Buxton 87]
> Myers, B., & Buxton, W. (1987). *Creating Highly-Interactive and Graphical User Interfaces by Demonstration.* In R. Baecker, & W. Buxton (Ed.), *Readings In Human-Computer Interaction: A Multidisciplinary Approach* Los Altos, CA: Morgan Kaufmann Publishers, Inc.

[Newell and Simon 72]
> Newell, A., & Simon, H. (1972).*Human Problem Solving.* Englewood Cliffs, NJ: Prentice-Hall.

[Norman 83]
> Norman, D. (1983). *Design Principles for Human-Computer Interfaces.* Proceedings of the Conference on Human Factors in Computer Systems, CHI '83, Boston, Mass.: American Association for Computing Machinery, 1-10.

[Norman 84a]
> Norman, D. (1984). *Stages and Levels in Human-Machine Interaction.* International Journal of Man-Machine Studies, 21, 365-375.

[Norman 84b]
> Norman, D. (1984). *Four Stages of User Activities.* INTERACT '84: First Conference on Human-Computer Interaction, Amsterdam: North-Holland.

[Norman & Draper 86]
> Norman, D., & Draper, S. (1986). *User Centered System Design: New Perspectives on Human-Computer Interaction.* Hillsdale, NJ: Lawrence Erlbaum Associates, Pub.

[Owen 86]
> Owen, D. (1986). *Naive Theories of Computation.* In D. Norman, & S. Draper (Ed.), *User Centered System Design: New Perspectives on Human-Computer Interaction* (pp. 219-238). Hillsdale, NJ: Lawrence Erlbaum Associates, Pub.

[Reilly 86]

Reilly, M. (1986). *User's Understanding*. In D. Norman, & S. Draper (Ed.), *User Centered System Design: New Perspectives on Human-Computer Interaction* (pp. 219-238). Hillsdale, NJ: Lawrence Erlbaum Associates, Pub.

[Shafer 88]

Shafer, D. (1988). Hypertalk Programming. Indianapolis, IN: Hayden Books.

[Shneiderman 87]

Shneiderman, B. (1987). *Designing the User Interface: Strategies for Effective Human-Computer Interaction*. Reading, Mass.: Addison-Wesley Publishing Co.

[Shneiderman & Mayer 79]

Shneiderman, B., & Mayer, R. (1979). *A model of experimental results*. International Journal of Computer and Information Sciences, 8(3), 219-239.

[Sibert et al. 86]

Sibert, J., Hurley, W., & Bleser, T. (1986). *An Object-Oriented User Interface Management System*. Computer Graphics, 20(4), 259-268.

[Topping et al. 87]

Topping, P., McInroy, J., Lively, W., & Sheppard, S. (1987). *Express - Rapid Prototyping and Product Development via Integrated, Knowledged-Based Executable Specifications*. Proceedings of the 1987 Fall Joint Computer Conference, Dallas, TX, Oct 25-29, 1987: AFIPS Press, 3-9.

[Walton & Shortliffe 89]

Walton, J. D., & Shortliffe, E. H. (1989). *Automated Design of a User Interface* (KSL-88-17). Knowledge Systems Laboratory, Stanford University.

[Wasserman & Shewmake 82]

Wasserman, A., & Shewmake, D. (1982). *Rapid Prototyping of Interactive Information Systems*. SIGSoft Software Engineering Notes, 171-180.

[Wixon et al. 83]

Wixon, D., Whiteside, J., Good, M., & Jones, S. (1983). *Building a User-Derived Interface*. Proceedings of the Conference on Human Factors in Computer Systems, CHI '83, Boston, Mass.: American Association for Computing Machinery, 24-27.

[Young et al. 89]

Young, R., Green, T., & Simon, T. (1989). *Programmable User Models for Predictive Evaluation of Interface Design*. Proceedings of the Conference on Human Factors in Computing Systems, CHI '89, Austin, TX: American Association for Computing Machinery, 1-5.1-5.

[Young & Whittington 90]

Young, R., & Whittington, J. (1990). *Using Knowledge Analysis to Predict Conceptual Error In Text-Editor Usage*. Proceedings of the Conference on Human Factors in Computer Systems, CHI '90, Seattle, Washington: American Association for Computing Machinery, 91-98.

Part IV

Evaluation

Contributions of a Social Science Based Evaluation for Adaptive Design Projects

Christoph Grüninger and Werner van Treeck

Gesamthochschule-Universität Kassel
Kassel, Germany

ABSTRACT

Conventionally designed software is too static to meet dynamically changing user requirements. User participation is a way to bring together designers and users in a joint development process. Yet, this brings little flexibility to pursue individual requirements. Adaptive systems seem to offer this potential now. However, the dynamic interdependence of cognitive, psychological, social, and organizational needs can be conflicting and lead to incompatible design orientations. There are different adaptive problems which call for different adaptive qualities. In order to arrive at concrete adaptive requirements an evaluation of the specific application context is needed.

1 ADAPTATION AND THE APPLICATION CONTEXT

1.1 Need for adaptation

The need for adaptive software has a comparably short history. Alan M. Turing, who would be 80 this year, and many of his colleagues believed that half a dozen number crunchers would be more than enough computational capacity worldwide. Yet, when he helped break the German codes with *Colossus* in World War II, he invented the theory of word processing along with it [Eurich 91]. Computers were no longer confined to numeric data but could process textual representations as well. An entirely new application domain of computer systems arose.

Then, from the seventies on, running on universal system platforms, applications have gone beyond machine room operations and have pervaded decentralized work places extensively. New design requirements emerged [Paetau 90]. With the widening use of computers, designers came to tackle increasingly non-repetitive and loosely structured tasks whose complexity and dynamic nature makes them difficult to specify.

At the same time a shift in entrepreneurial strategies gained momentum. While earlier emphasis on scientific management had sought a maximum efficiency in the production process, strategic management began to direct more effort into establishing a market orientation. Increasingly rapid market changes reduced the life cycle of existing products and demanded constant innovations. In accordance, new tasks have emerged quasi habitually. A new flexibility of organizations is required and tensions arise between the needs of adaptation and the inflexibilities of software.

Consequently, systems have to be equipped with a built-in flexibility to adapt to specific task requirements for two reasons. Firstly, because computers have become more pervasive; secondly, because tasks undergo constant redefinition.

Moreover, systems have to be designed for different end-users and even different groups of end-users. Such groups are often combined non-homogeneously and form an asymmetrical cooperative structure [Malone 89]. For example, in hospitals physicians constitute one group, the medical staff another. These professional groups do not differ just in their formal educational background or their position within the organizational hierarchy. While both groups contribute to a common overall task, namely the provision of medical services, they specialize in significantly different domains (e. g. patient care and diagnosis). This has a strong bearing on an individual´s work style, his or her usage pattern of computer systems, the learning approach, and the degree of autonomy. Factors such as these determine the potential to utilize adaptive options. So, without a thorough understanding of real users in a concrete domain, the production of adaptive features which are effective will remain unlikely. Thus, besides task requirements, systems[1] need the potential to adapt to very complex but specific user requirements as well.

Yet another adaptive need arises from the humanization of work life. From the early Scandinavian and British initiatives [French et al. 60, Mumford & Sackmann 75, Mumford & Henshall 79], it has become a widely acknowledged societal requirement. Since computers are an integral part of many workplaces this puts adaptive systems in a new context and introduces new criteria for the design process [Döbele-Berger et al. 88].

As we will show each one of the above aspects represents a complex set of adaptive needs. Many of them stand in contrast to each other.

1.2 Conflicts of adaptation

There is a need to bring together a system's functionality with the situational context and specific users' needs. A way to meet these adaptive requirements is an increased flexibility of systems at the interface level. Let the user participate in deciding, ad hoc via man-machine interaction, which operations to perform, in what order, and when. The user then has control of the best alternatives.

A suitable mode of interaction and process control is crucial to this design principle. It must be operable for the system, responsive to user needs, applicable in the organizational context, and, above all, it must facilitate task execution.

---

[1] As will become clear, we need no strict and exclusive distinction between the concept of system and interface in our discussion.

It is important to note that user-orientation should not be the sole objective of adaptivity. User-orientation is interdependent with other relevant criteria of system design which should not be neglected. The list of aspects we present below is just one of many possible classifications and perspectives [Reiterer 90, Harrison & Monk 86]. It is not meant to give here an extensive account of all criteria. We chose a variety of items to specifically illuminate their conflicting character[2].

- **Technical operability**
  Adaptations should be compatible with industrial standards and follow a uniform pattern. They must not interfere with the consistency of program structures, databases, or distributed applications. Relevant changes must be retraceable to ensure system maintainability and data security. The run-time performance of the overall system has to remain on an acceptable level. Adaptations of the software must be carried out in minimum time and with little effort.

- **Task-oriented functionality**
  Adaptive changes must lead to an improved usability. This could manifest itself in various ways: speeding up usage, reducing mistakes, lowering qualification barriers, facilitating learning. Users have to stay in a position to control the system. They should be freed of excessive routine work. This must not produce a mental overload of decision making activities. For some users the interface has to provide active guidance. The interface must adapt to cognitive styles and capacities of specific users. It has to support the user in moving to a higher level of expertise. An acquired qualification must be applicable in similar contexts. The overall system must be transparent and self-explanatory. The system must offer the potential to individualize it. Modes of system usage must follow ergonomic standards.

- **Organizational applicability**
  Adaptations of software components must not lead to breaks in the technological and informational infrastructure of an organization. Implementations may not become too personalized to be used by different users interchangeably. A system's features, including all adaptations, must be documented. Internal user models must remain subject to data privacy. The system's adaptive potential must correspond to the range of options the user could possibly adopt within his or her organizational autonomy.

- **Individual usability**
  The user's capacity to execute tasks has to be increased. Technical activities necessary to operate the system should be taken care of by the system itself.

---

[2] For a discussion of fundamental contradictions between technological and organizational requirements see [Brinckmann 91].

The user's problem-solving capacity should be increased. Modes of interaction and communication have to be uniform with the task environment. It must be possible to incorporate new task structures in the software. Repetitive and other specifiable activities should be easy to automate. The user must have insight into process states of the system.

The juxtaposition of the design criteria above shows that many of them are in conflict with each other or appear even self-contradictory. Attempting to providing a maximum of adaptivity as such or to fulfill cognitive criteria in isolation will not necessarily lead to any adaptive quality in the application context.

For example, if adaptive interfaces are designed to make boring routine work more interesting and users more attentive, this could be done through interfaces which attract more attention. But this attractiveness would turn out to be ineffective or even counterproductive if the system is used by people with highly variable tasks at hand. They would typically not use system components very intensively or repetitively in the first place. Being attentive would not be an issue for these users and adaptive features might quickly make a nuisance out of themselves.

Another example would be the fundamental problem of consistency. The more user-individualized an adaptive system gets the less compatible will it be in terms of user cooperation. There will be a noticeable cost for a user to individualize a system and to keep in touch with co-workers at the same time. Adaptive designs will have to take this into account and provide compatibility and common points of reference. This is not a trivial presentational problem which is free of functional implications. Practical differences between functionality and mere presentation blur because direct manipulation and iconization have already brought along concepts of visual programming. It is yet a problem to support user idiosyncracies and to match the differences in their deictic systems at the same time.

A third example would be an adaptive design for overly intuitive and self-adaptive human-computer interaction modes. Hiding all technical aspects of computers would hinder users to actually learn anything about the true technological basis of the adaptive system. This stands in contrast to agreed upon transparency requirements. An overly intuitive system would let the user elaborate on mental models which are plainly wrong and not suitable. Carrying out system-controlled adaptations, without disturbing the user, causes other fundamental problems as well. Exploratory system usage and user learning might be inhibited significantly because users do not like the idea of being monitored in their necessarily playful approaches. Moreover, adaptive systems which take too many initiatives would directly lead to a decrease in user autonomy. Such a system would simply not be up to motivational theory and would represent a very poor understanding of the true needs of people at work.

Such conflicts of adaptation as mentioned above show that there is no one best way for adaptive designs. There is a wide scope of adaptive forms which can be pursued but little is known about concrete adaptive requirements.

1.3 Adaptive requirements

System adaptation can take different, sometimes hybrid, forms [Edmonds 87, Oppermann 90]. Basically they vary in who or what is supposed to be the adaptive actor. A self-adapting system should be distinguished from a merely adaptable system. In the latter case, the scope of actors ranges from programmers or expert users to all end-users. A complementary way of distinguishing different adaptive forms is to look at the objects of adaptation. The scope ranges from the adaptation of defaults, presentation, and interaction, and can include the adaptation of functionality as the strongest adaptive form.

However, we do not intend to go into a description of adaptivity. A systematic and very elaborate taxonomy is presented in the chapter by [Dieterich et al. 93] in this book. Instead, we would like to concentrate on a complementary perspective. We are not describing adaptive *components* but adaptive *requirements*, a point which is crucial to our discussion. It is not conceivable to have a successful design project without a well-founded set of requirements. Identifying these requirements is part of the evaluation.

As we have shown above, identifying (and realizing) a problem-oriented balance of design criteria such as technical operability, task-oriented functionality, organizational applicability, and individual usability is not trivial. Maximizing the user-adaptive potential according to an assumed user ideal alone would meet few of the design requirements. Design problems would be attacked in an erratic, inefficient, if not counterproductive, manner. We therefore seek a development and a utilization of adaptive potentials which take a problem-oriented approach.

A problem-oriented approach to adaptive system design has to build on the real context under which a planned system will have to operate. Determinants of that context are often of a social nature. We name only a few of them in loose order.

- **Task**
  Adaptive needs will vary according to the type of task to be executed (e.g. various degrees of repetition and formalization have to be taken into account). The structures and hierarchies of task division have a strong bearing too (e.g. work processes may be holistic or fragmented). Other variances occur in such aspects as informational requirements, operational scope, or work objects.

- **Organizational framework**
  The size and architecture of an organization (e.g. function-oriented, product oriented, matrix, project team) have to be considered. Significant feature can be the number, span and interrelation of sub-units, autonomies, and authorities within an organizational unit (e.g. distribution of decision making), or

even the nature and role of external consumers of services (degree and quality of interdependence).

- **Work organization**
  Further determinants are the degree of routinization, the extent of buffers between the execution of sub-tasks, the degree of time-criticality, the flexibility in terms of sequence, and parallelism of sub-tasks. These variables have to be analyzed with regard to the degree of autonomy to arrange the work flow at a work place. The specific characteristics of work places (e.g. strictly personalized or shared) have to be taken into consideration as well.

- **Technological infrastructure**
  The existing quality and degree of computer support for task execution significantly determines the potential of adaptations. Such factors as size, complexity, and uniformity of the existing technology pool play an important role (e.g. occurrence of media breaks between different systems or instruments, degree of standardization in terms of qualification, or structure of maintenance services)

- **Informational interchange**
  Naturally, adaptive information technology can not be seen as isolated from the frequency, quantity, quality, and organization of information flow, for instance. Variances are to be expected in the extent of formalization as much as in the levels of and variances between formal and informal communication channels.

- **Internal social structure**
  The occurrence and effect of a specific task distribution according to social status (sex, age, long presence in the department, prestige) have long been underestimated, along with such aspects as the occurrence of political coalitions and informal groups competing for resources.

- **Management objectives and style**
  Authoritarian, humanitarian, or co-operative management forms exert a strong influence on the whole organization and the application context. The adaptive performance of a system is therefore subject to the existence and type of incentive systems, the design and flexibility of job profiles, and so forth.

- **Staff structure**
  Last but not least, it is the staff who are a crucial issue for adaptation. The design of a system has to relate to the turnover rate, for example, the education (academic profile or skilled worker), the departmental/task-related status (newcomer unfamiliar with job or experienced senior), the computer background (formal qualification or learning by doing), age, and sex.

For a system to be problem-oriented, any combination of the above features might be relevant. There may be a qualification problem with users with no computer background. There may be a very high turnover rate in a department, but with all of the staff being computer professionals. There may be a fairly permanent staff structure but the problem of using information systems for ever changing tasks in a consulting organization.

2 TOWARDS AN AUGMENTED EVALUATION CONCEPT

As we have shown above, we can speak of different adaptation problems. They make an evaluation of a system's adaptive potential in the light of the concrete application context necessary. In this section we want to outline the tasks of the evaluation in principle. Then we will discuss methodological aspects and will finally sketch an evaluation which runs parallel to the development process of an adaptive system.

2.1 Evaluation tasks

There are three evaluation tasks: a design-oriented evaluation has to identify concrete adaptive needs, contradictions, and areas of conflict, it has to provide mediation between project participants, and it has to make explicit the overall outcome of the development project.

An evaluation has to identify the specific need for an adaptive system in a given application context. There are objective and subjective sources to draw from. For valid design cues it is not sufficient to question the users. A part of the needs for adaptations have to be inferred indirectly from their daily struggles with the rigidities of their applications and their often improvised attempts to bridge such inflexibilities.

The design objectives will have to be narrowed down to an adaptivity concept which is feasible as well as suitable. The evaluation has to support the formulation of such a concept in close cooperation with the project participants. The design requirements derived from this serve as a basic frame of reference gaining in concreteness throughout the development process. Designers as well as users have to start out with unclear and incomplete conceptions of adaptive potentials and adaptive requirements. In order to find and maintain an optimal balance between different, probably conflicting user requirements and design activities, the evaluation has to initiate and support a close exchange and negotiation between project participants. Internally, the evaluators have to adopt a mediator's role in order to support a frequent knowledge exchange. A neutral third party has to suggest viable compromises and to improve the participants' readiness for necessary revisions.

From the external point of view it is the task of the evaluation to make explicit the overall outcome of the development project. Firstly, the evaluation has to provide insights into the achieved adaptive potential of the developed system. Secondly, it has to discuss prerequisites of the adaptive system's implementation in terms of organizational change, qualificational need, and cooperative potential. Thirdly, the evaluation has to give an outlook on possible effects of widespread use and consequences for the application context.

2.2 Methods and their implications

Now we would like to develop a suitable methodological approach to deal with the evaluation tasks as mentioned above. There is a huge variety of evaluation approaches [Howard & Murray 87, Karat 88, Malone et al. 84]. However, it is not useful to develop an elaborate taxonomy here. Instead, we exemplify relevant issues and assess implications for a design-oriented evaluation. To this end, a distinction of just three methodological elements is sufficient, i.e. interviews/questionnaires, controlled experiments, and checklists/guidelines.

- **Interviews/questionnaires**
  Such methods require comparably few resources and they are easy to carry out. Variations of these methods reach from highly standardized interviews to verbal reports. Verbal reports are especially prone to produce a very large bulk of data which is often difficult to integrate in a uniform framework ("noise"). Findings tend to be biased and not very reliable. Sometimes it is the lack of methodological qualification of users or their lack of insight in research objectives which accounts for disturbances. Thus, verbal reports usually give only a general impression about a system's overall acceptance. A strict standardization has implications, too. The higher the level of standardization, the more it is experience driven. In other words, a standardized questionnaire has to anticipate well in advance its implementation context and can only elicit such specific issues for which it was originally designed. Here, it is the authors and examiners who are prone to exert a bias. Yet, these methods do have a potential when combined. Loosely structured qualitative surveys and questionnaires help identify problem areas quickly and efficiently if they are carried out in a participative manner, leveling out misconceptions and misinterpretations. Highly standardized methods can be reserved for singling out, pin-pointing, and verifying specific details if carried out cyclically.

- **Controlled experiments**
  Conditions under which studies are carried out are made highly controllable through experimental settings. Since it allows an identical repetition of experiments, this method is ideal for comparative studies. However, the use of controlled experiments is limited because they are costly. Additionally, they are meant to produce simplified models of reality. So, only a fraction of the determinants of adaptive quality can be taken into consideration at one time. Moreover, techniques to elicit user knowledge of the application domain such as retrospective comment analyses, thinking-aloud protocols, interruption analyses, or incremental simulations [Salter 88] are relatively intrusive. They are confined to the selective reality of experimental settings. Typically, controlled

experimental studies are used for such questions as which of the given systems performs best in supporting a specific user-operation (bench-mark tests). As an element of a design-oriented evaluation, experiments can support the identification of best design alternatives, again, if carried out cyclically for incremental enhancement and if validated by a qualitative evaluation procedure running parallel.

- **Checklists/guidelines**
  Guideline-oriented or checklist-based evaluation methods usually have to be carried out by expert examiners and not by users (elements of interview techniques and observational studies are applied). They can produce a comprehensive and systematic description of a system according to the applied evaluation criteria. These methods address specific technical features while, for instance, interviews without a guideline approach often cling to perceived (overall) effects of a system. In comparison, a checklist or guideline approach therefore offers a better means to break down a system's complexity and adopt a concrete design orientation. A drawback is that there is not as yet any adequate theoretical foundation for the formulation of valid guidelines, especially for adaptive system design. However, guidelines exist, such as EVADIS [Oppermann et al. 89], which focus on the software-ergonomic dimension of software. When used in combination with complementary evaluation methods, EVADIS does offer a viable frame of reference to set the adaptive quality of a system in relation to concrete technical features. Because of this technological concreteness, it is valuable for a design-oriented evaluation.

Each one of the above methods can contribute to different evaluation goals or stages. Vice versa, most evaluation aspects require a mixed-method "toolbox" and an integrated methodology [Falck 91].

In earlier sections we have introduced a differentiation of adaptive requirements. Deriving from this, we have identified a multitude of design objectives and a range of uncertainties for system design which make it necessary to look at real application domains. We have discussed evaluation tasks and methods of software evaluation such as interviews, controlled experiments, and checklists and have assessed their potential contribution to a design-oriented evaluation. Now we would like to outline the evaluation process needed to integrate them.

2.3 Phases of an evaluation process

The specifics and implications of the evaluation methods described above suggest integrating them into a comprehensive evaluation process. The process concept basically consists of five phases which run parallel to a design project.

- **Phase I: Specifying the need for adaptation.**
  In its initial phase the design-oriented evaluation analyses a concrete application domain during a system's development. Carrying out intensive interviews and using observational techniques, the evaluation at this point identifies general adaptive requirements and assesses determinants of adaptive quality (whose complex nature has been illustrated above). For a further elaboration of adaptive design criteria, the participation of users in a real work context is required. Participating users are selected corresponding the findings of the first evaluation phase; that is they should be an adequate sample of the concrete field of application. Their selection then represents a far-reaching approximation of crucial design factors.

- **Phase II: Feedback of initial findings.**
  This phase presents a rapid feedback of findings from phase I. It addresses the designers, the participating users, and their department. In order to establish a constructive collaboration of all project participants special emphasis is put on adequate forms of presentation and interaction.

- **Phase III: Test of first prototype.**
  Prototypical run-time versions of the software are cyclically tested and evaluated in their real application context. This first test compares the adaptive requirements as specified in phase I with the adaptive quality of the system under real conditions. Deviations are detected by interview methods, observational studies, and similar elicitation techniques. Guideline methods (e.g. EVADIS) can help break down a system's technological complexity. If required, detected deviations can be narrowed down further by experimental settings.

- **Phase IV: Feedback of first test results.**
  This phase presents a rapid feedback of findings from phase III. The feedback addresses designers, participating users, and their department. In order to facilitate a constructive collaboration of all project participants, again, special emphasis is put on adequate forms of presentation and interaction. This evaluation phase helps to develop and convey design proposals for a revision of the prototype.

- **Phase V: Concluding evaluation.**
  This phase is carried out analogously to phase III. It presents a documentation of the design process and its outcome at the end of the design project. On the one hand, the concluding evaluation specifies the applicability and effectiveness of the adaptive system. On the other hand, it provides a body of data on the efficiency and effectiveness of the design process itself, including the validity of the evaluation.

3 CONCLUSION

There is a high potential for adaptivity and the need to develop adaptive systems is widely acknowledged. However, there are many success factors to ponder as well. We have shown that design requirements can vary according to different goals of adaptation. Only a few of them can be achieved at a time because they often conflict. Since adaptive systems are intended to be useful in a real work context, their design depends on a context-specific mixture of cognitive, psychological, social, organizational, and technical factors. Thus, successful adaptive design is not possible without a close exchange with real end-users. A design-oriented evaluation can bring end-users back in and provide a mediation in the development process of adaptive systems.

REFERENCES

[Brinckmann 91]
    Brinckmann, H. (1991). *Technological and organizational innovation. Contradictions in basic requirements.* In: Van den Besselaar, P. & Clement, A. & Järvinen, P. (eds.), *Information System, Work and Organization Design.* Proceedings of the IFIP TC9/WG9.1, Berlin 1989. Elsevier-North Holland, Amsterdam.

[Dieterich et al. 93]
    Dieterich, H.; Malinowski, U.; Kühme, T.; Schneider-Hufschmidt, M. (1993). *State of the Art in Adaptive User interfaces,* In: this book.

[Döbele-Berger et al. 88]
    Döbele-Berger, C.; van Treeck, W.; Zimmer, G. (1988). *Softwarenutzung am Arbeitsplatz und berufliche Weiterbildung. Eine explorative Studie.* Gesamthochschule Kassel, Kassel.

[Edmonds 87]
    Edmonds, E. A. (1987). *Adaptation, response and knowledge.* Knowledge-Based Systems 1, No. 1, 3-10, Butterworth & Heinemann, London.

[Eurich 91]
    Eurich, C. (1991). *Tödliche Signale. Die kriegerische Geschichte der Informationstechnik.* Luchterhand, Frankfurt/M.

[Falck 91]
    Falck, M. (1991). *Information system, work and organization design: How to do it?* In: Van den Besselaar, P. & Clement, A. & Järvinen, P. (eds.), *Information System, Work and Organization Design.* Proceedings of the IFIP TC9/WG9.1, Berlin 1989. Elsevier-North Holland, Amsterdam.

[French et al. 60]
    French, J. R.; Israel, J.; As, D. (1960). *An experiment on participation in a norwegian factory.* In: Human Relations, Tavistock Publications, 13th year, pp. 3-19.

[Harrison & Monk 86]
    Harrison, M. D.; Monk, A. F. (eds.) (1986). *People and computers: Designing for usability.* Cambridge University Press, Cambridge.

[Howard & Murray 87]

Howard, S.; Murray, D. M. (1987). *A taxonomy of evaluation techniques for HCI.* In Bullinger, H. J. & Shackel, B. (eds.). INTERACT '87, Elsevier-North Holland, Amsterdam.

[Karat 88]

Karat, J. (1988). *Software evaluation methodologies.* In: Helander, M. (ed.), *Handbook of Human Computer Interaction.* Elsevier-North Holland, Amsterdam.

[Malone et al. 84]

Malone, T. B.; Kirkpatrick, M.; Heasly, C. (1984). *Human computer interface effectiveness evaluation.* In: Shackel, B. (ed.) INTERACT '84. Elsevier-North Holland, Amsterdam.

[Malone 89]

Malone, Th. W. (1989). *Computer support for organizations: Toward an organizational science.* In: Carroll, M. (ed.). *Interfacing Thought*, 3rd ed. MIT Press, Cambridge/MA.

[Mumford & Henshall 79]

Mumford, E.; Henshall, D. (1979). *A participative approach to computer systems design.* Associated Business Press, London.

[Mumford & Sackmann 75]

Mumford, E.; Sackmann, H. (eds.) (1975). *Human choice and computers.* Proceedings of the IFIP Conference on Human Choice and Computers. Vienna, April 1-5, Elsevier-North Holland, Amsterdam.

[Oppermann 90]

Oppermann, R. (1990). *Möglichkeiten und Probleme individualisierter Systemnutzung.* Manuscript of a speech at the "Software-Ergonomie-Herbstschule" in Zurich, Switzerland.

[Oppermann et al. 89]

Oppermann, R.; Murchner, B.; Paetau, M.; Pieper, M.; Simm, H.; Stellmacher. *Evaluation of dialog systems.* GMD-Studien Nr. 169. Gesellschaft für Mathematik und Datenverarbeitung, Sankt Augustin.

[Paetau 90]

Paetau, M. (1990). *Mensch-Maschine-Kommunikation: Software, Gestaltungspotentiale, Sozialverträglichkeit.* Campus, Frankfurt/M.

[Reiterer 90]

Reiterer, H. (1990). *Ergonomische Kriterien für die menschengerechte Gestaltung von Bürosystemen, Anwendung und Bewertung.* Dissertational thesis, University of Wien.

[Salter 88]

Salter, W. J. (1988). *Human factors in knowledge acquisition.* In: Helander, M. (ed.). *Handbook of Human-Computer Interaction.* Elsevier-North Holland, Amsterdam.

Discussion Results

Uwe Malinowski and Matthias Schneider-Hufschmidt

Siemens Corporate Research and Development
München, Germany

INTRODUCTION

During the workshop a number of discussions took place, some after presentations of individual position papers, others at organized discussion meetings to analyze architectural issues and interesting fields of research in the area of user interface adaptivity. In this section we will summarize the major results of these discussions without following the course of these discussions too closely.

KEEP IN MIND WHAT YOU ARE DOING AND WHY

One of the predominant topics of all discussions was the question of how to justify adaptation in user interfaces. Adaptation is not a goal unto itself but rather a method to increase the usability of an application system in terms of effectivity, efficiency, and ease of use. Therefore, it has to be primarily motivated by the users' needs. When designing the user interface for a system, the first step has to be the elicitation of the user's requirements. The methods that allow the system to meet these requirements can subsequently be identified – and adaptation maybe only one among many. Many cases can be identified where existing user interfaces can be improved without using methods of adaptation. Implementing effective methods of adaptation is an expensive and error-prone process. Success stories are extremely rare, so if there are alternate ways to meet the users' expectations, it may be more efficient to implement these alternatives.

If the need for adaptation is identified in this first step it must be decided what components have to be adaptive and in which ways. Again, this step has to be driven by users' needs rather than by technology. We learned from many previous projects that it will normally not be successful if one takes the most technologically ambitious components and combines them into a system, hoping that this will meet all needs a user may ever have.

These experiences can be summarized as: Make sure to *do the right things* before starting to *do things right*.

It is commonly agreed that adaptation is helpful in a user interface for a system that is used by a heterogeneous user group. This is obviously the case if you have groups of users with different tasks and different access authorizations. The point could be made, however, that it is the case for any system with more than one user, because no two users are exactly alike. From this point of view it is important to identify whether the individuals differ in a way that is relevant for the communication of the user with the application system. If this is not the case, it is unreasonable to adapt to the individual user.

Adaptation to rapidly changing user behavior will generally result in confusion because the user is not able to construct a mental model of the adaptation process. It seems to be more promising to adapt to user characteristics that will not change in the near future, because then adaptation will be beneficial for a longer period of usage time and the interface will therefore not confuse the user through frequent changes.

MEASURES OF SUCCESS

To evaluate the quality of a user interface it is necessary to identify a measure or metric to estimate how well the goal of maximal usability and ease of use has been reached. For an adaptive user interface it has to be measured additionally whether the adaptation has been successful, i.e. whether the usability has been increased by the adaptation process. This measure can also be used to decide if additional adaptation steps might prove successful. Possible metrics are *number of errors*, *time needed*, or *mental effort* to complete a task.

If the necessary *mental effort for task completion* rather than *task completion time* is the metric for success, it is not necessarily true that it is useful to provide more powerful functions. It might be more appropriate for the individual user to press a well known sequence of buttons than to check whether a complex function is applicable for the current task.

ADAPTATION AND THE APPLICATION DOMAIN

The measure of success that has to be applied in a specific system is closely related to the goal of the adaptation process. The goal itself depends very much on the application domain. In process control systems safety comes first; in applications where casual users have to deal with computers, the adaptation should increase intuitivity and guidance; in most applications, e.g. in an office environment, it is the primary goal to make it obvious for the user how to complete the current task.

Likewise, the possible scope of adaptation is determined by the application system. In most systems some parts must never be adapted as they must be identifiable for different users. This may be necessary because different users physically use the same system or because they need to talk about the application system based on their individually adapted instances. This is especially important in CSCW systems.

SELF-ADAPTIVITY VS. ADAPTABILITY

The scope of adaptation and what type of changes are visible at the interface is the most important factor for the appropriate type of adaptation. Of course, scope and visibility of changes depend on the application area. Furthermore, the degree of control that can be given to the user and the style of user involvement are determined by the knowledge and skills of the user. Until now, it seems to be impossible to identify generally applicable rules to decide which type of adaptation is most appropriate.

Nevertheless, some rules can be identified. Self-adaptivity can be applied in help or explanation generation, where length and type of explanation can be adapted to individual knowledge. Although self-adaptivity helps the user in this case, users have to be enabled to adapt this on their own. On the other hand, self-adaptivity is not suitable for changes to interface design or selection of interaction style. This type of adaptation is far too complex to be handled automatically. As Cockton showed in his gedanken experiment, changing the user interface style can only be done by reprogramming. It was argued that the adaptation of the interface style might also be handled by self-adaptive mechanisms if the user is not aware of the changes.

The appropriateness of a type of adaptation is related to the complexity of the application system. On the one hand, the user has problems to construct a mental model of a high functionality system. Therefore, in a complex system the cognitive load on the user may not be increased by the customization task and only self-adaptivity is applicable. On the other hand, self-adaptivity increases the problems of building a mental model of the system because the user is confronted with the results of the adaptation and has to understand them.

The consequence is that the adaptation process has to be explicit, understandable, and controllable by the user, i.e. computer-aided adaptation is necessary. By this means, the construction of the mental model of the adaptation and of the application program can be supported.

It is obvious that the adaptation mechanisms are not understandable to any user on their own without further explanations. The mechanisms, however, have to be self-descriptive in a way that can be understood by any potential system user. It is not yet clearly understood what is the necessary knowledge that a user has to have in order to be able to control the adaptation process. It is also not clear how a user can be empowered to do this.

The discussion of the previous point showed that meta-dialog is necessary to control the adaptation. The regular communication between user and system deals with the completion of the current task. If the communication on this level becomes subject to adaptation, a first level meta-dialog takes place. On this meta-level, the system gives information about the adaptation to the user, and the user controls the adaptation. Furthermore, a second level meta-dialog is necessary if the user can adapt the adaptation process. On this level, information about the control must be given to the user.

This makes the interaction of the user with the system more complex and therefore contradicts the primary goal of introducing adaptation, namely to enhance the usability of systems. A restriction of the meta-dialog to the absolutely necessary topics is required. The consequence is that the adaptation mechanisms have to be simple and hence easy to understand. Furthermore, as much information as possible has to be communicated implicitly, for instance by extraction from the user's interaction with the application system. It should be clear that the additional effort of the meta-dialog has to be in an appropriate relation to the expected gain from the adaptation.

Although much of what we heard during the discussion points in the direction of *computer-aided adaptation*, this is only the partial truth. The overall result of the discussions about this topic is that in most cases a combination of *self-adaptation, computer-aided adaptation,* and *adaptability* would be appropriate. Depending on the situation, the system or the user should be able to choose the most suitable solution.

ARCHITECTURES

Until now, no generally agreed architecture for adaptive user interfaces has been identified. From an industrial point of view, however, this would be most desirable to make the development process for these interfaces more predictable. An architectural framework might be used to provide the components which can be combined into a specific system. During the discussions it became obvious, however, that we are currently not in a position to propose such an architectural framework. Since successful adaptive interfaces are extremely rare, it is necessary to build more examples of these interfaces before trying to generalize structural or behavioral properties.

Nevertheless, research seems to be not far from the point at which generalization from the examples is possible. This step is absolutely necessary to close the gap between research and product development.

MODELS

Although research is still far away from an architectural framework, something has been learned from previous projects. There are a number of models that have to be implemented in order to build adaptive user interfaces. They have to represent the information that is the basis for adaptation. Any of the models cited below has to represented explicitly and free of redundancies.

One of the models to be integrated into the system is an *application model* containing knowledge about the application domain and the tasks to be solved in this domain. If the complete domain has to be modeled, the background knowledge of any possible user has to be integrated into this model –and this is impossible. From this example the rule can be derived that all models, not only the application model, have to be adequate – they have to model only those aspects that are relevant for the adaptation of an application system.

One problem closely related to the application and the task model is the identification of the *users' plans and goals*. The complexity of this problem can be reduced if the system's guess can be confirmed by the user. On the other hand, this is once again an additional instance of a meta-dialog complicating communication with the system. The *user model* is important if the system has to be adapted to the individual users' needs. This model can be interpreted as a representative of the user inside the system. It supplies information about the user to the other components of the system.

In order to construct an adequate user model, the information represented in the model can be restricted to where differences between individual users might appear which are relevant to the interaction of the user with the system. In other words, only the characteristics of the user that might have an impact on the adaptation of the interaction have to be modeled.

One part of the user model is what is called a *discourse model* in the context of linguistics. In this part of the model the previous interaction between user and system is represented in order to provide access to the interaction history. Furthermore, the user model has to represent an overlay of the task model. The information represented in this overlay may be, for instance, the current task, tasks relevant for the individual user, and tasks successfully completed by the current user.

The information represented in the user model effects adaptation on different levels; a system can be adapted to the typical user, user groups, or the individual user. Access to the respective information can be facilitated by a hierarchical representation, distinguishing between aspects of the *typical user*, a *user group*, and the *individual user*. Additionally, a less redundant representation is generated by this means.

Often, the inference of information from the interaction of a user with the system is only possible on a high abstraction level. For instance, it is not sufficient to state that the fact that users do not use a specific concept identifies a lack of knowledge on their behalf. It needs to be determined as to whether this concept is not used because users don't know the concept or because it was not relevant in the situations under consideration.

Finally, it can be stated, that the user has to be in full control of the adaptation process. This control has to be guaranteed with a minimal meta-dialog. The control is necessary for both the adaptation strategy and for the models that are the information providing the basis for these mechanisms.

All models in an adaptive user interface have to be inspectable and changeable by the individual user. Without providing this feature, it seems to be impossible to make the adaptation understandable and acceptable for the user. Understanding and acceptance is not a problem that rises with adaptation. Any complex system is not naturally understood by itself. Therefore, adaptation is a means to make complex systems usable and understandable, but only if the adaptation itself is accepted.

RESULTS

It is difficult to give a short summary of the many interesting topics and findings that came up during the workshop. In our evaluation the two major results are that, firstly, research and development of prototype systems has to be *driven by the needs* of the users and the application context. They define whether adaptation is necessary, what is the appropriate scope of adaptation, and what type of adaptation is adequate.

Secondly, a *combination of adaptation types* is appropriate in most cases. On the one hand, the user should be able to change everything that the system can adapt. On the other hand, some parts of the system may never change, some parts can only be adapted automatically, and in most cases computer-aided adaptation seems to be the right choice.

About the Authors

David Benyon Computing Department
Open University
Milton Keynes, MK7 6AA, UK
E-Mail: D.R.Benyon@open.ac.uk

David Benyon is a Lecturer in Computing at the Open University, UK. He received his B.A. (Hons) in Mathematics and Politics from the University of Essex in 1974 and his M.Sc. in Computing and Cognition from the University of Warwick in 1983. His main research interests are in human-computer interaction (HCI), particularly in the application of knowledge-based techniques to HCI, and information systems design. He has obtained two grants from the National Physical Laboratory (NPL), UK for work on user modelling and adaptive systems.

Dermot Browne KPMG Management Consulting
8 Salisbury Square
London, EC4Y 8BB, UK

Dermot Browne is an Executive Consultant of KPMG Management Consulting. He holds degrees in Psychology, Ergonomics, and Computer Science. He has over ten years experience of designing Graphical User Interfaces and has published widely on the subject. He worked on the largest ever project to have researched the subject of Adaptive User Interfaces and was joint editor of the book "Adaptive User Interfaces."

Gilbert Cockton Glasgow Interactive Systems cenTre (GIST)
Department of Computing Science
The University
Glasgow, G12 8QQ, Scotland, UK
E-Mail: gilbert@dcs.gla.ac.uk

Gilbert Cockton is an HCI Lecturer in the Department of Computing Science in the University of Glasgow. His main research interests are: design knowledge; applying human sciences research to design; user-centered development notations; user interface design environments; and software structures for interactive systems. He is a member of IFIP WG2.7 (User Interface Engineering), and the ESPRIT CIM Interest Group on UIDEs.

Jairo Cote-Muñoz   Honeywell Regelsysteme GmbH
Honeywellstraße
D6457 Maintal, Germany

Jairo Cote-Muñoz studied Electrical Engineering at the Technical University of Darmstadt, Germany. While working for the Technical University of Darmstadt's Computer Graphics Research Center (Zentrum für Graphische Datenverarbeitung), he was involved in research in the fields of human-computer interaction, intelligent user interfaces, and adaptive interactive systems, and received his doctoral degree in Computer Science in 1990. He has been working for Honeywell Germany since 1992, and is responsible for the Honeywell Strategic Technology Research Center. He is currently involved in the areas of integrated dialog systems, multimedia applications, and CASE based design methodology.

Hartmut Dieterich   Siemens Corporate Research and Development
Dept. of System Ergonomics and Interaction
ZFE ST SN 7
Otto-Hahn-Ring 6
81730 München, Germany
E-Mail: dieteri@zfe.siemens.de

Hartmut Dieterich received a *Diplom* in Computer Science from the University of Stuttgart in 1989. Since then he has been a member of the System Ergonomics Department at Siemens Corporate Research and Development working on user interface design environments and interaction methods. His current research interests include adaptive and intuitive user interfaces.

Gerhard Fischer   Department of Computer Science
and Institute of Cognitive Science
Campus Box 430
University of Colorado at Boulder
Boulder, CO 80309-0430, USA
E-Mail: gerhard@cs.colorado.edu

Gerhard Fischer is Professor in the Computer Science Department and a member of the Institute of Cognitive Science at the University of Colorado, Boulder. His research interest include artificial intelligence, human-computer communication, cognitive science, and software design. His research has led to the development of new conceptual frameworks and to the design and implementation of a number of innovative systems in the areas of cooperative problem solving, integrated domain-oriented design environments, intelligent support system, end-user modifiability, and learning on demand.

About the Authors

James D. Foley
Graphics, Visualization, and Usability Center
Georgia Institute of Technology
Atlanta, GA 30332-0280, USA
E-mail foley@cc.gatech.edu

James Foley is Professor of Computer Science and Director of the Graphics, Visualization & Usability Center at Georgia Tech. He earned his Ph.D. at the University of Michigan. His research interests include user interfaces and interactive computer graphics; his work, which has been sponsored by DEC, NSF, NASA, Sun, the Software Productivity Consortium, and Siemens, focuses on building UIDE, the User Interface Design Environment. He is a Fellow of the IEEE, and a member of ACM, the Human Factors Society, and Sigma Xi. He is editor-in-chief of ACM Transactions on Graphics, serves on several editorial boards, and consults regularly for governmental and industrial organizations.

Christoph Grüninger
Forschungsgruppe Verwaltungsautomation
Gesamthochschule-Universität Kassel
Mönchebergstraße 17
3500 Kassel, Germany

Christoph Grüninger graduated from a technical college in Kassel and worked as a mathematical-technical assistant under various contracts. After studies at the University of Maryland and the University of Kassel, he graduated in 1989 from the University of Kassel majoring in Cognitive Science and Business Studies. He is currently a Research Associate in Computing and Social Sciences at the University of Kassel, and specializes in consulting and evaluating projects dealing with information system design for office applications.

Gernoth Grunst
German National Research Center for Computer Science (GMD)
Institute for Applied Information Technology
Schloß Birlinghoven
5205 St. Augustin, Germany
E-Mail: Grunst@gmd.de

Gernoth Grunst concluded studies of Communication Science, Psychology (M.A.), and Linguistics (Ph.D.). He was then involved in research and teaching in pedagogy for the deaf at the University of Köln, Germany. Since 1987 he is a member of the Human-Computer-Interaction research group of the German National Research Centre of Computer Science. There he is responsible for cognitive analyses guiding the design and evaluation of adaptive multimedia systems.

Heinz-Ulrich Hoppe　　　　　　　GMD-IPSI
　　　　　　　　　　　　　　　　Dolivostraße 15
　　　　　　　　　　　　　　　　6100 Darmstadt, Germany
　　　　　　　　　　　　　　　　E-Mail: hoppe@darmstadt.gmd.de

H. Ulrich Hoppe studied Mathematics and Physics at the University of Marburg, Germany. He was a Research Associate at the Pedagogical University of Esslingen, Germany. In 1984 he received his doctoral degree from the University of Tübingen. After a period of research at the Fraunhofer Institute (IAO) in Stuttgart he became Research Manager at the GMD Institute for Integrated Publication and Information Systems (IPSI) in Darmstadt. He is responsible for the research on user interfaces and cognitive ergonomics. Main research interests: task oriented, adaptive user interfaces, intelligent tutoring systems, logic based technics of machiné learning.

Judy Kay　　　　　　　　　　Software Systems Research Group
　　　　　　　　　　　　　　　Basser Department of Computer Science
　　　　　　　　　　　　　　　University of Sydney
　　　　　　　　　　　　　　　Sydney
　　　　　　　　　　　　　　　Australia, 2030
　　　　　　　　　　　　　　　E-Mail: jkay@cs.su.oz.au

Judy Kay is Senior Lecturer at the Basser Department of Computer Science, University of Sydney and a member of the Software Systems Research Group. Her research focuses on user modelling, especially for intelligent teaching systems and information filtering. She has developed a toolkit for user modelling with particular support for a range of acquisition methods. These are being used in a long-term research project involving modelling and coaching of a large number of users. Judy Kay is a member of the editorial board for the journal "User Modeling and User-Adapted Interaction."

Alfred Kobsa　　　　　　　　WG Knowledge-Based Information Systems
　　　　　　　　　　　　　　　Department of Information Science
　　　　　　　　　　　　　　　University of Konstanz
　　　　　　　　　　　　　　　78434 Konstanz, Germany
　　　　　　　　　　　　　　　E-Mail: kobsa@inf-wiss.ivp.uni-konstanz.de

Alfred Kobsa is an Associate Professor of Information Systems at the University of Konstanz. He received his master degrees in Computer Science and the Social and Economic Sciences at the University of Linz, Austria, and his Ph.D. in Computer Science from the Technical University of Vienna. He has also studied Cognitive Psychology, Linguistics, Formal Logic, and Philosophy of Science at the University of Salzburg. He has been a senior researcher and project director of a major AI project in natural language and expert systems at the University of Saarbrücken. His current research interests include knowledge-based methods, knowledge representation, inferences, user modeling, interface design, and computer-supported cooperative work. He is the editor-in-chief of the international journal "User Modeling and User-Adapted Interaction," which he founded in 1991.

About the Authors

Franz Koller
Fraunhofer Institut für
Arbeitswirtschaft und Organisation
Nobelstraße 12
7000 Stuttgart 80, Germany
E-Mail: F_Koller@iao.fhg.de

Franz Koller holds a *Diplom* in computer science from the University of Stuttgart. Since 1987 he is a scientific staff member and since 1989 project leader at the Fraunhofer Institute for Industrial Engineering (FhG-IAO) in the Human-Computer Interaction group. The focus of his research interest lies in the areas of software tools for interactive graphical and multimedia systems, design of multimedia interfaces and object-oriented user interfaces. Currently he is responsible for several national and international projects in the area of multimedia user interfaces at IAO.

Thomas Kühme
Siemens Corporate Research and Development
Dept. of System Ergonomics and Interaction
ZFE ST SN 7
Otto-Hahn-Ring 6
81730 München, Germany
E-Mail: kuehme@zfe.siemens.de

Thomas Kühme received a doctoral degree in Computer Science from the Technical University of Braunschweig, Germany. Since 1990, he has been a research scientist at Siemens Corporate Research and Development, München, Germany, where he is currently leading a project on adaptive user interfaces. His research interests include intelligent tutoring systems, user interface tools, and adaptive interfaces.

Uwe Malinowski
Siemens Corporate Research and Development
Dept. of System Ergonomics and Interaction
ZFE ST SN 7
Otto-Hahn-Ring 6
81730 München, Germany
E-Mail: malinow@zfe.siemens.de

Uwe Malinowski received a doctoral degree for his research on knowledge-based user support from the Technical University of Braunschweig, Germany. Since 1991, he has been research scientist at Siemens Corporate Research and Development, München, as a member of the research team on adaptive user interfaces. His current research interests include user modeling and the role of human factors in the user interface design process.

D. Peter Sanderson	Department of Computer Science
Southwest Missouri State University
Springfield, MO 65804, USA

Peter Sanderson is Assistant Professor of Computer Science at Southwest Missouri State University. He received the Ph.D. in 1991 at the University of Pittsburgh with a dissertation on the structured design of an adaptive user interface. He performed research in the areas of user interface design and simulation language design, and is also interested in software engineering and expert systems. He is a member of ACM.

Matthias Schneider-Hufschmidt	Siemens Corporate Research and Development
Dept. of System Ergonomics and Interaction
ZFE ST SN 7
Otto-Hahn-Ring 6
81730 München, Germany
E-Mail: msch@zfe.siemens.de

Matthias Schneider-Hufschmidt studied Computer Science and Civil Engineering at the University of Stuttgart, Germany, and at M.I.T. He received his *Diplom* and his doctoral degree from the University of Stuttgart. Since 1987, he has been a member of Siemens Corporate Research and Development. He has led the research group on human machine interaction at Siemens R&D, since 1991. He is a member of the CIM-Europe SIG UIDE. Current research interests: human computer interaction, user interface design, adaptive user interfaces, intuitive user interfaces, multimodality.

Eric H. Sherman	Department of Medicine
Columbia University
College of Physicians and Surgeons
New York, NY 10032, USA
E-Mail: sherman@cucis.cis.columbia.edu

Eric H. Sherman is currently an Assistant Professor at Columbia University College of Physicians and Surgeons in New York City where he is involved in research on and construction of medical information systems. The goals of this work are to improve user interface design and to implement automated medical decision making. He has an MD degree from New York University and an MS degree from Stanford University in Medical Information Sciences.

Edward Shortliffe	Section on Medical Informatics
Stanford University School of Medicine
Stanford, California 94305-5479, USA
E-Mail: shortliffe@camis.stanford.edu

Edward H. Shortliffe is Professor of Medicine and of Computer Science at Stanford University. He received a Ph.D. from Stanford in Medical Information Sciences in 1975, and an M.D. at Stanford in 1976. During the early-1970s, he was principal developer of the medical expert system known as MYCIN. He is currently Chief of the Division of General Internal Medicine in the Department of Medicine and Head of its Section on Medical Informatics. Edward Shortliffe is an elected member of the Institute of Medicine of the National Academy of Sciences, the American Society for Clinical Investigation, and the American Clinical and Climatological Society. He has also been elected to fellowship in the American College of Medical Informatics and the American Association for Artificial Intelligence.

Piyawadee Sukaviriya   Graphics, Visualization, and Usability Center
Georgia Institute of Technology
Atlanta, GA 30332-0280, USA
E-Mail: noi@cc.gatech.edu

Piyawadee "Noi" Sukaviriya is a member of the research faculty at the College of Computing, Georgia Institute of Technology. She received her doctoral degree from the George Washington University in 1991. Her dissertation was on automatic generation of context-sensitive animated help from user interface representations. Her current research areas include: model-based user interface environments, supporting evaluations in the user interface design process, automatic help generation, multimedia and animated help, and adaptive interfaces. She is a member of ACM SIGCHI and IEEE.

Werner van Treeck   Prof. für Arbeits- und Sozialpolitik
Fachbereich Angew. Sozialwiss./Rechtswiss.
Gesamthochschule-Universität Kassel
Nora-Platiel-Straße 5
3500 Kassel, Germany

Werner van Treeck is Professor of Industrial Sociology and Labour Politics at the University of Kassel. He received his doctoral degree in 1981 and finished his *Habilitation* in 1984, both at the Free University of Berlin. Major areas of interest: human-centered technologies, management strategies and labour politics, industrial accidents and environmental risks, relations between engineering and social sciences.

Siegfried Treu   Department of Computer Science
University of Pittsburgh
Pittsburgh, PA 15260, USA
E-Mail: treu@avid.cs.pitt.edu

Siegfried Treu is Professor of Computer Science at the University of Pittsburgh. Since receiving his Ph.D. (Interdisciplinary: Computer Science and Psychology) in 1970, he has conducted research on the design, measurement, and evaluation of user interfaces. Topics have included graphical, network-oriented, and adaptive interface designs, with special emphasis on structured approaches.

Subject Index

A

abstraction 79
accuracy of user models 290
action semantics 201
active help systems 168
adaptability 333
    level of 75
adaptable system 55, 56
adaptation 16
    agent 81, 90
    classification 80
    computer-aided 16
    conflicts of 320
    control 333, 335
    criteria 243
    dimensions 17, 89
    distance 79, 90, 99, 100
    domain 245
    goal 22, 332
    level 99
    locality 246
    long-term 229
    manner of 246
    means of 247
    mechanism 81, 90, 333
    methods 247, 255
    object 245
    process 15, 333
    purpose 244
    rules 258
    scope 332
    short-term 228
    strategy 23, 335
    support structures 247
    system-initiated 16
    timing 81, 90, 246
    within-session 81
adaptive help 204
adaptive interface 242
adaptive needs 325
adaptive requirements 323
adaptive system 56
adaptive user interfaces
    architecture 334
advisory system 133, 138
AID 69, 80
AIDA 204
Alvey 69
animated help 200, 201
animated procedural help 199
APEX 201
Apple Macintosh 83, 198
application knowledge base 199
application model 197, 230, 233, 334
architectural framework 334
architecture 28
areas of conflict 325
ART 217
ASSYST 183
attribute grammar 171
audiovisual recordings 271
AURA 183
automatic generation of help 201

B

BGP-MS 120, 140
blackboard 279
BNF 91
BUTTONS 55

C

C++ 217

Cartoonist 202
CENTAUR 253
change management 102
changeability
    dimension of 154
checklists 327
CHECS 135
chronological recordings 214
clinic chart 285
cognitive abilities 152
cognitive load 229, 333
Colossus 319
COMET 202
command interface 159
communication
    inter-component 90
component
    composition 79
    provision 79
composition 89
computer
    as agent 60
    as tool 60
computer-aided adaptation 16
conceptual design 208
conditional critiquing system 58, 59
configurational viscosity 88
connectionist network 117
consistency 322
constraint 210
context dependency 282
context-sensitive animated help 215
Control Panel Interface 292
controlled experiments 326
cooperative problem-solving system 49, 52
Cousin 200
critiquing system 52, 58
CSP 91
customization 141

D

description language 169
design
    structured ~ methodology 248

design environment 49, 53, 56
dialog
    adaptation of structure 89
    explicit 89
    explicit configuration 79
    history 137
    implicit 89
    modeling 35
    natural language ~ system 111
    net 183, 188
    sequencing 210
    specification 183
    structure 84, 85
    style 157, 161
discourse
    analysis 271
    model 335
disruption 91, 92
domain concepts 235
DON 200
dynamic user model 257

E

EAGER 204
EDDDL 183
EDIANE 189
editing 89, 90
EMACS 55, 142
embedded models 25
EMPR 84
enabling 89, 90
end-user modifiability 58
entrepreneurial strategies 319
errors
    number of 332
EUROHELP 133, 137
evaluation 303
    concept 325
    tasks 325
event
    ~-response system 91, 106
    graph 188
    management production rules 84
    queue 83
    rule-based ~ list 84

tagged ~-response system 106
ExcelinExcel 279
expert system 118, 247, 251
explanation generation 333
explicit dialogue configuration 79
exploratory learning 238

F

feature grammars 171
field dependence 156, 157
FLEXCEL 61
flexibility of organization 320
FlightFax 50

G

GAK 201
General Problem Solver 288
generality 72
generality metric 72
GKS 83
goal of adaptation 22
goal-oriented knowledge 254
GOMS 94, 169, 176, 288
granularity 246
GRINS 83
GRUNDY 134
guards 201
guidance 332
GUIDE 293
guidelines 327
gulf of evaluation 288
gulf of execution 79, 288
GUMS 118

H

HAM-ANS 115, 123
HCI 152
help
    active ~ systems 168
    adaptive 204
    animated 200, 201
    animated procedural 199
    automatic generation 201
    context-sensitive animated 215
    how 210

hypermedia ~ system 270, 272
textual 200, 215
variation of ~ contents 216
why 210
high-functionality systems 50
history
    chronological 213
    of help requests 213
    of interactions 212
    statistical 212
how help 210
HSL 241
HUMANOID 200
HyperCard 292
HYPERFLEX 116
hypermedia help system 270, 272
HYPERTEXT 292
hypertext 53
    navigation 116
HyPLAN 269
HyTASK 269

I

IBM VM/CMS 204
Iconographer 100
IDEAL 82
IMAGE 136
implementation metric 72
individual differences 129, 149, 151, 155
inductive learning 176
industrial standards 321
inference 117
information filtering 115, 129, 133
informational interchange 324
INFOSCOPE 60
intelligent information retrieval 115
intelligent teaching system 136
interaction
    natural language 112
    protocol 271
    scenario 258
    structured 248, 251
    technique 208
interface
    actions 207

software architecture 248, 260
system design structures 260
internal social structure 324
interviews 326
intuitivity 332
InVision 60
ISA Dialogmanager 183

K

knowledge
~-based system 50
acquisition 139
goal-oriented 254
model 198, 205, 256
plan-oriented 254
representation 253
shared 49, 62
structured ~ representation 248, 251
KN-PART 121

L

layered model. 233
Layout Appropriateness Metric 204
levels of system usage 51
LEXITAS 170, 171
LID 83
locality 246
logic
modal 117
predicate 117
logical input devices 83

M

machine learning 59
macro 279
macro generation 235, 238
MAID 77
malleable system 53, 58
management
objectives 324
style 324
manner of adaptation 246
MASTERMIND 201
means of adaptation 247
measure of success 332

medical clinic chart 290
mental effort 332
mental model 333
menu interface 159
Menulay 292
meta-dialog 333
metaphorical description 272
methodological assistance 264
methods of adaptation 247
metric 70
generality 72, 80
implementation 72, 80
objective 70, 80
of success 332
performance 80
recommendation 72, 80
theory assessment 70
trigger 71, 80
MICKEY 200
MIKE 200
modal logic 117
MoDe 97
model
embedded 25
system's 52
users's 52
modeling tools 141
modular interface design 264
monitoring 150, 230, 235

N

naive theory of computation 289
natural language 116, 168
dialog system 111
interaction 112
N-CHIME 203, 241, 243
NeXT Interface Builder 292
notation 236
NoteCards 55

O

objective metric 70
OBJECT-LENS 55
object-oriented design 260
Official Airline Guide 50

OLIT 217
OpenLook 200
OpenUI 188
OpenWindows 198
organizational applicability 321
OTTER 121
overlay scheme 257

P

PAC 97
parameterisation
    limits of 81, 84
partial specification 59
Peridot 292
personality traits 153, 154
Petri net 91, 188
    safe 106
PHIGS 82
plan
    ~-oriented knowledge 254
    construction 115
    library 114
    recognition 112, 114, 167, 269, 276
PLANET 269, 275, 279
PODIUM 285, 294
post-condition 193, 198, 199
power-law learning model 214
PRACSYS 183
practicality 74
pre-condition 193, 198, 199
predicate logic 117
presentation strategy 274
PRESENTER 82
procedural knowledge 198
production
    rules 254
    system 251
PROLOG 117

Q

questionnaires 326

R

Rapid/USE 292
RBEL 84

reason maintenance 117
recommendation metric 72
re-composition 91
recordings
    chronological 214
    statistical 214
representation 117
requirements analysis 73
revision 117
rule
    actions 255
    conditions 255
rule-based event list 84

S

sam 130
Sassafras 292
SB-ONE 121
Seeheim model 89, 95
self-adaptation 16, 225
    user-controlled 16
    user-initiated 16
self-adaptivity 333
    feasibility 102
SERUM 135
shared knowledge 49, 62
SINIX Help 202, 204
Smalltalk-80 217
SNI-Dialog Builder 188
software
    abstraction 81
    adaptability 79
    architecture 79
    disruption 79
spatial ability 157, 158, 161
SPIRITS 184
staff structure 324
statistical recordings 214
stereotype 112, 140, 185
    approach 112
    hierarchies 113
structural modeling 24
structural patterns 253
structured browser 279
structured design methodology 248

structured interaction 248, 251
structured knowledge representation 248, 251
student model 136
success
    measure of 332
    metric of 332
SuperCard 298
switching 89, 90
syntactic–semantic model of user knowledge 288
system
    adaptable 56
    adaptive 56
    advisory 133, 138
    conditional critiquing 58, 59
    cooperative problem-solving 49, 52
    critiquing 52, 58
    event-response 91
    high-functionality 50
    knowledge-based 50
    malleable 53, 58
    shared knowledge 62
    tagged event-response 106
system-initiated adaptation 16

T
TAG 171
TAILOR 135
Tailor 293
tailoring
    interaction and modality 135
    output 129, 134
task analysis 289
task knowledge 167
    acquisition 172
task model 167, 278, 335
task modeling 34
task-oriented functionality 321
task-oriented parsing 173
taxonomy 13
teaching 129
technical operability 321
technological infrastructure 324
TeleUse 188

textual help 200, 215
theory assessment 80
theory assessment metric 70
theory of action 288
thresholding technique 297
timing of adaptation 81, 90, 246
topology 90
training 185
transition network 86
trigger metric 71
Trillium 292
truth maintenance 119
tutorial system 269
tutoring strategy 272, 273, 281

U
UC 202, 204
UIDE 197, 199
UIMS 89, 188, 285, 296
UM 119, 130, 140, 142
UMT 120, 140
unification 171
UNIX 19, 116, 133, 135, 143, 170, 175, 202
Unix Consultant 133, 137
UofA* UIMS 200
usability 73, 150, 321, 334
user
    assistance 225, 226
    attention 229
    characteristics 112, 151, 231
    differences between ~s 335
    expertise 114
    goals 115, 335
    interface
        description 207
        development system 287
        management system 287
        separability 97
        toolkit 287
        tools 197
        variability 75
    knowledge 112
    map 296

Subject Index

      cumulative 297
    participation 319
    performance 229
    plans 114, 335
    preferences 115
    state graph 254
    subcommunity 294
    subgroups 112
    variance in ~ population 69
user interface
    building tools 297
User Interface Design Environment 198
user model 116, 129, 130, 167, 183, 184, 197, 198, 202, 230, 231, 257, 286, 335
    accuracy of 290
    acquisition 116, 139
    contents 131
    dynamic 257
    inspection of 142
    management of 140
    representation 139
    role of 136

    server 121
    usage of 137
    utility of 122
user modeling 29, 111, 287
    hazards of 111
    shell 140
    shell system 112, 118
user-controlled self-adaptation 16
user-initiated self-adaptation 16
users
    assessment of differences 156

V

variations of help contents 216
viability analysis 73

W

WEST 142
why help 210
widget 86
"Wizard of Oz" test 276
work context 282
work organization 324
Workspaces 293